Wellington's Engineers

Wellington's Engineers

Military Engineering in the Peninsular War

1808–1814

Mark S. Thompson

There's only one Corps that is perfect – that's us;
An' they call us Her Majesty's Engineers.

'Sappers' by Rudyard Kipling

Pen & Sword
MILITARY

First published in Great Britain by
PEN AND SWORD MILITARY
an imprint of
Pen and Sword Books Ltd
47 Church Street
Barnsley
South Yorkshire S70 2AS

Copyright © Mark S. Thompson, 2015

ISBN 978 1 78346 363 3

The right of Mark S. Thompson to be identified
as the author of this work has been asserted by him
in accordance with the Copyright, Designs and Patents Act 1988.

A CIP record for this book is available from the British Library.

All rights reserved. No part of this book may be reproduced or transmitted
in any form or by any means, electronic or mechanical including
photocopying, recording or by any information storage and retrieval
system, without permission from the Publisher in writing.

Printed and bound in England by
CPI Group (UK) Ltd, Croydon, CR0 4YY

Typeset in Times by CHIC GRAPHICS

Pen & Sword Books Ltd incorporates the imprints of Pen & Sword
Archaeology, Atlas, Aviation, Battleground, Discovery,
Family History, History, Maritime, Military, Naval, Politics,
Railways, Select, Social History, Transport, True Crime, Claymore
Press, Frontline Books, Leo Cooper, Praetorian Press,
Remember When, Seaforth Publishing and Wharncliffe.

For a complete list of Pen and Sword titles please contact
Pen and Sword Books Limited
47 Church Street, Barnsley, South Yorkshire, S70 2AS, England
E-mail: enquiries@pen-and-sword.co.uk
Website: www.pen-and-sword.co.uk

Contents

List of Plates vi
Acknowledgements viii
Foreword xi

Introduction 1
Chapter 1 1808 – Success, Controversy and Disaster 9
Chapter 2 1809 – Hard Lessons for All 29
Chapter 3 The Lines of Torres Vedras and the Defence of
           Portugal 46
Chapter 4 1810 – A Year of Waiting 69
Chapter 5 1811 – Goodbye to Lisbon 84
Chapter 6 1812 – Taking the Frontier 120
Chapter 7 1812 – Triumph and Failure 144
Chapter 8 1813 – The Road to France 160
Chapter 9 1813–14 – Into France 186
Conclusion 205

*Appendix 1: Commanding Royal Engineers (CRE) with
           Wellington's Army, 1808–14* 209
*Appendix 2: Engineer Officers who Served in the Iberian
           Peninsula* 211
Appendix 3: Military Reconnaissance and Surveying 216
Appendix 4: Military Bridging 222
Appendix 5: Military Education 233
Notes 249
Bibliography 265
Index 271

List of Plates

1. Lieutenant Colonel Sir Richard Fletcher RE. Portrait in possession of Royal Engineers Mess and used with their permission.
2. Monument at Alhandra to Sir Richard Fletcher and Neves Costa.
3. Major General John Thomas Jones RE. Bust from the Royal Engineers Museum, Chatham.
4. Lieutenant General Sir Stephen Chapman RE. Portrait in possession of Ronald Brighouse and used with his permission.
5. Field Marshal John Fox Burgoyne RE.
6. Contemporary image of Oporto from Villa Nova by Vivian.
7. Boat bridge across the Douro at Oporto by Landmann.
8. Flying bridge over the Tagus at Villa Velha.
9. Main entrance to Fort La Lippe, Elvas, Portugal.
10. Fort St Lucia, Elvas, Portugal.
11. Fort St Julian, defending the embarkation point that the British army would have used to evacuate Lisbon.
12. Section of the ditch of Fort San Vincente at Torres Vedras.
13. Gun emplacement at Fort 18, Ajuda.
14. Restored military road leading to the great redoubt at Sobral.
15. Drawing of a Portuguese single-arm telegraph, reproduced with the permission of the Municipality of Torres Vedras.
16. Reconstruction of a Portuguese single-arm telegraph.
17. Reconstruction of a British balloon telegraph.
18. Captain Charles Boothby RE, who lost a leg at Talavera.
19. Badajoz castle from Fort San Christobal.
20. The Tagus from the fort at Jerumenha.
21. The castle at Campo Mayor.
22. Defences at Almeida, Portugal.
23. Site of the main Allied breach in the wall at Ciudad Rodrigo.
24. Curtain wall of castle at Badajoz, Spain.
25. Major William Nicholas RE.
26. Bridge over the Guadiana at Badajoz seen from Fort San Christobal.
27. Bridge over the Guadiana at Merida.
28. Bridge over the Tagus at Almaraz.
29. Bridge over the Tormes at Salamanca
30. Bridge over the Tagus at Alcantara.

31. Siege of San Sebastian by Jenkins.
32. Passage of the Bidassoa by Jenkins.
33. Contemporary image of an ox cart and driver.
34. Fragment of memorial to Royal Engineer officers killed at the siege of San Sebastian.

Acknowledgements

Whilst I have always been interested in the Peninsular War, my knowledge of the Royal Engineers, like that of most people, was very limited. My interest stemmed from trying to find a topic for a PhD that had not been covered before. Ten years later, I have my bit of paper but also knowledge that I would like to share with others. There have been challenges in my research, mainly because the Corps is almost invisible in most histories of the period. Where an engineer appears in Wellington's dispatches it is usually difficult to find any further evidence of the events mentioned. Even the official Corps history, although admittedly written over 100 years ago, has big gaps in its coverage of the Peninsular War. Fortunately we have a number of diaries and letters that we can use to reconstruct the Engineers' story one piece at a time.

Information on the other units involved in engineering activities is even scarcer. The Royal Staff Corps, the army's equivalent, has no history and no personal diaries; similarly the engineers of the King's German Legion. Although almost completely ignored in the Anglo-centric writings on the Peninsular War, the Portuguese and Spanish engineers did play their part. I have not done much better, but have tried to acknowledge their presence where I found it.

In my search to rebuild the engineer's story, I have had help from many people who have given their time, knowledge and enthusiasm freely and I thank them all. The first and foremost came from a chance encounter at the Royal Engineers' Museum in 2004. Julia Page, known for her excellent book on Edward Charles Cocks[1] and also for many years as an expert tour guide, shared my interest in the Royal Engineers. Later that year, with the battlefield tour group the Forlorn Hope, we spent a week going over the ground of many of the events recounted in this book. She is the only other person in the world with whom I can share my enthusiasm. Julia also planned to write a book on the Corps and had even started it. Unfortunately lack of time has interfered and it is left to me to bring this subject to the reader. This book is as much Julia's as mine.

It is difficult to know where to start with the others who have helped me. Rory Muir is a hidden presence behind many modern works. His knowledge of the history is unparalleled and I have learnt so much from reading his books and talking to him. The other side of Rory is the man who willingly shares his knowledge with all and is always there when you have a question. He feels more like my next-door neighbour than someone who lives 10,000 miles away. I know that I am not the only person who has benefited from his generosity, so on behalf of us all, thank you.

During my research, I have made a number of visits to the Royal Engineers' Museum and Library at Chatham. They have met with my many requests with patience and diligence and I would particularly like to thank Rebecca Nash and her team. I would also like to thank serving and retired members of the Corps for their assistance and encouragement, particularly Gerald Napier, Séan Scullion and Martin Stoneham. I first met Gerald Napier when we co-presented a session on the Lines of Torres Vedras and this led to my involvement in the Friends of the Lines of Torres Vedras (please look up our website and Facebook pages). I would also like to thank Nick Lipscombe for his advice and support.

In Portugal there are two people to I particularly need to mention. Firstly, Clive Gilbert, Chairman of the British Historical Society of Portugal. If you are ever visiting Portugal and need a local expert, you need Clive. He is heavily involved in local activities to protect and promote the Lines of Torres Vedras and is a superb interface between Portuguese and British interests. Secondly, I would like to thank Isabel Luna who works on the preservation of the Lines and is particularly heavily involved at Torres Vedras itself. She has been very supportive of my research and particularly in the efforts to identify the names of places and people in the unpublished diary of Edmund Mulcaster. There have been several others in Portugal who have contributed to my research, including José Paulo Berger, João Torres Centeno, Carlos Cunha, Flor Estavo, Moisés Gaudencio, Rui Moura, Jorge Quinta-Nova, Rui Sa Leul and Sergio Tavares. In the same group, although not Portuguese, is Anthony Gray.

From the British Commission for Military History (BCMH), I would particularly like to thank Dick Tennant and John Peaty. We have had a number of healthy debates about the war in general but particularly around bridging and military surveying. It was Dick who invited me to one of their conferences where I found myself speaking at Sandhurst next to the late, great Richard Holmes, an experience I will not forget for many reasons. The battlefield tour with them in 2012 is also a memory I will treasure.

Whilst not a regular contributor myself, I must recommend the Napoleon Series (www.napoleon-series.org) as a tremendous source of information both in the website content, but also the discussion forum. Over the years I have received help from many people but would particularly like to mention Bob Burnham, Howie Muir, Ron McGuigan and Tony Broughton. Bob Burnham and I have also corresponded on military bridging and he has written an excellent chapter on the subject in the book *Inside Wellington's Peninsular Army*.[2]

One constant in my life as a historian has been the presence of the British book dealer Ken Trotman, run by Richard and Roz Brown. I have been buying books from them for over thirty years and many of the books on my shelves came from them. I also owe them special thanks for allowing me to use images from some of their reprints.

I cannot end without giving my thanks to Chris Woolgar and Karen Robson at Southampton University, both for answering my questions and for arranging the Wellington Congress. I also must thank the staff of the British Library, the National Archives and the National Army Museum for their help in providing material for my research.

My final thanks are to my family who have lost me for a second time to Fletcher and his officers. Their understanding when I locked myself away for days on end and over my 'business' trips to London, Portugal and Spain have always been met with understanding and patience. This book and the PhD that preceded it are the result of the support of 'Team Thompson'. The credit for this book should go to you, Trish, my wife and daughters, Ruth and Katherine.

Mark S. Thompson
October 2014

Foreword

It is well over one hundred years since Major General Whitworth Porter included an account of the Peninsular War when writing Volume One of the *History of the Corps of Royal Engineers*. This book now draws on much new material, not previously available, to tell the story from the perspective of engineer officers and explains how they supported the victories of the Duke of Wellington in the Iberian Peninsula. These officers from the Royal Engineers, never more than fifty at any one time, played a highly significant, but mainly invisible role in supporting Wellington's army and the operations in Spain and Portugal. They were present at almost every major engagement, but their roles as staff officer, liaison officer, bridge and road builder, and fortifications engineer are not well recognised. A number of them lived to enjoy rank and high reputation, while others died in the breach of a stormed city, leading the infantry into the gap in the enemy's defences as Sapper officers should. It is now time that all their various contributions are better understood.

Further into the nineteenth century some of these same officers continued their careers in both military and civil roles, to high acclaim. Field Marshal Sir John Burgoyne (the first Royal Engineer to achieve that rank), who served on both Sir John Moore's and the Duke of Wellington's staffs, would forty years later advise Lord Raglan in the Crimean War. Another, General Sir Charles Pasley, had been at the Battle of Corunna and would pioneer much-needed improvements in the training of engineer officers before going on to establish at Chatham what is now known as the Royal School of Military Engineering. Others were called upon to oversee a variety of famous civil endeavours. For example, Lieutenant Colonel John By played a major role in the early development of Canada, including the building of the Rideau Canal between Montreal and Kingston in the 1820s – now a World Heritage Site. Indeed, Ottawa, the capital of Canada, was originally called Bytown. Sir Joshua Jebb played a leading role in prison reform and would later become the first Surveyor General of Prisons in 1844. Sir William Reid, who was a Lieutenant at the time of the Peninsular War, became chairman of the committee for the planning of the Great Exhibition in 1851. Others continued the work of their forebears in the Ordnance Survey by conducting survey operations across the British Empire, and many made names for themselves as directors of railway companies and as colonial governors in the West Indies and Australia.

The bi-centenary of the Peninsular War has created renewed interest in the period and I am delighted that we have a new evaluation of the role of Royal Engineer officers, who did much to lay the foundations for the many military and civil engineering feats that were accomplished in the Victorian era. Their legacy to our nation's history deserves greater recognition.

Lieutenant General Sir Mark Mans KCB CBE DL
Chief Royal Engineer

Introduction

On 27 July 1808, a very wet Royal Engineer officer, Captain Peter Patton, was washed up on the beach at Mondego Bay in Portugal, after his boat capsized whilst trying to ride over the rough Atlantic waves. Fortunately for him and his fellow Engineer passenger, Lieutenant John Neave Wells, there was no lasting injury.[1] This was the first step of an officer from the Corps of Royal Engineers in the Peninsula and the reason he was there will come as a surprise to many people. He was not there to conduct a siege, but to undertake a range of tasks for which he had been fully trained but is understood by few today.

The stereotypical view of the engineers as just being employed for sieges is outdated and this book will provide a more balanced description of their role and their contribution to the war. Today, we have a greater emphasis on all the components that make up war. Gone are the descriptions of battles with no consideration of what came before the first shot or after the last. Recently, there have been a number of studies on logistics, the role of the Royal Navy, the effects of political considerations and the impact of other campaigns on the Peninsular War, e.g. the central European campaigns or the War of 1812. One area that has not been looked at for over 100 years is the role of the engineers who supported Wellington in his campaigns in the Iberian Peninsula. This support was provided by a number of different corps. These were the Royal Engineers, the Royal Military Artificers (later to become the Royal Sappers and Miners), the engineers of the Portuguese army, the Spanish army and the King's German Legion, the Royal Staff Corps and the officers serving with the Quarter Master-General's department (QMG staff, exploring officers and the Corps of Guides).

This myriad of different units is partly the cause of the confusion about who did what during the war. Whilst on paper the roles of these units were clear, there was a level of pragmatism in the field, where whoever was available was used. This showed clearly in two particular areas, bridging and mapping. This pragmatism was not always shared or understood at home where inter-service rivalry remained intense. An early example was the engineer Captain Peter Patton being asked to explain why he had jointly signed a survey report with an officer from the Royal Staff Corps, as the Board of Ordnance were not aware of any arrangements for joint working between the different corps. The nonsensical view from home was that each officer should have submitted a separate report.

Whilst this book is primarily about the role of the Corps of Royal Engineers, it will try to put in perspective the valuable contribution made by these other units. It will also focus on the campaigns of the Duke of Wellington and will not cover in detail the role of the Royal Engineers at Cadiz and Gibraltar, nor the east coast operations. This is not to say that these were not important. The constant threat from the two southern strongholds meant the French could never concentrate their forces against Wellington. Similarly, the continued defiance of the Spanish forces, regular and irregular, kept many thousands of French troops tied down and contributed to the massive drain on their resources. The Allied campaigns on the east coast were generally co-ordinated to have some value to Wellington. Even though they were not always successful, they kept the French looking over their shoulders for six years.

The role of an officer in the Royal Engineers was unique in the armed forces at the time. Like their fellow officers in the Royal Artillery, they were not under the command of the army. Their chain of command was entirely separate, reporting through the Board of Ordnance. Additionally, an engineer officer was very different from an artillery officer in that they typically reported to and lived with the senior unit commanders. A lieutenant in the Royal Engineers could receive orders directly from Wellington, a level of exposure that a typical army subaltern would only dream of, or more likely dread.

The number of engineer officers was so small that they often worked alone and this required a great deal of self-confidence in their professional capacity and in dealing with authority. There was no one to ask if you did not know what to do. There is some evidence that this was true up to the highest levels. One example is Captain Henry Anderson, the commanding engineer on Madeira, who in April 1808 complained he had not received any correspondence or orders for eight months! Communication between Richard Fletcher and the Board of Ordnance was also decidedly one-way. Engineer officers were literally on their own for most decisions. The engineers felt they were the elite in the armed forces and even within the Ordnance the top students almost always elected for the Royal Engineers in preference to the Royal Artillery. The army, for its part, had mixed views about engineer officers. Words like arrogant, distant, aloof, stand-offish and serious were typical descriptions. There is no doubt that some were arrogant and opinionated. Their unusual roles and responsibilities meant they behaved differently and were treated differently.

In August 1808, when Captain Howard Elphinstone stepped ashore in Mondego Bay, he was the first engineer to command in the Peninsular War. He was the first of four officers who held the position of Commanding

Royal Engineer (CRE) with the Allied army during the war (see Appendix 1). The CRE with the Allied army had another daunting challenge; his commander was Sir Arthur Wellesley, who was not known to be an easy person to work for. He was also not well known for taking advice from others, which was going to be an unavoidable role for the senior engineer. The CRE was part of Wellington's management team that included the Quarter Master-General, the Commissary General and the Commander of the Royal Artillery. Typically, when on campaign these officers would meet with Wellington every day. The person who held the unenviable role of CRE for most of the war was Richard Fletcher, a lowly captain in 1808 and probably the most junior person by rank on Wellesley's staff. We will come back to him later.

Because the number of engineers was so small, this book can talk about the engineer officers as individuals. It means we can examine their hopes and aspirations, their arguments and their friendships, their roles and what they thought of them. George Landmann, who was officially attached to the Gibraltar garrison, managed to spend most of the war being in places where he was not supposed to be, sometimes with great value and sometimes not. Reading Rice Jones' diary there seems to be a relationship between his health when he was ordered on services which looked interesting, and his illnesses when they looked less so. Howard Elphinstone arrived with a reputation of being difficult and did his best to live up to it. But aside from my cynicism, there were some deep friendships formed between engineers and senior officers in the army. This was often based on previous service together, John Squire and Sir John Moore and John Burgoyne and Sir Thomas Picton being examples.

The main thing the engineer officer brought was flexibility – staff officer; liaison officer; builder of roads and bridges, destroyer of them too; siege master; builder of defences both static and field; surveyor; well-digger; and negotiator. Also, whilst it was not their primary role, engineers, like their fellow officers in the army, wanted to be on active service in preference to being 'stuck' working on fortifications or lines of communication. An engineer officer would never miss an opportunity to be present at a battle.

The Ordnance and the Army
As mentioned above, the provision of military services to the British government came from a number of different sources. The main source of soldiers came from the army, centred on the Commander-in-Chief at Horse Guards. The army provided infantry and cavalry, but had no control over where they were used, their funding or their movement. These

responsibilities were firmly held by the government. Completion of the martial forces came from the Board of Ordnance who provided the artillery and engineers. The Board of Ordnance had immense responsibilities, being responsible for the upkeep of military establishments worldwide, e.g. the major facilities at Plymouth, Portsmouth and Chatham were all under their control. The Board of Ordnance was also responsible for the supply of guns and ammunition to the army and the navy, both at home and overseas. The other main difference between the Army and the Board of Ordnance was in their representation in government. The army had none, whilst the Master-General of the Ordnance was a member of the Cabinet and consequently had a greater opportunity to influence policy.

The presence of two different military hierarchies led to a number of difficulties. The first and most obvious was that the general commanding the army did not have direct command over Ordnance officers. Operationally, this did not usually present problems as they expected to get their day-to-day instructions through the army hierarchy. It was more of a problem for the bigger decisions. A general could not influence the appointment of specific officers or the number of them on service. Such requests had to be made to the Board of Ordnance for their consideration. At the start of the war there was a level of concern at the Board of Ordnance, mainly around Wellington not officially recognising (through his Dispatches) the contribution of the Ordnance officers. Later on, as Wellington's successes grew, there was a greater willingness to meet his needs.

The second area that caused problems was the award of brevet ranks. Brevet rank was awarded to army officers for exceptional service, usually in the field. A frequent way to obtain a brevet promotion was to be mentioned in dispatches. A brevet rank entitled the officer to use the rank in terms of seniority, but without the associated pay. Ordnance officers were entitled to be awarded brevet ranks, but these were army ranks only and did not count in the Ordnance. So, a Royal Engineer captain awarded a brevet majority would not outrank his fellow Ordnance captains on the basis of his brevet rank, but he would outrank an army captain. The engineer officers serving in the field had greater opportunity to obtain brevet ranks and this caused great resentment amongst the home based officers. This was particularly true in 1812 where a small number of engineer officers gained two brevet promotions in the year for their efforts in the great sieges at Ciudad Rodrigo and Badajoz. There were also a number of occasions in the Peninsula when an engineer officer tried to claim seniority over his fellow engineers by use of his brevet rank. Everyone knew that this was not acceptable but it did not stop them trying. Apart from the kudos of being in command, engineer officers received substantial command pay.

Brevet ranks also caused friction in one other area. The Board of Ordnance had slightly different ranks to the army. The main difference was the rank of Second Captain (junior to a captain) in the Ordnance. This rank was not entitled to brevet promotions. As the war progressed there were more and more occasions when Second Captains were overlooked when their fellow officers gained brevet rank. Following a plea to Wellington in 1813 the ruling was changed.

A Brief History of the Royal Engineers from its Inception

The Corps of Royal Engineers was formed in 1717 to provide trained specialists for the British military. Prior to this time, the Board of Ordnance kept a small number of officers to advise on engineering matters, but generally when the British Army went on campaign it hired foreign specialists to provide these services. When first formed, the Corps had twenty-eight officers. This number grew slowly until the start of the Napoleonic Wars when there was a large increase in numbers to keep up with the demand from across the world.

Number of Officers in the Royal Engineers[2]			
Year	Number	Year	Number
1717	28	1806	157
1759	61	1808	172
1782	75	1809	201
1796	94	1811	229
1802	113	1813	262

With the exception of India, where the East India Company appointed its own engineers, the Royal Engineers served as far afield as the Indian Ocean, the West Indies, the Cape and North America. Unlike their peers in the army, an officer in the Ordnance had to undergo professional training and pass examinations before they were commissioned. The commissioned Ordnance officers would then choose or be assigned to the artillery or the engineers. The best students typically chose the engineers. Engineer and artillery cadets received the same training and this was not just about fortifications and guns. The syllabus included chemistry, physics, military engineering, languages, fencing and dancing. These last two were often seen as interchangeable: fencing was dancing with more serious consequences if you got the steps wrong.

Unlike the army, commissions could not be purchased. Entry was by application to the Master-General and subsequent promotion was strictly by seniority. Ordnance officers were also not able to sell their commissions and this led to stagnation in the senior posts as there were limited opportunities to obtain a pension. The oldest officer in post (until he died) was eighty-four! Whilst the common view is that promotion by seniority was much slower than by purchase, an analysis of promotions in the Royal Engineers during this period does not support this view. What did change was that the rapid increase in the size of the Corps of Royal Engineers and the promotion opportunities caused by casualties meant that engineer officers gained promotion much faster than their predecessors.

The Royal Military Artificers and Royal Sappers and Miners
One of the anomalies of the Corps of Royal Engineers at this time was that it was an officer-only organisation. There were no rank and file. Manual labour and tradesmen were provided from the infantry regiments whilst on campaign and by local civilians for static establishments. The first steps to redress this omission were taken at the garrison in Gibraltar in 1770 when the senior Royal Engineer suggested that skilled tradesmen should be transferred from the garrison regiments there and formed into a permanent body to carry out military engineering work. A Royal Warrant was issued in 1772, to raise a 'Company of Soldier Artificers' to serve only at Gibraltar.[3] In 1786, a second company was raised.[4] As tensions grew in Europe, and the need to defend the shores of Great Britain became more apparent, a further six companies were raised in 1787, under the title of the 'Corps of Royal Military Artificers' (RMA). They were to serve at Woolwich, Chatham, Portsmouth, Gosport, Plymouth and the Channel Islands. Again, each company was destined to serve only in the one location. A further four companies were added in 1806 to serve at Dover, Cork, in Nova Scotia and in the West Indies.

The intention behind the formation of the RMA was to provide skilled workmen at the main Ordnance facilities around Britain, Europe and eventually the globe. There was never any intention that these troops would be mobile and available to travel in significant numbers with an army. The lack of their own officers meant that they were never properly managed and they were allowed levels of freedom that should never have been tolerated in any military organisation. Captain Charles William Pasley RE commented on the soldiers 'going grey' in the corps, while stagnating in the same location, for life. He also commented on the effects of receiving volunteers from the line regiments, which allowed units to get rid of their worst men.[5]

The Formation of the Royal Staff Corps

Friction between the Army and the Board of Ordnance about the supply of officers and equipment was not unusual, the campaigns in the Low Countries in the 1790s being a low point in the relationship. The Duke of York, who commanded one of these unsuccessful campaigns, felt that he was let down badly by the Ordnance and took steps to ensure it never happened again. In 1800, the Royal Staff Corps (RSC) was formed to provide the same services that historically had been provided by the Royal Engineers. This small corps contained both officers and artificers and initially was a single company strong, although it did later grow to battalion size. Both officers and artificers had to have training either at a military school or through an apprenticeship. A number of officers, including Henry Sturgeon, transferred in from the Ordnance, but subsequently they provided their own officers.

The RSC was not meant to be a direct replacement for the Royal Engineers, but was designed to work alongside them. In theory the Royal Engineers focussed on static defences (sieges and fortifications) and the RSC concentrated on operational work (reconnaissance, mapping, bridging and field works), but in practice the line between them became blurred very quickly. The formation of the RSC was to ensure that the Army had some engineering expertise under its direct control.

The Contribution of the Portuguese Engineers

One area that remains overlooked and needs further research is the contribution of the Portuguese engineers to the Peninsular War. They tend to make fleeting appearances in English works but clearly played a larger role. Some senior Portuguese engineer officers were appointed as military governors in various towns and they had a constant presence in most Portuguese fortresses. The defences around the city of Lisbon were under their control throughout the war. Their involvement in the design and construction of the Lines of Torres Vedras remains a little controversial. They clearly had more involvement than they have been given credit for. The name of Neves Costa was virtually unknown outside of Portugal until recently, but his contribution to the Lines is now better understood.

The Portuguese engineer service was also complete in the way that the British was not, They had both officers and artificers and these were deployed with some Portuguese army brigades. This was something that Wellington could not even consider until late 1813. When Wellington advanced towards the French border in 1813, Portuguese engineers went with him. The English pontoon trains were actually operated by Portuguese seamen. The Corps of Guides, formed in Portugal in September 1808 by

8 Wellington's Engineers

George Scovell, appears to have been mainly Portuguese and some of them were certainly involved in mapping over the coming years.

There is an absence of significant recent work on the engineering services supporting the British army. The relevant volume of the history of the Corps was written over 100 years ago. The history of the Royal Sappers and Miners is even older. There is almost nothing in print on the Royal Staff Corps. The situation is no better in Portugal. Sepluveda's work on the Portuguese engineers is also 100 years old. It is time for a re-evaluation. This book tells the same story of the Peninsular War, but from a different perspective. This is not about the detail of the major battles or sieges, it is about the unseen and little-understood work that went on around the major events and contributed to their success.

Chapter 1

1808 – Success, Controversy and Disaster

The first campaign in the Iberian Peninsula saw the piecemeal arrival of British troops from all over Europe. Various fleets converged on Mondego Bay in July and August 1808 from England, Ireland, Sweden and the Mediterranean. The first engineers to arrive from Cork with Sir Arthur Wellesley were Captain Howard Elphinstone with Second Captain Patton and Lieutenants Williams, Boteler, Wells and English. Captain George Landmann with Lieutenants Mulcaster and Mercer arrived from Gibraltar with Sir Brent Spencer. Captain Richard Fletcher with Captains Squire and Burgoyne, Lieutenants Smith, Forster and Stanway arrived with Sir Harry Burrard and Sir John Moore.

Elphinstone had recently returned from the ill-fated South American expedition to the Rio de la Plata and was assigned to Sir Arthur Wellesley's new South American task force. Following requests for support from the Spanish provinces that had risen against Napoleon, the task force was rapidly diverted to the new Iberian adventure. In the early euphoria following the French surrender at Bailén on 19 July 1808, the Spanish were keen to get assistance in the form of arms and money but were reluctant to allow British troops on their soil. Wellesley's original plan was to land his troops at Corunna but the Spanish suggested he would be better employed supporting the Portuguese. Wellesley accordingly moved south to Oporto and then on to Lisbon for talks with the Portuguese authorities.

Elphinstone wrote frequently to his wife and provides entertaining although not always accurate commentary on what was going on. As the senior engineer present he became, by default, the Commanding Royal Engineer with the army. Writing home to his wife on 27 July 1808, he expressed his initial impressions and hopes for the campaign.

> We anchored in this bay [Mondego Bay] yesterday morning and are to land in the course of a day or two. The inhabitants are friendly to

us and there is no danger in landing . . . Junot has but a small force in Lisbon such as I think will surrender upon our appearance . . . I am only afraid that the opposition will be so trifling that I shall not get a Majority [i.e. promotion] from the French rogue.[1]

He also noted that he dined with Sir Arthur Wellesley on his first night ashore and said 'from what I can perceive at present everything will go on alright with him'.[2] His first intention was to get transport for himself, but, as the whole army was discovering, horses were in very short supply and his demands on the commissariat fell on deaf ears. As Elphinstone was riding a mule at the first battle, his high hopes of securing a thoroughbred were obviously dashed. Having said that, you should not confuse an Iberian mule with a British seaside donkey, these were big, powerful brutes! He noted he paid 94 dollars for his 'neddy'.

In the days following Elphinstone's landing, other engineers started arriving including Captain George Landmann, whose father was Professor of Fortifications at the Royal Military Academy. Landmann had powerful delusions of grandeur and soon would get his brief moment of glory. But first, like Elphinstone, he needed personal transport and bought a pony without a personal inspection. You can hear Landmann making fun of himself as he described the first ride on his new pony on 10 August 1808:

> . . . at the sounding of the bugle next morning, I jumped up and ordered my famous pony to be accoutred with my handsome new Mameluke saddle, holsters and ornamented bridle etc; then swinging over my left shoulder, my spy glass . . . and my haversack . . . over my right shoulder, I mounted [and found that whatever encouragement was applied] my pony advanced no faster than a walk.[3]

Landmann's movements in these early days of the war are fairly well known through his self-publicising two-volume memoirs.[4] But he does also tell us what Wellesley and Elphinstone were doing.

Beginning a trend that continued throughout the war, engineers were assigned to each infantry brigade and would report directly to the unit commander. Landmann was appointed to General Fane's brigade. Elphinstone as CRE would have remained with Wellesley at his headquarters.

On the morning of 11 August the troops were raised around 3 a.m. and stood to arms until after daybreak when it was confirmed there was no sign of a French attack. The army remained around Leiria until the morning of the 14th when after a cold, foggy start the warm weather quickly turned into a hot, dry day with copious amounts of dust covering everyone. Staying close to the coast, the army advanced to Alcobaça where the first contact with the French under Delaborde occurred. The Allied army then moved on to Caldas da Rainha on the 15th. The next day, at Óbidos, Landmann describes his Engineers' training kicking in.

> My first object was to reconnoitre the whole of the surrounding country [around Óbidos]. Having quickly inspected the ground to the west, I crossed the valley to the eastward of the town . . . where there is a good road . . . which I suspected might join . . . the more direct road to Lisbon which is by Roliça. Having questioned several of the country people . . . they confirmed my conjecture.[5]

He then rode back to Óbidos to brief General Fane, reporting that the French could be clearly seen on the heights of Columbeira. Although Landmann recounts as his own idea the decision to reconnoitre in front of the advancing army, it is more likely that such activity was being ordered by Wellesley and co-ordinated through Elphinstone.

On the morning of 17 August, Landmann was back in the Moorish tower at Óbidos watching the French 'with my famous three-feet telescope, by Watson'[6] when Sir Arthur Wellesley arrived. Landmann's account has him passing his telescope to Wellesley and then briefing him on the terrain based on his reconnaissance the day before. Five engineer officers were present at the first battle of the war at Roliça on 17 August 1808. They were Elphinstone in command, Captain Landmann and Lieutenants English, Mulcaster and Wells. Landmann was with the flanking force under General Fane and Elphinstone remained with Wellesley. Late in the day, Elphinstone was wounded, a musket ball shattering his lower jaw. Landmann related that Elphinstone was watching the assault of the 29th Regiment at Columbeira through his telescope when he was hit, the shock knocking him from his mule. 'He was raised by Lieutenant Mulcaster'[7] and Elphinstone described, as he retired, 'a second ball did me the favour to graze my thigh – a third saluted me on the rump'.[8] Landmann lost no time in personally visiting Wellesley at headquarters and writing to the Board of Ordnance reporting he was now the Commanding Royal Engineer, but could not find the time to visit the injured Elphinstone until the following day. He reported the action as follows:

> I have to report that yesterday the army under the command of Sir Arthur Wellesley, proceeded from Óbidos, and engaged the French

troops under the command of General La Port [*sic*], who had taken a very strong post in the mountains we now occupy, which we carried after a very severe action of about four hours – It is with the deepest regret that I have to say that Captain Elphinstone was severely wounded by a musket ball in the face, the surgeons report is very favourable, and I hope he will be again able to take the command, although I fear it may be some time. I was unfortunately not able to see him myself, as we had advanced too far before I heard of the accident. Lieutenant Mulcaster was with Captain Elphinstone at the time, and has seen him last night who says he was in good spirits, and well taken care of in a small village about three miles in the rear of our present situation. I am happy to add that all the other officers of the corps have escaped unhurt.[9]

The Allied army now moved south to Vimeiro to cover the landing of Acland and Anstruther's brigades. Junot, realising that any chance of success would diminish once these troops were ashore, attacked on the morning of 21 August. Although Sir Harry Burrard had arrived in Maceira Bay to take over command, he had not yet landed and Wellesley was able to retain command during the battle. During the battle, Landmann described the situation around Wellington who was ignoring the French skirmishers shooting at him, causing much anxiety to the young engineer Lieutenant Edmund Mulcaster. After the second time that Mulcaster brought the situation to Wellington's attention, he was ordered to chase them away, which he promptly carried out with the assistance of some orderly dragoons.

Landmann's report on Vimeiro was short and to the point:

I have the honour to report to you that a little after eight o'clock this morning we were attacked by a large force of the enemy said to be about sixteen thousand under the command of General Junot. We obtained a complete victory by 12 o'clock, the enemy having left in the field about 15 pieces of ordnance and a great quantity of ammunition. It is with great regret that I have to report that Lieutenant Wells is missing. I have no doubt of his being a prisoner, for had he been killed or wounded we should have found him, as the field of battle remained in our hands. The last accounts I had of the state of Captain Elphinstone's wounds were very favourable, and I expect him to be able to return to duty in about a month.[10]

There may have been a practical reason why his report was so short. He recorded in his book that it was written in the rain, under an umbrella picked up on the battlefield. Lieutenant Wells had been assigned to General Acland's brigade and was asked to ride to a unit of Portuguese cavalry to give them orders. Being short-sighted, he got lost and mistook a group of French staff for his intended target, whereupon he was made prisoner. Wells was then taken to Junot and spent the remainder of the battle with the French commander. He remained a prisoner until he was released as part of the terms of the Convention of Cintra.[11]

Captain Richard Fletcher RE had arrived with Sir Harry Burrard on the eve of Vimeiro but neither got ashore until after the battle. Burrard replaced Wellesley as commander of the army and Fletcher took command of the Royal Engineers. Fletcher, because he was not present at the battle, allowed Landmann the honour of reporting to the Board of Ordnance the victories of Roliça and Vimeiro to the Board of Ordnance.

Elphinstone had held the position of CRE for sixteen days and Landmann for a mere four days. Elphinstone showed his character very early with his annoyance when he discovered a French émigré engineer, Captain Preval, was on board HMS *Crocodile* with Wellesley and who quite rightly, being his senior, would not accept Elphinstone's authority. Preval, who was under the command of the Royal Engineers, had been sent out to Lisbon in advance of the main force to evaluate the situation there. Wellington sought his advice when he briefly visited the city and took him on board before returning to Mondego Bay. Elphinstone lost no time writing home reporting the situation and also complained to his wife that it was very 'shabby' that Fletcher had been sent out above him. Elphinstone's reason for requesting leave to go home was more about his injured pride rather than his injured chin.

Issues around seniority were a constant theme for engineer officers in the Peninsula. The senior officer of engineers at any location or an officer acting on his own was entitled to claim the title of Commanding Royal Engineer. This could lead to a greater chance of recognition in dispatches and the potential for brevet promotion in the army lists. Apart from the kudos of commanding, positions of authority also came with increased pay and allowances. This additional pay was significant. Fletcher noted the award of 5s [shillings] *per diem* command pay in 1808.[12] A captain's daily pay was 11s, in this case doubled to 22s as engineers received double pay when on active service to help cover their additional costs.[13] Before Fletcher left England in July 1808, he wrote to his superiors at the Board of Ordnance asking for clarification on his role. He pointed out that Colonel Harding was likely to be appointed to command the Royal Artillery and would be a senior Ordnance officer. He asked for clarification that he would command the engineers with the Army and that this would also be independent of the engineering command at Gibraltar.[14] Fletcher received the confirmation of his appointment as CRE in Spain and Portugal in early September 1808.[15]

Why was Richard Fletcher selected for this very important role? This was the biggest expedition organised by the British Army for many years. At first glance the decision seemed odd. Fletcher's seniority in the Corps was a lowly 24th out of 143. However, when you go through his superiors and strike off those holding senior posts at Ordnance headquarters, those commanding major stations in the UK, those commanding stations abroad, the choice came down to two officers, Robert D'Arcy and Richard Fletcher, with three less likely possibilities (Alexander Bryce, Augustus De Butts and John Rowley). It looks likely that Fletcher was selected as he had the most recent field experience. D'Arcy went on the ill-fated Walcheren campaign in 1809 where he narrowly avoided a court-martial for insubordination but was still offered a baronetcy, something Fletcher did not get until the end of 1812! It should also be noted that some of Fletcher's superiors were VERY old, with several being over 60. Fletcher was a sprightly 40 years young. It also says something about his views on his duty that despite having lost his wife a few weeks earlier, he left his six children in the care of relatives to go on this expedition.[16]

The day after the Battle of Vimeiro, the French asked for a ceasefire to discuss terms for their evacuation of Portugal. These negotiations led to the unpopular Convention of Cintra where the French and their 'personal possessions' (in many cases including items stolen from Portugal) were transported home in British ships with no restrictions on the troops serving again. Following widespread outrage at home and in Portugal, the Allied commanders Dalrymple and Burrard, along with Wellesley, were recalled for an inquiry with Sir John Moore taking over command of the Allied army. Under the terms of the Convention, the French troops started to embark at the beginning of September 1808 and Fletcher was assigning his officers to various tasks. These included:

- Trying to obtain maps and plans from the Portuguese archives before the French removed them.
- Ordering plans to be made of the defences at Lisbon and St Julian to the south of Lisbon, St Julian being a possible point of embarkation.
- John Burgoyne ordered to Almeida and Ciudad Rodrigo to report on the defences.
- John Squire assigned to General Hope's division that was marching to Elvas to take control of it from the French.
- George Landmann ordered to survey Peniche as a place of defence and possibly for embarkation.

- Peter Patton being ordered to review the defences at Setuval, south of Lisbon, that was also being considered as a point of embarkation for the army.
- Edmund Mulcaster being ordered to survey the Tagus at Villa Velha and Abrantes for possible crossing-points.

In addition Moore had ordered Lieutenant Boothby RE to the Portuguese frontier fortress of Elvas with the party sent to demand the surrender of the French garrison under the terms of the Convention of Cintra. Leading this group was John Colborne who was required to make three journeys between Lisbon and Elvas. At first, the terms were challenged by the French garrison and then the Spanish refused to let the French garrison leave. Boothby took the opportunity to review the defences and look for plans whilst at the fortress.

In early October 1808, the first reports on the roads and rivers were being returned, with details of the routes from Lisbon to Almeida and Abrantes being some of the first received. This was the start of a mapping exercise that would be carried out by Staff Corps, Engineer and QMG's staff continually to the end of the war. The targets of these surveys quickly spread with reconnaissance in the Alentejo and south of the Tagus towards Setubal.

Advance of Moore's Force

Sir John Moore was officially confirmed as commander of the Allied forces on 7 October 1808 and immediately started considering how best to support the Spanish armies, an operation that was expected by both the British and Spanish governments. On the 8th, Fletcher reported home that orders had been issued for the advance of Sir John Moore's army into Spain and most of the engineers would accompany it. Much to their disappointment, Captain Patton and Lieutenants Williams, Stanway and Forster were ordered to remain in Lisbon.[17] Captain Landmann also remained in Lisbon as technically he was part of the Gibraltar garrison and not attached to the army in Portugal. Landmann appeared entirely happy with this arrangement. He always seemed to find a way of not coming under the direct control of any of his seniors, a situation that he used to his advantage throughout the war.

Fletcher's attention turned to how to move the engineer stores with the army, a task that proved nearly impossible due to the shortage of transport. He expected the Ordnance store ships would move to Corunna or Grijon and, writing home on 22 October, he reported that he could only obtain transport for entrenching tools for 1,000 men.[18] The Army was in a very similar position, with transport only for the most basic supplies.

Moore's army started its advance from Lisbon on 18 October although the General did not leave Lisbon until the 27th. Fletcher left Lisbon on the 26th, although other engineers were already moving ahead of the army surveying the various routes, e.g. on 1 November, Lieutenant Wells wrote a report on the road from Almaraz to Salamanca.[19] On the same day Fletcher reported that the army was moving to Abrantes and the route from there would depend on the reports that were coming in. However, one important decision had been made, based on inaccurate information on the state of the roads. Burrard had come to the conclusion that the artillery could not follow the route of the army to Ciudad Rodrigo through Coimbra and Almeida and planned to send the artillery via Elvas. Moore came to the same conclusion and made the dangerous decision to split his forces. He sent his artillery protected by Hope's division, by the main road through Elvas to Almaraz and then north.[20] This led to several days' delay at Salamanca whilst Moore waited for his forces to concentrate. If time had not been so critical and Moore could have justified delaying his advance for a couple of weeks, he would have been in possession of accurate reports on the roads and he would have had more confidence that the artillery could have moved with the army via Coimbra and Ciudad Rodrigo. Having said that, the early surveys by engineer officers warned of the difficulties of moving artillery over the route. John Burgoyne described the roads in the first part of the journey from Lisbon to Coimbra as 'good' and 'frequently extremely fine'. He then reported that they deteriorated:

> from Coimbra [towards Almeida] the road is very bad, steep and narrow, and in its present state not practicable for artillery, the country carts do pass it, but with much difficulty that they can scarcely get from Coimbra over the mountains 10 miles in a whole day; from the foot of the mountains the road is bad but passable for carriages.[21]

Fletcher also noted that the few light guns travelling with General Hill 'will find many difficulties as the roads are said to be almost impassable for carriages of any description'.[22] Whilst it may have been possible to move the artillery by the more northerly route, with winter approaching and an inexperienced army and commissariat the decision to send the artillery by the best road may have been the correct one.

Moore arrived in Salamanca on 13 November with Fletcher arriving on the 15th. Moore now waited for his forces to concentrate, most of his infantry arriving by the 23rd, but his artillery did not arrive until early December. He was also waiting for a further 16,000 troops under Sir David

Baird which had arrived at Corunna on 13 October but could not get permission to land until the local Junta had received approval from Madrid. Baird finally concentrated his troops at Astorga by 22 November, but by then Moore had decided to retreat and Baird was instructed to head for Vigo to re-embark.

Fletcher, whilst stationed at Salamanca, continued to receive reports from engineer officers on the state of the various roads. This extract from one of Fletcher's reports indicates the type of activity underway:

> I have now sent Captain Burgoyne and Lieutenant Meineke, to reconnoitre the province of Avila, its roads, rivers, bridges etc and Lieutenant Boteler is gone from hence to Zamora, and . . . will proceed up the Douro as far as he can with safety, to examine that river and the roads leading to and from it. Lieut. Wells arrived this morning, from Elvas, by way of Badajoz, Merida, Truxillo, Almaraz and Plasencia, and he is going on towards Madrid, to meet the head of Lieut.-Gen Hope's column, and report on the country he has passed through.[23]

When he arrived at Avila, Burgoyne heard that General Hope with the cavalry and artillery were at Madrid and, taking the initiative, rode overnight, arriving on 21 November. Burgoyne then worked with Hope's Quarter Master-General, De Lancey, to plan the route for the artillery over the Guadarrama mountains and on towards Salamanca.[24] Lieutenant Meineke, who travelled with Burgoyne, wrote two detailed reports on the route for Fletcher. Whilst Fletcher makes no reference to receiving direct orders from Moore, he was building a detailed picture of the operational environment whether it was ordered or not. Officers had realised very quickly that most of the maps had serious errors. The engineer John Squire remarked:

> All the maps of Portugal, particularly in this part of the country, are extremely incorrect, Faden's last map . . . is as bad as any of them. The Carta Militar published at Lisbon can never be depended upon. To form a good judgement, it is necessary to actually visit every part of the frontier.[25]

The activities of the engineer officers over the last three months now meant that the British had detailed descriptions of the area around Lisbon and the three main routes from Lisbon to Elvas, Castello Branco and Coimbra and the routes into Spain via Badajoz to Madrid and Ciudad

18 Wellington's Engineers

Rodrigo to Salamanca. There were also reports of the condition of the four border fortresses. We will leave Moore at this time and look at what had been happening in the north of Spain.

Military Liaison in the North of Spain between the British and Spanish
Whilst the main engineering activity was concentrated around the British army in Portugal, a completely separate activity was underway further north. Following the Spanish risings against the French occupation in mid-1808, a number of emissaries had been sent to London to request support from the British government. In the absence of a central Spanish government, which was not formed until late September 1808, in June the British government ordered out a number of military agents 'acquainted with the Spanish Language'[26] to liaise with the Spanish provinces and report on the situation.[27] These officers initially arrived in the northern provinces of Asturias and Galicia and then, with more enthusiasm than good sense, encouraged the Spanish into uncoordinated actions against the French with vague promises of British help. They also wrote a stream of misleading reports to the British government, which rapidly regretted these appointments. On 29 August, Canning (Foreign Secretary) wrote to Castlereagh (Secretary of State for War and the Colonies) expressing horror at what Colonel Doyle was promising the Spanish authorities:

> Nothing can be more unlucky than the orders which Colonel Doyle has given [to prepare accommodation at Corunna in expectation of the arrival of a British force] . . . as it appears to excite expectations which will be disappointed, and the disappointment of which may lead to disasters of great extent.[28]

Realising that the situation in northern Spain needed better control, Generals Leith and Broderick were dispatched in August to Santander and Corunna respectively. Four officers from the Royal Engineers were also appointed under the command of General Leith. These were Captains Charles Lefebure, John Francis Birch, Charles William Pasley and John Thomas Jones. General Leith set out on 17 August, arriving in Santander on the 23rd. Castlereagh's detailed instructions to Leith were delivered by Lefebure when he and John Jones joined him at Oviedo: 'This letter will be delivered to you by Captain Lefebure whose talents as an engineer will be of much use in accelerating the survey of the military line of the Asturias and the principality of Santander.'[29]

The engineers' orders were to carry out surveys of the northern provinces and report on the state of the Spanish forces. This seems like the same brief that was originally given to the first group of military agents who were now running almost out of control. The main difference was that the engineer officers were clearly under military control.

Leith-Hay, in his *Narrative of the Peninsular War*,[30] responded to what he felt was unjustified criticism by Napier describing the engineer officers as follows: 'That, in point of zeal, intelligence, military knowledge, or sound judgement, four more distinguished persons could not have been selected from any army . . . these officers were active and zealous, constantly moving from one point to another.' Leith-Hay, who was present as ADC to General Leith, went on to remark that finding suitably-qualified persons in the British Army at this time would have been difficult due to the state of practical knowledge (or more precisely, the lack of practical knowledge).[31] Leith-Hay's defence of the engineer officers was unnecessary, as Napier's criticism was almost certainly directed at the originally appointed military agents Doyle, Dyer, Roche, Whittingham and Patrick.

Pasley, who was waiting to sail with Sir David Baird's force, received orders directly from Castlereagh on 30 August to proceed to Gijon 'on a particular service' and set off immediately for Portsmouth, reporting two days later that the fleet was ready to sail as soon as the 'dollars' arrived.[32] The dollars were of course the funds that the British government were sending out to support the Spanish revolt. Pasley joined General Leith at Oviedo on 11 September.[33]

Through the early part of September the engineer officers, Lefebure, Jones and Pasley, stayed close to General Leith as he moved between Oviedo, Gijon and Santander.[34] On 20 September, the Spanish under Blake pushed the French out of Bilbao and Lefebure and Jones moved into the town to liaise with the local authorities. At the same time, Pasley was ordered to carry out a survey of the Asturian mountains and Birch was ordered to join the Spanish Army of the Centre under Castaños to report on his intentions and the condition of his army. The French, stung into activity by the advance of the Spanish, regrouped and started closing in on Bilbao. On 26 September, Lefebure and Jones carried out a forward reconnaissance[35] and found the French under Marshal Ney advancing on the town, necessitating a rapid withdrawal by the Spanish and the loss of Jones' baggage.

General Leith, who was present when the French marched back into Bilbao, then went inland to Frias, accompanied by Jones, where he expected to find General Blake. He eventually found him at Lastras de la Torre and having discussed the situation with him, Leith, returned to Santander. Leith-Hay, who was with General Leith, expressed surprise at the lack of knowledge Blake had of the location and movements of the French.[36]

Meanwhile Pasley had returned from his survey of the Asturian mountains on 30 September, writing a detailed report for General Leith and also later copying it to General Sir David Baird.[37]

There was now a lull in Spanish activity as their generals and juntas discussed the next steps. Agreements had been made to form three armies: the Army of the Left under Blake around Bilbao and Valmaseda; the Army of the Centre under Pignatelli around Logrono; and the Army of the Right under Castaños between Logrono and Tudela. Another force, mainly levies under Palafox, were around Zaragossa.[38] Lefebure wrote an update for the Board of Ordnance on 7 September:

> I lay before you a letter from Captain Pasley, in the hope that you will be pleased to find that the officers of your corps are gaining the good wishes of the generals on the spot. General Leith's statements to Lord Castlereagh are all very flattering to each and every engineer with this mission.[39]

On 8 October, the Spanish army received some welcome news when HMS *Defence* arrived at Bilbao with a convoy carrying 9,000 Spanish troops that had been serving in northern Europe with the French.[40] They had been secretly embarked from Nyborg in Denmark. Unfortunately for them, their commander, General Romana, had travelled separately via London and Corunna. Pasley, commenting on the event, wrote:

> I have been here since I wrote you last with Major-General Leith, and have been witness to the happy return of the Spanish army of the north to their country, who are very fine looking and well-disciplined troops. The greatest part is still here either waiting orders from Madrid or the arrival of their general, the Marquis de la Romana. At present they are commanded by the Conde de San Roman, who is a fine soldier-like man. On his arrival he gave out a very impressive order to his troops which was read at the head of each regiment on King Ferdinand's birthday; A Major of one of the regiments who was reading it was so much affected that he could not proceed. They all seem full of ardour and patriotism and their presence will inspire confidence whatever army they may join.[41]

Blake, taking full advantage of his unexpected reinforcements, advanced on Bilbao, pushing the French out again on 11 October.[42] He then settled into a period of inactivity that allowed the French to regroup and to absorb the large reinforcements that were pouring over the Pyrenees. Jones noted with great satisfaction that the personal possessions that he had lost when the French retook Bilbao on 29 September had been hidden by the Spanish and were returned to him when he went back to his billet.

On 13 October, around 16,000 reinforcements under Sir David Baird arrived at Corunna. Travelling with Baird was Captain James Carmichael-Smyth RE. The junta at Corunna would not let Baird land without permission from the Central Junta at Madrid. Riders were sent for their approval, which was received on the 22nd. Much to his displeasure, Baird was instructed to move his troops in small numbers to limit the impact on the local population. The landings began on 26 October but it was not complete until 13 November, on which day Baird set off for Astorga.[43] Like his fellow generals, Baird had sent his engineers forward to reconnoitre the route to Astorga and to review the terrain around Villa Franca 'with a view to its defence'.[44]

On 21 October, Pasley wrote an update report for the Board of Ordnance in England. Jones, Lefebure and himself were at Santander with General Leith and Birch was attached to Blake's army to report on its activities. He said that Lefebure had been ordered to go to Bilbao to assist in arming the inhabitants. Pasley went on to express concern on the state of the Spanish armies: 'That great portion of the Spanish troops, being newly raised, imperfectly disciplined, and officered by peasants, so that you cannot reckon a Spanish army of 30,000 equal to more than a veteran army of 20,000 or less.'[45] Similar sentiments were expressed by Jones: 'The new regiments (I mean the armed and organised peasantry) have not sufficient confidence in themselves to contend with the French veterans, and it is to be doubted whether the men are under sufficient command to be kept together should the French follow up.'[46]

Although working completely independently, it is interesting to note that the engineers serving under Leith in the north of Spain were corresponding with Fletcher who was with Moore's army and we can assume that this information was passed on to Moore.[47] Moore was expressing concern about the limited information he was receiving from Leith on the activities of the various Spanish forces.

Birch, who had been with Blake for some weeks, was ordered to join the Spanish Army of the Centre under Castaños and find out his intentions. Jones and Pasley were sent to replace him at Blake's Headquarters. Birch, writing from Burgos in early November, described the formation of a Spanish grand strategy to outflank the French forces. He arrived at Castaños' headquarters on 27 October and then travelled with him to Saragossa where they met Palafox:

> The result of which I understand from General Doyle was that the army of the centre should unite itself to the army of the right on the Aragon near Sanguesa . . . and that at the same time the army of the left should move along the mountains in the rear of the enemy and form a junction with the two others. General Blake had sent an officer to arrange his movements with General Castaños. He [Doyle] was present when the above measures were decided upon, and told me . . . that he had little doubt of their success, and hoped to . . . accompany General Castaños to carry to General Blake the notice of the time when the movements were to commence.[48]

The British military agent Colonel Doyle, who was now using his new honorary Spanish rank of Major-General, claimed the idea for this strategy was his. Birch noted that Doyle was 'on the most intimate footing' with Palafox. Birch found the Spanish plans 'very extraordinary' and felt 'the army of the left . . . would be exposed to entire destruction', and said he planned to go to Blake 'to take the liberty of explaining my sentiments'. Before Birch had an opportunity to do this and before the Spanish grand plan had commenced, their moment had passed.

In late October the French reacted to Blake's further advance. Although Napoleon had ordered that no action should be taken until he arrived, General Lefebvre decided to attack, pushing Blake out of Zornosa on 29 October. Jones, who was present at the battle, reported the action as follows:

> It was my fortune to be present in the action, and I have great pleasure in being able to state that the Spanish troops behaved with the greatest gallantry and the success of the French is to be attributed to their superiority in numbers and in artillery, and not at all to their superior courage – the ground having been disputed inch by inch – and when General Blake saw it was useless contending any longer, he took up a new position about two leagues in the rear of his former position, which was occupied with so much skill as to deter the enemy from renewing their attack that afternoon, in the night General Blake drew off all his forces and retreated towards Valmaseda – the retreat was conducted with so much order that no loss was sustained, and scarcely a musket left behind.[49]

Jones stayed with Blake for a few days after the action reporting on the situation and then returned to Santander. This repulse meant that Bilbao again became indefensible. Captain Lefebure, who had been sent to organise distribution of arms to the Spanish was ordered to send the supply ships back to Santander and then return there himself.[50]

Meanwhile Blake, realising that some of his troops had been cut off by his retreat, pushed forward again on 5 November, allowing the stranded troops to rejoin him. For the next six days the French applied constant pressure on Blake, steadily pushing him back. Birch, who had rejoined Blake's army, was wounded in a skirmish on the 7th and was shipped out to Corunna.

Despite the best efforts of General Leith, the situation with the Spanish armies remained unclear. Conflicting reports continued to be circulated. Pasley, writing on 7 November, described as 'absurd' the report dated 3 November from the British Military Agent, Captain Caroll, saying that Blake had been cut off after the battle at Zornosa on 29 October.[51] Four days later Pasley wrote:

> You will recollect my mentioning that we had very desponding accounts from Captain Carroll, who by letter to Gen Leith dated the 3rd instant from Headquarters expressed his fears that the army would be cut off – What grounds he went upon he did not state but the next thing we heard from him was the account of a splendid victory . . . This morning a dispatch arrived from General Blake who notwithstanding all these favourable accounts it appears has retreated from Valmaseda.[52]

Moore, who was in the vicinity of Salamanca, needed clear information on the state and intentions of the Spanish armies if he was to have any chance of making a successful strike against the French. This he was not getting. On 16 November, Moore wrote to John Hookham Frere, British Ambassador to the newly-formed Spanish Central Junta, as follows:

> Officers employed to correspond, . . . might have been useful before you or I were sent to Spain . . . but I . . . disapprove of any person being authorized to correspond officially with Government but you and me . . . my wish is to overset the whole system; to send them with their Spanish rank to England, and to send, as they may occasionally be wanted . . . officers . . . who will look to no rank or emolument but from their own country, in whose duty they should consider themselves employed.[53]

Moore clearly had a problem with the British agents being awarded Spanish commissions and the potential conflict of interest that it created. Doyle had been given the honorary Spanish rank of major-general and Caroll was made a lieutenant-colonel.

With Moore arriving in Salamanca and being able to communicate directly with the Central Junta and with the Spanish commanders, the need for a separate military authority in northern Spain came to an end. This seemed to be recognised by both Moore and Leith. Writing on 17 November, Jones, who was still with Leith, reported that Lefebure had been sent to Moore to deliver dispatches and to provide any further information requested. He also reported that Pasley had been sent to join Sir David Baird's force. Jones then returned to Santander to remove any remaining British money and provisions.[54] His final task (according to himself) before winding up his military adventures was to return to Corunna and take charge of a delivery of 100,000 dollars for General Romana. Jones recounts leading his forty-mule convoy against the flow of troops heading for Corunna before being dispersed in the disorder at Astorga. He wrote that half was handed over to the British commissary 'without receipt or acknowledgement'. The other half was thought to be lost but was handed back by the Spaniard in charge of it after the Battle of Vitoria in 1813. The whole story seems implausible if it were not mentioned in a letter to the Board of Ordnance by Pasley.[55]

On 19 November, Moore wrote to John Hookham Frere complaining that he had received no correspondence from Leith 'who is employed with that army to correspond'. He went on to say that as he had a shortage of general officers, he had ordered Leith to join Baird at Astorga.[56] Moore's complaint about the lack of communication from Leith was resolved soon after when Lefebure arrived at Moore's headquarters to brief him.[57] Leith had clearly realised his role in northern Spain had come to an end. At the same time that he ordered Lefebure to Moore's headquarters, he added Jones to his staff as an extra ADC and dispatched Pasley to Astorga. There, Pasley briefed General Craufurd and passed over a dispatch to be sent to Moore at Salamanca (probably a duplicate of the information that Lefebure was delivering in person). Baird then kept Pasley on his staff on account of his knowledge of Spanish. Pasley later transferred on to Moore's staff for the same reason.

The role of these four engineer officers during the period from September to November 1808 showed their flexibility. Whilst their initial brief was to carry out surveys of the northern Spanish regions, this turned out to be a minimal part of their work. Their primary task was liaison with Spanish military and civilian bodies and accurate evaluation and reporting of the rapidly changing situation. They also became heavily involved in the distribution of arms, supplies and money to the Spanish.

Moore's Retreat and Corunna

Moore, having arrived at Salamanca on 13 November 1808, now started receiving reports of the reverses suffered by the Spanish armies and also the advance of the French as far as Valladolid, which would threaten his plans to join with Baird. When Moore heard on 29 November of Castaños' defeat at Tudela, he felt he had no choice but to order a retreat to Lisbon. He urgently needed good intelligence of the position of the advancing French. Amongst others, engineer officers were employed to probe for the French forces. Lieutenant Charles Boothby noted in his diary that he set off on 30 November to reconnoitre north-east towards Valladolid. That morning they met a Spaniard carrying a French requisition for rations and a proclamation from the French announcing the defeat of Castaños. He continued out in advance for some days before joining General Paget at Villapando on 17 December 1808.[58]

In the first days of December Moore had communications from Castaños informing him that he was reforming his army, and from Stuart and Hookham Frere, who were both strongly against Moore's retreat. Also Moore finally met up with his artillery on 4 December at Alba de Tormes. The claims that the Spanish intended to defend Madrid swayed Moore to make one last effort on their behalf. He recalled Baird to Astorga and then planned a move north to Zamora and Toro. Even whilst cautiously moving forward, Moore made plans and arranged depots in case a retreat was needed. Corunna and Vigo were being considered as likely points of retreat. On 14 December, he learned from a captured French dispatch, that Soult was unsupported and moved his forces against him. Lieutenant Charles Boothby RE, who was attached to the reserve under Paget, excitedly reported on 19 December 'Sir John [Moore] dines with General Paget, Battle is the word!'.[59] Two days later, Paget's cavalry surprised and dispersed the French cavalry at Sahagun. Three days later, when about to launch his offensive against Soult, Moore received information that Napoleon was advancing north to cut off his retreat.

Realising the danger, Moore immediately ordered the retreat, with Allied and French forces racing each other in terrible weather to the river Esla around Benavente. The first of the Allied troops crossed the river on 26 December. The following day, most of the infantry were across the river and work started on destroying the bridge, which was blown on the morning of the 29th. The bridge was prepared for destruction by the Royal Engineers, Burgoyne's biography reporting that the destruction was left to the last moment to allow stragglers to cross with 'the French cavalry reaching the farther end of it before Burgoyne exploded the charge'.[60] Boothby noted that he rode with a message for Moore 'through devilish rain and numbing wind'. He spent the night of 28 December sawing through the woodwork with 'cursed saws that refused to do their duties' and setting fire to the buildings on the enemy side of the bridge.[61]

On the morning of the 29th, General Lefebvre-Desnoettes' cavalry of the Guard managed to find a ford over the river but were repulsed by the British cavalry, Lefebvre-Desnoettes himself being captured. While the French failed to cross the river Esla at Benavente, they succeeded further north at Mansilla. The weather remained very bad with snow and rain hampering every step of the journey. Moore ordered a further retreat to Villa Franca on 30 December, with discipline in the Allied army disintegrating. Fortunately, the rearguard under Paget kept the French at bay all the way to Corunna where the Allies turned to face their pursuers, the French having refused a similar challenge at Lugo.

On 30 December, Moore had ordered a number of engineer officers ahead of the army to survey routes and more importantly provide information on where Moore's force should retire to. The original plan was to retire to Vigo and that was where the Allied transports had been sent. However, Corunna was also being considered. Fletcher rode with Edmund Mulcaster to Corunna and Captain John Burgoyne RE headed for Vigo, both producing reports for Moore. Fortescue wrote that Moore reviewed the engineer reports on 4 January 1809 and determined on falling back on Corunna although the reports from Fletcher and Burgoyne are dated later.[62] Interestingly, Captain John Birch RE, who was at Corunna recovering from his wounds, commented:

> From what I have seen of this place, I may venture to say that it is an exceedingly bad and improper one for the re-embarkation of the Corps of the Army pursued by the enemy; the fortifications of the town are indefensible, and defenceless, and were the town in the hands of the enemy, the citadel would be presently untenable, and it would be difficult if not impossible to embark from it. The bay is commanded from all the shore around it, which might expose the shipping to the enemy's fire from thence, and the vessels might be detained in the harbour under it by a contrary wind.[63]

Also on 30 December, Lieutenant Charles Boothby RE and Lieutenant William Forster RE were ordered to

> obtain the correct information of any movements of the enemy from Benavente towards Orense and to transmit the same by the most expedition and secure route to Sir John Moore. Also to endeavour

to induce the Spanish troops now at or near Sanabria to defend the passes as long as possible, and also to defend the fortress of Puebla and that of Monterey, and throw every impediment in the way of the advance of the enemy.[64]

The orders from George Murray, the Quarter Master General, also included instructions to order a party from the 76th Regiment to retire from Monterey and any supplies there to be removed or destroyed. Boothby carried out his orders and then rejoined the army in time to be present at the Battle of Corunna.

Fletcher remained in the vicinity of Corunna and began work on the defences, starting at the village of Betanzos. Orders were given to destroy one of the bridges at Betanzos, mine the other and also mine a third bridge at El Burgo. Mulcaster, who carried out the work at the latter on 10 January, noted 'the pavement [was] so hard and well laid as to turn all the picks'. Mulcaster noted with satisfaction that the 3cwt (150kg) of gunpowder 'answered perfectly'. The general view of the engineers involved in this task was that their limited operational experience and training in destroying bridges led to numerous failures. Charles Pasley, who went on to form and command the School of Military Engineering from 1812, wrote 'all attempts to blow up stone bridges . . . made by officers of the Corps, myself amongst others, failed . . . with the exception of only one, which Lieutenant Davy . . . succeeded in completely destroying, but at the expense of his own life, which he lost from not understanding the very simple precautions necessary'. Mulcaster noted that Davy 'was killed by the explosion of it going off immediately on his lighting the portfire'. The blowing of the other bridge at Betanzos failed when one of the two charges was displaced when the first went off. The French cavalry had to be removed from the bridge before the mine could be re-laid and blown again at 8 p.m. on 11 January.[65] A few days earlier Captain Evelegh RA noted 'we retired over a bridge which Pasley attempted to blow up, but did not succeed. Chester and Barlow remained with two guns to defend the blowing up of the bridge.'[66]

Over the next few days the engineer officers were involved in strengthening the defences at Corunna and destroying stores. Mulcaster wrote in his diary on 13 January 1809, 'The transports came in sight and some of them anchored in the evening. Hard at work making cask traverses; laying platforms'. Boothby noted on the day of the battle that he was 'charged with the erection of a battery in the town'. When the firing started, having not taken part in a battle before, he managed to obtain a horse and joined General Hope's party, Moore and Baird having already been wounded. Boothby's description of the role of an engineer in battle is worth repeating as it will happen again many times throughout the war: 'An engineer has no appropriate place or defined duty in an open battle, but he is always acceptable in the field if mounted, because he is generally a good sensible smart fellow that looks about him, and is trustworthy in the communication and explanation of orders.'[67] He goes on to describe how he 'was very glad to find myself so little disturbed by the whizzing of the balls'. Mulcaster was not so fortunate, complaining 'Being nailed in the citadel and now dismounted I could not go into the action, a circumstance I shall regret to the last hour of my life'. The day after the battle, Boothby claimed that he and General Hope were the last two to embark after all other troops had been loaded on to the transports.

The end of January 1809 saw the British army returning to England in a sorry state. Many saw Moore's campaign as a humiliating defeat, but it had in fact achieved its objective, which was to disrupt the French aims in the Iberian Peninsula. Without the British intervention, it was likely that Portugal and Spain would be fully under French control. The British army still had a foothold in Lisbon and were much better prepared for the following years' campaign through accurate information on the geography of Portugal and western Spain. The Portuguese and Spanish governments were also turning their thoughts to resisting the French. As the Battle of Corunna was being fought, other engineer officers were setting off for the Peninsula. Captain Stephen Chapman wrote that a fleet of forty transports, with six engineer officers on board, had set off from Spithead on 14 January destined for Lisbon.[68]

Chapter 2

1809 – Hard Lessons for All

Throughout late 1808 and the first part of 1809 there was still a small British presence at Lisbon, and work continued to make the place more defensible. Engineer officers were also ordered to improve communications by building bridges over the river Tagus.[1] Edmund Mulcaster had been sent in early October 1808 to survey the possible sites and reported back to Fletcher on the 19th. General Mackenzie, commanding at Lisbon, wrote to Moore on 13 December reporting:

> Captain Landmann of the engineers has been sent to Abrantes to assist in throwing the bridge across the Tagus there, and also to strengthen the flying bridge [floating platforms made of boats or pontoons, secured and moved by ropes] at Villa Velha and at Punhete on the Zezere. When he has accomplished these objects he is to examine as far as he can the best positions in Upper Beira, where almost all the best Portuguese engineers are now employed on surveys.[2]

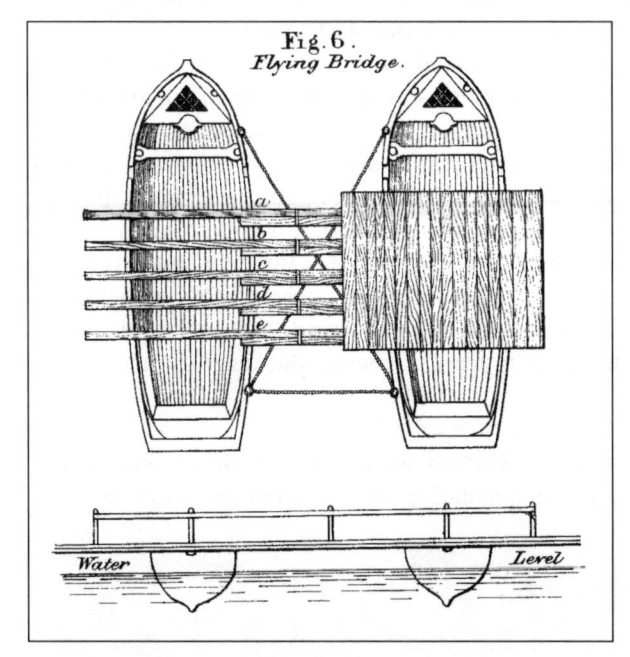

The flying bridge over the Tagus at Villa Velha.

Whilst there is no doubt that this bridging work was essential, Mackenzie had unwittingly set off an internal disagreement about seniority. As Fletcher had noted in his letter of 23 September, Landmann was not part of his command and had been ordered back to his official role as part of the Gibraltar garrison. The commander-in-chief at that time, Sir Hew Dalrymple, had 'expressed himself in strong terms of approbation as to the zeal, activity and intelligence with which he had acted during the period he had served with this army'.[3] A few days later Fletcher reported that Landmann had been ordered to carry out a survey of Peniche before he returned to Gibraltar. Four weeks later, on 21 October, Fletcher wrote again to Landmann, asking for copies of his report to be sent to England and also left with Captain Patton at Lisbon. On 26 November Fletcher again asked for the report on Peniche and said that the Inspector-General of Fortifications had ordered that Landmann proceed 'to Gibraltar at the first opportunity'.[4] On receiving Mackenzie's order to work on the bridges over the Tagus, Landmann wrote to Captain Peter Patton, the senior engineer at Lisbon, assuming command of the engineering activities at Lisbon and ordering Patton, who was working on the defences at Setuval, to return to Lisbon.[5] This left Patton in a difficult position and when Landmann did not communicate any further, he was left with no choice but to raise the matter with the commander-in-chief at Lisbon and subsequently with the Board of Ordnance. On 21 January 1809, Patton wrote that Landmann had confirmed to Sir John Craddock that he had been ordered to return to Gibraltar and he was to be considered 'unattached to the army'.[6] Landmann appeared to have an ability to slip through the command net and, writing to his commander at Gibraltar on 21 February apologising 'after so long a silence', he explained he was now at Cadiz with General Mackenzie.

Landmann now became involved in the unrest at Cadiz where the population, fearful of a French attack, were objecting to the authorities' refusal to allow British troops to land. The Spanish were still suspicious of British intentions and were reluctant to allow their troops into the city. Unfortunately they did not want to make this public due to the popular unrest. To prove they did not need British aid, they had marched in Spanish troops, but when the population discovered that the regiment was full of French deserters, they rioted. The compromise agreed between the British and Spanish authorities was to appoint two British officers to speak to the population and appease their fears. General Mackenzie described the situation:

> . . . [A] deputation of Spanish arrives at the British consul's residence and said the population were 'extremely tumultuous'

because they thought the city had been betrayed and the only way to appease them would be a declaration from the British that they would assist in the defence of the town and appoint two officers (one of them artillery) to assist the Spanish defenders. I in consequence sent Captain Landmann of the Royal Engineers and Lieutenant Wills of the Royal Artillery to the Governor about 9 o'clock in the evening.[7]

The actions of these two officers appeared to have the required effect and in gratitude Landmann was given a lieutenant colonel's commission in the Spanish army. Writing to Mackenzie, Frere, the British Ambassador, reported:

I have according to your desire procured the rank of Lieutenant Colonel for Captain Landmann, and intend to apply for additional rank for Lieutenant Wills. I should hope that you might be able to dispense with the services of these two officers, who may be so usefully employed in the situation to which they have been invited.[8]

A few days later, Landmann turned up at Seville, with Captain Henry Evatt RE, who was stationed there, noting that he did not know why Landmann had arrived. Writing in April, Evatt reported that Landmann had still not returned to Gibraltar. Landmann is one of those interesting characters who plays a role in many events but does not appear to be under the direct control of anyone. He was at Cadiz for most of the period up to mid-1810, when he returned to England for the recovery of his health. He did return to the Peninsula and spent several months in some vague Military Agent role, until he was ordered home by Lord Liverpool personally. In true Landmann style, he wrote from Corunna that he would do so, as soon as he had returned some papers in his possession to Cadiz![9]

Evatt, along with Lieutenant Hustler RE, had been sent from the Gibraltar garrison to Seville at the request of John Hookham Frere 'to aid in forming the defences'.[10] His initial report on the activities of the Spanish was pessimistic:

On my arrival here, they were supplying a working party of about four hundred men constructing a breastwork around the town under the direction of a Brigadier-General and colonel of engineers, but in my opinion the work was inadequate to any kind of defence as the parapet was not more than four feet thick . . . [I recommended] not less than 5,000 men [are required] so as to carry on the whole with vigour, but from the unaccountable stupor of the supreme junta it was not till last night I could get any satisfactory compliance.[11]

Captain Patton appears again in Board of Ordnance correspondence in February 1809, when the other tricky issue of inter-service co-operation was raised. Patton had jointly signed a report on the defences around Lisbon with Major Worthy of the Royal Staff Corps. This generated a query from the Master-General:

> The report was signed first by Major Worthy, and under his signature that of Captain Patton appeared. The Master-General could not avoid considering this measure rather out of rule, as he is not aware of any other instance when the Corps of Royal Engineers and Staff Corps were blended in a professional report; His Lordship can readily understand that the Commander of the forces in Portugal might require the opinions of Captain Patton and Major Worthy on questions of position; but it occurs to the Master-General that their sentiments should have been submitted in distinct reports, unless Lieutenant General Sir J Craddock <u>should have ordered</u> the report to be signed by both these officers, in which case or even under any view, it was the duty of Captain Patton to have stated all the circumstances that accompanied this transaction.[12]

This response showed the sensitivity at home about the potentially conflicting roles of the Royal Engineers and the Royal Staff Corps. In the field, there appeared to be a more pragmatic approach, where they remained on amicable terms and in the subsequent campaigns often worked together. Having finished his work around Lisbon and Setuval, Patton was then sent to Abrantes in April 1809 to assist the Portuguese in the defence of the bridge and the castle.[13]

At the end of the last chapter it was mentioned that Captain Stephen Chapman was ordered to Lisbon and had set sail on 14 January 1809. Whilst he had been ready at Portsmouth since 28 December 1808, bad weather delayed his arrival in Lisbon until 5 March. With him travelled Captain Henry Goldfinch and Lieutenants Anthony Emmett, Edward Fyers, Rice Jones and Alexander Thomson. Already at Lisbon were the engineers Captain Patton, Lieutenants Emmett and Williams and also Lieutenant Wedekind of the King's German Legion. The fleet that brought Chapman to Lisbon also contained a force under General Sherbrooke that was expected to move swiftly on to Cadiz. Sir John Craddock, commanding at Lisbon, asked Chapman to assign engineer officers to join Sherbrooke's force 'at a moment's notice' and Goldfinch, Wedekind and Thomson were assigned.[14] Two weeks later the situation had changed, with news of Soult crossing the northern Portuguese border and advancing on Oporto. Chapman reported that:

> In consequence of the commands of Lieutenant General Sir John Craddock, I have directed Captain Goldfinch and Lieutenant Thomson to proceed to Oporto with all possible dispatch. Captain Goldfinch will take upon himself the command of the Engineer department and has been directed to put the city in such a state of defence as circumstances will permit.[15]

There were few trained troops in the north and the militia and civilian defenders were swept aside with terrible casualties. On 29 March, Soult took Oporto and Goldfinch and Thomson were taken.

In the same letter above, written on 22 March 1809, Chapman explained the other tasks that were ordered:

> Lieutenant Jones and Stanway are gone into the interior for the purpose of ascertaining whether gunboats can act with effect up the Tagus upon the flanks of an army as far as Santarem, and whether carronades in ships' launches will be beneficial as far up as Abrantes. I have also directed Lieutenant Jones to examine the Zezere where it joins the Tagus, and to proceed from there by Thomar as far as Leyria and to report to me in writing on his return, the result of his observations upon these positions. Lisbon is to be placed immediately in a state of defence and a project has been presented to General Beresford by the Portuguese Chief Engineer for that purpose . . . [the plan has] been submitted for my opinion; I have therefore been employed upon the examination of the several points upon the ground and I hope to make a beginning to the works immediately.[16]

The work described above appears to fit some of the components of what would become the Lines of Torres Vedras. Gunboats on the Tagus below Santarem were certainly a feature of the scheme. Lieutenant Rice Jones was a twenty-year-old Welshman. He was offered the Adjutancy of the Corps in Lisbon, which whilst it meant extra work, also meant extra pay which was very useful when buying the necessaries for campaign. He commented that Chapman had paid fifty guineas for a horse and he paid only slightly less. This was three months' pay for a captain, and five months' pay for a lieutenant! Jones wrote home saying that his survey of the Tagus required riding 270 miles and as had been discovered by other engineer officers, wearing his blue uniform was risky as he was often taken for a Frenchman. Jones also noted that 'I am extremely glad I went as in the event of our being obliged to evacuate this country, I may not have another opportunity of seeing it'. His view on the likely outcome of the campaign against the French was shared by many others. Although Jones initially expected Chapman to accompany him, 'he [Chapman] was detained in Lisbon commencing batteries on both sides of the Tagus'.[17] Jones noted with regret that both himself and Chapman lost their additional pay when Fletcher arrived on 23 April to take command of the Royal Engineers and appointed Edmund Mulcaster to the post of Adjutant.

On 22 February a number of officers in England received preparatory orders from the Board of Ordnance for foreign service 'at the shortest notice'. This included Fletcher, Burgoyne, Squire, Pasley, Boothby and Mulcaster.[18] Fletcher immediately set to work trying to equip his engineer force for the return to the Peninsula.

> As I am ordered to prepare for foreign service, I beg to submit for your consideration the expediency of being supplied with the following maps – the map of the Pyrenees about to be published by Arrowsmith which will include the provinces of Aragon, Catalonia, Navarre and Biscay. The map of Portugal by Lopez – the Mentelle map of Spain. The best plan extant of Cartagena and Barcelona and also that of Cadiz by Faden. I would further request that the following instruments etc. may be sent with the engineers department should it meet your approbation. One barometer, three small theodolites, three small sextants, six pocket compasses with sights, a proportion of stationary, ten quires of oiled tracing paper.[19]

William Fadden, the famous map-maker, wrote personally to the Board of Ordnance, saying that he could not provide the Lopez maps of Portugal and offered the Jefferey map as an alternative.[20] Other maps and plans were provided from the personal collection of Lieutenant Colonel Frederick W. Mulcaster RE, who had been in Lisbon in 1797 and 'took them by stealth'. Fletcher also asked for a small detachment of twenty Royal Military Artificers to be attached to the expedition. This was clearly approved as Fletcher noted that a detachment was present on his arrival in Lisbon on 2 April. With Fletcher were Captain Burgoyne and Lieutenants Boothby, Hamilton and Mulcaster. Sir Arthur Wellesley would not arrive for another three weeks. What is interesting to note is that two experienced engineer officers who were included in the preparatory orders, Charles Pasley and John Squire, did not sail. Both of these officers subsequently went on the Walcheren campaign later in the year. What is not clear is whether their orders were changed or whether they tried to avoid going to the Peninsula as it was seen as a lost cause.

On arrival in Lisbon, Fletcher had to quickly get up to speed on the activities of the Portuguese government, the British commander and the engineer officers who had preceded him. He found that two of his engineers who had been sent to assist in strengthening the defences of Oporto had been captured when it was overrun by the French. Other engineer officers were working on Portuguese proposals to fortify Lisbon. He reported 'The outer line is I fear very extensive but I have not been over the ground'.[21] Writing a few days later, Fletcher's opinion had not changed:

> I do not think there is any good point of retreat for an army near Lisbon, as there is no work or position in which a moderate rear guard could effectually cover the embarkation of the main body, if closely pursued. Positions are to be taken in front of the town but I feel they are too extensive to be defended by the present British force, and on the discipline and firmness of the Portuguese but little reliance can be placed – they are now deserting by whole regiments – The tract of country to be enclosed within the positions will, I should imagine, be quite insufficient to subsist the inhabitants of this populous city, and therefore once completely invested they must soon be compelled to surrender as I do not conceive they could bring any considerable supplies by water when an enemy possesses the left bank of the Tagus.[22]

His initial pessimistic view was based on two points that eventually proved erroneous. The first point was that the Portuguese army and militia would be incapable of playing their part in the defence of Portugal. Fletcher's view on the quality of the Portuguese troops was common amongst the British officers, Jones commenting 'I am of opinion we shall embark and leave the French in quiet possession of Lisbon, for I fear we can place but little reliance on the Portuguese fighting'. The second point was that the French would take possession of the south bank of the Tagus, meaning that supplies could not be brought in by sea. This concern was also shared by Wellesley who wrote on 9 April 1809, just before he left for Portugal, 'I have long determined to fortify the heights of Almada, so as to be able to hold them with a small body of men, as the first step I should take on my arrival'.[23] This was eventually done, but not for another eighteen months.

Fletcher commented again a few days later on the planned fortification of Lisbon:

> The Portuguese are doing little or nothing to their entrenchments immediately covering the town of Lisbon. Sir John Craddock considers the fortifying and defending this line as exclusively a concern of their own. Upon an extent of six miles they have now a hundred and sixty nine men employed though I have [stated] in the strongest way the necessity of having at least some thousands constantly at work if they mean to fortify it. I have twice seen their Minister at War who promises great things; but I confess I have but little confidence of any good effects from his exertions. I have Lieutenant Wedekind in Lisbon to assist the Portuguese engineers.[24]

Fletcher initially formed a good working relationship with Sir John Craddock, commenting 'I have the pleasure of being on the best possible terms with Sir John Craddock, and Mr Villiers [Envoy to the Court of Portugal] certainly treats me with the most unlimited confidence. He and the General do not, perhaps pull remarkably well together, so that I hardly know how to manage between them.'[25]

Most engineer officers were assigned to the army brigades, but Fletcher did not assign Chapman as he found him very useful and wanted him to stay close to headquarters. Mulcaster was also attached to headquarters as Adjutant. Burgoyne and Boothby were assigned to the right column under General Mackenzie, Williams to the centre column and Hamilton and Rice Jones to the left column. Jones had been originally ordered to remain in Lisbon and work on the defences, much to his disappointment, but Chapman had taken up his case and persuaded Fletcher to send Lieutenant Wedekind back to Lisbon and allow Jones to join Murray's brigade. In a youthful show of ingratitude, Jones now applied to be assigned to the cavalry brigade of Major-General Cotton as he thought 'he should like the active service of a dragoon brigade'.[26]

Craddock started moving his troops north out of Lisbon, establishing his headquarters at Sobral, and Fletcher travelled with him, stopping at Runa on 15 April and Caldas the next day. On 18 April, Fletcher rode to Peniche, with a caustic comment in Mulcaster's diary that they 'could not find the level country mentioned by Landmann to exist near this place'.[27] This I assume is a reference to the report that Landmann was ordered to produce in 1808 and took some months to be completed. Chapman and Mulcaster were sent to repair a bridge on the army's route to Alcobaça, but finding it could not be repaired to take the weight of artillery they improved the riverbed at the nearby ford. By 23 April the advance guard under General Hill had reached Pombal. News now arrived that Wellesley was at Lisbon. Fletcher was anxious about how he would get on with Wellesley, writing:

> As an individual I am not glad of the change as nothing can exceed the kindness and attention shown me by Sir John Craddock; and as I rather think that any engineer is not likely to be taken into the confidence of his successor. I confess should I not be employed or considered at all. I should be most heartily glad to be removed from this situation, altogether. I find Elphinstone was hardly ever spoken to. However, I hope and trust I may be mistaken.[28]

Writing a few days after Wellesley's arrival, Fletcher was clearly still very concerned about how he could work with him: 'Sir Arthur is very civil to me, but I do not think I shall ever be so much in his confidence . . . From what I saw in Zealand I do not believe that Sir A attaches much importance to our department.'[29]

The value of Captain Chapman had been recognised by others and Beresford asked for him to be sent back to Lisbon to co-ordinate the defence of the capital. Wellesley noted in his dispatches, 'I have sent two officers of Engineers with orders respecting the defence of Lisbon, the Tagus, Palmela and Setuval'.[30] Chapman's brief also included working on the embarkation point at St Julian, a task that was assigned to the second officer, Lieutenant Anthony Emmett. According to Burgoyne this order was to 'their great annoyance'.[31]

Wellington joined the army at Coimbra on 2 May for the advance on Oporto. He believed that the capital was safe for the moment and he could concentrate his forces against Soult without any chance of support reaching the French. They advanced with minor skirmishing until 11 May, when there was more determined resistance around Grijó before the French retired across the Douro into Oporto, burning the boat bridge behind them.

On 12 May, Fletcher and his adjutant, Lieutenant Edmund Mulcaster, rode to Oporto ahead of the army to obtain intelligence and then remained with Wellesley during the assault. Burgoyne and Rice Jones moved upriver towards Avintes with General Murray's brigade to look for boats or crossing-points. The French clearly thought they were safe, with the Douro, 250 yards wide at this point, between the opposing forces, but in an area where boats were used for most transport it was inevitable that some would be found. The inattention of the French just made it easier. Several engineer officers were present at the battle with only one casualty, Lieutenant George Hamilton. Mulcaster recorded 'He had been sent by General Murray to post the German Riflemen – on his return he met the cavalry on the road about [to] charge. He knew it was impossible to get by them therefore turned about and was the first man wounded at their head'.[32] A musket ball passed through one thigh, lodging in the second. It was eventually removed but Hamilton never fully recovered from his wounds and died a year later at Lisbon.

Fletcher took command of replacing the boat bridge at Oporto and work was started that night. With assistance from a number of the Royal Military Artificers the bridge was completed on the following evening.[33] The other good news following the capture of Oporto was that the engineer officers Captain Goldfinch and Lieutenant Thomson managed to escape from the French in the confusion. The Allied army pursued the retreating French until 18 May when they abandoned almost all their equipment to avoid being surrounded, Burgoyne and Mulcaster reporting repairing a bridge near Ruivães to assist the pursuit.

The bridge over the Tagus at Alcantara, by Boothby.

Bridge of Alcantara.

Fletcher now returned to the routine tasks of an engineer officer and dispatched Burgoyne to survey the course of the river Douro from Oporto to the river Agueda, over 100 miles inland.[34] At the same time, Lieutenant Williams was also dispatched to survey the river Tamega. Other engineer officers were carrying out independent roles in central Spain. Lieutenant Frank Stanway was with Sir Robert Wilson and the Loyal Lusitanian Legion, strengthening the defences at the key crossing-point over the Tagus at Alcantara. He also took the precaution of laying a mine on the bridge. When it was approached by a French force on 10 June, Stanway initially commanded the batteries defending the bridge and when there was concern it would be taken, blew an arch.[35] Clearly some progress had been made since Corunna, where Charles Pasley complained the engineers had failed to effectively destroy bridges during the retreat. Stanway disabled a bridge that had withstood everything nature and man could throw at it for 1,700 years. I am sure it is something he would not want to be remembered for.

The rigours of field operations were already having an effect, with three engineer officers being unfit for duty and there being too few to meet the demands on them. On 31 May, Fletcher wrote home saying Wellesley had asked for ten more engineer officers to be sent out.[36] This request generated a petty response back in England: 'It seems very extraordinary Sir Arthur should be applying for more Engineers, since it does not appear from his public dispatches that he had made any use of those already with him.'[37] Being mentioned in dispatches was important to both individuals and their units. It was the only public recognition of their services and could lead to promotion for the officers involved. The Board of Ordnance was particularly sensitive about how they were reported since they were not part of the army and their relationship with it was often strained. Whilst the Royal Engineers were generally well treated in dispatches, the Royal Artillery had a much more difficult time.

Fletcher's correspondence shows that he continued to dispatch officers to survey the country. He was clearly trying to build a comprehensive picture as surveys in June and July 1809 included Burgoyne surveying the Minho and the province of Entre-Douro-e-Minho; Jones reported on the route of the river Alagon; Chapman on the fords on the Tagus below Abrantes; Williams reported on the Tagus, Mondego and Sierra Estrella and Jones reported on the River Tietar. The latter reconnaissance was likely done for Wellesley's planned joint operation with the Spanish General Cuesta.

This constant movement was having a terrible impact on the finances of the engineers, particularly the younger ones. Jones recorded in June 1809 that he bought a pony for 60 dollars as the back of his horse was too sore to ride. The horse that had cost him 90 dollars died later in the month and

Jones was faced with the expense of replacing it. When Fletcher ordered him to survey the river Zezere he had to report that he was unable through lack of transport. The nature of the duties they carried out meant that they had to employ a servant to take care of their personal belongings, which as a minimum meant they had to provide three horses or mules. Whilst the military provided basic rations for man and horse, the cost of the horses and servants had to be provided from the officers' pay. This huge expense was recognised and the basic pay for an engineer officer was doubled when on active service. However, this was still insufficient and there was a constant stream of letters throughout the war from the commanding engineers to the Board of Ordnance complaining about the huge personal expense. This was one of the hidden barriers to being an officer in the military. Without personal wealth it was very difficult to survive on army pay and the higher you rose in the ranks the more difficult it became. An army officer was in a slightly better position as he had some access to regimental transport and could use soldiers as servants, which significantly reduced personal costs.

From Oporto, Wellesley's army now started moving south, travelling through Coimbra and arriving at Abrantes in early June, the army remaining there whilst the troops concentrated and Wellesley waited for money to be delivered from Lisbon, without which he would be unable to buy supplies as he moved across central Spain. Transport and food remained major concerns for the commander. On 28 June the army moved forward, reaching Plasencia on 9 July. Jones was active through this period surveying the Alagon and Tietar rivers in the vicinity of Plasencia. He noted in his diary that Lieutenant D of the Portuguese engineers accompanied him. There is little evidence that the Portuguese engineers were working outside of their country early in the war, but clearly they were. Jones also recorded being asked by the local junta at Plasencia to identify a spot to place a bridge across the river Tietar. Jones met with Sir Robert Wilson and spent some time at his headquarters. Over the next few days, Jones carried messages between Wilson and Wellesley before arriving at Talavera on 22 July where he was appointed adjutant with a welcome three shillings a day extra pay. Fletcher and Mulcaster also visited the bridge at Alcantara to determine if a repair was possible 'but seeing [that it] was an undertaking of too great magnitude to be executed without much time, labour, means and money neither of which appeared to be forthcoming the Colonel determined to report accordingly to Sir Arthur.'[38] Fletcher had taken the time to find and speak to Senor Miranda, the local master mason, who stated that the repair was beyond him.

On 11 July Wellesley rode to meet Cuesta near Almaraz. A plan of action was agreed and the two armies met at Oropesa, just short of Talavera where the French awaited them. The British army left Plasencia on 17 July and the next day, according to Fortescue, 'the whole army passed over a flying bridge at La Bazagona'.³⁹ This was the first major bridge built by the Royal Staff Corps, two companies being present under the command of Captain Alexander Todd. Rice Jones' report, mentioned above, from his reconnaissance of the river Tietar was written on 11 July. In it, he mention the ford at Bazagona as being readily passable, but more importantly states that the roads to the ford were good, I would assume that Wellesley had seen the report before he issued his orders for the placement of the bridge.

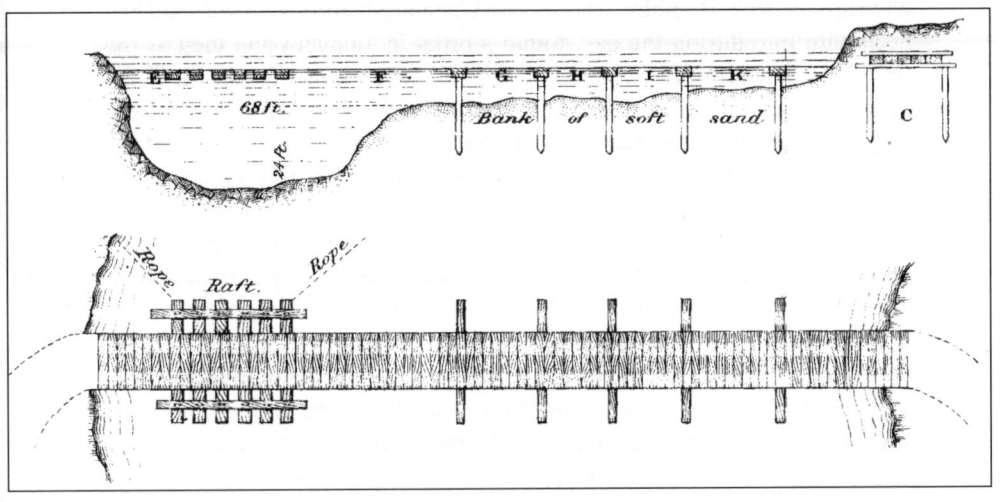

The bridge over the Tietar, from Douglas,

First contact with the French was on 22 July and Wellesley wanted a full attack the following morning whilst the Allies had a great superiority in numbers. Cuesta would not agree to this and when they advanced two days later, the French, having realised their inferiority, had retired. Cuesta then pursued them alone, coming up against the reinforced French army near Toledo. The Spanish were forced into a rapid retreat and were back at Talavera on 27 July. Fletcher remained with Wellesley at Talavera but was keeping his officers busy. On 25 July, Lieutenant Richard Mudge RE was sent forward to reconnoitre the Alberche and Mulcaster was sent to the Tagus at Arzobispo and Almaraz. Mulcaster was impressed by the bridge at Almaraz saying 'It is forever to be lamented that as fine an edifice should have been ruined'. He also recorded that the bridge of pontoons put in place by Cuesta depended on dry weather.⁴⁰ The following morning Mulcaster returned to Arzobispo and, hearing accounts of a defeat the day before, rushed back to Talavera but arrived too late to take any part in the battle.

On the morning of 27 July, the Allied army was now facing a stronger French force than expected and the supply system had failed, with the British troops already on half rations. Jones recorded that after Wellington and Cuesta had discussed the situation, at around 11 a.m. he was ordered to construct a redoubt for ten guns in the centre of the Allied position. This was carried out using 200-strong working parties from the British brigades.[41] This redoubt was to play a vital part in the battle the following day.

The French attacked unexpectedly that night but after some confusion were driven back. Boothby, who was on General Sherbrooke's staff and had been with him during the day, found a billet in Talavera and then as the firing continued into the evening rode out to find his general who was 'glad of [his] timely arrival' as few of his staff were present. Boothby was used to convey orders and as darkness fell, he found himself out in front of the British line as the French approached: 'It instantly struck us both that in the confusion of night the fire would spread down the whole line in which case we should be blown to pieces . . . I found myself galloping up into an interrupted sheet of fire [when] I was struck in the leg by a musket ball, which brought me to the ground.'[42] General Sherbrooke found Boothby later and ordered him carried from the field where he had to wait until the 29th for his leg to be amputated. His book goes into graphic detail of the process of amputation. Boothby was one of the wounded captured by the French when Cuesta abandoned them after the battle. He received good advice from fellow engineer Henry Goldfinch who had been captured at Oporto; 'You must cry out "*Capitaine Anglais*" and you will be treated well'. This proved to be true although Boothby remained in captivity until the middle of 1810.

The main battle was on 28 July, where several French attacks were repulsed but not without significant Allied casualties. Fletcher, with his new adjutant Rice Jones, remained at Wellesley's side throughout the battle with Jones recording he took messages to the Allied cavalry on the left flank of the army. Lieutenant Stanway was wounded 'in the belly' whilst serving on General Mackenzie's staff, the two other engineer officers, Goldfinch and Forster, being unhurt. Forster was thanked for his services in the general orders of the 4th Division. There was also another unexpected casualty amongst the small group of Royal Engineer officers. Lieutenant Edward Fyers had become unwell with mental health problems. Burgoyne described finding him on 2 August at Oropesa 'with a fever and insane'. Mulcaster commented that 'Fyers had got off' on 9 August. Fyers, who was the son of Colonel William Fyers RE, was eventually committed to a mental asylum in 1819 but still held his rank in the Corps up to that time, including promotion to captain in 1813.

The day after the battle Wellesley was faced with failing rations for the troops and around 4,000 wounded. Believing he was safe, he remained on the battlefield, unaware that Soult was descending on his rear with superior forces. Soult arrived at Plasencia on 1 August, seizing Wellesley's stores and then advanced to attempt to take the crossing-points over the Tagus at Almaraz and Arzobispo, thereby cutting Wellesley's communications with Portugal. Wellesley, still believing that Soult only had a small force with him, set off to intercept him on 3 August, leaving his wounded in the care of Cuesta. The reality of the situation was then discovered and Wellesley chose to retreat, rejecting Cuesta's preference to again face the French. The British passed over the Tagus at Arzobispo on the morning of 4 August, leaving the Spanish in possession of the crossing-point. Wellesley also ordered Craufurd's brigade to reinforce the Spanish holding the crossing at Almaraz as its loss could once again threaten the retreat. They arrived there on 6 August with Fletcher visiting on the next day and marking out additional batteries to defend the crossing. Jones commented 'we were a little disturbed by the firing of the enemy' from the other side of the river. Captain Chapman, who had arrived from Lisbon on 30 July, was sent the following day to construct the batteries. On 8 August, the French took the crossing at Arzobispo from the Spanish. The next few days the armies faced each other across the Tagus, the French finally recognising that the Allied armies had evaded them. Wellesley was able to retire unmolested back to the Portuguese border around Badajoz. Whilst the British government tried hard to sell Talavera as a great victory, many were unconvinced, reading of a British army retreating before a French one for the second time in a year. Wellesley, now Viscount Wellington, had learnt the same hard lessons as Sir John Moore. The Iberian Peninsula was a difficult environment in which to move and feed an army, operations with the Spanish were fraught with difficulties and if the French could concentrate their forces they were too strong to resist.

During the retreat after the Battle of Talavera, it is interesting to note that within days of receiving a report from Chapman,[43] both Fletcher and Wellington had separately written home mentioning the defence of Lisbon.[44] Chapman, who was now with the army, dated his report 18 August 1809, so it was probably completed whilst the army rested at Truxillo. The options were clearly being discussed as the troops retreated westward. On 10 August, Canning, in a letter to Marquess Wellesley (Sir Arthur's brother), the newly-appointed ambassador to Spain, had also posed the question, could Portugal be defended? Wellington's view was outlined to Castlereagh, Secretary of State for War and the Colonies:

> My opinion is, that we ought to be able to hold Portugal, if the Portuguese army and Militia are complete. The difficulty upon this sole question lies in the embarkation of the British Army. There are so many entrances into Portugal, the whole country being frontier, that it would be very difficult to prevent the enemy from penetrating; and it is probable that we should be obliged to confine ourselves to the preservation of that which is most important, the capital . . . However, I have not entirely made up my mind upon this interesting point. I have a great deal of information upon it, but I should wish to have more before I can decide upon it.[45]

Wellesley had held his positive view on the defence of Portugal since his first visit. When he wrote his *Memorandum of the Defence of Portugal* for the British government in March 1809 he clearly stated 'I have always been of the opinion that Portugal might be defended, whatever might be the result of the contest in Spain . . . The French would not have been able to overrun Portugal with a force smaller than 100,000 men'.[46] Although his argument must have been at least partially accepted by the government, Fletcher, like most others, was more pessimistic:

> The practicability of defending the Capital to the last extremity and of afterwards embarking the British troops I confess I have always doubted. Sir Arthur Wellesley is naturally anxious to combine these two objects, but I believe that he now begins to feel that the doing so, would be certainly difficult if not altogether impossible. The ground is in itself unfavourable and a very long line must be established to save the retreat of the army . . . Even admitting that the city of Lisbon, as a fortified position were tenable . . . I should imagine that a population of perhaps three hundred thousand souls cannot be long supported in a town without magazines . . . These ideas generally, I have continued to submit to the consideration of Sir Arthur Wellesley, who now seems to be of the opinion, that these are almost insuperable difficulties opposed to the measure of defending Lisbon to the last extremity, and then embarking the British troops.

Fletcher finished his letter saying: 'He [Wellington] however means to revisit that place in a short time to determine what steps can be taken.'[47]

Once the army was safe and settled, Wellington's primary task was to make this decision. One of the few advantages the Allies had at this time was the inability of the French to concentrate their forces. There were a number of reasons for this. Firstly, the French marshals were not good at working together, their egos and characters often making co-operation difficult. Secondly, Napoleon tried to conduct the war from a distance, never giving overall command to any one of his subordinates. This made formulation of an overall strategy almost impossible. Thirdly, the resistance of the Spanish population required the use of large numbers of French troops to keep order. This meant these troops were not available for field operations. Finally, the presence of islands of resistance across the Iberian Peninsula meant the French had to spread their immense resources thinly. There was not only Lisbon, but Gibraltar, Cadiz, Tarragona and Alicante, all of which needed to be watched and could launch attacks with little warning. This factor was a key component in Wellington's thinking on the defence of Portugal.

Whilst the army settled into winter quarters, there was no let-up for the engineers in the reconnaissance work. Fletcher continued to receive a flurry of surveys from across central Portugal and Spain, all of which will have added to Wellington's knowledge of the operational area. Many of these were based around the route of the retreat with surveys of the Guadiana, the border roads and towns and the routes back to Lisbon. Goldfinch, Mulcaster and Stanway were principally involved in this work.

On 7 October, Wellington invested Sir John Sherbrooke with the Order of the Bath. Mulcaster succinctly described the event as a 'grand let off and dance in the evening with ugly women and bad singing'.[48] The following morning Wellington left Badajoz for Lisbon, the primary purpose of the visit being to decide on the defensibility of Portugal. With him travelled the engineers Fletcher, Chapman and Rice Jones. The planning for the following year had started.

Chapter 3

The Lines of Torres Vedras and the Defence of Portugal

Most people interested in the Peninsular War will have heard of the Lines of Torres Vedras, but probably not much more. Even modern works on the Peninsular War have treated it very lightly. For example, Esdaile's recent single-volume work has a chapter of twenty-eight pages entitled Torres Vedras, but all mention of the Lines has ended by the second paragraph of the second page.[1] David Gates' book takes even less space to deal with them. Oman sets aside seventeen good pages of description (out of 5,000 in total) and Fortescue a mere three pages out of several thousand. Recently, we only have Norris and Bremner's rare booklet, Ian Fletcher's Osprey book and John Grehan's work on Torres Vedras as the only serious attempts to describe the Lines since John T. Jones's secret work of 1829, which later became Volume 3 of his third edition of 1846 on the sieges of the Peninsular War. It is understandable that there is less interest in this part of the war as it does not involve any battles and the Lines were never assaulted. However, the Lines of Torres Vedras were every bit as important to Wellington as his victories on the field of battle.

The situation in the Peninsula at the end of 1809 was not good for Britain, neither politically nor militarily. Initial enthusiasm for the defence of the Iberian Peninsula had waned in the light of events. Wellesley's early victories at Roliça and Vimeiro were followed by the deeply unpopular Convention of Cintra. Worse followed with Moore's valiant attempt to assist the Spanish that turned into the costly retreat and evacuation of the British army from Corunna in January 1809. Wellesley's return to the Peninsula in April that year had early success at Oporto followed by the dubious victory at Talavera, and the year ended with the British still in the Iberian Peninsula but back in Portugal with no-one being happy with the situation, neither the Spanish, the Portuguese, the British nor even the French! If we take into account the wider strategic context of the last few years, including the British surrender in South America and the problems in Sweden and Walcheren, the public perception of the British military was not good.

The Anglo-Portuguese and Spanish military only survived in 1808–9 thanks to the difficulty the French had concentrating their more numerous troops, but the French knew they could not allow this to continue. The British presence needed to be crushed quickly to stop it bolstering the weak Spanish and Portuguese resistance. The main difficulty for the French in achieving this was their war with Austria. An Austrian success would distract Napoleon's attention from the Iberian Peninsula for the foreseeable future, but a defeat would allow the massive French military machine to swing in the direction of Spain. Events in central Europe were being watched anxiously in both London and Lisbon and when Austria's defeat at Wagram in July 1809 was announced, everyone knew this meant that Napoleon would send more troops to the Peninsula. Wellington, writing to Castlereagh in August 1809, commented: 'Napoleon is reinforcing his armies in Spain, you may depend on it. He and his marshals are desirous of revenging on us the different blows we have given them, and when they come to the Peninsula, their first and great object will be to get the English out.'[2] In the army these events were also being followed carefully, Ensign John Aitchison of the 3rd Guards commenting: 'We have it from the French that peace was signed on 1st October – they say B [Bonaparte] himself is to come to Spain.'[3] Mucaster commented in a similar manner: 'There is an account that Austria has given up Trieste to France to settle the existing differences. Should this be the case we cannot expect a very long residence in this country.'[4]

The British government was in a difficult situation. They could not match the size of the vast French armies and were continually concerned about the loss of their largest (and only) land force. It had to be protected from destruction. This left the conundrum that England needed to stay to support the Iberian defenders, but in the last resort it would have to evacuate the army rather than risk losing it.

Wellington would have been aware of his government's concern when he arrived back in the Peninsula in April 1809 and will have also watched from afar the events unfolding in central Europe even whilst he was campaigning in central Spain. As well as the events in Europe, there was also turmoil at home in both the government and the monarchy. About the same time that Wellington heard of the Austrian defeat, he also learnt that the government at home had fallen as a consequence of the ill health of the Prime Minister, Portland, and the political fall-out of the Walcheren campaign that led to the duel between Castlereagh and Canning. King George III was also seriously ill, and as the Prince Regent was aligned to the Whig party, who were strongly against the war, it was likely there would be a change in government soon.

Whilst the pessimists in the British army in Portugal and England, and that included pretty much everybody, were saying that the army was only pausing momentarily before it ran for the ships, some people were thinking about how to stop the French tidal wave. Once the army was safely back at the Portuguese border, Wellington's thoughts turned to future operations and the security of the Allied forces. He left Badajoz on 8 October 1809 and arrived in Lisbon on the 12th. His party included George Murray, Quarter Master-General, Benjamin D'Urban, QMG of the Portuguese army and three engineer officers; Lieutenant Colonel Richard Fletcher, Captain Stephen Chapman and Lieutenant Rice Jones. The next few days were spent reconnoitring both the hills to the north of Lisbon and the terrain as far south as Setuval.

Rice Jones, writing to his father who was a Captain in the Denbeigh Militia, commented:

> I know that his Lordship and the Col [Fletcher] have been riding all over the country for 30 miles round, and have nearly knocked up Colonel Fletcher's stud; from which it is easy to conclude that the ground to be occupied for the defence of Lisbon is a material part of the Commander of the Forces' business at this place.[5]

Rice Jones continued in the typical style of the British officer of that period writing home and divulged confidential information: 'I will also tell you what is an impenetrable secret at present even to our officers; viz., that *all* our Corps are ordered from the army to a place called Castanheira . . . and understand there are a great many works in contemplation.' His letter concludes with the other typical theme of officers writing home:

> These measures look too much like a determination . . . to defend Portugal to the last extremity; that extremity will certainly arise as soon as the French are able to advance in any force, and we shall then very likely have just such a scramble to get off as the army at Corunna last year.

It appears that Fletcher was not always with Wellington when looking at the area. Fletcher and Chapman visited St Julian on 15 October and Fletcher reported his finding to Wellington in a letter of the same date.[6]

The result of this visit led to Wellington's famous memo to Fletcher of 20 October 1809, describing the work that was to be carried out. This was an outline of the task which he would have developed through riding through the hills, by talking to the Portuguese and looking at previous analyses of the area, particularly by the French engineer Vincent and the Portuguese engineer Neves Costa. Wellington had also operated in this area during the previous year's campaign and would have built up some knowledge of the terrain. The detailed design of the Lines was developed over the coming months by Fletcher and the British, Portuguese and German engineers. Each redoubt was individually designed to fit the terrain and its operational needs. If you break down the many paragraphs of Wellington's memorandum into general tasks it looks like this:

Wellington's Instructions, 20 October 1809	
Build dams	3
Destroy bridges	2
Construct redoubts	15
Scarping	1
Build roads	3
Destroy roads	4
Build signal posts	1

Of the twenty-nine activities listed, only just over half were related to building forts. The original plan was to build a single line of defence. This eventually became the second line. In front of this line, two major forts were to be built at Torres Vedras and Sobral to blunt any French advance. As more time became available, the basic plan for the Lines was expanded to include many more forts and other defensive measures.

Wellington's memorandum was very detailed in terms of where needed to be surveyed and the purpose of the defences, but there was generally no detail about what was to be built. The only exceptions were for the major forts at Torres Vedras, Montachique and Sobral, but even for these Wellington described no more than the capacity of the fort (e.g., for 4,000 men) with no specifics on the design or the number of guns. These details was left to the engineers to plan and implement. Wellington wrote to Beresford on 26 October ordering nearly 2,000 Portuguese militia to report to Torres Vedras, Sobral and St Julian and on the 31st ordered the commissary to prepare 19,000 palisades and 10,000 fascines. Wellington returned to Badajoz on 27 October 1809 and then travelled on to Seville, leaving Fletcher to co-ordinate the work.

The primary purpose of the Lines of Torres Vedras was to defend the four main routes to Lisbon though the passes at Mafra, Montachique and Bucellas and the river route past Alhandra. Descriptions of the Lines usually focus on the two defensive lines to the north of Lisbon and the embarkation point at St Julian. In addition, a fourth line was built on the left (south) bank of the Tagus opposite Lisbon and defences were strengthened at Setubal and Peniche. There were also defensive works around the perimeter of the city of Lisbon. The key defences were:

Number of Forts in the Lines of Torres Vedras			
Line	**Forts**	**Guns**	**Troops**
First Line	70	319	18,700
Second Line	69	215	15,000
Third Line (St Julian)	13	94[7]	5,300
Fourth (Almada)	17	86	7,500

Following the issue of Wellington's memorandum of 20 October, Fletcher issued a general recall to all Royal Engineer officers except two, Burgoyne and Emmett who were with the army at Badajoz. By the end of the month almost all the engineer officers in the Peninsula had arrived in Lisbon.[8] Work started in early November 1809, as soon as the engineer officers began arriving. The initial focus was on the embarkation point at St Julian and the two major advance posts at Sobral and Torres Vedras. Once these were under way, the focus moved to the extensive fortifications of what became the second line.

Dates Work Started on the Lines		
Location	**Officer in Charge**	**Start Date**
St Julian	Wedekind	3 Nov 1809
Sobral	Williams	4 Nov 1809
Torres Vedras	Mulcaster	8 Nov 1809
Mafra	Ross	17 Feb 1810
Ericeira	R. Jones	19 Feb 1810
Montachique	Mulcaster	19 Feb 1810
Via Longa	Stanway	24 Feb 1809
Arruda	Forster	19 Mar 1810
Ponte do Rol	Thomson	26 Feb 1810[9]

Rice Jones' excitement diminished rapidly when he was left in Lisbon by Fletcher to co-ordinate the various activities for his commander whilst the other engineers started work on the Lines. He complained 'I am the only officer here except Hamilton who continues so lame since he was wounded at Oporto.'[10] The reason Fletcher had left him in Lisbon was because Jones' health was not good. One of the tasks that fell to Rice Jones was paying the civilian workmen. He noted in his diary on 29 November, riding 'to Sobral where I mustered and paid the artificers' and similarly on 17 December he 'rode to Torres Vedras . . . and settled with the artificers'.

Fletcher continually moved around the area north of Lisbon and corresponded with Wellington on his findings and his recommendations. He wrote a long and detailed report to Wellington on 25 December making recommendation on redoubts to be built at various points. He also noted his concern that the number of workers requested for St Julian and Sobral had not been provided despite a number of requests through Marshal Beresford and this would delay completion of the defences. Complaints about the shortage of workmen were a constant theme thoughout the whole period of the construction, with Fletcher, Beresford and Wellington writing to the Portuguese authorities at different times. Fletcher finished his letter by reporting that Captain Goldfinch was assisting the Portuguese engineers on the defences of Lisbon[11] 'as requested by Marshal Beresford' as well as superintending the work at St Julian. Another engineer officer had been sent to Abrantes to assist Captain Patton in fortifying the town. A few days later, Fletcher wrote another extensive letter on the position at Castanheira on the Tagus. Although he did not make any specific recommendations, leaving the decision to Wellington, the work to make the area defensible appeared significant. Although initially Wellington was in favour of carrying out the works, when he visited a few weeks later the decision was made to move the position back to Alhandra.[12]

Through December 1809 and January 1810 Fletcher and Wellington kept up a detailed correspondence that described the planned and actual work at Castanheira, Mafra, Montechique and Ericeira. Wellington showed particular concern about both extremities, describing the western end as being the most important to the 'English'. In early January 1810, Mulcaster, who was leading the building work at Torres Vedras, reported the progress to his friend Burgoyne:

> My entrenchments are getting on, but not so rapidly as I had hoped . . . I wish you could see my entrenchments, unlucky dogs that ever want to attack them if they are defended by Englishmen. They will bite the dust wholesale. The Merinos had not arrived when

Goldfinch wrote but he was entreating for a passage for them . . . I like his system on this occasion, which is 'damn the expense'.[13]

Whilst war was a serious affair, it did not mean that some private business could not be conducted. Burgoyne had arranged to buy twenty Merino sheep on behalf of a number of officers to ship back to England, the others being the engineers Mulcaster, Goldfinch, Major Dundas of the Royal Staff Corps and Mr Pickering the Commissary. He noted on 20 December that 'he had shipped off some Merino sheep consigned to Goldfinch at Lisbon, four of them belonging to me'.[14] Whilst Mulcaster might have been proud of his work on the Lines, he, like most of his colleagues, wanted to be with the army. Writing a few days later: 'I wish that I could get to the army afterwards but fear some [more] vile redoubts are in store for me. I have as yet been afraid to ask Fletcher what is to become of me. He is here to stay and flies about the Country like a Jack Snipe.'[15]

The importance of this defensive work is perhaps best illustrated by the fact that during his visit in February 1810 Wellington gave orders that all requests made by Fletcher were to be accepted without question: 'All orders . . . drawn by Lieutenant Colonel Fletcher upon the Deputy Commissary General may be paid . . . [and] . . . the Deputy Commissary General may supply to Lieutenant Colonel Fletcher . . . without waiting for further orders from me.'[16] Wellington was not known for giving any authority or decision-making powers to his subordinates, but throughout this period the senior engineer officers were given such authority. These included Fletcher, Captain John Jones and later Captain Henry Goldfinch when he was building the defences to the south of the Tagus. The engineer officers were given similar civilian powers to make demands for men and materials in any of the districts in which they were working.

As mentioned earlier, the Lines of Torres Vedras were not just made up of forts but included a range of other defensive features. There were extensive salt pans on the banks of the Tagus near Via Longa, and the banks of these were broken to flood the whole area, and at the western end of the Lines the river Zizandre was dammed to achieve a similar result. On the low-lying area around Alhandra, extensive abatis were constructed by cutting down cork and olive trees and laying them down whole in a continuous line. All other cover was removed by destroying walls and buildings so that the French would be exposed to Allied fire when advancing to attack the defences. The hilly terrain to the west of Alhandra was made impassable by scarping over a mile of the hillside, using gunpowder to blow away the crests of the hills to create an impassable vertical face. Both ends

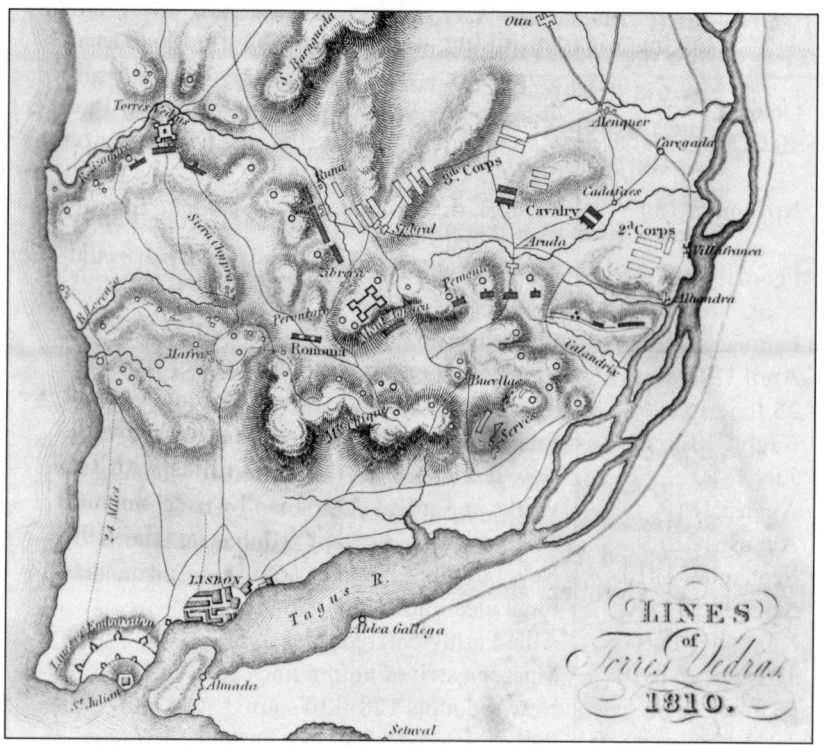

The Lines of Torres Vedras in 1810, from Napier.

of the Lines were covered by the Royal Navy with warships patrolling the Atlantic coast and gunboats patrolling the river Tagus.

To complement the work to make the defences as difficult as possible for the French to attack, significant work was also expended on roads and bridges. In front of the Lines, roads and bridges were broken up or mined to inhibit French movement, while behind them roads were built or improved and bridges repaired to facilitate the movement of Allied troops. Wellington intended to keep the bulk of his regular troops mobile to react to any attack and was able to move his troops faster than the French could.

The Lines were also part of a wider defensive network in southern Portugal. Setuval to the south of Lisbon was strengthened as a potential embarkation point, as was Peniche. Abrantes was strengthened to deny access to the French both to the locality for supplies and to the major crossing-point on the Tagus. Whilst the French were in front of the Lines, Abrantes and Peniche were used to launch attacks on French convoys and foraging parties. Work on strengthening these three towns was under way long before work on the Lines themselves began.

54 Wellington's Engineers

Timeline for the Building of the Lines of Torres Vedras	
October 1809	First visit by Wellington accompanied by Fletcher
20 October 1809	Memorandum from Wellington to Fletcher on the lines
November 1809	Work started on redoubts at St Julian, Sobral and Torres Vedras
February 1810	Second visit by Wellington. Work at Castanheira scrapped
February 1810	Work started on defences of the passes
April 1810	New redoubts 103–108 started at St Julian
25 June 1810	Fletcher reports that 108 redoubts are complete
6 July 1810	John T. Jones left in charge of construction work
July 1810	New redoubts 114–120 started at Alhandra
August 1810	Works at Setuval completed
August 1810	Further work agreed at St Julian
September 1810	New redoubts 121–124 started at Calahandrix
September 1810	Final clearance work commenced
8 October 1810	Allied army entered lines
11 October 1810	Masséna arrives before lines at Sobral
October 1810	New redoubts 128–130 started at Monte Agraça
10 December 1810	Work started on defences on south of Tagus
1811	New redoubts 131–144 started
July 1811	Four permanent jetties built at St Julian

   The majority of the work to build the Lines was carried out by Portuguese civilians, generally under the control of officers of the British or King's German Legion Engineers. Two militia regiments were involved from the start to provide labour. As the scale and urgency of the work grew, thousands of Portuguese civilians were conscripted to help. There were constant problems with getting sufficient labour and there were numerous complaints to the Portuguese Secretary of War about the local governors and town officials not providing the required numbers.

   As well as the small number of engineer officers, never exceeding twenty, there was a similarly tiny number of Royal Military Artificers. An additional number of tradesmen were provided through volunteers from the British line regiments stationed at Lisbon, although this number never exceeded 150. Spread in one and twos across the works, at the peak of activity they managed the work of several thousand Portuguese.

According to John Jones, the historian of the building of the Lines, there were very few Portuguese engineer officers involved in the construction. Fletcher's letter passing command of the construction to Jones, names three of them.[17] The Portuguese have a different view and claim that many more were involved. It is highly likely that this was the case as their local knowledge, language and understanding of the culture would have made managing the authorities and population much easier. My research had identified several other Portuguese engineers who worked on the Lines at some stage during their construction. This does not include those working directly on the defences around the city of Lisbon. Mulcaster names two engineers officers not mentioned by Jones, and Rice Jones a third. On 12 November 1809, Mulcaster wrote that:

> I forgot to tell you I have an old Captain of Portuguese Engineers here under my orders. He complained to Thomson that I don't tell him my plans. I must treat him with more confidence in the future. I think I have been too civil and formal with him . . . There is a [Portuguese] Major at Sobral under their orders [that is, of Williams and Forster]. We don't treat our allies with much respect.[18]

The officer working for Mulcaster was Captain Bellegarde and the officer working for Williams was probably either Major Lourenco Homem da Cunha D'Eça, or Major Manuel Joaquim Brandão de Sousa. The issue of ranks is interesting as it is unlikely that a major in the Portuguese engineers would agree to work under a British captain. Wellington was clear that he expected the most senior officer to command although there was always some ability to be flexible in its application. It is more likely that the Portuguese major was under the direct command of Fletcher or his Portuguese superiors and not Captain Williams.

Although the conscription of Portuguese civilians was compulsory, the workers were paid. Men women and children were employed, with differing levels of pay. Whilst the money was probably gratefully accepted by the displaced civilians, many of the labourers were from the surrounding villages, and were taken away from their normal employment in the fields. As the numbers grew it became more difficult for the civilians to find food. Eventually, they were also provided with rations, which were of course deducted from their pay. The engineer officers found themselves single-handedly managing not only the engineering work on the Lines, but also the administrative side of obtaining, feeding and paying the workers. This put an additional demand on their already limited resources. Eventually, commissariat staff were appointed to undertake the administrative duties, leaving the engineers to concentrate on their proper priorities.

The engineer John Squire writing to Henry Bunbury, Undersecretary of State for War, on 27 May 1810, reported nearly seventy redoubts had been constructed including the major forts at Torres Vedras and Sobral. By 25 June, Fletcher was reporting to Wellington that 108 forts had been completed.[19] This was a considerable achievement in about eight months and averaged about three forts per week. A week later, Fletcher wrote home updating the Board of Ordnance on his progress. His letter is really surprising in that he was still uncertain that the Lines could be defended, writing:

> The length of the lines to be defended is however so great that but a small proportion of them can be occupied by troops, and as the ground is in many places practicable for artillery . . . and in general very easy for infantry to pass over, I do not feel sure to say that against any superior numbers we are by any means secure.[20]

With the work progressing well, Fletcher and Chapman left Lisbon to join Wellington's army on 6 July and Captain John T. Jones was left in charge of completing the works with full authority. The work was not without its difficulties in dealing with civilians who were unhappy about the damage to their land and possessions. Most civilians were given no choice (e.g. the destruction of mills) but some had to be handled with more consideration. On 12 July, Jones reported:

> I am going to Via Longa to examine into a complaint by the Marchioness of Abrantes of the injury we are doing to her salt pans. I have in consequence of a memorandum from Mr Stewart stopped the cut and will after seeing it again make some proposition to you for another expedient if I find I cannot give the cut a direction by which it shall do no harm to the pans.

The problem was resolved to everyone's satisfaction, as Jones reported a few days later:

> Arranged with Stanway to widen and deepen an old ditch which crosses the whole breadth of the ground a few yards in advance of the salt pans of the marchioness of Abrantes and which I think will answer every purpose of the originally requested cut without causing the slightest damage to the property of anyone.[21]

After the disaster at Almeida (see next chapter), Fletcher wrote to Jones on 29 August, saying movement towards the Lines had started and that they should be made ready for immediate occupation.[22] Fletcher identified completion of the defensive works around the embarkation point at St Julian as a priority.[23] Two days later, after he had discussed the situation further with Wellington, Fletcher wrote again to Jones asking for the abatis to be formed by felling trees, for several bridges and roads that had been previously identified to be mined, and for ammunition to be moved into the forts. Wellington still held back on breaking the banks of the Tagus to flood the salt pans at Via Longa, but a week later, on 7 September, he gave the order to do so. Between July and October 1810, around 50,000 trees were felled for use in the Lines.

As we now know, the French did not move directly on Lisbon and another three months was gained to work on the defences. This time was used primarily to strengthen the first line to a point where it would stop the French rather than just delay them. The scale of the works completed when the lines were occupied was 126 redoubts with 427 guns requiring 30,000 men, plus the thirteen forts at St Julian which housed a further 94 guns and 5,350 men.[24] By 1812 the number of forts had grown to 152 redoubts with 524 guns requiring 34,000 men, excluding the fortifications to the south of the Tagus where another seventeen forts were erected.

In December 1810 Captain Goldfinch RE, assisted by Rice Jones, started work on redoubts to the south of the Tagus comprising of seventeen redoubts and repairs to the castle at Almada.[25] The original plan had been for thirty-five of them,[26] but this was considered excessive and was cut back. The works to the south of the Tagus had been under consideration for some time. Wellington had originally intended to do it in April 1809 but did not. He wrote to Admiral Berkeley in March 1810 on the subject, referring to a report from Fletcher.[27] Fletcher's letters from early 1809 also mention the threat to the south of the Tagus. What is not clear is, if Wellington expected a French attack on Portugal to use both sides of the river Tagus, why did he leave reinforcing the south side so late?

Improvements and repairs went on throughout the war. As many of the redoubts were built of earth, the heavy rains took their toll, and keeping the defences in good condition took constant attention. Even through the first winter of 1810, there are numerous comments on having to repair the defences. As late as February 1811, Fletcher reported there were still 'several thousands of workmen employed'.[28] Whilst the Lines were never used again, Wellington had greater confidence to press the French knowing that he had an impregnable position he could retire to if the need arose.

Before moving on from the building of the Lines of Torres Vedras, I am going to review some particular aspects of them.

The Portuguese Thought of it First, or Did They?
There were two contemporary proposals for the defence of Lisbon that are frequently mentioned. The first was prepared by the French engineer officer Vincent for Junot after he arrived in Lisbon in 1807. This report focusses on the defence of the city and the harbour by fortifying both banks of the Tagus. It does not really cover the hills to the north of Lisbon. The second was prepared by the Portuguese engineer, José Maria Neves Costa, for the Portuguese government. Neves Costa produced the report in May 1809 describing his plans for the defence of Lisbon and subsequently claimed that the original idea was his.

There is certainly evidence that the Portuguese were working on defensive positions around Lisbon in early 1809, but that is not to confirm that they were working on the proposals made by Neves Costa. However, I have to say that I think it is possible. Stephen Chapman, the Commanding Royal Engineer, reported as early as March 1809 that the Portuguese Chief Engineer had presented a proposal for the defence of Lisbon to Beresford.[29] It is probable that Wellington was aware of the earlier plans of Vincent and Costa but he never acknowledged that they were the basis of his proposals in 1809.

The Portuguese certainly believe that Neves Costa had a role in the development of the proposals for the defence of Lisbon and that his contribution has been overlooked. The memorial erected to Fletcher by the Portuguese Engineers in 1911 has two plaques on its base, one to Fletcher and one to Neves Costa.

Who Led the Work on Building the Lines?
Mistakenly, the credit tends to be given to John Jones (working under Fletcher) as he published the comprehensive book on the subject. But the majority of the work was overseen by Captain Stephen Remnant Chapman. He had been involved from the very start, arriving in Portugal on 4 March 1809. He was the Commanding Royal Engineer until Fletcher arrived on 2 April and was working on the defences from that time. By July 1810, when he handed over to John Jones, much of the planned work planned originally had been completed. Jones did not arrive in the Peninsula until April 1810, Fletcher having asked for him to be sent out to act as Brigade Major. Although it is fair to give credit for Jones' effort to complete the defences in the final months before the Allied troops arrived, he was only in overall command from July to October 1810, when Fletcher arrived back at the

Lines with the Allied army. Through that period Jones was in constant communication with Fletcher and indirectly with Wellington.

Whilst Chapman's contribution is not well understood today, it was at the time, which is why he is mentioned in Wellington's dispatches and Jones is not: 'We are indebted for these advantages to Lieutenant Colonel Fletcher and the officers of Royal Engineers; among whom I must particularly mention Captain Chapman who has given me great assistance upon various occasions.'[30] Wellington agreed to a request to write in support of the claim for a brevet majority for Chapman in 1811. This can only have been for his work on the Lines.

When did Construction Start and When did it Finish?

The common view is that the work on the defence of Portugal started in October 1809 when Wellington visited Lisbon. Typical comments being:

> [Work on the] celebrated Lines commenced in Oct 1809 [and] were fully completed late in 1810.

> The lines which were to check Masséna had been thought out in the British general's provident mind exactly twelve months before the French army appeared in front of them.

> Exactly a year had passed since Wellington had had the foresight to investigate the viability of a project that was taking shape in his mind.[31]

This view is not correct, either for the Lines or for the wider defence of Portugal. The earliest work started in some of the surrounding towns. Captains Patton and Landmann of the Royal Engineers, along with Lieutenants Stanway and Williams, had been in the country since August 1808 and were employed strengthening the defences at both Setuval and Abrantes as well as making plans of the various towns and countryside including Peniche and Coimbra. In September 1808, Fletcher reported that he had seven officers working on drawings of the area around St Julian.[32]

The Portuguese had started work on the defences around Lisbon in early 1809. On 22 March, Chapman reported that Portuguese plans for the defence of Lisbon had been put to Beresford and that he was planning to start work on them straight away.[33] In the same letter Chapman reported that he had sent Lieutenants Jones and Stanway to investigate the feasibility of using gunboats on the Tagus as far upstream at Abrantes to protect the flank of the army, a key component of the final scheme of the Lines of

Torres Vedras. Richard Fletcher, who took over command of the Royal Engineers on his arrival on 2 April 1809, wrote the next day to say that work was underway for the defence of Lisbon.[34] In a separate letter of the same date, Fletcher reported 'arrangements are being made for entrenched positions in front of Lisbon – The outer line is I fear very extensive but I have not been over the ground'. Three weeks later Fletcher was still concerned about the progress with the defences:

> The works carrying on by the Portuguese in the neighbourhood of Lisbon go forward very slowly; though I desired Lieutenant Wedekind [KGL engineer under the command of Fletcher] to make his application for working parties in writing to the Portuguese Secretary at War.[35]

Fletcher was also expressing concern about the south bank of the Tagus as early as 9 April 1809, commenting that supplying Lisbon by sea would be impossible if the French held the south bank.[36] When Wellington moved north from Lisbon in early May, Fletcher and Chapman accompanied him and Fletcher was very unhappy when Chapman was recalled to Lisbon by Beresford to work on the defences.

> Captain Chapman is ordered to Lisbon to assist the Portuguese in fortifying the positions for covering that city and to report on the practicability of defending both banks of the Tagus by detachable independent works. He is also to visit Palmela and Setuval, to give his opinions of the strength and local importance of the towns, and of the general state and utility of the works . . . The loss of this active and intelligent officer from the duties of the field at this moment I cannot but truly regret.[37]

In the same letter, Fletcher said that Wellington wanted to establish ten to twelve permanent works.[38] Wellington also refers to this decision: 'I have sent to Lisbon two officers of Engineers with orders respecting the defence of Lisbon, the Tagus, Palmela and Setuval.'[39] The other officer ordered to Lisbon was Lieutenant Anthony Emmett, who noted in his diary: 'Ordered to attend Captain Chapman in Lisbon to examine the ground from Belem to St Julian's for covering the embarkation of the army, should that be necessary.'[40] Wellington remained concerned about the ability to embark the army if it was threatened and the defences of St Julian were repeatedly reviewed. Even though Emmett did this in May 1809, Lieutenant Rice Jones was sent to look again in October that year. The first detailed British report on the position around St Julian was written by Fletcher himself a year earlier.[41] Finally, on 14 October 1809, Wellington wrote, 'I am down here to arrange finally for the defence of Portugal'.[42] This is several months if not a year after work had started on the defences of Portugal.

Signalling
The use of signalling stations was not new to Portugal when the Lines of Torres Vedras were built. They had been used for some time, particularly between the main cities of Lisbon, Coimbra and Oporto and also connected the border fortresses in the north and south of the country. The telegraphs used by the Portuguese were typically either a shutter or single-arm design.

Signalling stations were part of the original design of the Lines, although their actual completion became a bit of a battle against time and circumstance as the occupation approached. The First Line had five main signal stations at Alhandra, Sobral, Pero Negro (Wellington's headquarters), Torres Vedras and Ponte do Rol at the western end. Jones claimed that these stations were able to send a signal from end to end in about seven minutes. Modern trials have not been able to replicate this feat.

There were two very different types of telegraph used on the Lines. The primary system was based upon signalling used in the Royal Navy with land-based masts on which to display the signals. The codebook was similarly based on Home Popham's naval codebook with additional phrases added where necessary. The masts were operated by seamen provided by the English Fleet in Lisbon under the command of Lieutenant Leith RN. As a backup, the much simpler Portuguese single-arm telegraph was available at each signal station in case the main mast was damaged.

On 1 June 1810, Rice Jones recorded buying eleven telescopes for use by the signal stations.[43] Initial trials showed that reading the signals was very difficult. Attempts were made to improve the situation by clearing hilltops that were in the line of sight of the signal stations. Eventually, it was decided that the telescopes were not powerful enough and John Jones wrote on 18 July that he would purchase better telescopes if they could be found in Lisbon. Modern trials with replicas of the telegraphs have confirmed how difficult it was to read the signals.

As well as the difficulties in reading the telegraphs, there were also problems with their construction. The first examples were not strong enough and collapsed under the weight of yards, lines and balls. Jones reported to Fletcher:

> I am sorry I cannot give you a very favourable account of the signal stations – at every post I have visited the sailors in charge say the

VOCABULARY.

A 1

First Part, or original Edition.		Second Part.	
26	Able	1026	Aback
27	Above	1027	Abate-d-ing-ment
28	About	1028	Abrupt-ly
29	Abreast	1029	Abundance-tly
30	Absence-t-ed-ing-tee	1030	Accommodate-d-ing
31	Absolute-ly	1031	Accomplish-ed-ing-ment
32	Accept-ed-ing-ance	1032	Account-ed-ing
33	Accident-ally	1033	Accurate-ly
34	Accompany-ied	1034	Accuse-d
35	According-ly	1035	Acknowledge-d-ing-ment
36	Acquaint-ed-ing-ance	1036	Acquire-d-ing
37	Act-ed-ing-ion	1037	Acquit-ed-ing-al
38	Active-ly	1038	Across, *athwart*
39	Add-ed-ing-ition-al	1039	Actual-ly
40	Adjourn-ed-ing-ment	1040	Adapt-ed-ing
41	Admiral	1041	Adequate-ly
42	Admiralty	1042	Adhere-d-ing
43	Advance-d-ing-ment	1043	Adjacent, adjoining
44	Advantage-ous-ly	1044	Administer-ed-ing-ration
45	Advise-d-ing	1045	Admit-ed-ing
46	Africa-n	1046	Admonish-ed-ing-ition
47	Aft, abaft, after-wards	1047	Adrift
48	Again-st	1048	Advice-s
49	Agree-d-ing-ment-able	1049	Afar-off
50	Aid-ed-ing, assist-ed-ing ance, abet-ed-ing.	1050	Affair-s
51	All	1051	Affect-ed-ing-ly
52	Alone	1052	Affirm-ed-ing-ation
53	Also	1053	Afford-ed-ing
54	Alternative-ly	1054	Afloat
55	Am	1055	Ago
56	America-n	1056	Aground
57	Amicable-ly	1057	Alacrity, alert-ness
58	Ammunition	1058	Alarm-ed
59	An	1059	Allot-ed-ing-ment

c

A page from Home Popham's telegraph signal book.

distance between the stations is too great and that the masts are all too light for the yards – it blew rather hard on Sunday evening and two were sprung, that on Mount Socorro so badly that we were obliged to replace it. I shall endeavour to see Mr Leith the [Royal Navy] Lieutenant in charge of the signals and obtain his ideas as to a new construction and in the meantime I have ordered stronger masts and yards to be prepared for each post.[44]

Jones followed this up a few days later saying he had spoken to Admiral Berkeley who stated that Lieutenant Leith had not expressed any concerns to him. Jones then wrote to Lieutenant Leith 'offering all the means of the [Engineer] Department to perfect the stations'.[45]

In the final few weeks before the Lines were occupied, the whole plan for Wellington's vital communications was thrown in jeopardy in circumstances that could only be described as farcical today. An argument broke out about proving additional rations for the sailors manning the telegraphs. When the Navy were informed that Wellington could not authorise this, they threatened to recall the sailors to their ships. Wellington, who must have had more urgent business, was forced into writing a constant stream of letters on the subject. When on 7 September 1810 the Royal Navy reported they were planning to withdraw the sailors if the army would not provide rations, Wellington was forced to suggest that the signalling should revert to using the simpler, but less effective, Portuguese telegraph which could be operated by 'old seamen at Lisbon'. In the days immediately before the arrival of the Allied troops in the Lines, Wellington was still asking 'are new telegraphs complete?' and saying 'I am very anxious about our signal posts'. One can only assume that the situation was remedied to Wellington's satisfaction as they were not mentioned again.[46]

Was it a Secret – or Was it Not?
The question of how secret the building of the Lines was is an interesting one. It is easy to find many examples of people who did know, but it seems puzzling that others did not appear to. The engineer George Ross commented on 28 January 1810 that guards were stopping inquisitive people approaching the works. Interestingly, Ross also said that when he mentioned the works in his previous letters 'he was at liberty to do so . . . but could not repeat now being one of the confidential agents'. As he was writing almost to family, it is clear that they had been told to keep quiet. This did not last long!

In Portugal, steps were taken to stop inquisitive people gaining access to critical places. Wellington showed his continual concern about having a secure place for embarkation by issuing instructions about the works at St Julian: '[You] will allow no-one into or inspect them excepting officers of engineers . . . or persons having orders in writing from Marshal Beresford or me.'[47]

In the Allied army there clearly was some knowledge of the Lines. As early as 23 October 1809, Ensign Aitchison reported home that Wellington had been reconnoitring the area around Lisbon, and it is said that the packet had been delayed so that he could send home his opinion on defending the city,[48] and Captain Duffy of the 43rd wrote about the existence of the Lines when he passed through the area in April 1810.[49]

Amongst the Ordnance officers, that is the Artillery and the Engineers, there was clearly a better understanding. Alexander Dickson first mentions the lines in his diary on 16 July 1810, but he said the Engineers had been working on them for some time so we can assume that Dickson had also known about them for some time before that. Dickson was not near Lisbon during this whole period. John Burgoyne noted in his diary on 22 November 1809 that he had 'Heard from Mulcaster at Torres Vedras. The engineers are throwing up field works at that place and Sobral.' Burgoyne noted in a different letter that he did not know the detail of the works due to the secrecy surrounding them. Mulcaster had said 'you will not mention this to anyone, all being a most profound secret'.[50]

George Ross, writing home to Dalrymple on 25 April 1810, said:

I have now my hands full having commenced twenty-three redoubts . . . Our line of redoubts commences in front of Ericeira a few miles – and continues . . . to the Tagus . . . In front of this short position Torres Vedras and Sobral have been made as strong . . . field works . . . so as to put them out of the chance of being stormed without being breached.[51]

Hew Dalrymple was in the UK at this time and it is difficult to believe that this sort of information will not have been discussed with his peers. Similarly John Squire was writing home regularly to Henry Bunbury who was Under Secretary of State for War.

There is a very noticeable lack of mention of the Lines in Wellington's dispatches. Was he deliberately not saying much to the government because he felt that some of the leaks of confidential information appearing in the newspapers were coming from government sources? There is no real discussion in Wellington's dispatches about the detail of the Lines. Maybe Liverpool was concerned about the security of the British force because he did not know about the lines. It is interesting to note that immediately after

Wellington's visit to Lisbon in October 1809, when he ordered the start of work on the lines, his correspondence on the subject is quite vague unless absolutely necessary. Writing to Castlereagh on 20 October, he said: 'I came here [Lisbon] a few days ago in order to be better enabled to form a judgement on the points referred to in your Lordships dispatch on 14 September.'

Writing to the Marquis Wellesley on 25 October 1809 and Lord Burghersh three days later, he refers to 'business' in Lisbon but makes no comment on the nature of the business. However, he goes into some detail in a letter to Admiral Berkeley the next day, when asking him to advise on the best embarkation point. It is surprising that Wellington, writing to the Earl of Liverpool on 14 November 1809, which is about the first opportunity after his visit to Lisbon, makes no mention of ordering construction of the Lines and just makes a general reference to being able to 'successfully resist' a French attack. Bearing in mind that Wellington was also writing to Liverpool at the same time complaining about the publication of confidential information in the British press, it is maybe understandable why he was being economical with the details.

I find the most surprising comment on the Lines is in the January 1811 edition of the *Royal Military Chronicle*.[52] It lists the number of forts and guns present in the Lines. This seems like far too early to be making such information publicly available! Masséna was still in front of the Lines at this time. It is also interesting to note that the numbers of redoubts, men and guns mentioned in the account of Masséna's ADC, Pelet, match exactly those given in the *Royal Military Chronicle*, but do not match any other report I have seen.

What I am sure of is that although there were many on the Allied side who did know about the Lines, the French did not. They had been given some warning but did not believe that the defences would be able to stop them. Pelet tried hard to justify the failure of the French to be aware of the lines, saying;

> The cruel ravages carried out by the enemy reinforced our ignorance [of the existence of the Lines], for it seemed they would not have abused a country they wanted to save. One must never lose sight of this central idea, for otherwise we could be accused, with reason, of a lack of foresight, and even stupidity.[53]

Stupidity is too strong, but I think the French were guilty of arrogance, ignoring the information they were receiving. They did not consider that Wellington was eventually going to stand, but at a place of his choosing, like he did at Bussaco.

What did the Engineers Think of the Lines?

Over a period of more than a year many engineers were involved in the construction of the Lines and the surveying and planning work that preceded construction. Their private letters often show their true feelings about the work they were involved in. What is surprising is their lack of understanding and confidence in the defences they were building.

John Squire, writing on 27 May 1810 to the Undersecretary of State for War Henry Bunbury, said:

> I cannot however understand our defensive operations in the interior of the country, we seem to entirely abandon the defence of the frontier . . . we find all our strength applied to fortifying a line, which surely neither ought nor can be defended . . . I feel persuaded that this extraordinary line will never be defended; and . . . expose us to the ridicule of both our friends and enemies.[54]

George Ross wrote to Hew Dalrymple in a similar vein on 25 May 1810:

> If they [the forts] should ever be named as a sin we have to answer for, I hope the military world will be kind enough to consider that we make them but do not invent them. If the twenty-seven redoubts in my neighbourhood were upon wheels and could travel quick as thought – they might by a fortunate application of them prevent a French column penetrating with impunity.[55]

and again on 20 June 1810:

> Your friend Colonel Murray seems to like to keep us useless gentleman as far from the army as possible. The armies are contending on a frontier where certainly fortresses have some influence. Twenty of us are kept here making useless works and one Captain [Burgoyne] is with the army fortifying alone a fort which may perhaps be disputed.

Burgoyne commented in a letter to Pasley on 26 March 1810 that he did not think Wellington could hold the Lines, although he did admit that he did not know much about them because of the secrecy. He surmised that Wellington was not confident about the strength of the defences due to him demanding sufficient transports to carry off the army. Burgoyne cynically suggested that Wellington's reason was – I will show them I can do anything Sir John Moore could, i.e. fight a battle before withdrawing by sea.

As the campaign progressed and the size of Masséna's army fell in the imagination of the British officers, there was a growing confidence that perhaps the French could be stopped short of the British transports. In a more positive mood, Squire wrote to Henry Bunbury on 10 October 1810:

> When I told you in one of the letters written soon after my arrival in Portugal that the lines in front of Lisbon neither could nor ought to be defended I calculated that the enemy would not have committed the unpardonable error of invading this country with an army inferior in numbers to those who defend it.[56]

Even after the Allied troops had entered the Lines there was no praise for the Lines or Wellington's strategy, only criticism of the French.

Was Masséna Starved Out?
An essential part of Wellington's strategy was the 'scorched earth' policy that would lead to the rapid starvation of the advancing French army. Despite his best efforts, several proclamations and threats of punishment for people who did not destroy usable goods, there is no doubt that there were still substantial supplies available when the French arrived in front of the Lines. Schaumann records in his diary that he was often sent out with foraging parties to find and remove stores 'hidden' by the Portuguese, using the same techniques that the French were well practised in. The Allied cavalry were also engaged in disrupting French foraging. The abandoned mills, which were supposed to have been completely disabled, were in many cases quickly back in action again. Whilst Wellington was very unhappy that the Portuguese civilians had not followed exactly their instructions to destroy everything of value, it is not surprising that they did not. They were being asked to destroy everything they owned with no promises that they would receive any help to replace their possessions. Many Portuguese civilians starved to death on the streets of their capital city during that terrible winter.

There were a number of engineer officers who commented on the supply situation whilst Masséna was in front of the Lines. Soon after the French arrived, Burgoyne wrote:

> The country they are now occupying is a very fertile one and the harvest was got in entirely when they arrived. No measures were taken for driving the country . . . Even at Villa Franca a town . . . only one league in front of our line, a very large quantity of grain was left. Therefore all things considered the idea of starving the enemy out of their ground is out of the question.[57]

A few days later, on 6 November 1810, John Squire wrote to Bunbury:

> Do not my dear friend believe that the enemy are in want of provisions. As they arrived just at the conclusion of the harvest I believe they are most amply supplied . . . their granaries were left full of corn and their cellars filled with the wine of the recent vintage. Large herds of cattle also remained for the enemy and while lately on the opposite side, on the left bank of the Tagus I saw an abundance of stacks of straw, Indian Corn etc. untouched, which convinced me that their supplies were by no means exhausted.[58]

Whilst this meant that the French had adequate supplies for a few weeks, as the winter progressed the foraging parties had to cover larger areas, the brutality of their methods of extraction increased and ultimately the success of the foraging decreased. But even into 1811, there were still reports of the French having food. Fletcher wrote on 2 February: 'They are said still to find an abundance of cattle'; Squire also commented on 1 March: 'They display on their side of the Tagus a great abundance of sheep and cattle and are in no greater danger of starvation than ourselves.'

In the end Masséna had no choice but to retreat as his force had steadily diminished throughout the winter to a point where it was no longer strong enough in numbers or in health to attack the Allied positions. It is likely that Masséna also knew that Allied reinforcements had arrived in the first days of March. It may have been that this, combined with no possibility of substantial reinforcements of his own, was the trigger for his decision to retreat. In the end Masséna did not even try to take the Lines. I will leave the final comment on the Lines to John Jones: '[This was the] first and only instance of a military enterprise planned and matured by Napoleon . . . being defeated by the . . . superior foresight of an opponent.'[59]

Chapter 4

1810 – A Year of Waiting

With the recall of all engineer officers to Lisbon to work on the Lines in October 1809, there was little engineering activity further afield. Burgoyne and Emmett, who were based at Badajoz, continued surveying work in southern Spain. Emmett carried out a survey of the Guadiana south of Badajoz including the crossing-point at Jerumenha which would be of importance in 1811. Burgoyne surveyed the towns in the area including Campo Mayor which he described as a fortified town 'but the ground is favourable for its approach and attack'. He also commented that it had very few guns, 'all the places on the frontier having been dismantled to supply Elvas'.[1] Royal Staff Corps officers were carrying out similar tasks, for example Alexander Todd surveying of the ground between Castello Branco and Punhete.[2]

The end of 1809 saw the army moving from Badajoz back into Portugal, and in January 1810, Wellington moved his headquarters to Viseu with Craufurd's light troops being pushed forward to the Spanish frontier. Apart from a feint by the French in February, when they advanced on Ciudad Rodrigo and summoned the fortress without having any guns to undertake a siege, things remained quiet until the end of April when Ciudad Rodrigo was properly invested. Despite pleas from Herasti, the governor, for Wellington to lift the blockade, no action was taken. A second summons was made on 12 May and Herasti again refused. The French now settled down to conduct a regular siege.

Whilst the Allied army monitored the siege at Ciudad Rodrigo, surveying work continued, including Henry Goldfinch being ordered to survey the Bayonne islands off the Spanish coast near Vigo. Like the Berlingas islands off Peniche, these islands could become strongpoints if the Allied army was forced to evacuate the mainland. At the end of May, Burgoyne was ordered to repair the fort of La Conception near Almeida. Three days later, realising that they could not risk the repaired fort falling into French hands, Burgoyne was tasked with preparing mines to destroy the fort even as he carried out the repairs. On 18 June Burgoyne reported the breaches were repaired and the mine shaft was ready to be filled with gunpowder.

Wellington knew he was going to retreat, whilst the French did not. His planning included surveying the routes for his retreat and identifying choke points where the French could be delayed. Burgoyne had surveyed Wellington's probable line of retreat several months earlier. In January 1810, Wellington had ordered Burgoyne to

> survey the course of the Cris and to ascertain its course, by how many bridges and fords it is crossed, where the roads crossing it head to; whether it fills in winter, and how long it remains full; and whether the destruction of the bridge between Mortagua and Sao Comabadao [*sic*] and the destruction of the road leading from the bridge on the right of the river would be a serious impediment to the use of the road from Vizeu to Coimbra by Mortagua and Mealhada. Let him calculate the means of destroying that bridge and road. I would wish to have the same information regarding the Dão which joins the Cris immediately below Sao Combadao.[3]

The siege of Ciudad Rodrigo dragged on for two months until 10 July, Herasti surrendering just before the French launched an assault on the breach. The French had lost ten weeks before the fortress.

Fletcher joined the army from Lisbon in early July 1810, leaving John Jones in command of completion of the Lines of Torres Vedras. He was corresponding almost daily with Jones on the progress towards finishing the works. It is clear that Fletcher's role was to manage the range of very different tasks carried out by his officers, each of which had a part to play in Wellington's overall strategy. Fletcher was commanding individuals spread over hundreds of miles in the Peninsula where, signal stations excepted, news travelled at the speed of a horse, or more often a mule! One of Fletcher's first tasks when he arrived at headquarters was to visit Almeida on 16 July and discuss its defence with the governor, Brigadier-General Cox. Fletcher, Chapman and Rice Jones also visited Fort Conception to see the preparations carried out by Burgoyne.

Further delays now occurred as the French replenished their supplies before moving on Almeida, although a strong reconnaissance by the French had caused the fort of La Conception, near Almeida, to be blown up on 21 July. Mulcaster described the event in his diary:

> Burgoyne rode to show me the picquet and returned – going on with them through the village of Barquilla they encountered the enemy's

advance and a skirmish commenced against superior numbers; about 5 o'clock the picquet retired and I rode by desire of Major Hervey [Major Felton Hervey, 14th Light Dragoons] to tell Gos [Burgoyne] to lose no time in setting fire to the mines – Finding nobody there I was riding up the ramp when I heard the burning of the portfire and saw the smoke issuing from the gallery – I therefore rode with all possible speed out of the fort to the dragoons who were continuing to skirmish – the fort exploded about ¼ of an hour after I left it and the mines appeared to answer fully all the flanks, one face and the outworks being breached.

Burgoyne also noted in his diary that:

Captain Mulcaster went up to warn me to light them [the mines], but it was already done; the dragoons I had sent down to give everyone they met notice; neglected to tell him, and he was going up to the ramparts to look for me, when, smelling powder strong, he looked into one of the passages and saw the portfire burning. Of course he made off as fast as he could.[4]

Brotherton of the 14th Light Dragoons noted that his skirmishing troopers were so close to Fort Conception that he 'lost several horses and men by the explosion'. He also noted with regret that he saw the body of his Colonel who had been buried on the glacis at Fort Conception a few days before 'blown into the air'.[5]

Going back to Mulcaster's diary:

General Craufurd came up at Val de la Mula in front of which the enemy paraded for near an hour – they appeared to have 3 regiments of infantry and a battalion of light troops – The 14th [Light Dragoons] continued to retire very slowly and finally halted about 2 miles in front of Almeida at 11 o'clock – the enemy who had been extremely shy all day drawing off all but a small picquet – only 2 or 3 men and 6 or 8 horses wounded – At Almeida they have reformed the parapets and made some traverses in the most exposed fronts and are mounting a gun on a windmill about 900 yards from the covered way and entrenching it.

Burgoyne had recorded in his diary on 30 June that he had been sent for by General Cox to 'consult on a project of Lord Wellington's' to fortify the windmill and entrench the ground as far as a convent about 1,500 yards to the right of the mill. The purpose of the fortification was to preserve communications with the bridge over the Coa.[6] Clearly this plan did not work, as the French advanced again on 24 July and gave the Light Division a bloody nose through Craufurd completely misreading the situation. It was forced to rapidly retreat across the Coa over the single small bridge. The engineers were very active over the next few days, riding round the outposts and reporting on the activities of the French, Fletcher riding out most days with Chapman and Rice Jones.[7] Rice Jones also noted in his diary that Burgoyne and Thomson had been ordered to mine the Ponte de Murcella which was one of the major crossing-points on the river Mondego near Coimbra. The beginning of August saw a lull in French activity as they settled before Almeida.

Wellington, to make sure he was fully aware of the movements of the French, stationed troops well forward of his main positions. This included numerous cavalry patrols led by some of the more enterprising officers under his command like Cocks and Krauchenburg. Wellington also ordered Rice Jones and Mulcaster to construct a number of telegraphs to allow communication between Almeida, Celorico and Guarda. Stations were also built at Freixadas and Alverca, Mulcaster noting on 8 August that he had been ordered to 'construct a telegraph on the Lisbon principle'. The following day he said that the Portuguese telegraph was coming from headquarters.[8] This would suggest that the army was carrying telegraph masts with them for such an eventuality. On 15 August, Rice Jones reported that 'Captain Ross of the artillery rode to Linhares, from whence he distinguished the signals made by the Portuguese Telegraph with one arm, fixed upon the castle here [Celorico]'.[9] The distance being about ten miles, they were having better success than their fellow engineers on the Lines of Torres Vedras.

The French opened their trenches in front of Almeida on 15 August and the batteries were ready ten days later. Then came the disastrous explosion in the main magazine that led to the surrender on the 27th. Engineers remained active at the front, erecting further telegraphs and monitoring the activities of the French. Following a period of reorganisation the French army began their advance which led them to the ridge of Bussaco, where, on 27 September, Wellington repulsed the French attempts to dislodge him. Part of Wellington's meticulous planning for his retreat included preparing the defences at Bussaco in case he decided to make a stand. Engineer officers were on the site several days before the battle, constructing a lateral road behind the Allied position to allow rapid redeployment of troops. Mulcaster also noted on 23 September 'at work all night on a fleche [an earthwork with an open rear] . . . to secure a picquet from a cannonade'. Prior to the battle, Wellington had also began the destruction in his rear. Mulcaster was sent on 19 September to destroy the bridges over the Dão and Cris rivers near Santa Comba Dão which was completed on the 20th and 21st respectively.[10]

The French now turned Wellington's position, Fletcher reporting he 'was sent forward yesterday to reconnoitre the enemy and finding that his movements threatened our left, Lord Wellington has this day ordered the . . . Army to cross the Mondego'[11] and continue his retreat towards Coimbra. Wellington also ordered Burgoyne to conduct a last-minute survey of the river below Coimbra to identify how many crossing-points there were and to decide if it was necessary to blow the main bridge in the city.[12] Burgoyne reported that there were numerous crossing places and blowing the bridge would be pointless. He also noted with some exasperation that he sent five copies of his letter before he received an acknowledgement.

When the French reached the city they embarked on an orgy of looting that delayed their advance for a few days and gave Wellington's troops an opportunity to retreat in a more leisurely fashion. As Wellington withdrew before the advancing French, another element in his defensive plan was initiated. Using the traditional Portuguese principle of calling the population to arms, the countryside over which the French advanced was abandoned with the people fleeing and all supplies (supposedly) being destroyed. This meant that the French advanced into a wasteland where there was insufficient food for the troops. When the French eventually came up to the Lines, they would find themselves with a formidable obstacle in front and limited means to stay or even retreat.

The weather in the final days of the retreat was awful, Boutflower describing it as 'the most uncomfortable day of my life without exception . . . It blew and rained with the most dreadful violence, and in a very short time rendered the roads nearly impassable'.[13] The poor weather was probably more of an advantage to the Allied cause than the pursuing French. The first British troops arrived at the Lines on 9 October, with the forts already being occupied by militia. John Squire, writing to Henry Bunbury on 10 October, described the defences at Alhandra as follows:

> General Hill's division occupies the position of Alhandra, which is now by dint of excessive labour become almost unassailable. It consists of a ridge of heights, which commences about 600 yards from the Tagus and extends about 2½ miles in a westerly direction, where the country becomes less difficult of access. The interval between the heights of Alhandra and the Tagus is occupied by low

marshy ground, across which is an entrenchment having a double ditch and since our arrival I have added an impenetrable abatis, so that I consider our right as secure as if we were in the fortifications of Malta.[14]

When the Allied army entered the Lines in October 1810, engineering officers were assigned to each district with responsibility to continue construction work and repairs. This continued throughout the winter. Wellington was very pleased with the effort of the engineers, writing to Liverpool:

> It is but justice to Lieutenant Colonel Fletcher, and the officers of the Royal Engineers, to draw your Lordship's attention to the ability and diligence with which they have executed the works, by which these positions have been strengthened to such a degree as to render any attack on that line occupied by the allied army very doubtful, if not entirely hopeless.[15]

Fletcher had also recorded praise for the efforts of John Jones in the final months. Writing home he reported the 'works are directed by Captain Jones with a degree of zeal and ability that no language of mine can do justice to'.[16]

Occupation of the Lines, October 1810 to March 1811

Wellington's general strategy, which seems to have been missed by many of the 'moaning' Allied officers at the time, was for the forts to be occupied by second-line troops, that is Militia and Ordanenza, leaving the regular troops to remain mobile to move to any threatened point using the roads that had been constructed or repaired for this purpose. The troops were initially concentrated at three main points, Alhandra, Monte Agraça and between Torres Vedras and Monte Agraça.[17]

Wellington's headquarters was at Pero Negro, in the rear of Monte Agraça, which was close to the centre of the Lines. Hill commanded two divisions at Alhandra, with four further divisions concentrated to the rear and left of Monte Agraça. This gave Wellington great flexibility to quickly move the bulk of his strength to any threatened point.

When the Lines were initially occupied, they were formed into six districts with a general officer in command and an engineer appointed his staff as regulating officer.[18]

District	Location	Regulating Engineer	Supporting Engineer
First Line			
1	Sea to Torres Vedras	Capt Mulcaster	Lt Thomson
2	Sobral to Calahandrix	Capt Goldfinch	Lt Forster
3	Calahandrix to Alhandra	Capt Squire	Lt Piper
Second Line			
4	Tagus to Bucellas	Capt Burgoyne	Lt Stanway
5	Bucellas to Mafra	Capt Dickinson	Lt Trench
6	Mafra to the sea	Capt Ross	Lt Hulme

Later, when the area on the first line between Sobral and Torres Vedras was strengthened, a seventh district was formed to cover this area.

The French first arrived in front of the Lines at both Alhandra and Sobral on 11 October. Reconnaissance quickly showed that there was a strong line of defensive forts on the hills in front of them. On 12th, the French attacked the town of Sobral and dislodged the British outpost. A strong cavalry reconnaissance down the Alhandra road achieved nothing but the loss of General Sainte Croix to a shot from one of the Royal Navy gunboats. The following day the French probed west of Sobral and again in front of Alhandra, and on the 14th and 15th, Masséna personally reconnoitred around Sobral and towards Alhandra. There was a difference of views amongst the French on what to do next. Junot wanted to launch an attack from Sobral. Marbot was of the opinion that it should be possible to break through somewhere by using feint attacks to tie down the defenders. But the majority of opinion, including Masséna, Ney and Reynier was that without reinforcements, they would not be able to breach the lines. John Jones noted in his diary on 19 October: 'A Mameluke who deserted yesterday reports that Marshal Masséna and Ney after spending five days in making a complete reconnaissance of our line had declared it to be "trop forte" and that it was intended to wait for reinforcements.'[19] Masséna felt his decision needed to be explained carefully to Napoleon and General Foy was dispatched to Paris, not arriving until 22 November. In the meantime, the French army dispersed to forage. Masséna ordered work to start on preparing bridging material at Santarem, which would give the French access into the Alentejo.

The daily routine for the Allied troops after entering the Lines was for them to assemble two hours before dawn and stand ready until an hour after dawn. Wellington rode up from his headquarters at Pero Negro each morning to the great redoubt above Sobral. When it had been confirmed that there were no changes in the French dispositions, the troops were allowed to return to their bivouacs to prepare food. Initially, for many of the troops these were very rudimentary, built with whatever wood and cloth that could be found making makeshift shelters against the cold and wet weather. Wellington quickly ordered tents to be provided to give some protection to the troops.

The impasse in front of the Lines continued until 14 November when Masséna withdrew to Santarem. Due to a foggy start to the day, this was not immediately detected and the Allies followed cautiously until the intentions of the French were clear and Wellington realised they were staying. On 24th, Masséna withdrew to Cartaxo and these positions remained static for the next four months with the Allied advanced guard facing the French across the bridge at Santarem.

Conditions for the Allied troops improved once the French retreated, with many being housed in the villages in front of the Lines. The situation also settled, with little or no skirmishing between the armies. In fact Kincaid, who spent most of this period living in some farmhouses at the end of the bridge at Santarem, reported that 'we lay four months in this situation, divided only by a rivulet, without once exchanging shots'.[20]

Despite this period of relative stability, there was no slowdown in the work on the Lines, Fletcher writing home:

> The most vulnerable part of our present front is on the left of Torres Vedras – We have already established six guard redoubts upon this ground, and are now throwing up seven for forty eight pieces of artillery . . . as his Lordship seems inclined to do all I have proposed to render us secure, we shall have to employ seven thousand workmen at different points at the same moment.[21]

In this same letter Fletcher reported that Wellington had asked for another 100 Artificers to be sent out to Portugal but Fletcher had reduced this to fifty 'lest it should appear unreasonable'. Wellington was already planning for next year. On 29 October, Captain Wedekind of the King's German Legion Engineers received orders directly from Wellington to start preparing material for three bridges across the Tagus to be used when the French retired.[22] He was clearly planning for the worst, as several days later he told Admiral Berkeley that boats at Villa Velha had been burnt, the bridge

The bridge over the Tagus at Abrantes, by Leith-Hay.

at Punhete had been dismantled and moved to Abrantes and the bridge at Abrantes was still intact. He had given orders that the boat bridge at Abrantes was to be destroyed if there was any possibility that it would fall into French hands.[23]

In December, Captain Henry Goldfinch was ordered to begin building defences to the south of the Tagus. This was to counter the threat that if the French took the southern bank, shipping at Lisbon would be endangered. A number of engineer officers were employed on this task through the winter including Captain Wedekind and Lieutenants Rice Jones, Meineke and Hulme.

Wellington's greatest concern during this period was that the French would force a passage across the Tagus and be enabled to forage in the fertile Alentejo region. On reports reaching Wellington that the French were collecting and building boats around Santarem, he first dispatched troops to defend the southern bank and then the engineer John Squire on 19 October to carry out a reconnaissance. Squire reported back that 'the story of the 40 boats is a mere tale – five bullock carts with their standing poles on the sides were mistaken for 40 boats!!! At Santarem there are two large boats not yet launched.'[24] However, Masséna's ADC Pelet tells a different story, suggesting that many boats were built. We will come back to this. In the coming months, Squire would come to the attention of the commander of the forces a number of times, but not in a good way.

John Squire was one of the most experienced engineer officers in the Corps. He was educated at Charterhouse school before attending the Royal Military Academy, where he was commissioned in 1797. He served in the Helder campaign in 1799 where he served under Sir Ralph Abercromby. He served again under the same commander in Egypt in 1800–1. On the conclusion of the Egyptian campaign, Squire obtained leave of absence, and made a tour through Syria and Greece. Not to be outdone by his colleague Stanway who damaged Trajan's bridge at Alcantara in 1809, Squire can claim to have been part of one of the biggest heists in antiquity. He left Greece for Malta in the brig HMS *Mentor*, in Lord Elgin's party. The ship was laden with the Elgin marbles taken from the Acropolis. The ship was wrecked on the island of Cerigo on 17 September 1802, and he narrowly escaped death. The marbles were later recovered from the wreck.[25] He was Commanding Royal Engineer under General Whitelocke in the disastrous South American campaign of 1806 and was called as a witness during his court-martial. He was with Sir John Moore in Sweden in 1808 before serving in the Walcheren campaign in early 1809, which he published a book about the next year.[26]

The first situation where Squire came to Wellington's notice arose on 10 November 1810 when he got into an argument with General Craufurd after refusing an order to change the design of one of the forts. Squire thought the change unnecessary and argued that such an order had to come from Wellington or Fletcher. He then appears to have been subjected to one of Craufurd's 'foul-mouthed' tirades and felt so strongly about it that he wrote to Fletcher asking for him to raise the matter with Wellington and seek clarification on whether he was within his rights to refuse. Whether it was related is not clear, but a few days later, Squire was ordered to join General Hill on the south of the Tagus and remained there for the remainder of the winter. Squire felt so strongly about the incident that he wrote again to Fletcher on 25 December asking for clear direction on the relative authority of engineer officers and general officers in the army. Fletcher responded that 'the custom of the service with reference to officers of engineers seems to be well understood [i.e. engineer officers take orders from their superiors]; but I am not aware of any positive regulation on the subject, and shall therefore transmit your letters of the 24th ult and of the 10th November last to the Inspector-General of Fortifications, that you may have the decision of a superior authority.'[27] Fletcher wrote home the next day explaining the situation and asking for guidance:

I have the honour to submit to your consideration, two letters from Captain Squire of the Royal Engineers – the first relative to a discussion which took place between Brigadier-General Robert Craufurd and himself on the 10th of November last – the other dated the 24th ult on the subject of the control and authority possessed by officers of the corps, in the construction of the works entrusted to their charge. The former of these letters I referred (by desire of Captain Squire) to Lord Wellington, who answered me verbally nearly as follows: That 'he thought it would be injurious to Captain Squire to bring this matter publicly forward. That I might have observed his (Lord W's) wish to lean towards the engineers whenever it was possible; That he hoped and believed they experienced very little interference but that he would not <u>set-off</u> a Captain of Engineers against a General officer in the force of the army.' His Lordship concluded by saying that however if I wished it, he would order a public investigation of the matter to be made; but which, on the whole, I did not think advisable. The second letter which I enclose, requesting my instructions as to the control of officer on works, and expressing the opinions of Captain Squire on that subject, seems to embrace so much, that I can only refer it to you.[28]

Clearly, the Board of Ordnance thought Squire had exceeded his authority and an order arrived in early February for him to be recalled to England. Fletcher reported the order to Wellington, who was clearly trying to play down the whole incident:

I have to acknowledge receipt of your letters of the 4th and 5th instant relative to Captain Squire and containing an order for that officer's return to England. In conformity with your directions I submitted these letters to Lord Wellington's perusal. His Lordship expressed his regret that the affair should have been carried so far and a hope that Captain Squire whose conduct had left an unfavourable impression on his mind, might yet be allowed to remain in this country – He desired me to address you confidentially, and to say that if at the time he thought Captain Squire somewhat unreasonable, he did not consider General Craufurd as by any means free from blame. He observed that perhaps at the moment there was something faulty on both sides; but that his wish was to conciliate, and he had hoped and believed the occurrences would have been heard of no more – Lord

> Wellington desired I would not give Captain Squire the order to return to England until I could receive an answer to this letter – His Lordship added that if Captain Squire wanted for another duty the case would be very different; but that on the mere grounds of having written the two letters in question, he should be very sorry to lose the services of so intelligent an officer.

A few days later, Fletcher wrote home again:

> I continue to hope the wish expressed by Lord Wellington that Captain Squire should be allowed to remain in this country will not be disappointing to you – I feel confident that the steps already taken will operate as a salutary warning to that officer; and I trust they will prevent the [repeat?] of anything of the same nature for the time to come – It is extremely gratifying to observe the disposition of Lord Wellington, to uphold the consequences of the Corps of Engineers on every occasion.[29]

Jones noted in his diary that Fletcher went to see Squire on 3 March 1811. It is likely that this was to explain how close he was to being sent home.

Squire's argument was not an isolated incident. Captain John Williams wrote to Fletcher on 8 November 1810, explaining that he had an argument with Brigadier-General Pack over the building of a stable for his horses. He also said that he had done several things for Pack that were not strictly his responsibility (e.g. tracing out kitchens) but was concerned that Pack would raise the incident at a later date.[30] One wonders if everyone was getting bored and tempers were becoming short?

Soon after Squire's argument with Craufurd in November, Squire was ordered south to serve with General Hill's corps on the south of the Tagus where he remained throughout the winter. When Hill became ill at the end of the year, Beresford took command. Initially, he concentrated on the possibility of Masséna attempting to cross the Tagus where it was joined by the Zezere river. On 1 January 1811, Beresford viewed the French positions around Punhete and ordered the construction of three batteries opposite the mouth of the Zezere. The building of these batteries occupied his attention for the next few days until word started arriving of Soult's movements to the south. Like many other simple events around this period, the purpose and position of these batteries was used by Napier to criticise Beresford.[31] Napier found a supporter of his views in John Squire, who claimed that they were built 'against the advice of the engineers, he [Beresford] placed them at too great a distance from the river'.[32] Squire went on to say: 'Thank God, for my own credit, I protested against these batteries from the first, in my reports which were sent to Lord Wellington, and I now verily believe that the Marshal himself is ashamed of their construction.'[33] This claim was strongly denied following the publication of Napier's work, and even at the time D'Urban noted that 'Lord Wellington sent over Colonel Fletcher, the Chief Engineer, who approved of the sites of the batteries fixed upon by the Marshal'.[34]

The debate seemed to focus on whether the purpose was to command the mouth of the Zezere only, or to attack the French boat yard and bridge, which were half a mile from the mouth of the Zezere. Defending the mouth of the river only would have been solely for the purpose of opposing any French attempt to cross the Tagus and move into the Alentejo. Installing heavier-calibre artillery to directly threaten the bridge and boat yard would have destroyed the ability of the French to launch such an attack, but required finding and installing heavy guns, which would then be susceptible to the opposing French artillery unless it was disposed of first. This would have been a much larger undertaking, and it is debatable if the Allies could have brought sufficient weight of artillery to bear to overwhelm that of the French opposite them. D'Urban seems quite clear of the purpose, stating in his journal that they were to 'command the entrance of the Zezere'.[35] Wellington, however, was not. Writing to Beresford on 5 January 1811, he said:

> I think, however, that this is deserving of some further consideration. First; I observe that Capt. Squire's report on the relative state of things at Punhete is so far defective that he has not stated at what distance from the river the enemy's ground rises, and becomes superior to ours: I believe close to the bank. Secondly; What is our object in establishing a heavy battery on the ground opposite the Zezere?

He then went on to suggest:

> I therefore think that we should confine ourselves to commanding with our cannon the communication between the two rivers; and that if we attempt more, it should be by a more powerful artillery [than 6- and 9-pounders], which should be opened at once upon the bridge of boats, and continued as long as any of them swim or can be seen.[36]

Wellington's criticism of Squire probably reflected his unhappiness over his re-igniting the issue of his argument with Craufurd. Squire's letter to

Fletcher of 24 December 1810 would have been brought to Wellington's attention in the past few days. Pelet, Masséna's ADC, writing about the batteries, stated that they 'were directed against the mouth of the Zezere',[37] but then later said they 'actually raked the canal and even our workshops'.[38] Squire was clearly not convinced that the lighter guns could achieve their objective of commanding the mouth of the Zezere, and reported this to D'Urban on 3 January 1811. The answer became apparent very soon after, when the French 4- and 8-pounders on the opposite side of the Tagus began bombarding the emplacements that were being built. The Allied view during the early part of January was that Soult, who was moving north from Seville, would be making a dash to support Masséna. They believed the work by the French opposite Punhete signalled the most likely crossing-place, as they were building a large number of boats and bridging equipment at this point. It became clear a few days later that Soult was besieging Olivenza and not making a dash for the Tagus. The boat-building at Punhete was watched with anticipation, D'Urban noting that 'the enemy is still busy about his boats in the Zezere and has perhaps about 80 completed. I can't imagine his attempting the river till the Southern army [Soult] can come near.'[39] In the end, the French never made an attempt to cross the Tagus, so the preparations came to nothing.

North of the Tagus, work also continued on the Lines, both repairing damage caused by the rains and starting new redoubts. The demand for workmen remained strong and on 21 December 1810, posters were put up in the surrounding villages asking for workmen for the Lines.[40] Mulcaster started a new redoubt at Ribaldeira on 18 December 1810, and on 7 January 1811 another for 300 men and four guns between Forts 32 and 111. On 18 January, Lieutenant Meineke started a redoubt for 200 men between Mount Agraça and Sobral. A few days later he started another for six guns at Alcoentre and marked out three further batteries. The rain was particularly bad in early February 1811 and Jones noted 'breaches have been reported in almost every work but most from Sobral to Alhandra'.[41]

As well as work on the forts, a number of bridges were mined in case the French made another advance from Santarem. On 20 February, an attempt to raise the river in front of Alcoentre by rolling casks into it failed. Wellington also wanted to improve his communications across the Tagus and on 8 January, Wellington and Fletcher looked at the possibility of putting bridge across the Tagus at Benavente. Fletcher discussed this with Squire on 20 January and the work was completed on the 27th, the bridge being made up of fifteen boats.

The French position continued to deteriorate over time, with supplies becoming progressively harder to obtain. Eventually a few reinforcements did fight their way through to Masséna, but their numbers did not offset the losses that he was suffering. The French finally retreated on 5 March 1811 and started the year's campaigning that culminated in the Allied victories at Fuentes del Oñoro and Albuera. The French had made no attempt to force the Lines and never saw them again. The loss to the French should not just be measured in casualties. Wellington now knew had had a secure base in Portugal, and the French realised that it would be very difficult if not impossible to eject the British, and the loss of face in having to retreat provided great encouragement to the defenders in Spain and Portugal and a glimmer of hope across Europe.

Chapter 5

1811 – Goodbye to Lisbon

Away from the Lines of Torres Vedras, the French started 1811 with some success. Soult was finally stung into action by repeated demands from Napoleon that he make an attempt to support Masséna's beleaguered forces, and proposed a diversionary invasion of Estremadura and the capture of Badajoz rather than direct support of Masséna. With this in mind, he set off from Seville with 20,000 men on 30 December 1810. Wellington, aware of the risk but assuming Soult was advancing to the support of Masséna, asked for the bridges at Merida and Medellin to be destroyed and for the ferries on the Guadiana to be removed, forcing Soult into a lengthy detour. Unfortunately, this was not done and the French took control of the bridge at Merida on 7 January 1811. Whilst Soult waited for his main siege train to arrive, he besieged the weak Spanish fortress at Olivenza, which was defended against Wellington's wishes by 4,000 good Spanish troops. This decision may have had more to do with politics than strategy. Olivenza had been part of Portugal until 1801 when it was ceded to the Spanish as part of the peace treaty after the War of the Oranges. It was possible that if the Portuguese had thrown a garrison into the fortress, they would have taken advantage of the significant improvements in their armed forces to decline to return it to the Spanish at a later date. Soult's guns opened against Olivenza on 22 January and the weak walls collapsed immediately, with the Spanish governor surrendering the same day. The Portuguese telegraph system meant that Wellington was informed of this by 24 January. Soult now moved on Badajoz, destroying the large Spanish army under Mendizabal at Gebora on 19 February before the fortress surrendered on 10 March.

This could not have come at a worse time for Wellington. Masséna had finally started his retreat from the Lines on 5 March and Wellington was cautiously pursuing him north, only to find his flank threatened. Wellington had hoped that he could dispatch a force south to relieve Badajoz, but the late arrival of expected British reinforcements meant that he did not have sufficient troops to act against Masséna and Soult at the same time.

The unexpected loss of Badajoz to the French disrupted Wellington's whole strategy for 1811. His intention when Masséna retreated from the Lines of Torres Vedras was to advance and re-take the fortresses of Almeida and Ciudad Rodrigo and then, having secured the northern passage, turn his attention to the south. The loss of Badajoz left both the southern and northern routes into Portugal in French hands, and put Wellington on the defensive. Replying to a question as to his priorities from Lord Liverpool on 7 May 1811, he wrote that retaking Badajoz was his first priority as it dictated his whole strategy for the rest of the year.[1] Speaking to Earl Stanhope in October 1836, Wellington said 'Had it not been for the last, [the surrender of Badajoz] I could have blockaded Almeida and Ciudad Rodrigo at once; and when I had taken them carried the war to the south'.[2] Strategically, it was vital that Wellington recover the fortress as quickly as possible.

Fletcher and John Jones travelled north with Wellington's headquarters. A number of engineer officers remained at Lisbon to continue work on the defences north and south of the Tagus, while others, including John Squire and Lieutenant Forster, were with the Allied force on the south bank of the Tagus. As Wellington pursued Masséna north, the French destroyed several bridges to impede pursuit, so the Royal Staff Corps constructed crossings at Pernes, Foz d'Arouce and Ponte de Murcella. The first was constructed from wood taken from local buildings, the second was a trestle bridge thrown across the river Ceira and the third was 'an ingenious' raft bridge.[3] Masséna having been chased back across the Coa, the RSC now repaired the bridge below Almeida.

While this was going on in the north, the French continued their operations in the south. They commenced the siege of Campo Mayor on 14 March, which after a brief but heroic resistance surrendered on the 21st. The governor, Tallia, had been told on 19 March that the Allies were marching to his relief but there was no way he could have resisted until they arrived on the 26th.

It was mid-March before Wellington was confident enough about Masséna's retreat to dispatch a force south for the relief of Badajoz. These troops under Beresford concentrated around Portalegre before moving forward to Arronches on 24 March. The Allied army was now within ten miles of the French at Campo Mayor, who did not appear to be aware of the threat. March 25th saw the French surprised at Campo Mayor and they rapidly retreated back to the safety of Badajoz. Badajoz is located on the river Guadiana and the only bridge in the area ran through the city itself. The next bridge, also under French control, was at Merida, forty miles to the east, so Beresford's first challenge was to get his army across the river.

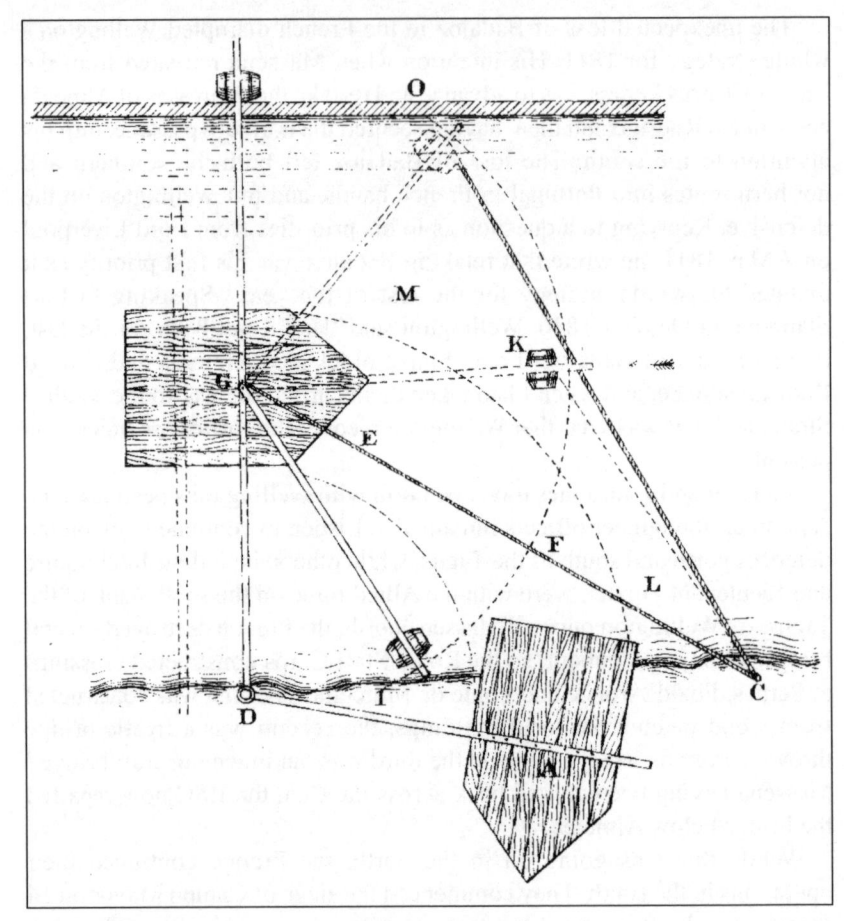

The floating bridge over the Douro at Puente Murcella.

As usual Wellington, although not present, directed operations. Writing to Beresford on 20 March 1811, he said 'lay down your bridge, and make a tête de [*sic*] pont opposite Jerumenha; and in the first instance invest Badajoz on the left of the Guadiana, doing the same with the cavalry only, or Spanish troops, or militia, on the right'.[4]

Jerumenha was ten miles south-west of Badajoz and was the closest point to Badajoz where the river was fordable with the least chance of French interference. The plan to rapidly cross at Jerumenha and drive on to Badajoz before the French could finish their repairs now came to a complete halt. Beresford had been assured that a pontoon bridge was available for his use at Jerumenha. Unfortunately, the Allied pontoon bridge had been captured at Badajoz, even though Wellington had asked Mendizabal to remove it during the early part of the French siege. Anticipating the need for pontoons, Captain Wedekind, one of the engineers from the King's German Legion, had been ordered on 8 March to bring up six pontoons from Lisbon. They arrived at Elvas on the 23rd.[5] Unfortunately, these were nowhere near sufficient to bridge the river which was about 200 yards wide at this point. Having surveyed the area, Squire decided that a bridge could be built by putting the pontoons in the deepest part of the river with trestles at either end. Work started on 30 March, with Squire promising to have it ready by 3 April. Through great effort in collecting materials locally, the bridge was completed on time and plans were made for the troops to cross early in the morning of 4 April. Unfortunately, fate once again turned against Beresford's plans. Overnight, the Guadiana rose three feet, washing away the trestles and making the bridge unusable. Although the first of four flying bridges was set up during the day, it left the picket on the left bank of the Guadiana very exposed. The largest of the ferries could only take 100 men or 25 horses,[6] the smallest 'were not able to carry over more than 16 persons at a time. They were so little buoyant that the smallest weight made them sink.'[7]

The picket was reinforced slowly over the next three days and nights until the bulk of the army was on the left bank by the morning of 7 April. The French commander, Latour-Maubourg, retreated south to protect his lines of communication, leaving 3,000 troops in Badajoz under the governor, Phillipon. On the morning of 9 April Beresford's force advanced towards Olivenza. When they arrived there, it became clear that the French had retired, leaving only a small garrison of 400 to block the advance. 'The Marshal sent Colonel Reynell, his English Adjutant General, to summon the place . . . the Governor, a Colonel named Neboyer, [said] that he was determined to defend the place to the last extremity; that if his garrison was small he could depend upon it.'[8]

Although the garrison was totally inadequate to defend the fortress, the decision was made not to risk an escalade and to make a formal approach to the place. A reconnaissance on the afternoon of the 9th determined that the abandoned work to the south of the fortress was the ideal site for a breaching battery. Dickson set off the same afternoon to Elvas to arrange the necessary artillery for the siege. There he selected six 24-pounders which were dispatched on 11 April, each with 300 rounds of ammunition. The same night, the 4th Division, which had remained to carry out the siege, took possession of the abandoned outwork and started work on the battery under the command of Squire, who was still working on securing the passage of the Guadiana at Jerumenha. He reported:

We have completed an infantry bridge of casks across the Guadiana which may be passed by a front of three and have [built?] a tête du pont on the left of the Guadiana for 15 or 1600 men and leave Captain Wedekind to take charge of these works while I am engaged in establishing a breaching battery of five guns against Olivenza.[9]

It took until 14 April for the guns to arrive, due to the difficulty of getting heavy artillery across the Guadiana at Jerumenha. General Cole, who had been left in charge of the siege, reported:

> Having succeeded in getting the guns into the battery during the night, and got everything ready before daybreak on the 15th . . . I sent a summons to the Governor, a copy of which I have the honour to enclose with his answer, which being a refusal to accept the terms I offered, our fire immediately commenced, and was returned with some spirit from the town. At 11 o'clock a white flag was hoisted by the enemy, and an officer came out with a letter from the Governor, a copy of which I have the honour to enclose with my answer and the Governor's reply, to which I sent none, and recommenced our fire. After a few rounds a white flag was again hoisted, and they surrendered at discretion, and the Franciscan gate was taken possession of by the grenadier company of the 11th Portuguese Regiment.[10]

The French gained no benefit whatever from the defence of Olivenza, and lost 400 good troops.

The First Siege of Badajoz

The focus now turned to the greater challenge of Badajoz, which was a major fortress with a strong garrison and an able governor. The main problem Wellington faced was that because the loss of Badajoz had been unexpected, no provision had been made for siege equipment in that area. Oman criticised the British government for not providing a siege train for Wellington's use, writing, 'The British army in Portugal was absolutely destitute of artillery destined for and trained to the working of siege guns'.[11] On this point he was wrong. At that time, there was a brand-new British siege train aboard the transports at Lisbon. Wellington knew it was there and planned to (and did) use it for the future siege of Ciudad Rodrigo. There was simply no practical way to move it quickly from Lisbon to Badajoz, even if its safety could be guaranteed.

Timeline for the First Siege of Badajoz.	
20 April 1811	Wellington visits and agrees plan for siege
23 April 1811	Bridge at Jerumenha swept away
29 April 1811	Bridge at Jerumenha restored
4 May 1811	South side of Badajoz invested
8 May 1811	North side of Badajoz invested
8 May 1811	Trenches started that night
10 May 1811	French sortie against Fort San Christobal
11 May 1811	Allied guns opened fire against Fort San Christobal and Fort Picurina
11 May 1811	All stores moved to north bank in preparation for raising siege
11 May 1811	Work started on attack against castle at night and stopped in early hours of 12 May
13 May 1811	Siege raised

Wellington, still in the north, was considering his next move. He ordered Fletcher to carry out a close reconnaissance of the fortress of Almeida to determine if it could be carried by escalade. Fletcher's opinion was that this could not be achieved without significant loss. Having discarded that possibility, Wellington and Fletcher now hurried south to review the situation at Badajoz, arriving on 20 April 1811.[12] After speaking to Dickson and Squire about the artillery and engineering requirements, he decided to make a personal reconnaissance of Badajoz and arrangements were made for Alten's brigade of the King's German Legion light infantry and two squadrons of Portuguese dragoons to escort him. Coming across a French working party, Wellington's escort was caught between them and a relieving force from Badajoz and roughly handled. George Ross, who had recently arrived from Lisbon, described the incident as follows:

> The Duke of Wellington crossed the Guadiana at the ford of Lavadora (just below the Caya) from Elvas and reconnoitred Badajoz. The morning was fine, the ford passable notwithstanding considerable rains had fallen, and the reconnaissance was completed. But I plainly saw an instance of what I had often heard. His Lordship's unwillingness to leave the slightest operation to any of his generals. General Alten had moved . . . to cover the reconnaissance. Which instead of being left to him to manage; and

notice given him of the points from whence the noble commander meant to view the place, he was desired occasionally to send on two companies as his Lordship was going to such a point, which he did without waiting a moment. To General Alten's evident surprise he found by this means his little corps quite dispersed. When we came to the first ground before the place, information was given that a detachment of the garrison was in our rear; having gone out with a number of wagons to cut timber on the Valverde road. This was sneered at, and not even a patrol sent to ascertain it. But as his Lordship was returning from his recce on the east side of the place, he had the pleasure of seeing this small detachment with a number of heavy wagons drawn by horses, pass through his scattered troops and enter the place, covered by a detachment which came out of the garrison. Instead of taking this escort which would have depressed the spirits of the garrison, our reconnaissance cost us above 30 killed, wounded or prisoners and I do not hear of more than 2 Frenchmen being taken. Of course the garrison must laugh at such bungling, as it must have appeared to them, and will gain confidence.[13]

Wellington returned north on 24 April but left three instructions with Beresford. The first outlined the strategy he should follow for the siege and how he should respond if a French relief force was sent. The most important point in this letter was that Wellington authorised Beresford to fight a battle if he felt it was appropriate. It also included clear instructions that if the siege was raised, any stores from Elvas must be returned as the fortress' resources had been severely depleted to furnish stores for the siege.

The second detailed the siege operations which were to be carried out against Badajoz. As was typical of Wellington, the instructions were very detailed and left nothing to chance. The main points were:

• To establish a flying bridge over the Guadiana below the junction with the Caya.
• To simultaneously lay siege to the outworks of San Christobal, Picurina and Pardaleras.
• Only when these three outworks were taken was Beresford to start operations against Badajoz itself.
• Wellington suggested that the most likely point of attack would be the south face, but left the decision to Beresford.

Most of the responsibility for the failure of the first two sieges against

1811 – Goodbye to Lisbon 91

Badajoz must lie with Wellington, as these orders were clearly not practical, as we shall see.

The third memorandum was a letter to three senior Spanish generals in the area, Castaños, Blake and Ballesteros, asking for explicit acceptance of Wellington's operational plan. Any move against Badajoz was dependent upon their agreement.[14] Wellington made his views absolutely clear to Beresford on 6 May, writing 'If General Blake does not positively agree to everything proposed in my memorandum, and does not promise to carry it strictly into execution, I think that you ought not to be in a hurry with the siege of Badajoz'.[15] The following day he informed Liverpool that he had told Beresford to delay the siege until agreement had been received from the Spanish generals.[16] It is significant that Beresford did not take any positive steps to start the siege until 8 May, following the Spanish generals' agreement to the proposals in Wellington's memorandum. Beresford had been ready to start a few days earlier and the artillery and engineer officers were puzzled by the delay. Overall, the siege was not off to a good start. The lack of siege stores at Elvas, the loss of the temporary bridge at Jerumenha, which provided their primary means of communication across the river Guadiana, and the delays in resolving issues of command meant that eight weeks had passed since the French had taken Badajoz. Beresford heard that Soult was marching to relieve the fortress on 10 May, before the first gun had even opened fire. The day the first gun fired, 11 May, Beresford was already making preparations to raise the siege.

There is some debate about the plan chosen for the siege of Badajoz. According to John Jones, when Wellington arrived at Elvas on 20 April he was

> determined to lay immediate siege to Badajoz, if any plan of attack could be offered which should not require more than sixteen days open trenches, as in that period, and the time required to make the necessary preparations for the siege, it was calculated that Marshal Soult would be able to collect a force equal to its relief.[17]

The preference of most of the officers, including Wellington, was for an attack on the southern front. No plan could be developed that would meet the sixteen-day target, normal calculations for such an attack indicating that twenty-two days would be required. Jones continued that 'it was of the greatest consequence to the future operations of the army that Badajoz should be retaken'.[18] Probably under pressure from Wellington, Fletcher proposed a plan that he felt could be achieved within the sixteen days. The plan was to take the fort of San Christobal which overlooked the castle and once it was taken, to form batteries to batter the old castle walls which would then be stormed when there was a practicable breach. It was also proposed to make simultaneous feint attacks on the other two outworks to mask their real intentions. According to Jones' diary, these discussions occurred before Wellington's reconnaissance on 22 April, and Wellington approved this plan after he had examined the fortress.

There is a confusing difference in the accounts at this point. Jones' published *Journal* described Fletcher's plan above. This *Journal* also printed Wellington's memorandum of 23 April, but crucially left out his last point, which stated that all three outworks must be taken before the attack on the fortress began. He also made no mention of feint attacks and suggested an attack on the southern front. Wellington's instructions do not appear to be the same as Fletcher's plan. Jones' original diaries, which he kept at the time, do not specifically detail Fletcher's proposal. He did, however, detail Wellington's memorandum including the crucial last point, which was not printed in his published *Journal*. On 8 May, he noted in his diary 'Fletcher marked out a work against the Picurina redoubt and to conceal from the enemy the real point of attack, it was decided to carry out a false attack against the Pardaleras'.[19] Later in the diary entry for that day, he noted troops breaking ground for the feint attack against the Pardaleras fort, but no mention was made of the attack on the Picurina being a feint. In his published *Journal*, and in his original diary, Jones made continued reference to feint attacks on the Pardaleras.[20] Alexander Gordon, who was one of Wellington's aides-de-camp travelled with him to Badajoz. He commented on 23 April, the day Wellington inspected Badajoz, that he expected the attack would come from the south side, after opening against the three outworks.[21] A later letter still talked about taking all three outworks.[22]

Oman was highly critical of the decision to attack San Christobal and puts the blame firmly on the shoulders of Fletcher, the commanding engineer. He criticised the decision to make it a requirement to capture all three forts before attacking the castle, noting that 'none of these were to be mere false attacks'.[23] In Oman's work there is no mention of Jones as a source for the first siege although he does use Jones for the subsequent sieges of Badajoz. Although Oman's text is explicit, the map of Badajoz in his book marks both the Pardaleras and Picurina forts as 'False attacks'.[24] It is possible that Oman did not have, or chose not to use, the comprehensive third edition of Jones' work when writing about the first siege. The original first edition of Jones' *Journal*, published in 1814, had a shortened account of the first siege. This edition described the attack on San Christobal, but did not mention the false attacks on the Picurina or Pardaleras. Fortescue

1811 – Goodbye to Lisbon 93

used Jones' *Journal* and recognised that the engineers had a preference for taking San Christobal over the other two outworks. He also criticised the decision to attack San Christobal rather than follow the French lead and attack the southern front.

The above analysis leaves two unanswered questions:

- Was the decision to attack San Christobal due to the time constraints reasonable?
- Why did Jones' published account completely ignore Wellington's final instruction to take all three outworks before attacking the fortress?

In answer to the first question, it is necessary to acknowledge the experience of the engineers. Their judgement was that twenty-two days would be necessary to attack from the south. This did not meet Wellington's requirement of sixteen days. The plan proposed by Fletcher was certainly risky, but quickly taking the outwork would have given the army a great chance of meeting the short timescale. Certainly, the strength of San Christobal had been underestimated by everyone, Dickson noting that it 'might easily be taken'.[25] On 26 April, Wellington sent Beresford copies of the French plan of Badajoz and their plan of attack which had been intercepted by Castaños. With this information, there was time to change the Allied plan of attack, but no change was made. In the end it was the limited resources that led to failure against San Christobal, not the decision to attack it.

The answer to the second question is more difficult. The plan followed by the engineers, which is clearly reported in Jones' *Journal*, was to attack all three outworks, but only the attack on Pardaleras was meant to be false. The map in Dickson's Diaries shows the attack on the Cerro del Vinto (Pardaleras) as being a 'false' attack.[26] Rice Jones similarly talks about only this attack as being false.[27] These do not match Fletcher's original proposal described in Jones' *Journal*. Neither does it appear to follow Wellington's instructions of 23 April. His instruction to take all three outworks, does not appear to be logical when time was critical. It would have taken significantly longer to capture all three outworks, where the possession of two or even one would allow the start of an attack on the fortress. The plan that was actually followed will be discussed below.

The biggest problem Wellington faced with the loss of Badajoz was getting together the resources to try and re-take it. Both Oman and Fortescue criticise Wellington's preparations but neither are accurate. Fortescue stated that Wellington did not ask about resources at Elvas until 6 April, with deficiencies being made up from the 'English' battering train at Lisbon.[28]

Wellington did not actually write 'English' battering train, but 'our' battering train, probably just referring to resources at Lisbon. Wellington was reluctant to use the new train, writing that it would 'cripple' future siege operations.[29] He did subsequently send a number of siege guns from Lisbon, but these were not from the new train. Oman wrote that Wellington did not start preparations for assembling the guns until 18 April, when Dickson was sent to Elvas.[30] Dickson, the commander of the artillery, was writing as early as 21 March that the artillery would come from Elvas.[31]

Wellington's first letter to Beresford on the subject of the siege was written on 27 March 1811, where he stated: 'Elvas must supply the means [for the siege of Badajoz], if possible: if it has them not, I must send them there; this will take time, but that cannot be avoided.'[32] Writing to Beresford again on 6 April, Wellington explained: 'In respect to Badajoz, the first thing to do is to blockade it strictly . . . and I am most anxious to receive the accounts of what Elvas can supply for this purpose that I may order up from our battering train the deficiency'.[33] Beresford had sent for Dickson on 2 April and asked him to prepare a return of the 'ordnance, ammunition etc' in Elvas for Wellington.[34] Clearly the answer he received was that Elvas could not provide the necessary resources,[35] because on 9 April Wellington was ordering siege material to be sent up from Lisbon.[36] At the same time, he also ordered heavy guns to be sent from Lisbon to replace the guns that were being moved from Elvas.[37]

Writing to Beresford the next day, Wellington stated:

I was in hopes that the return of ordnance at Elvas would have been accompanied by a return of stores in the garrison, by which I should have seen what the garrison could spare for the siege of Badajoz, and we should have been spared the time, the trouble, and expense of sending up the articles of which I enclose the list. I enclose the list of our ordnance and ammunition at Elvas, which Fletcher thinks ought to be prepared to be taken out for the siege of Badajoz, and a list of stores, which I have ordered from Lisbon to Setuval.[38]

At this time Fletcher was still in the north with Wellington, in the vicinity of Almeida, and was clearly providing advice. On 12 April, Squire received a comprehensive enquiry from Beresford:

The Marshal requests you to give out an estimate of all that may be requisite to undertake the siege of Badajoz. It is my[?] desire to commence against that place with as little delay as possible. Elvas cannot probably furnish much more than guns, powder and shot of which Major Dickson can probably give you information. He begs you will consider and specify the means which you conceive the country on both banks of the Guadiana can supply in gabions, fascines, timber for platforms etc. which the Marshal imagines can be prepared in the neighbourhood of the place and that the Militia and country people can make them [from] the dimensions or models being given – sand bags it will probably be difficult to obtain in sufficient quantities – Entrenching tools will be my principal want but the Marshal begs your attention to the working tools made use of by the country people, and whether with those from Elvas or now in your possession, it may not be possible to undertake the siege of the place applying to this object the means of every description which Elvas, the army, and the country can provide. Should the country tools be considered applicable, you will be so good as to state the nature and numbers required and the other articles likely to be procured in the country – and which the Marshal will endeavour to obtain. He desires me to remind you although it will not have escaped your attention, that the repaired breach may not be very perfect, and that you may judge it advisable to conduct your approaches by those recently made and since filled up by the enemy and which may render the insufficiency of the tools less a matter of importance than it would otherwise be. He also desires that you will take into consideration the circumstance of the strength of the enemy garrison which he has reason to suppose does not exceed 1,500 men.[39]

Squire responded the following day:

I enclose a return of stores and according to the Marshal's wish; the difficulty with respect to our bridge satisfies me that no timber for platforms etc. can be had at or near Elvas. By a requisition made on the country as I before said, I think we may collect a sufficient number of entrenching tools. From what I observed in the works at Elvas, I should have no doubt that gabions and fascines may be made in the neighbourhood. If the enemy intend seriously to defend Badajoz I am of the opinion that to undertake the attack of that place we ought to be provided with the stores specified in the inclosed return and also think that twelve officers of Engineers besides Forster and myself indispensible. It will also be necessary to create a corps of artificers or Sappers and Miners.[40]

The criticisms of Oman and Fortescue mentioned above appear to be unfounded. Similarly, Fortescue's comment that Beresford must have told Wellington that Elvas could supply the stores appears equally unfounded.[41] Heavy material for a siege took time to get together and Wellington had no warning that this would be required for Badajoz. In comparison, it took from May to October 1811 to transport the siege train by sea and land to be ready for use at Ciudad Rodrigo in January 1812.

There were also problems with the delivery of the requested stores. Wellington was informed that there was insufficient transport to move all the stores he had requested from Lisbon and on 23 April, he reduced the amount of stores to be brought forward. The stores ordered from Lisbon did not arrive at Elvas until 12 May, and the first items did not get to Badajoz until that evening, by which time the siege was effectively over.

There were similar difficulties with the guns. There were no modern siege guns immediately available for this operation. The guns that were used were supplied from Elvas and, as has been widely recorded elsewhere, they were generally old and in poor condition. Through the efforts of Dickson, a siege train of thirty guns was put together.[42] Some of these were the guns used at the siege of Olivenza and were still there. Yet again, the most immediate problem was transport. Dickson reported on 22 April, that there were only three carriages at Elvas for transporting guns. To get the guns to Badajoz would require moving the six guns at Olivenza as soon as possible so that their carriages could then be sent to Elvas to move the remainder.

Apart from material, the engineers were concerned about the availability of experienced troops. Although this became more prominent in the later sieges, the concern was there from the very first siege. Squire raised concerns before the siege started about the lack of sappers and miners and the need for men who 'know how to carry on an approach under fire'.[43] He knew that in their siege of Badajoz the French sapped right up to the glacis and this required trained and experienced sappers. Squire's view was that if the British had to do the same, there would be significant casualties.

Wellington was impatient to get started on the siege. On 30 March, he wrote to Beresford commenting that 'the breach can be barely more than stockaded'.[44] He wrote again on 6 April, stating that Badajoz must be blockaded as soon as possible. Writing to Liverpool three days later, he mentioned that he 'hoped' Beresford would have been blockading Badajoz from 3 April. These timescales all appear unrealistic as there had been problems establishing a crossing-point over the river Guadiana in early April due to the level of the river rising unexpectedly. Beresford also had to take Olivenza before he could move on Badajoz. At that time he also did not know the exact whereabouts of Soult. Wellington also wrote to Beresford on 21 April, when he heard that Soult was fortifying Seville. He saw this as indicating that he could be planning to relieve Badajoz. He explained that it was even more urgent that not a moment was lost in starting operations against Badajoz.[45]

Immediately after the siege of Olivenza was concluded, Dickson and Squire were ordered to start preparing for the siege of Badajoz,[46] and from 19 April they were preparing the siege train of thirty guns and howitzers. On the 27th, Beresford issued an order for one hundred troops to be permanently assigned to the engineers as artificers. John Squire, who was the engineer in charge of the siege of Olivenza, had requested these on 10 April:

> I request you will submit to His Excellency Marshal Beresford the propriety of forming a corps of artificers amounting to 100 men from the British Regiments of the line who would be attached to the Engineers Department during the attack of Badajoz. Viz. Miners – 50; Carpenters – 20; Masons/bricklayers – 24; Smiths – 6. Such men as have been employed in the lines in front of Lisbon will be best calculated for this service.[47]

Ten days later, Beresford confirmed he could have them.[48] The men arrived at Olivenza on 2 May, and some were immediately put to work cutting timber and making siege materials. The remainder were given some basic training in siegecraft along with the small number of Royal Military Artificers who were present, none of whom had any previous training in siege works.[49] In addition, eighty-four carpenters and miners from the British divisions and twelve officers were to serve as assistant engineers (these were officer volunteers from the army). Beresford told Wellington in a letter of 3 May that he was waiting for Fletcher to confirm that all the stores were ready and would then order the investment of the north side of the river Guadiana.[50] Dickson and Squire certainly thought everything was ready to start the investment of Badajoz before this date.[51] The final delays were likely to have been caused by waiting for confirmation that the bridges had been restored at Jerumenha; that the troops allocated to assist were present; and that the additional shovels had arrived from Abrantes. All these events happened on or around 2 May.

Following the investment of the fortress on the south side of the river Guadiana on 4 May, the guns at Olivenza were moved up and placed in the park behind the Cerro del Vinto on the 6th. The carriages were then sent off to Elvas to be available to bring up the next batch of guns. The guns for the attack on San Christobal had been available since 5 May, and were only waiting for the north side of the river to be invested. Dickson recorded that it would take two trips (that is, two days) to transfer the eight guns required for the north side. In the same letter he mentioned he was still waiting for two companies of Portuguese artillery, who were essential to progress the siege on the south side of the river.[52]

Dickson expressed his confusion on 1 May, and again on 7 May, as to why the siege had not commenced.[53] Similarly, there were a number of comments from engineer officers, the earliest being 25 April.[54] The engineers believed that arrangements had been made for the right bank of the river Guadiana to be invested on 4 May. They moved stores and pontoons up and had to make rapid arrangements for their protection when no troops arrived on the right bank. Jones commented on 8 May that the stores for the attack on San Christobal had been waiting on carts for two days.[55]

There appears to have been a change of plan around this time. Jones' diary recorded that the plan of attack was put 'on paper' on 5 May, and agreed by Beresford on the 7th. Wellington's earlier memorandum had not specified exactly how the attack was to be carried out, noting that after taking the three outworks, Beresford was to decide where to attack the castle. Although Wellington had suggested the south side of the fortress, he had not ordered it. The engineers had a clear preference under the time constraints for an attack on the castle, rather than the south side. It may have been the lack of trained sappers and miners that influenced the decision to attack San Christobal and breach the walls from a distance, as such an attack would require fewer sappers and miners. Based on the comments at the time from the engineers, it is probable that the plan Fletcher presented to Beresford on 7 May included a proposal to start the attack on the castle before San Christobal was taken. It was necessary to attack the Picurina outwork to do this; but it was not necessary to take the Pardaleras outwork. This was earlier than had been proposed in Fletcher's original plan as documented in Jones' *Journal*. Fletcher would have been looking for quicker ways to take the fortress to mitigate the impact of the additional delays since the original plan had been agreed. It was now two weeks since Wellington had sent his memorandum to the Spanish generals (and eight weeks since the French took Badajoz) and as yet, there had been no answer from them. That there was a change in the plan is indicated by the numerous comments from engineer officers which refer to attacks on San Christobal and Picurina and false attacks on Pardaleras. These include:

> It had however been previously decided to attack the castle at the east extremity of the town . . . the intention was to breach the castle,

while batteries were established on the right bank of the Guadiana to take in flank and reverse. With this view it was necessary to take Fort Christobal . . . The whole was intended to be a simultaneous operation, so as to have divided the attention of the enemy. If we had had sufficient tools it was also proposed to make a fake attack to the westward by re-opening the trenches of the enemy.[56]

On the 8th . . . we broke ground on this side against Fort Christobal in earnest and they in joke opened the old French parallels on the other side.[57]

The project was to commence a parallel embracing the castle having its right on the river, and to attack that part, the castle being like most others on a hill accessible and the wall not covered; at the same time attacks were to be carried on against the fort of San Christobal on the opposite side of the Guadiana.[58]

The attacks to be directed against the castle and Fort Christobal.[59]

On the same day that Beresford approved the plan (7 May), Jones recorded that a working party was preparing materials near the spot where it was intended to start the battery against Fort Picurina.[60] This would suggest the plan to attack the castle had been accepted. Significantly, Jones also noted that Lieutenant Forster RE was employed that night to cross the Rivellas stream and ascend the height to the castle wall to determine the feasibility of British troops approaching the walls. It is difficult to think of any reason to carry out such a dangerous reconnaissance unless the plan was to attack the castle at this point. It is probable that the actual plan followed by the engineers was what had been agreed with Beresford, but it has not subsequently been recorded in that way. It is inconceivable that the engineers would have been allowed to alter Wellington's plans without his or Beresford's agreement.

Fletcher was marking out the positions for the trenches against the Picurina during the day on 8 May and Squire was doing the same on the other side of the river against San Christobal. The trenches were started against all three outworks on the night of 8 May. Jones started marking out the ground for the attack on the castle the following morning with the expectation that the trenches would be started that night. However, Beresford 'forbade' any work to start. Jones then wrote that the noon reliefs on 10 May for the attacks against the Picurina and Pardaleras were 'nominal' to make a 'show of work'. Beresford agreed to start the attack on the castle on that day, but on hearing news of the French plan to move against him, he deferred the work again.[61] At the evening relief on 10 May, because 'Beresford was still forbidding' work against the castle, 'it became necessary to devise some means to amuse the enemy',[62] and further trenches were dug against the Picurina and Pardaleras. Jones again mentioned small parties working against the two outworks the next day.[63]

The delay in starting the attack against the castle also had a major impact on the attack against San Christobal in that the fire from Badajoz was almost wholly directed against the attack on that fort. On the morning of 10 May, the French made a sortie against the works around San Christobal. They briefly took control of the trenches. They only did minor damage before they were repulsed, but the British covering party rashly chased them up to the very walls of the fort and suffered 400 needless casualties. Squire, who was commander of the attack on San Christobal, reported:

> I have the honour to report to you that at 7am the enemy made a sortie from Fort Christobal and from the line between that place and the bridge – They gained the [?] of our battery, but were immediately repulsed – our loss I believe has been rather severe – Lt Reid [RE] was in the battery at the time and he has received a slight contusion but is not incapacitated from doing his duty – it gives me the greatest pleasure to report to you the very handsome manner in which Col. Harcourt and all the officers of the covering party speak of the gallantry and zeal of that officer.[64]

The delays caused by Beresford not allowing work to start against the castle was causing some frustration amongst the engineers:

> Still we were urged on . . . with the reason . . . that we were to take the fire off the main attack . . . by attracting it to ourselves!!!!!! . . . The daylight of each succeeding day however affording us the mortification of seeing that our promised support from the main attack had been withheld . . . Marshal Beresford not allowing the original plan to go on.[65]

> The project was to commence a parallel embracing the castle . . . at the same time attacks were to be carried on against the fort of San Christobal . . . This latter one however only was commenced, Marshal Beresford, who commanded saying he would take that first, the consequence was that the small attack [on San Christobal] . . . had to support for three days the whole fire and efforts of the place and fort.[66]

On the evening of 10 May, Beresford finally gave permission for work to start against the castle on the following evening but insisted that it must not start until Fletcher could guarantee that the workmen would be fully protected from French fire by the morning. To achieve this the tools ordered from Lisbon were needed, and these were expected to arrive until the next day. The batteries finally opened against San Christobal on the morning of the 11th. D'Urban and Oman both suggested that the battery at San Christobal started too early[67] and took all the return fire from Badajoz. Ross, one of the engineers working at San Christobal, wrote clearly that 'on the 11th by order, our battery of three 24-pounders and two 8-inch howitzers opened upon San Christobal having [the whole of] Badajoz opposed to it'.[68]

The battery against the Picurina had been ready since 9 a.m. on the 10th. There is no specific information on when this battery opened fire, but Jones commented that the Picurina battery fired 160 rounds on 11 May, hitting the target only four times.[69] This would strongly suggest that the battery had been firing for most of the day.

Dickson said that his and Fletcher's wish 'was not to begin the fire from any one battery until the whole attack should be more advanced'.[70] Their view was that the Picurina battery was not sufficiently far forward to support San Christobal. The effect of the two batteries fire was negligible due to the inexperience of the artillerymen and the faults in the guns. The battery against San Christobal was overwhelmed by fire, with four of the five guns being disabled by mid-afternoon. It was decided to build another battery next to the one that had been badly damaged, and this was started on the night of 11/12 May. This battery did not open fire before the siege was raised.

At 5 p.m. on the 11th, Fletcher received news that the tools required to begin the attack against the castle would not arrive that night. He complained to Squire that the tools they had were so defective as to be almost unusable and told Beresford that the works against the castle could not start until the following night. When the new tools finally arrived, the trenches were started against the castle on the night of 12 May. Good progress was being made when at 1 a.m. an order was received from Beresford for the work to stop immediately and for the troops to be withdrawn.

Activities over the next 48 hours became very confused, with most of 13 May being spent removing stores. However, work was still continuing against the forts of San Christobal and Pardaleras. According to Jones, at 6 a.m. on the 14th, Beresford wrote to Fletcher and suggested that the attack could continue against San Christobal, as he believed the French were only manoeuvring. Fletcher had started recalling the stores when he was informed that orders had been issued to the army to raise the siege and he then had to countermand his orders. On the night of 14 May, the batteries were dismantled and any remaining stores that could not be removed were burnt. Beresford, who had advanced to meet Soult, was very concerned about his rear as the temporary crossing-point over the Caya river had been dismantled and floated down to Jerumenha, leaving the bridge at Jerumenha as his only point of retreat if his army was beaten. He would have been very aware that these crossing-points had twice been made impassable in the last few weeks. He wrote to Fletcher asking him to make sure it was secure 'as the ultimate safety of the army might depend upon it'.[71] Fletcher personally inspected the bridges on the evening of 15 April 'on his way to join the army'. The final covering forces did not leave Badajoz until the night of 15/16 May and marched straight to the battlefield at Albuera. Thus ended the first siege of Badajoz.

Oman's account of the siege is flawed in a number of places. He claimed that Wellington's orders were for the siege of Badajoz to begin the moment that the guns and material were ready.[72] This is not true. Wellington had told Beresford not to start the siege until the Spanish generals had agreed to his memorandum of operations. This did not happen until 8 May. The evidence shows that the siege was ready to start before that date. Oman states that the south side was invested on the 6th and the north side on the 7th.[73] He also wrote that Beresford only invested the south side after Fletcher and Dickson said all the stores were ready on the 5th.[74] These dates should in fact be 4 and 8 May, respectively. Wellington's only comment on the investment dates are in a letter to Liverpool on 15 May, where he said both sides were invested on the 8th. Beresford, writing to Wellington on 3 May, stated that he intended to invest Badajoz on the 4th, but this did not happen.[75]

Oman's summary of the strategy accurately reports Wellington's memorandum of 23 April 1811. He goes on to say that none of the attacks were to be false attacks and that the engineers had given Wellington 'bad counsel as they certainly did to Beresford during the subsequent weeks'.[76] He then concluded by saying that planning three attacks when the engineers knew they had limited resources was inexcusable. Oman's criticisms are based on the premise that the engineers were following the plan described by Wellington on 23 April, but the diaries of the engineers show that they were not. A more plausible explanation is that the engineers were operating to a plan based on that originally proposed by Fletcher, but with a change to bring forward the attack on the Picurina and castle to make up some of the additional lost time and this is what was agreed with Beresford on 7 May.

Without even looking at the actual work undertaken during this first siege, the timescale for its completion was unrealistic. The whole operation started too late and was too hurried. Wellington was desperate to recover Badajoz, as his whole strategy was dependent on it being in Allied hands. Wellington pressured the engineers to come up with a plan to meet his tight schedule. The plan was risky, but could have worked. The strength of San Christobal was certainly underestimated but at the time both the engineer and artillery commanders believed it was possible to take the fort in a few days.

There was real confusion both at the time and amongst later writers about which plan was being followed. The plan Wellington wrote up was not that proposed by Fletcher. The plan implemented was not that proposed by Fletcher either, but was much closer to it. The engineers believed they were working to a plan that Beresford would not let them implement fully, after he had approved it. Their frustration comes through clearly in several of their letters.

The resources required were not available, either in terms of guns or siege materials. The siege train was too small and ineffective. Although thirty-two guns were available for the siege, only thirteen of these made it into the batteries. Five guns[77] opened against San Christobal on 11 May, four of which were damaged the same day and were not replaced before the siege was raised, although a new battery for four guns was started. The eight guns for the attacks on the two outworks on the south side were too far away to cause any significant damage. During the whole siege there were only five siege guns firing to make a breach from 7 a.m. to around noon on 11 May. The stores in terms of tools, shot and powder were insufficient and had to be shipped in from Lisbon. Even the reduced stores ordered from Lisbon did not arrive until the 12th.

There were too many delays in starting the siege. It appears that the decision to besiege Badajoz had developed a level of momentum and rather than stop it, each problem just delayed the start, with no-one re-evaluating the costs and benefits of continuing with the siege. Most of the delays were not the fault of the engineers. These included the problems with the bridging across the Guadiana, getting the stores to Badajoz and getting the agreement of the Spanish commanders to Wellington's operational plan. The loss of a week between 24 April and 1 May, due to the river rising, was the last in a series of delays that severely affected the plan to attack Badajoz. Wellington's correspondence shows that the deciding factor for starting the siege was the agreement of the Spanish commanders to his memorandum. Beresford did not want to commit to starting the siege until he knew he would have their full support. Neither Oman, Fortescue or later historians pick up on this.

Beresford knew on 10 May that Soult was advancing to relieve Badajoz. He was in a difficult situation. There was no way that there would be sufficient time to complete the siege before Soult arrived. But if Soult was just making a demonstration, or decided that his force was not strong enough and retired, Beresford would be criticised for raising the siege too early.

The engineers all wanted to start the attack on the castle on 9 May, but Beresford would not allow them. From the 11th, Beresford was trying to protect the siege materials and conduct the siege at the same time. The result was that neither was done successfully. The siege was half-hearted in its application and many stores had to be destroyed when the siege was raised. A better strategy would probably have been to suspend the siege and keep a tight blockade around Badajoz until Soult's intentions were clear and then restart with all the materials and resources immediately at hand. In the end there was no way that the siege could have succeeded. There were only five days between the investment of the fortress and the raising the siege. It was impossible to take the fortress in that time. It should be remembered that the French took forty-two days to take Badajoz and that was through surrender. It would have taken them longer to take the fortress by storm.

One impact of the first siege of Badajoz was the effect it had on Beresford's reputation. There was a growing lack of confidence in his leadership that had started with the action at Campo Mayor. Gordon, Wellington's ADC, had very little good to say about Beresford before they rode down to sort out the problems. Squire described the leadership as all 'doubt and indecision'.[78] Boutflower, the surgeon of the 40th Foot, complained that they were 'victims of some shameful mismanagement'.[79] Following the Battle of Albuera, there were many more officers complaining about Beresford's leadership.

The first siege resulted in nearly 750 casualties with no visible benefit, although the bulk of the casualties were caused by the reckless pursuit of the French sortie on 10 May. Of the twenty-one engineers present, two were killed and three wounded, all in the attack on San Christobal.[80] The troops were despondent, and after the bloodbath at Albuera they were to come straight back to Badajoz to try again.

The engineers played no part in the battle, being employed removing or destroying the siege stores. Fletcher, who was at Jerumenha on the morning of 16 May, heard of the battle and rode with Rice Jones, arriving after the battle was over. The two of them spent an uncomfortable night out in the open and waited the next day with Beresford to see what Soult intended to do next. On the 18th Rice Jones followed the retreating French with the Allied advance guard and was used as a messenger between the Spanish cavalry and Beresford. Realising that Soult was indeed retreating, Beresford ordered Hamilton's Portuguese division and Madden's cavalry brigade to re-invest Badajoz. That night the engineer officers retired to Olivenza and 'procured good quarters', their thoughts going back to the challenge of besieging Badajoz.[81] In the period since the siege had been raised Phillipon, the governor, had worked hard to make repairs. He also ordered the soil to be removed from the area where the batteries would be sited for any subsequent attack on San Christobal.

The Second Siege of Badajoz
Wellington arrived at Elvas on 19 May 1811, having ridden from the north after defeating the French under Masséna at Fuentes del Oñoro. While Beresford followed Soult south, he took control of the plans for a second attempt on Badajoz. He ordered Dickson to collect the necessary siege materials. Jones believed that it would take around eleven days to have the guns ready, primarily because the carriages used to transport the siege pieces needed significant repairs after the first siege.[82]

Timeline for the Second Siege of Badajoz	
19 May 1811	South side of Badajoz invested by Hamilton
25 May 1811	North side of Badajoz invested by 7th Division
25 May 1811	Flying bridge installed at the mouth of the Caya
27 May 1811	3rd Division joined investment on south side
29 May 1811	Work started on false attack against Pardaleras
30 May 1811	Work started against San Christobal and Picurina
3 June 1811	Guns opened fire on both sides
4 June 1811	Seven guns moved forward to new battery on night 4/5 June
5 June 1811	Seven guns opened from Battery No. 6, south side
6 June 1811	1st assault on San Christobal, night 6/7 June
7 June 1811	Three guns opened from Battery No. 7, south side
8 June 1811	Ten guns opened from Battery No. 7, south side, including six iron 24-pounders which had arrived from Lisbon
9 June 1811	2nd assault on San Christobal, night 9/10 June
10 June 1811	Siege raised and guns removed by that evening

It was not until 29 May that the convoy set off from Elvas. During this ten-day delay, Allied reinforcements had also arrived to replace the losses at the Battle of Albuera. The 7th Division arrived on 25 May and reinvested the northern bank of the Guadiana, once again completely cutting off the fortress. General Picton arrived with the 3rd Division on the 27th and took up a position on the southern bank. Wellington was in no doubt that this siege would also have to be conducted against the clock. Although Soult and Masséna had been temporarily repulsed, it quickly became apparent that the French were preparing once again to come to the aid of the fortress. As early as 23 May, Wellington noted the movement of reinforcements to the south which would give the French 50,000 troops to use against him. Whilst the French still held Ciudad Rodrigo to the north, Wellington could not bring enough troops south to face this force. Consequently, when Soult advanced, Wellington would once again be forced to raise the siege unless the fortress could be taken by that time. Fletcher also reported that 'it seems highly probable that our siege may again be interrupted'.[83]

Wellington now considered the plan to be followed for the second attempt, Jones noting that 'After much consideration, [he] determined . . . to follow the plan . . . for the last attack'.[84] This infers that the plan that the engineers actually followed for the first siege was known to Wellington, even though it was not documented, as discussed above. The plan was for attacks against the San Christobal and Picurina outworks (which would ultimately become the attack against the castle), with a false attack against the Pardaleras outwork. Some changes were made to the overall plan, to increase the number of guns available, to set up counter-battery fire and to start both attacks simultaneously. There was one major boost to the planning, in that the stores that Wellington had ordered from Lisbon in April 1811, for the first siege, had eventually arrived at Elvas and were now available for use. But there were still not enough tools for the planned activities as 1,000 more picks and shovels were ordered from Lisbon on 22 May.[85]

The siege train that Dickson put together comprised thirty 24-pounder and four 16-pounder guns, and eight 8in and four 10in howitzers. As before, these were all supplied from Elvas and were of the same age and poor quality as those used previously. To bolster these limited resources, orders were sent to expedite the arrival of the six iron guns that had been ordered from Lisbon around 10 April and also to assign a company of British artillerymen to support the Portuguese artillerymen. Wellington, clearly still had no intention of using the new battering train that was at Lisbon. As early as 14 May, he was arranging for it to be moved north for the planned siege of Ciudad Rodrigo. Fletcher also requested that Beresford assign 250 soldiers to the engineers and that the assistant engineers who volunteered for the first siege would be made available again.

All the officers knew that this was going to be another race against time, Dickson, writing on 29 May, said 'Reinforcements are on their march from Masséna's army to the south, so that we must soon take Badajoz, or we probably will be interrupted again'.[86] Similarly, Jones' view was 'anything to be undertaken against Badajoz, must therefore be of a rapid nature'.[87] As with the first siege, collecting men and material together with the limited resources that were immediately available proved time consuming and it was not until 30 May that everything was in place to start the attacks.

Between 30 May and the morning of 3 June, the batteries and trenches were formed for the attacks against San Christobal and the castle. The attack against San Christobal suffered the same problems as before, through the lack of soil and the incessant bombardment from the French. Due to the limited number of workmen available on the south side, the parallel was not as long as proposed and on the night of 31 May 1811 it was decided to prepare the main battery at the end of the current parallel rather than wait a further twenty-four hours for the parallel to be extended nearer to the walls. The decision was made to accept the extra distance for the sake of speed.[88] The batteries were completed and opened fire on the morning of 3 June 1811.

Siege guns available	1st Siege	2nd Siege
Attack on San Christobal	5[89]	23[90]
Attack on Castle	8[91]	20

There was an impressive increase in the number of guns brought forward. Compared with the first siege, three times the number of guns were available on the morning the firing commenced. On the north side, there were four batteries in action. On the south side all the guns were initially placed in one large battery. Fletcher had written to Wellington on the evening of 3 June, stating that as 'the guns employed are so uncertain in their effects it may become necessary to push yet further forward'.[92] He told Wellington that he had ordered work to be started that night on the second parallel and a new battery that would bring the range to the castle walls down to 650 yards. This work was completed and seven guns opened fire on the morning of 5 June. Again that night, the parallel was extended further to the right and another battery was started at 520 yards from the castle. This battery opened with three guns on 7 June, and that night the six iron 24-pounders, which had eventually arrived from Lisbon were installed with one other gun, bringing the battery up to ten guns on the morning of the 8th.

Guns Available Each Morning of the Second Siege of Badajoz							
	3 June	4 June	5 June	6 June	7 June	8 June	9 June
San Christobal Attack	23	21	15	14	13	20	17
Attack on Castle	20	18	19	17	18	13	13

The table above shows the number of guns that were available each morning. The old brass guns continued to exhibit all the problems that had been apparent during the first siege. Most were made inoperative through use rather than through enemy action. Both Jones and Dickson remarked on the improvements when the first iron guns became available on the morning of 8 June.

As predicted by the engineers, the wall of the castle was quickly destroyed on the first day of firing. However, what was not expected was that the wall was actually just a facing for the ground behind which refused to collapse and peeled off in sheets leaving a near-perpendicular slope. This was battered incessantly until 10 June, and it was only at this point that there was some hope that the breach might be practicable. Captain Mulcaster reconnoitred the Rivellas stream on the night of 5 June, and identified two fords where troops could cross near the proposed breach.[93] Captain Patton was mortally wounded making a further reconnaissance of the Rivellas stream and the castle walls on the night of 8 June 1811.[94]

The fire against San Christobal was also more successful than it had been during the first siege. The breach was declared practicable following a reconnaissance of the breach on the night of 5 June by Lieutenant Forster RE. An assault was ordered for midnight on the 6th, led by Lieutenant Forster. Writing to the Earl of Liverpool on that day, Wellington said 'I have strong hopes that they will not be able to keep us out of the place [i.e. Badajoz]'.[95] His optimism had gone by the following morning, and it seems it had been for public consumption only. Cocks recalled overhearing him talking to Dickson the day before, saying 'If we succeed with the means we have it will be a wonder'.[96]

The assault failed, primarily due to the prompt action of the French who had cleared away the rubble from the breach between dusk and midnight when the attack was made. The attacking party made valiant attempts for nearly an hour to find a way in, but eventually retired with losses of twelve killed and eighty wounded. Jones noted that 'the storming party, I am afraid, did not march until midnight', which suggests that the engineers thought the delay before the assault was too long.[97]

The siege batteries recommenced firing the following morning and battered the walls of the fort for a further two days, when the breach was once again declared practicable. To reduce the time for the French to clear away the rubble, the assault was scheduled for 9 p.m. The size of the assault force was increased but a similar result occurred, with the garrison showing great energy in clearing the rubble from the breach and blocking the breach itself. The leader of the assault, Major McGeechy, and Lieutenant Hunt RE, who was guiding the party, were both killed in the first minutes of the attack. Casualties this time were fifty-four killed and eighty-five wounded.[98] Squire, writing just before the second assault took place, showed that despondency was creeping in:

> This night Fort Christobal will be again assaulted. On the last occasion we lost one of the bravest and finest young men in the Corps of Engineers. He was a real hero, he lived and died like a Roman in the best ages of their glory. In this unfortunate attack I have now buried three of my comrades – two of them, Dickinson and young Forster, I knew intimately and I sensibly feel their loss. I have called our attack unfortunate because of our miserable means. In every other aspect we have done well and the Corps of Engineers have at least endeavoured to deserve an honourable distinction – Our guns are infamous all Portugueze – and two or three became useless every day – I think a practicable breach may possibly be made tomorrow evening in the castle. Captain Patton of the Engineers was severely wounded yesterday.[99]

Two days later, he updated the situation:

> On the night of the 9th, the assault of Fort Christobal was again attempted, and a second time it failed although I am persuaded if success had been possible, we should have succeeded. The enemy made a most noble and obstinate defence they had cleared away the rubbish from the foot of the breach and filled the ditch with 5½ inch shells, hand grenades, light balls etc. When our ladders were planted the enemy rolled down upon our men large stones or rubbish or pushed them into the ditch with poles. They cried out from the parapet *Venez Monsieurs Anglais, Venez Portugaise*. The Portugueze amidst all this fire behaved as nobly as the English. We lost 130 men killed and wounded; amongst the killed Lieutenant

Hunt of the Royal Engineers, who was the first man shot on the occasion. Our losses on this side have indeed been severe. I have certainly suffered great anxiety but my calamity is now at its height for we must raise the siege, time and means completely failing us. In a day or two a large French Army will be collected in this neighbourhood; our breach in the castle will not be practicable for three or four days and to take Christobal we must go to the crest of the glacis. We have neither time nor means. Our guns are most infamous, nearly half of them have been disabled by our own fire. The artillery is Portugueze most of the vents of the guns are now 1 ½ inch in diameter! We have had no mortars whatever.[100]

At noon the following day, 10 June 1811, Wellington called together his officers and told them he was raising the siege. The guns and stores were removed over the following two days. The comprehensive reasons Wellington gave for his decision were:

- The poor quality of the siege guns.
- The even poorer quality of the gun carriages.
- The resistance of the castle wall. He was 'astonished' by it.
- Failure to take the fort of San Christobal.
- The expected arrival of French relief forces.
- The depletion of the ordnance stores at Elvas to a point where it would not be able to defend itself; the lack of replacement stores from Lisbon and the lack of transport to deliver replacement stores.
- The depletion of provisions to the point where there were less than a fortnight of supplies for Elvas.
- The need for the transport used at the siege of Badajoz to replenish the ordnance stores and provisions at Elvas.[101]

The two sieges of Badajoz were dismal failures. The reasons need to be re-evaluated with emphasis on the performance of the engineers rather than on the events themselves.

There are some common threads running through both sieges:

- They were carried out against time pressures.
- There were limited resources available: manpower, materials and guns.
- There were transport problems.
- The choice of point of attack was strongly criticised both at the time and later.

The two most significant English writers on the war, Oman and Fortescue, are highly critical of the sieges, blaming the engineer officers and to a lesser extent Wellington. Myatt generally takes the same line, but he is more sympathetic to the problems that the Allies faced.[102] In the analysis below both sieges will be treated as one, because they were effectively the same siege, undertaken twice.

Both Oman and Fortescue criticised the decision to attack San Christobal in the strongest terms. Whist criticism with hindsight is always easy, the views of the experts who were making decisions at the time must be considered. On two separate occasions the engineers advised that there was insufficient time to carry out a regular approach. The admittedly high-risk attack on San Christobal and the castle was the only possible solution they could see to meet the time limits.[103] Wellington and Beresford approved their plan on both occasions. Dickson, the senior artillery officer, expressed no concern about the strategy before, during or after the sieges. On both occasions, the siege was raised because of an approaching army. Oman, when commenting on the second siege, stated that Wellington had four weeks to take Badajoz. The fact is that Wellington only had ten days from opening the trenches to raising the siege. He had even less time in the first siege, just four days. The remainder of the time that the Allies had available was taken up arranging guns and stores or sorting out communications across the river Guadiana. If the plan chosen was believed to be the fastest, then there was absolutely no chance of an attack on the south side succeeding. The French took seven weeks to take Badajoz and that was by surrender, not assault. It is difficult to understand why most writers believe that Wellington could achieve the same in seven days.

D'Urban stated in his diary that the breach in San Christobal was never practicable and noted on 10 June that a French sapper who had deserted said that the castle wall could never be breached at the point chosen as it had solid rock behind (which was shown to be untrue). D'Urban thought the engineers had chosen the wrong point of attack and should have attacked the south side.[104] He reserved more serious criticism for the overall strategy, in that he believed that Wellington should have focussed on destroying Soult's army first and then turned on Badajoz at his leisure. There is also an interesting comment by George Ross RE who wrote that Beresford believed that the siege of Badajoz should not have been undertaken.[105]

The two assaults on the fort of San Christobal need further consideration. It was a small but very strong fort, each side being around 100 yards long. The first assault used less than 200 men and the second a few more. During the first assault, the French had less than 200 troops in the fort and probably not more than 400 during the second assault. Oman and Fortescue both commented that the storming parties were too small.[106] There was no reason why they could not have been larger. With the forces Wellington had available, he could have made an attempt to overwhelm the fort. Brute force may not have led to any greater casualties, as the losses were caused by these small groups spending up to an hour trying to get into the fort. Ladders could have been used at different points as well as at the breach. At no time did the French have enough troops in the fort to defend all the faces at the same time. When Wellington finally took Badajoz in 1812, it was the secondary attacks that succeeded, not the main one. A similar approach, attacking at multiple locations, should have been used in the assault on San Christobal in 1811, particularly due to Wellington's strong desire to re-take Badajoz quickly.

There is no doubt that the guns available from Elvas were not up to the task of performing siege work. There is no doubt that the lack of trained sappers and miners had an effect in that there were no experienced troops who could take the sap forward. There is also no doubt that the transport problems meant that not all the materials were there when they were required. But the single inescapable reason why these sieges failed was time. None of the other factors would have prevented the sieges' success had Wellington not been working against deadlines. Wellington had known for days that he could not continue the siege past 10 June.[107] In a letter to Charles Stuart, he wrote, 'Badajoz may fall; but the business will be very near run on both sides . . . I have never seen walls bear so much battering, nor ordnance, nor artillery so bad as those belonging to Elvas'.[108] He also knew that Badajoz only had supplies for two weeks.[109]

Added to the above, there were some other factors. San Christobal proved to be stronger than Wellington, the artillery and the engineer officers expected. It must also not be forgotten that the governor proved his skill many times during the three sieges of Badajoz. With a less energetic governor, the fortress would probably have fallen in June 1811. Overall there were too many factors working against the sieges succeeding, but they had to be tried because of the strategic importance of Badajoz.

What is surprising in looking closely at the writing of Oman, Fortescue and many modern authors is that the sieges have been skipped over and not really understood by them. Examples of this include Oman's criticism that Wellington could have ordered up better guns in early May 1811 for the second siege of Badajoz.[110] Wellington had ordered additional guns for the first siege of Badajoz around 10 April, a full month earlier than that. The lack of transport made moving them very difficult. These guns finally arrived near the end of the second siege of Badajoz on 8 June, two months after they were ordered. Fortescue gets similarly confused over the guns.

First he suggests that time constraints meant that Wellington would not wait for the 'English' siege train.[111] Later he writes that they sent for some British iron guns from Elvas.[112] The iron guns from Lisbon were actually Portuguese naval 24-pounders. They were also old and worn, but much better than the old brass 24-pounders that were being used prior to their arrival.

In summary, the first two sieges of Badajoz were attempted with insufficient time and material available. The choice of point of attack was not the preferred option for any officer but circumstances led them to believe that this was the only option that might succeed. The engineer officers felt that they were not allowed to follow the plan that had been agreed. There is no strong evidence to support the view that another point of attack under the same circumstances would have been successful. The French, realising that the Allies were once again intending to besiege Badajoz, in a rare show of cooperation combined their forces into a joint operation. Marmont, who had replaced Masséna, came south with around 30,000 troops and Soult came north from Seville with a similar number.

Once Wellington had made the decision to abandon the siege, the artillery was quickly removed and on its way back to Elvas the following day. By the end of 12 June, all the stores had been removed. Over the next few days Wellington closely monitored the movements of the French, waiting until 16 June before deciding to raise the blockade. The next morning the Allied army crossed the Guadiana, primarily by the fords around Jerumenha. Soult and Marmont met at Merida on 18 June and not knowing that Wellington had already retired, made plans to advance to Badajoz on the 19th. It quickly became clear that there were no Allied troops in the vicinity, the two Marshals triumphantly entering the fortress the next morning, which fortuitously was also the last day for which Phillipon had provisions for the garrison.

Following their withdrawal, Wellington placed his forces in defensive positions to wait the advance of Soult and Marmont. His lines stretched from the village of Oguella on the river Gebora on his left, through Campo Mayor, to the bridge over the Caya on his right. The engineers were employed building field defences to strengthen Wellington's positions, Burgoyne noting he was employed in this activity near Campo Mayor and Captain MacLeod and Rice Jones were working between there and the castle at Oguella.[113] This activity is interesting since the Royal Staff Corps were officially responsible for field works. This is a good example of the blurring of responsibilities between the engineering services and Wellington's pragmatic use of whatever resources was available. As there is no mention of the Staff Corps during either siege, it is certain that the bulk of the Staff Corps were with Wellington's army in the north where they played their part at the Battle of Fuentes del Oñoro (see below).

Having found no sign of the Allies on the south side of the Guadiana, the French pushed out a large-scale reconnaissance on the morning of 22 June, finding the Allies in strength at Jerumenha and Campo Mayor. No further action was undertaken before the 24th, when Soult expressed concerns to Marmont on receiving the information that the Spanish General Blake was not, as believed, with Wellington, but was in fact moving south into Andalusia. Soult argued that the protection of Badajoz was probably of more importance to Marmont than it was to himself and consequently he should take responsibility for its safety. However, Marmont did not agree and believed that Soult was trying to pass the responsibility for Badajoz on to him as some of the other French generals had said he would. He then insisted that unless the whole of V Corps and Latour-Maubourg's cavalry were left with him, he too would abandon Badajoz and move off towards Truxillo. The honeymoon period of good relations between the French commanders had lasted less than a week and Soult, realising he had no option, consented.

The first indications of Soult's return to Seville came to Wellington on 27 June, when he heard that the defences at Olivenza had been destroyed. On the 28th, Soult set off for Seville. Wellington held his position to protect Elvas and the Portuguese countryside from French attention. This standoff continued until mid-July when Marmont had managed to collect six months' supplies for Badajoz. Marmont retired north towards the Tagus and D'Erlon, re-established links with Soult. Wellington, as soon as he was certain that the French had dispersed, took the opportunity to do likewise. The countryside around the Guadiana and the Caya was known to be unhealthy due to the marshy terrain, and plans were in hand to move the Allied troops away as soon as practicable. As early as 30 June, Cocks clearly knew what was intended:

> We have been quietly encamped here between Elvas and Campo Mayor and scarcely see anything of the enemy; indeed, I believe the greater part of his force has already been drawn off from our front and that the remainder will go as soon as Badajoz is revictualled. In this case it is said we shall go into cantonments during the unhealthy season.[114]

Between 18 and 24 July, the bulk of the Allied troops moved away to their summer quarters, with Wellington's headquarters moving back to

Portalegre. Squire had recovered from his earlier despondency and was able to reflect on the events of the last few months:

> Every branch of the service has had an opportunity to profit by the extraordinary events, which have occurred. They will give rise to reflections, perhaps not very agreeable to our feelings, but highly important to us; who are now contending against the first military nation in the world. Those who command will see the necessity of proportioning their means to the end they have in view: – they will feel, that first to think deeply and combine with precision – then to execute with promptitude and secrecy is the surest road to success. When the passage of rivers is the object, they will, it is to be hoped, look forward and be provided with the means of passing them: they will not for the future despise difficulties, but be prepared to meet them: – when they intend the attack of fortified places, they will be previously provided with ample means for such an operation. The moment of execution is not the time to deliberate yet have I observed this to occur in more than one instance during our late campaign. . . . The Engineer Department (I speak without partiality, for you know I am a lover of truth) is capable of being made one of the best Departments in the Army: – but, as it is without means or organisation, it is one of the most inefficient from my own observation and experience I have no hesitation in saying, that there is more zeal, spirit and intelligence in that Corps, than in any other Department of the Army. Its best executions are however checked and though we may try (as I think we always shall) to deserve a reputation, it is almost impossible to obtain it.[115]

The army spent the remainder of 1811 quietly, but typically there were many things for the engineers to do. Before I describe these activities, I need to pick up the activities of the Royal Staff Corps at the Battle of Fuentes del Oñoro in May 1811. On the second day of the battle, to safeguard his retreat in the case the battle went against him, Wellington ordered the two companies of the Staff Corps under Captain Todd to construct a temporary bridge over the river Coa. Several large trees that were found two miles from the selected location were floated down the river. Two separate bridges were then constructed, each by placing the tree part-way across the river and artificers then crossing the remaining distance to the far side to complete the construction. The bridges were not required, due to Wellington's victory but would have been vital if he had suffered a reverse.[116]

Having failed to relieve Almeida, Masséna now ordered it to be abandoned, the garrison escaping on the night on 10 May due to failures in the Allied blockade. Fletcher ordered Captain MacLeod and Lieutenant Trench to work on the repairs at Almeida. It had been extensively damaged during the French siege and further damage was done when the French abandoned it. One of the engineer officers assigned to this task at Almeida was tragically killed whilst trying to clear the ditches, Fletcher reporting 'it is with infinite regret I have to report to you that Lieutenant Trench died on the 10th instant [June] of several wounds he had received . . . by the explosion of several barrels of powder and some shells'.[117] Progress in repairing Almeida was reported in a letter from Burgoyne:

> Lascelles [Lieutenant Lascelles RE] writes from Almeida that they have begun its repair (the Portuguese engineers) for which a regiment of Militia has been assigned, which from various causes can only produce a daily working party of 3 masons and 80 labourers – this is not a rapid way of building up more than three entire fronts of escarp – this scarp work is to be of 12 to 14 feet only the rest of earth. No measures were taken to provision this unfortunate regiment of Militia, many have deserted, many sick and the remainder are starving.[118]

The Portuguese engineer commanding the repairs at Almeida was probably Lieutenant Colonel Carlos Frederico Bernardo de Caula.

Recognising the impact in the previous two sieges of the lack of trained artificers, engineer officers were ordered to start training line infantry in the basics of sapping and mining to support future sieges. Burgoyne and George Ross worked with the 3rd and 1st Divisions respectively through the late summer. Burgoyne noting in his diary 'An order arrived from headquarters that I am to instruct 200 men of the 3rd Division in the art of carrying on the sap etc'. Burgoyne made his opinions clear in a later letter:

> My principal business now is training 200 men of different regiments to the duties required in a siege, which, to our disgrace and misfortune, we have no regular establishment equal to, notwithstanding the repeated experience of the absolute necessity of such a corps to act under the Engineers in a campaign. For want of such an establishment we are frequently led to the loss of valuable officers, and very undeserved discredit.[119]

These troops, whilst not perfect, formed a skills base that would be used in

Lieutenant Colonel Sir Richard Fletcher RE. Portrait in possession of Royal Engineers Mess and used with their permission.

Monument at Alhandra to Sir Richard Fletcher and Neves Costa erected by the Portuguese Engineers.

Major General John Thomas Jones RE. Bust from the Royal Engineers Museum, Chatham.

Lieutenant General Sir Stephen Chapman RE. Portrait in possession of Ronald Brighouse and used with his permission.

Field Marshal John Fox Burgoyne RE.

Contemporary image of Oporto from Villa Nova by Vivian.

Boat bridge across the Douro at Oporto by Landmann.

Flying bridge over the Tagus at Villa Velha.

Main entrance to Fort La Lippe, Elvas, Portugal.

Fort St Lucia, Elvas, Portugal.

Fort St Julian, defending the embarkation point that the British army would have used to evacuate Lisbon.

Section of the ditch of Fort San Vincente at Torres Vedras.

Gun emplacement at Fort 18, Ajuda.

Restored military road leading to the great redoubt at Sobral.

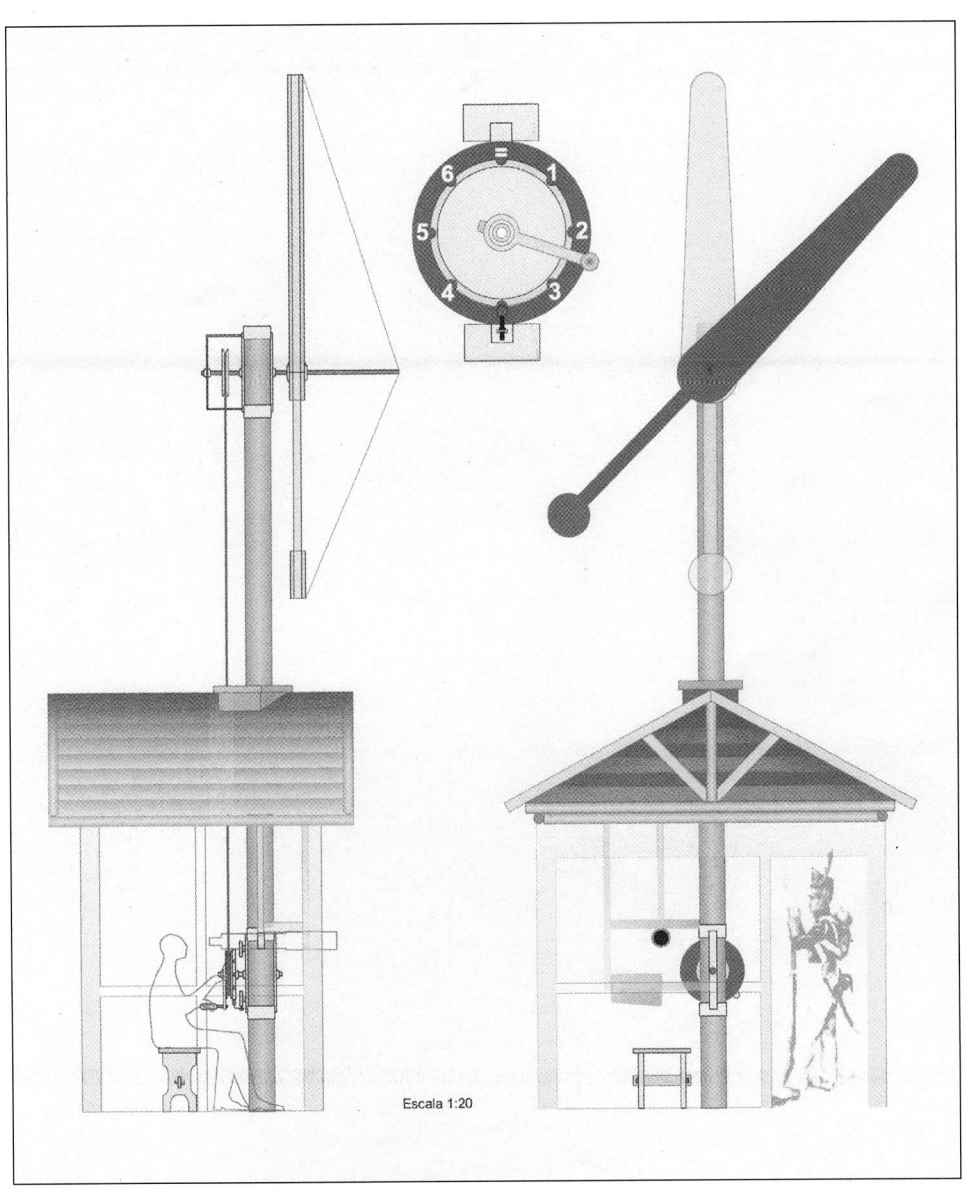

Drawing of a Portuguese single-arm telegraph, reproduced with the permission of the Municipality of Torres Vedras.

Reconstruction of a Portuguese single-arm telegraph.

Reconstruction of a British balloon telegraph based on naval signalling techniques.

Captain Charles Boothby RE, who lost a leg at Talavera.

Badajoz Castle from Fort San Christobal.

The Tagus from the fort at Jerumenha.

The castle at Campo Mayor.

Defences at Almeida, Portugal.

Site of the main Allied breach in the wall at Ciudad Rodrigo.

Curtain wall of castle at Badajoz, Spain.

Major William Nicholas RE. Killed at the siege of Badajoz in 1812.

Bridge over the Guadiana at Badajoz seen from Fort San Christobal.

Bridge over the Guadiana at Merida.

Bridge over the Tagus at Almaraz.

Bridge over the Tormes at Salamanca

Bridge over the Tagus at Alcantara.

Siege of San Sebastian by Jenkins.

Passage of the Bidassoa by Jenkins.

Contemporary image of an ox cart and driver.

Fragment of memorial to Royal Engineer officers killed at the siege of San Sebastian, including Richard Fletcher.

the forthcoming sieges. Similar training had been started in England under the control of Charles Pasley. His developments will be discussed later.

In September, Wellington moved forces near to Ciudad Rodrigo to prevent the French getting supplies and reinforcements into the town. Burgoyne wrote that Wellington had been told the fortress was short of supplies and was hoping that a short blockade might force the place to surrender. Several engineers were present preparing for the planned attack on Ciudad Rodrigo but also assisting in resisting any French advance to relieve the place. Burgoyne noted:

> Three or four different positions have been sketched by order of our Colonel who has marked on the plans numerous batteries and slight field works; these positions are in front of Guinaldo and between that and Rodrigo having their right on the bold ravine of the Agueda and their left on the steep fall of the range of heights which is about 4 miles in a parallel direction with that river. The object of a position in the situation I cannot conceive as the enemy by attacking have much to lose by defeat and little to gain by success.[120]

When the French advance came, Wellington found himself facing superior forces. Burgoyne was present at the action at El Bolden on 25 September and was ordered by Wellington to stay with the 21st Portuguese Regiment which was under great pressure from the French. Anthony Emmett RE, who was also present, described what happened:

> On this day Marmont advanced in great force towards . . . El Boden and after a little manoeuvring opened his artillery on the position near El Boden held by two Portuguese guns supported by the 21st Portuguese Line . . . After a smart cannonade the French cavalry cut through the Portuguese guns, which made the 21st Regiment in some trouble and Lord Wellington passed by the regiment and posted himself on the right to see what passed, telling Burgoyne in passing to keep by the regiment and see if he could keep it together.[121]

Surprisingly, Burgoyne does not mention this incident in his diary or when he wrote to Squire a few days later. Eighteen months later he wrote in detail about the event:

> In talking over the general arrangements of the Corps for the ensuing campaign, his Lordship agreed it would be advisable to

attach officers of Engineers to the different divisions of the army, and said they might be useful in a thousand instances. 'There was Burgoyne,' said he 'in the 3rd Division, always took the command of the Portuguese. After the business at El Boden, Marmont told my Aide-de-Camp, who went in with a flag of truce, that he observed we were forced to attach a British officer to encourage the Portuguese regiment on that day and keep it to its duty, and that was Burgoyne' . . . This business of El Boden was on 25th September 1811, and Lord Wellington himself was present; our small force retired for six miles across a plain, in presence of a much superior body of the enemy, particularly cavalry. There being some difficulty in moving the 21st Portuguese regiment, I volunteered, to interpret to them all orders, and regulate their movements, and ultimately, the Portuguese Colonel being an inactive old fool, I took complete command of the regiment through the day. They were frequently threatened but never absolutely charged, though it would appear by Marmont's observation, that he particularly watched for an opportunity against them, as the party on which he was most likely to make an impression. Lord Wellington appeared most pleased at the time, but I imagined it was all forgotten. This remark, of Marmont's, however, appears to have fixed it in his memory as a point in my favour.[122]

The flexibility of Fletcher's officers was demonstrated in a number of ways over this period. Captain Ross and Lieutenant Emmett spent several weeks working on improving the navigation of the river Douro for the next major operation that would occur in early 1812.[123] Lieutenant Reid was serving on the staff of the Spanish army under General Carlos D'España at the specific request of the general and with the agreement of Wellington.[124] Squire, who was still with General Hill in the south, was present at the action at Arroyo dos Molinos on 28 October where Hill surprised a French force under General Girard and destroyed it. Writing to his friend Bunbury a few days later in great excitement, he said:

Never was a surprise more complete than that which took place at Arroyo del Molino [sic] on the 28th October . . . The Colonel of the 40th French infantry told me that the first notice he had of the attack was the appearance of two British officers galloping through the streets of the village . . . All the French officers (our prisoners) say that Girard ought to be shot and that General Hill deserves the highest praise for his conduct.[125]

Squire concluded his account with:

> During our late excursion General Hill has treated me with the most unbounded confidence, since our return he has expressed himself to me in the most kind and flattering language. He has written to Lord Wellington recommending me very strongly for promotion; should any communication on the subject pass through your office I trust you will exert yourself in my favour; for as I only aim at distinction, military rank is my chief object, and I am conscious of this, that (small as my exertions are) I always do my utmost to deserve it.

Promotion was never far from an officer's thoughts. As Squire was promoted to brevet Major in December 1811 it looks like the recommendation from Hill was successful.

The year ended with Wellington poised in the north of Portugal waiting for an opportunity that would come sooner than many expected.

Chapter 6

1812 – Taking the Frontier

Whilst the end of 1811 was quiet, 1812 started with a bang, literally, with Wellington besieging and taking Ciudad Rodrigo, almost before the French knew it was happening. It had taken several months to plan and to move the new battering train into position. Bizarrely, whilst Ciudad Rodrigo is seen as being the best-organised and most successful of Wellington's sieges, the engineers had many misgivings. Captain George Ross commented:

> I am now on the eve of being very differently employed. . . . Lord Wellington is anxious to break ground tomorrow night for which he has not afforded the means . . . I expect his lordship will have another lesson in the school of sieges . . . as far as a loss of men goes . . . he expects to take the same places from the French in a few days which cost them [the French] 30 or 40 to take from the Spaniards. Can anything but chance prevent his being disappointed?[1]

Two days later Ross was dead, hit by a cannon ball whilst directing troops in the trenches.

The siege of Ciudad Rodrigo was probably the only British siege during the Peninsular War that was successfully planned and executed. Unlike the two earlier sieges of Badajoz, Wellington knew this siege was inevitable so could plan when to begin it as part of his overall strategy. The operation started a full eight months before the siege itself, when Wellington gave orders in May 1811 for the new British siege train which was lying in transports at Lisbon to be moved north by sea to Oporto.[2]

The scale of the planning and the time required to move this siege train reinforces the reasons why it was not possible to arrange something similar at short notice for the previous sieges of Badajoz. The siege train was made up of thirty-eight guns, eighteen mortars and twenty-two howitzers, totalling seventy-eight pieces of ordnance. Wellington's memorandum of 19 July 1811 details 1,092 carts and an additional 768 bullocks to move the train and supplies from Oporto.[3] Even with this large number of carts, they had to make two trips. One hundred and fifty boats were also needed for the river passage of the siege guns.[4] Collecting this amount of transport together was a major task and keeping the carts and bullocks together for an extended period leading up to the siege was even more difficult. In his autobiography, John Jones described the Iberian ox-cart:

> The peasant clad in wooden shoes, carrying a ten-feet staff in his hand, and goading on his oxen whilst they pushed forward their rude cars, the wheels of which, formed of one solid piece, sent forth a loud noise, lugubrious, and startling. Trains of these cars were frequently passed, their music having been heard for miles before they appeared.

The siege train was ordered forward to Almeida in mid-November 1811[5] and work started on preparing materials for a bridge to be used to cross the river Agueda at the same time.[6] The troops to undertake the siege had been in the vicinity for many weeks and they were ordered to start preparing the siege materials on 18 December. In freezing winter weather, the Royal Staff Corps built a trestle bridge across the river Agueda to allow the gun carriages and stores to approach the town.

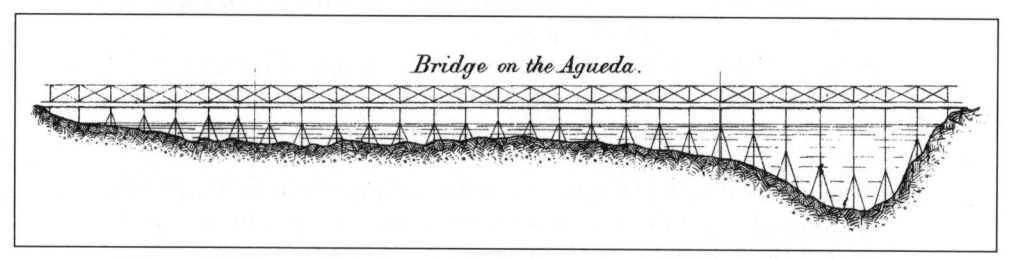

The bridge over the Agueda at Ciudad Rodrigo.

On 1 January 1812, Wellington saw an opportunity to attack the fortress and ordered it to be invested on the 6th. Due to the shortage of transport he decided not to wait for the howitzer ammunition to be delivered and attacked the fortress with guns only.[7] Edward Charles Cocks, who was a great favourite of Wellington, said that he did not like using mortars.[8] This may have come from his witnessing the British bombardment of Copenhagen in 1807 and the terrible effect it had on the civilian population. The use of mortars against San Sebastian in 1813 would cause great anger amongst the Spanish due the damage and civilian casualties they caused.

Engineer resources for the attack comprised of Fletcher in overall command with eighteen other officers[9] and eighteen men from the Royal

Military Artificers. A company of Royal Military Artificers had been ordered up from Lisbon on 18 December 1811, but they had not yet arrived.[10] Burgoyne and Ross were assigned as siege directors, taking 24-hour shifts in turn. Additional support was made up of twelve assistant engineers and 180 soldiers, all from the 3rd Division. These were the men who had been given basic training under Burgoyne in the preceding months.

Timeline for Siege of Ciudad Rodrigo	
14 May 1811	Wellington ordered siege train to be moved from Lisbon to Oporto
1 December 1811	Siege train moved up to Almeida, ready for use
8 January 1812	Fortress invested
8 January 1812	Reynaud redoubt stormed on night of 8/9 Jan 1812
8 January 1811	Trenches opened on night of 8/9 Jan 1812
13 January 1812	Convent of Santa Cruz stormed on night of 13/14 Jan 1812
14 January 1812	French sortie from fortress
14 January 1812	Siege guns opened fire on fortress
14 January 1812	Convent of San Francisco stormed on night of 14/15 Jan 1812
18 January 1812	New battery opens to form second breach
19 January 1812	Fortress stormed on night of 19/20 Jan 1812

Heavy snow delayed the investment due to the difficulty in bringing the stores forward. The fortress was finally invested on 8 January and on the same night the Reynaud redoubt was stormed by troops under the command of Colonel John Colborne.[11] Work started on the trenches immediately and the following night the breaching batteries were started. The plan was to place the first breaching batteries on the Great Teson hill and then move nearer to build a second one on the Little Teson.[12] George Ross, one of the siege directors, was killed early on the night of the 9th and was replaced by Charles Ellicombe, an officer with less experience.

On 10 January, one of the batteries being constructed was found to be partially masked by the Reynaud redoubt and some of the guns had to be moved to another battery. Jones remarked, with some irony, 'that it was thought less labour to remove five of the guns [to another battery] . . . than to cut away the redoubt'.[13] Overall progress was good, but the troops were suffering due to the freezing weather and because they had to march from their camp that was ten to twelve miles away. *En route* they had to ford a river so they spent most of their 24-hour shift cold and wet.

There was a change of plan on 13 January, when Wellington asked Fletcher if the second, closer, set of breaching batteries could be dispensed with as he had received news that Marmont was moving to relieve the fortress. This was agreed, although work continued on the trenches to keep Wellington's options open if Marmont did not advance. That night the convent of Santa Cruz was stormed as it directly threatened the second parallel. On the morning of the 14th, the French made a sortie from the fortress and briefly took control of the trenches, but only limited damage was done and the breaching batteries opened later that day. Burgoyne described it as follows:

> On the evening of the 14th, our batteries opened and made an hour's very bad practice, partly however from opening the embrasures in a hurry. In this operation, while standing on the parapet, poor Skelton [Lieutenant Thomas Skelton RE] received a mortal wound, a round shot taking his hip and the hand he had upon it . . . On the same night Mulcaster received a musket ball through the fleshy part of his thigh (of little consequence, but disables him for the present) while superintending the zig zags on the right, on which they keep up a constant fire of musketry and occasionally grape.[14]

There was another error in the siting of the guns, as it was now found that two 18-pounders could not see the foot of the wall of the convent of San Francisco which they were supposed to attack. Two new batteries were started to create a second breach in the wall and these opened fire on the 18th. The new guns had an immediate impact and the next day the wall collapsed, creating the second practicable breach. Wellington inspected the breaches and wrote orders for an assault that night. The 3rd Division was to storm the main breach and the Light Division the second breach. The storming parties were led to the breaches by Major Sturgeon, Royal Staff Corps, Captain Ellicombe RE and Lieutenant Wright RE.[15] The assault was planned for 7 p.m. that evening and both attacks succeeded, the troops then dissolving into a disorderly mob to ransack the town. Order was restored by the morning and work commenced at once to restore the fortress to a defensible state.

This siege was generally seen as being very successful, both at the time and by later writers, with the fortress falling in twelve days. However, there are circumstances that need further evaluation. Wellington's decision to attack on 1 January 1812 was a consequence of intercepting orders from

Napoleon reorganising the French command structure and simultaneously detaching troops to the east coast of Spain,[16] the result being that the French forces covering Ciudad Rodrigo were reduced in numbers and moved further away, thereby increasing their response time to any actions by Wellington. The assault on Ciudad Rodrigo was clearly a snap decision, as on 30 December 1811, Dickson wrote 'Wellington thinks in about a fortnight we shall have sufficient [ammunition] here to commence operations'.[17] Two days later, he wrote that the 'operation will be undertaken immediately . . . and . . . the trenches will be open in six or seven days'.[18] Dickson, who was many miles away, was slightly behind with the decision-making. John Jones noted in his diary on 28 December 1811 that 'Wellington determined to start the siege instantly he could get up the smallest possible proportion of stores and ammunition'.[19] Once again Wellington was starting a siege with a very small window of opportunity, which meant that the normal rules of sieges had to be ignored. The weather was atrocious and the stores were not ready. One engineer remarked 'Lord W is anxious to break ground tomorrow night, for which he has not afforded the means'.[20]

This quick decision meant that there was no transport to deliver the howitzer ammunition and Wellington took the risk of starting the siege with only a limited ability to carry out counter-battery fire. This would explain why there was no attempt to silence the French guns until the day of the assault. After the siege, Wellington appeared to justify this decision as a new tactic: 'We proceeded at Ciudad Rodrigo on quite a new principle of sieges. The whole object of our fire was to lay open the walls'.[21] The disadvantage of this principle was that many more Allied troops were injured through the consistently effective fire from the numerous French guns. The French were certainly surprised by the lack of counter-battery fire.[22] Colville, commanding the 4th Division, commented that Fletcher had requested counter-battery fire on 18 January and that when the guns were directed at the French batteries just prior to the assault they had an immediate effect. Colville also noted that whilst he thought counter-battery fire was necessary, Wellington did not.[23]

One of the main reasons why Ciudad Rodrigo was taken so quickly was because it was a second-rate fortress with nothing like the strength of Badajoz. Burgoyne, after a visit to the fortress in 1808, described it as 'incapable of defence . . . its works . . . possessing nearly every fault a fortification can have'.[24] In 1810, Squire described Ciudad Rodrigo as 'merely a walled town',[25] and after it was taken, wrote to Charles Pasley: 'We succeeded in taking the place more from its own weakness, than from any means we possessed'.[26] Wellington took full advantage of this weakness and was able to breach the walls from the position of the first batteries. The governor and the garrison were similarly weak. Barrie, the governor, was 'the only general of brigade available at Salamanca when his predecessor, Renaud was taken'.[27] Renaud described Barrie as a 'miserable fellow, perfectly unfit for the job'.[28] His performance matched the expectations set: 'all British accounts agree in condemning Barrie for his lack of energy'.[29] There was no serious resistance to the taking of the redoubt, the convents or the fortress. Barrie has to take responsibility for this.

The greatest success of the siege and the single event that made the siege so quick was John Colborne's taking the Renaud redoubt on the first night. Typically four to five days would have been needed to prepare to attack and take such an outwork. It is worthy of note that to take this small redoubt Colborne used more troops than Wellington did during the two failed attempts on the much stronger Fort San Christobal at Badajoz. The outcome at Badajoz may have been different had a similar strategy been used.

The size and quality of the guns used during the siege also had a significant effect on the outcome. Wellington had none of the problems with inaccuracy and overheating that plagued the old brass guns at Badajoz. Had he been able to bring up the howitzer ammunition, there would probably have been substantially fewer casualties both before and during the assault.

The performance of the engineers tells a different story from the previous two sieges. At Badajoz, the engineers had neither time nor resources to complete their task. At Ciudad Rodrigo they had better guns and more time, although time was still a constraint. Whilst the result was positive, there were some worrying mistakes. Three significant errors were recorded; a battery being placed behind the Renaud redoubt; the guns to attack the convent of San Francisco being too low to see the base of the wall; and the embrasures for the main batteries being misaligned when originally opened. The first error, the misplacing of the battery, was made on the night of 8/9 January, when Ross who was siege director for the night was killed. Burgoyne was strongly critical of the time and effort wasted, writing:

> It was placed behind the French redoubt, it was nearly finished, some platforms laid, and we had worked two nights to level the parapet of the redoubt, when it was at length ascertained that not a single gun of the nine could see the object to be fired at.[30]

He continued: 'Our Headquarters party have sent home a journal of the siege, in which I presume this battery does not make its appearance – it makes a very ugly one in my journal.'[31] Burgoyne and his comrades do not specifically identify who they thought was at fault. Fletcher certainly marked out the batteries previously at Badajoz and it is difficult to believe that he was not present when this, the most vital stage, was being carried out, even if Ross actually did the work. Similarly, the failure to open the embrasures properly occurred after the engineer in command, Lieutenant Skelton, was killed whilst standing on the top of the parapet encouraging the troops to perform the task. His death was unlikely to have helped with the troops' willingness to expose themselves to French fire. Burgoyne noted that when the batteries originally opened on 14 January, many of the shots were passing over the top of the town. Jones' published Journal notes Skelton's death but not the problem with the embrasures. However, his unpublished diary noted 'the want of [a] qualified . . . Engineer . . . to superintend the opening of the embrasures . . . caused such a delay that the day was lost'.[32] This problem was corrected that night and the guns were firing effectively from the following morning.[33] The loss of Ross so early in the siege probably had a continuing effect. Ellicombe who replaced him, whilst being a senior officer, had no operational experience. After some years in Ceylon he had been in the UK for the preceding three years. All three errors were avoidable and should have been identified earlier. Whilst Burgoyne is highly critical of the errors, he took no personal responsibility for them, which as one of the siege directors he should have. Ultimately Fletcher must take responsibility as the commanding engineer. None of these errors had a material effect on the timescale or the outcome of the siege, but they must have had some effect on the reputation and confidence of the engineers.

Burgoyne was critical of most elements of the siege of Ciudad Rodrigo, even though this was seen as the most successful Allied siege of the war. The Commanding Royal Engineer at the siege, Richard Fletcher, gave high praise to Burgoyne who 'gave me every assistance, and executed the works under his charge with great zeal and ability'.[34] Burgoyne's initial comments in his diary were quite mild : 'Our works were certainly not carried on with great expedition'.[35] In private letters he was much more critical. He wrote lengthy letters to John Squire and Charles Pasley criticising most aspects of the siege including the preparation (the gabions and fascines were made without proper supervision and too far away, leading to poor quality and delivery problems) and the daily operations (the siting of the batteries and guns, the want of arrangement in bringing up stores and the organisation of the working parties). In a letter to Squire, Burgoyne complained: 'We go on most miserably, no superintendents, no arrangements, it is said that Wellington objects to give any assistance the Colonel proposes, but I can't think this would be the case to a man of firmness.'[36] In a later letter he wrote:

'His Lordship can have but little confidence in Colonel Fletcher, as it appears from what we hear that he objects to nearly every proposal made by him . . . for some reason or other Colonel Fletcher had not influence enough to get the smallest assistance from the army.'[37] This appears to be the first suggestion that there was a lack of confidence in Fletcher's command both amongst his subordinates and Wellington. This is a marked change from what Burgoyne said two years earlier about the relationship between Wellington and Fletcher: 'He [Wellington] has universally treated Fletcher with the greatest consideration and attention'.[38]

Burgoyne's criticism was not restricted to his engineering superiors. He believed that Wellington summoned the French governor too early and that the French would have been much more likely to ask for terms had they had been summoned on 19 January, just before the assault, when there were two significant breaches.[39] The commitment (or lack of it) from the army that became very evident at Burgos was also an object of criticism. Burgoyne noted that the line officers 'do not seem to think it a point of duty or honour to interest themselves in the exertions of a working party'[40] and suggested that having a general officer with the troops in the trenches would help to maintain progress.

In terms of resources for the siege, all the senior engineers, Burgoyne, Jones and Ross, commented on Wellington refusing to provide line officers to assist.[41] This should, in fairness to him, be offset against the fact that the engineers had been allocated around 200 soldiers and officers from the 3rd Division who had been given some rudimentary training in the previous few months. In addition to this the division on duty each day had to furnish a further group of carpenters and miners.

There were some lighter moments during the siege. Jones described being asked by Wellington to show the newly arrived Prince of Orange round the trenches 'being his first exposure to fire'. Jones recorded he was cautioned 'not to expose the royal personage unnecessarily' but lost track of time and ended up trying to leave the trenches during the change of guards when the firing was heaviest from the defenders and 'HRH got a good peppering'.[42] He did not elaborate on what the punishment would have been had he been responsible for the death of the future King of the Netherlands.

In summary, the siege of Ciudad Rodrigo was a great operational success that materially strengthened Wellington's position and put the French firmly on the defensive. The success was due to three main factors: the weakness of the fortress, the strength of the Allied battering train and the lack of energy of the French governor. Overall, the engineers had performed their duties well, but as Fortescue wrote 'the engineers themselves . . . were by no means faultless in their plans'.[43] As mentioned above, the first signs of criticism within the engineers were also appearing. This situation was not helped when, due to an oversight, Burgoyne's name was omitted from Wellington's dispatch and only Jones and Captain George MacLeod RE were mentioned. Both received brevet promotions and only a subsequent appeal got the same recognition for Burgoyne. The promotion of Macleod in particular would have caused annoyance as he was mentioned in connection with the troops from the 3rd Division who had been trained as sappers. Burgoyne was responsible for their training but received no thanks for his work training these troops or for his performance as siege director. It appears that Wellington also asked for a brevet promotion to colonel for Fletcher. This was, however, refused with the following explanation:

> HRH is most fully impressed with a high opinion of the merits and services of Lieutenant Colonel Fletcher, and would gladly attend to your recommendation in his favour, if it were not for the difficulty which would attend the establishment of such a precedent, particularly in the case of the lieutenant colonels who have eminently distinguished themselves at the head of their regiments and who would naturally look for similar indulgence.[44]

The frustration around the lack of trained sappers and miners was more apparent during the siege. Writing home to Liverpool after the siege, Wellington said:

> I would beg to suggest to your Lordship the expediency of adding to the Engineer establishment a corps of Sappers and Miners. It is inconceivable with what disadvantage we undertake anything like a siege for want of assistance of this description . . . we are obliged to depend . . . upon the regiments of the line; and although the men are brave and willing, they want the knowledge and training which are necessary.[45]

Fletcher had written a similar note to the Board of Ordnance about two weeks earlier. Wellington had no-one other than Fletcher at hand to take his frustrations out on. One wonders if this was becoming a source of friction between them. Jones in his autobiography said he also wrote to the Board of Ordnance and was suitably chastised for the suggesting the inactivity of the Board of Ordnance was the equivalent of Nero fiddling whilst Rome burned.[46]

Casualties among the nineteen engineer officers were two killed and five wounded. Two of the wounded sailed to England and did not return to the Peninsula.[47] Three of the four fortresses covering the main routes in Portugal were now in Allied hands. It was not difficult to see what was coming next.

The Third Siege of Badajoz
As soon as Wellington had the repairs for Ciudad Rodrigo under way, he turned his attention to the next challenge, the retaking of Badajoz. On 25 January 1812, Dickson arranged for all the 24-pounder roundshot and shells along with 900 barrels of powder to be moved to Oporto for onward transmission to Elvas.[48] The following day Wellington ordered sixteen 24-pounder carronades (howitzers) and a number of gun carriages to be moved by land to Elvas from Almeida.[49] On the 28th, Wellington met Borthwick (the senior artillery officer in the Peninsula), Dickson and Fletcher to discuss moving the 24-pounder guns from Almeida to Elvas, but Dickson argued that the state of the bullocks and the availability of forage made it impossible.[50] This meant another cobbled-together siege train using guns from Lisbon and Elvas. Wellington revised his plan to use sixteen 24-pounder guns that were on transports in Lisbon, supplemented by twenty 24-pounder guns which Wellington hoped could be supplied by Admiral Berkeley from the fleet. Wellington also sent orders to Lisbon for the engineering stores to be collected and dispatched to Elvas, which would allow the garrison to start work on gabions and fascines. Captain George MacLeod RE was ordered to Elvas to superintend the preparations. Wellington had previously made arrangements for a pontoon train to be assembled, ready for use to cross the river Guadiana which would be in full flow at that time of year.[51]

All this preparation looks a little odd. Wellington had been planning the siege of Ciudad Rodrigo since May 1811. He knew that Badajoz was likely to be his next target but there seemed to be a distinct lack of planning for this eventuality. All the discussions of the previous days appear to be trying to work out how to get hundreds of tons of siege equipment across central Spain. When this was seen to be impossible, the Allies were then trying to find other, less-suitable guns that could be used instead. Was Wellington's original plan to besiege Badajoz later in the year, or did he have some other plan and then changed his mind to go after Badajoz? If he had known that he was going to besiege Badajoz after taking Ciudad Rodrigo, why was there not another siege train prepared for that purpose? The plan to attack Badajoz feels like a last-minute decision as he *hoped* to get guns from Berkeley that the Admiral did not have or was unwilling to release. Wellington clearly did not know this.

Timeline for the Third Siege of Badajoz	
28 January 1812	Wellington agreed there was insufficient transport to move main siege guns from Ciudad Rodrigo to Badajoz. Arrangements made for alternative supply from Lisbon
5 March 1812	Wellington hands Ciudad Rodrigo over to Spanish governor and sets out for Badajoz
8 March 1812	Last guns of siege train arrive at Elvas
11 March 1812	Wellington arrives at Elvas to direct the siege
16 March 1812	Fortress invested
17 March 1812	Trenches opened night of 17/18 Mar
19 March 1812	French launched sortie from Picurina fort. Colonel Fletcher wounded
22 March 1812	Pontoon bridge washed away
25 March 1812	Batteries opened fire on fortress
25 March 1812	Picurina fort stormed night of 25/26 Mar
5 April 1812	Fortress stormed night of 5/6 Apr

Dickson found out on 10 February that Admiral Berkeley was planning to provide twenty Russian 18-pounders instead of the hoped-for English 24-pounders.[52] This caused Wellington and Dickson great concern as 18-pounders were significantly less effective in siege work. The guns were also in poor condition, which meant that both their accuracy and power were further reduced. Wellington complained to Berkeley, but at the time Berkeley would not offer an alternative. Berkeley did eventually provide ten new English 18-pounders but Dickson argued that he did not want to mix 18-pounders (Russian and English) or to delay the siege to bring them up. Myatt notes that he was unsure if they were used in the siege, but Jones' journal clearly stated that they were not used.[53]

Wellington remained in Ciudad Rodrigo while all the preparations were being made. The main reason for this was to keep the French guessing. Although the siege of Badajoz was an obvious next step, there were other possibilities and until Wellington signified his intention by going to Badajoz, the French had to keep their options open. He wrote to his brother:

> You are aware of the great operation, which I have in hand. If I should succeed, which I certainly shall, unless those admirably useful institutions, the English newspapers, should have given Bonaparte the alarm, and should have induced him to order his

Marshals to assemble their troops to oppose me, Spain will have another chance of being saved.[54]

Jones' diary described a meeting to discuss the plan of attack on Badajoz. There had been much criticism of the point of attack the year before and a decision had to be made on whether to follow the same plan as last year, the previous French plan, or some other alternative. At the meeting were Wellington, General Castaños, the Spanish Chief Engineer and Fletcher. Jones recorded that Wellington and the Spanish engineer wanted to attack the southern front as the French had done in early 1811, while Fletcher wanted to attack the south-western corner from the Picurina redoubt. Fletcher was initially reluctant to admit openly that his recommendation was due to the lack of skilled sappers and miners to deal with the mines that the French were known to have placed on the southern face. Wellington, on being reminded of the situation, reluctantly agreed saying 'he regretted extremely our deficiencies and it obliged him to undertake an attack he did not approve, but that knowing the means he believed it to be the only attack in our power to get through'. Jones added 'though adopted through necessity, . . . it was never for one moment approved by any one employed in drawing it up, or in the execution of it'.[55] Jones summed up his thoughts with the comment, 'what a reflection on those who have governed the engineering service for the last nineteen years of war'.[56] Jones added further comments in his published Journal to the effect that the attack on the southern side would have required a further thirty guns and significantly more engineering stores and that this was beyond the available resources and transport.[57]

The Siege
Like the year before, the attack on Badajoz started with the engineers placing a pontoon bridge across the river Guadiana. And, like the year before, keeping it in place proved a real challenge. The south side of the fortress was invested on 16 March. Fletcher had twenty-three engineers including Squire and Burgoyne, who acted as siege directors, and Jones as Brigade Major. At least one and possibly four of this number did not arrive until the very end of the siege.[58] For the first time in the war there was a significant number of men from the Royal Military Artificers present, 115 in total. A further thirty had been ordered up from Cadiz, but they did not arrive before the end of the siege. Fletcher also had at his disposal the remainder of the men from the 3rd Division who had been previously trained in sapping, now reduced to around 120 from their original strength of around 200. Finally, there were also ten assistant engineers from the line regiments.[59]

Fletcher marked out the first trenches on 17 March, and these were commenced that night. The weather over the first few days was poor with constant rain and this made work in the trenches very difficult. The French launched a sortie at noon on the 19th, and once again caught the Allies unprepared. A small body of French cavalry made it to the engineers' depot where they attacked the unarmed soldiers and captured two officers before they were driven off. Little damage was done to the works, but many tools were carried off as the French troops had been promised a reward for every one they collected. Allied casualties were around 150 men including the Chief Engineer, Fletcher, whose wound confined him to bed until 5 April but he retained command. The routine for the remainder of the siege was for Wellington to meet with Fletcher and Jones each morning to discuss progress and agree the tasks for the next twenty-four hours.

The wet weather led to the river Guadiana rising until it swept away the pontoon bridge on 22 March. This was a major concern to Wellington as the bridge was both the source of his siege supplies and also his line of retreat. A complete loss of communication across the river would require Wellington to raise the siege, the nearest alternative bridge being at Merida, twenty miles away. Lieutenant Piper RE was sent to investigate the damage to the pontoon bridge and reported that twelve of the twenty-four pontoons had sunk. Two were subsequently recovered from the river, but the rest were lost. Wellington, with his normal attention to detail, wrote further instructions:

1. Lieutenant Piper to be desired to supply six pontoons as row boats near the flying bridge, to carry over principally powder and shot.
2. Care must be taken that they are not overloaded; not more than forty 24-Pound shot to be put in each, or an equal quantity or weight of powder.
3. Plank must be placed in the bottom, and the lower part of the sides should have a plank in order to prevent the shot from rolling against them and making holes.
4. The pontoons must not be used as passage boats.
5. Lieutenant Piper to be requested to mention in his report whether he has bullocks in sufficient numbers, and in good order, to move the bridge.[60]

For the remainder of the siege the pontoons were used exclusively as rowing boats for the transport of powder and shot across the river.[61] The poor weather had probably delayed completion of the batteries by two or three days but they finally opened on the fortress on the morning of 25 March and started to batter the fortress and also the Picurina and San Roque outworks. No significant damage had been inflicted on the Picurina fort when Wellington ordered it to be stormed that night, Oman suggesting that this was to make up lost time.[62] Due to the delay between the siege guns ceasing fire and the attack, the French had time to make repairs and although the attack was successful, fifty-four were killed and 265 wounded out of 500 attackers. Once the fort had been taken, the second parallel and associated batteries could be started.

From 27 March, the trenches were extended towards the San Roque lunette with the intention of taking it and destroying the dam that kept the ground in front of the fortress flooded. Wellington's intention was to launch the assault across this ground but until the water was drained this was not possible. Progress by the partially-trained sappers was not fast enough and casualties were high. An attempt was made on 2 April to mine the dam near the San Roque lunette. Lieutenant Stanway RE led a party forward and placed 450 pounds of gunpowder on the dam, but the explosion did not have the desired effect. The attack on San Roque was now abandoned and Wellington accepted that the attack would have to work round the flooded area. The danger involved in trenching is well described in a letter from Lieutenant Vetch RE:

> I was employed . . . in advancing the approaches; we were three or four officers, at least half an hour laying out the work not 80yds from the French parapet. The sap was marked out with a white cord, and the men put down as near as they could work along the line. They squat down and worked away as hard as they were able, in order to cover themselves . . . the moment we were perceived they opened a very sharp fire of musketry, and killed seven men in the first half hour, after which our men got too much cover to be hit.[63]

As the days moved on into early April, Wellington once again found himself balancing the time needed to batter the fortress against the advance of the French to relieve it. He was aware that Soult was collecting troops and was moving north towards Badajoz, so he needed to decide between rapidly concluding the siege, or putting it on hold and advancing to meet Soult, leaving a force to guard the trenches, or raising the siege. Marmont was also demonstrating in the north against Almeida and Ciudad Rodrigo, but Wellington cannot have been seriously concerned about their safety at this time.

By 5 April, the breaches looked ready and Wellington issued orders for an assault that night. Later in the day the assault was postponed for twenty-four hours to allow a third breach to be battered in the curtain wall. It would appear that Wellington asked Fletcher to look at the breaches and give his opinion.[64] Following his inspection, Fletcher advised that the defences the French had constructed behind the breaches were strong and that a third breach should be made where they would have little time to prepare new defences. The original plan was to make a third breach at the last moment. The concentrated effort of the siege guns on 6 April quickly battered the wall and the third breach was ready in the afternoon. The three breaches would be attacked by the 4th and Light Divisions. Separate attacks would also be made on the castle by the 3rd Division and on the San Vincente bastion by the 5th Division. Sunset was just after 7 p.m.[65] The siege guns stopped firing at about 7.30 p.m. but the assault did not get underway until around 10 p.m., leaving the defenders with plenty of time to prepare for the assault that they knew was coming. The main attacks through the breaches all failed, with huge casualties, due to the obstacles put across them and the heavy fire from the garrison. When it became clear to Wellington that they had failed, he ordered the troops to be withdrawn and planned to make another assault just before daybreak, but about this time, he was informed that Picton's 3rd Division had managed to scale the walls of the castle and that the 5th Division had also entered the town. He ordered the 4th and Light Divisions forward again, using these footholds to break out and finally take the fortress. As at Ciudad Rodrigo, there followed an uncontrollable sack by the troops and it took two days before order could be restored.

Lieutenant James Vetch RE who had just arrived from Cadiz with a detachment of thirty miners from the Royal Military Artificers described the events:

> When we got intelligence of the siege of Badajoz, and as I knew we were wanted there I pushed on the party as fast as possible . . . I got to Badajoz on the morning of the fifth . I did duty in the trenches and lost, of my small working party, seven men the first half hour . . . The enemy had been very active in throwing every obstacle they could think of in the way . . . I was posted between the castle and breaches, at the ravelin of San Roque, which was to be escaladed by 200 men. About 10 p.m. a brisk firing began from the castle and they threw some light balls which gave them great advantage. When the castle had been attacked for half an hour, the parties in the breaches commenced. That moment produced such a scene as no man can conceive. The night was dark; the castle on high and all the lower points of attack involved in one sheet of fire, a well pitched

light ball now and then bringing out the scenes more fully to view; at the breaches the springing of mines, bursting of large shells, which they rolled into the ditch, with the fire from the whole of the batteries made a sight which I believe never was seen in so small a space. My party of 200 men, which attacked the ravelin, carried it immediately and marched their prisoners through the breaches. General Picton carried the castle about 10 p.m. The parties at the breaches were completely repulsed; those escalading on the left succeeded about 2 a.m. with great slaughter. At 3 a.m. we had pretty good light and we discovered the enemy had left a gate open near the ravelin, which three of our companies took possession of. I was in the town at 3 a.m. and it was completely in our possession by 4 a.m. I had been sent out to give notice of the gate being in our possession, and got in again about 5 a.m. in good daylight to behold the most shocking scenes of dead and wounded, and the soldiers pillaging the houses. Not many of the inhabitants were killed, but all were left without a rag to cover them or a morsel to eat. Broken chairs and tables only were left. The pillage [had] lasted two days when two gallows were erected to show the pillage was over. When looking about for quarters, I was implored by a lady to take my abode under her roof for her protection, and I remained there two days. I found my hostess was a Marchioness; Lord Wellington called twice at my billet, and the poor lady had scarce a gown to cover her back.[66]

Casualties from the assault were shocking, with 800 killed and 2,900 wounded out of an overall total for the siege of around 1,000 killed and 3,800 wounded. As always with the sieges it was the officers and better soldiers who took more than their fair share of the injuries. Engineer casualties were similarly heavy. Of the twenty-four officers present, four were killed and eight were wounded, three of whom went home.[67]

Wellington had taken Badajoz in twenty-one days. His estimate before the start was twenty-four days, not taking into account the bad weather that surely delayed progress. Mulcaster, one of the engineers, had estimated twenty-seven days for the siege.[68] In 1811 the French took forty-five days to get the fortress to surrender and in reality it should have held out for much longer. The cost of this rapid success was once again measured in casualties. In this case they were all from the very experienced British divisions, troops Wellington could not afford to lose. Although there were criticisms at the time of the decision to postpone the assault for another day to make the third breach, it is probable that this decision tipped the balance by spreading the defenders thinner which meant they were not able to resist the secondary assaults. Once order had been re-established in the town, work started immediately to repair the defences. As a sign of the importance that Wellington placed on its speedy and effective repair, Fletcher was left to oversee the work and did not rejoin Wellington at headquarters until September 1812.

Analysis of the siege
As in the previous year, time was of the essence and taking the fortress on 6 April 1812 required brute force, inflicting enormous casualties on Wellington's best divisions. The huge casualties at the siege of Badajoz finally pushed Wellington into writing a strongly-worded private letter to Liverpool demanding that something be done about the lack of trained men available to undertake siege work. His criticism overflowed into a more general complaint about the skills of the engineers. An analysis of his complaints will be detailed below, but first the other components of the siege that were not within the control of the engineers will be evaluated.

Wellington's strategy of keeping the French guessing about his plans by staying north worked well. Soult made arrangements for Marmont to come to his aid if Wellington attacked Badajoz, but he then appears to have become distracted and, even though warnings had started filtering through, he was at Cadiz until 20 March. Soult then rushed back to Seville and spent the next ten days putting together a relief force which did not exceed 25,000 men, believing that Marmont would be doing the same. Marmont, in the meantime, had received direct orders from Napoleon not to support Badajoz, this being Soult's responsibility. He was ordered to threaten Ciudad Rodrigo instead, which Napoleon believed would force Wellington to break off the siege of Badajoz and race north to protect it.[69] Soult did not discover until around 6 April that Marmont was sending no supporting force. By that time it was too late for the French to relieve the fortress.

The habitual problem of transport once again caused the siege train to be much less powerful than Wellington would have liked. At Ciudad Rodrigo the siege train was made up of thirty-eight new English iron guns, thirty-four of which were 24-pounders. Since these could not be transported to Badajoz, reliance had to be placed on a combination of sixteen new English 24-pounders and twenty old Russian 18-pounders in poor condition. There were an additional sixteen 24-pounder carronades but these were of no use for breaching work and appear to have been used for enfilade fire. Jones commented that the 24-pounder iron howitzer (carronade) 'should never be admitted into a battering train . . . [as] it only served to waste ammunition'.[70] General Colville commented 'we have for the third time undertaken the siege . . . deficient of means . . . half the guns are 18-pounders. We have not a single mortar'.[71] This siege train was a little better than the one used at the second siege of Badajoz, primarily due to the guns being made of iron, but it was much less powerful than that used at Ciudad Rodrigo, which was a much weaker fortress, so the time taken to make a significant impact on the breaches was extended. The lack of heavy howitzers limited the besiegers' ability to undertake counter-battery fire and this led to heavier casualties in the trenches and during the assault.

The weather also had a material effect on the early stages of the siege. It rained continuously until about 25 March, and this slowed down work in the trenches and certainly stopped any attempt to put guns into the batteries until the ground had dried out. Of more concern to Wellington was the loss of the pontoon bridge and the difficulties with the flying bridge as the river rose. At this time, around 22 March, Wellington did not have a clear picture of the movements of Soult and Marmont. The loss of his only bridge was a serious matter. If the French had forced him to lift the siege and retire, his army would have been able to do this, but the siege train would probably have been lost. The wet weather also ensured that the inundation around the walls of Badajoz caused by the damming of the Rivellas stream was higher than normal and was impossible to cross. This was what made the attack on the San Roque outwork important. If heavy howitzers had been available to suppress the French guns, it might have been possible to take the San Roque lunette, which would have enabled the destruction of the dam and the draining of the area in front of the breaches. Wellington could not reasonably blame the bad weather for unexpectedly hampering his plans. He understood what the weather would be like at this time of year and used the poor weather as an argument to explain his timing of the siege, as it would hamper the movements of the French. Of course there was also a chance that it would hamper his own plans and in the event it did.

The French governor, Phillipon, showed the same energy and determination that he had in 1811. The garrison was made up of seasoned troops and the experienced chief engineer, Lamarre, had been at the fortress for some time and knew it well. The defenders' energy, particularly in clearing the debris from in front of the breaches and in blocking them up, made the assaults much more difficult. As described above, the assaults on the breaches all failed with heavy casualties and it was only due to the secondary attacks that the fortress was taken. With another thousand men, Phillipon would have probably repulsed the assault. It is doubtful that the British troops would have had the energy to make a further serious assault as Wellington planned on the morning of 6 April.

One question that needs further consideration is why did Wellington decide to make the assault on 6 April? Wellington was clearly concerned that the French would try to relieve the fortress, but there does not appear to be the urgency that he felt. He was aware of the movements of Soult and he had a reasonable idea of the size of his force. Wellington also must have been reasonably certain that Marmont was not marching to the aid of Soult, having had a report on 4 April that Marmont had been in front of Almeida the previous day, which suggested he was not making any immediate plans to move south.[72] He was also clearly concerned that the breaches were only just practicable. His decisions to order and then postpone the attack on the night of 5 April show a level of indecision that was very unusual for him. He had made preliminary plans to suspend the siege and move to face Soult who he believed had up to 35,000 men. When he realised that he had around 25,000 men, he would have known that Soult could not possibly interfere with the siege without the support of Marmont. Marmont did not receive permission from Napoleon to directly support Soult until 27 March, and would have needed ten to fourteen days to concentrate sufficient troops. A week later he had not moved south and Wellington knew that, so the earliest he could have arrived would have been the end of the second week in April.

There are two areas where the lack of trained artificers appeared to have made a difference to the planning. The first was in selection of the point of attack. As mentioned above, Wellington's preference was to attack the south front, as it appeared to be the weakest. This was the point that the French attacked, but the French, realising the same, had significantly strengthened it by reinforcing the Pardaleras outwork and also by placing mines in the approaches to the walls. The approaches to the southern wall that Wellington last saw in June 1811 were significantly stronger in March 1812. The second was in the attempt to take the San Roque lunette and allow the destruction of the dam behind it. This was abandoned due to the heavy casualties and poor progress made by the partially-trained sappers from the army. If trained sappers had been available, better progress would have been made and casualties should have been lower. But the major difficulties were caused by the heavy fire from the defenders and without some attempt to reduce this, the results might not have been any different. The siege train at Badajoz did not contain weapons that were ideal for counter-battery and breach clearing activities. The 24-pounder carronades were the only 'high-angle' weapon available and as they were equivalent to the smallest 5½in howitzer, they did not have the punch that was required.

It could be argued that Wellington moved too quickly to the assault, when he could have waited a few more days and continued battering the defences. This would have reduced his casualties although it is unlikely that

Phillipon would have considered surrender. Wellington's complaint about the lack of trained sappers and miners causing the additional casualties was justified, but even with the trained artificers he would still have needed to give them time to work and it is unlikely that the siege would have progressed any faster. As in all the previous sieges in 1811 and 1812, Wellington was pushed into attacking early because of the need to take the fortress before the relieving force could intervene. Badajoz was no different and trained artificers would not have made a significant difference.

On 7 April Wellington wrote his dispatch informing the government of the success at Badajoz. With it was sent a private letter to Liverpool in which he complained about the lack of trained engineers and artificers and blamed the heavy losses at Badajoz on the lack of such troops:

> It is quite impossible to expect to carry fortified places . . . unless the army should be provided with a regular trained corps of sappers and miners . . . The consequences . . . are – first, that our engineers although well educated and brave, have never turned their minds to the mode of conducting a regular siege, as it is useless to think of that which it is impossible in our service to perform. They think that they have done their duty when they construct a battery, with a secure communication to it, which can make a breach in the wall of a place; and, secondly, these breaches are to be carried by vive force by an infinite sacrifice of officers and soldiers . . . I earnestly recommend to your lordship to have a corps of sappers and miners formed without loss of time.[73]

His frustration at his losses extended his complaints from the reasonable towards what many engineers saw as an unreasonable attack on the whole engineering profession. His complaints about the lack of sappers and miners were fully supported by the engineer officers themselves. One example was Squire, who used almost the same words as Wellington in his letter after the assault: 'This siege has served to confirm . . . that constituted as our Corps is, we are decidedly not equal to the attack of a place; whose scarp is covered by a good counterscarp and glacis . . . Sappers and Miners are as necessary to engineers during a siege, as soldiers to the General'.[74]

Wellington's critical comments in his letter of 7 April 1812 were lost until 1889, but a subsequent letter on the same subject to Major-General Murray was published in the dispatches.

> I trust . . . that future armies will be equipped for sieges, with the people necessary to carry them on as they ought to be; and that our

engineers will learn how to put their batteries on the crest of the glacis and to blow in the counterscarp, instead of placing wherever the wall can be seen, leaving the poor officers and men to get into and across the ditch as best they can.[75]

This was responded to in Jones' Journal: 'the officers ... were fully equal to the difficult duty of crowning the crest of the glacis had they been assisted by a proper trained body of men'.[76] Wellington's complaint about the casualties during the assault on the Picurina fort is particularly unreasonable, since the fort was stormed on his orders the same day the batteries opened when it was clear that no material damage had yet been inflicted. Wellington rushed the assault to make up time lost due to the bad weather. There is no doubt, based on the available evidence, that Wellington's criticism of the engineer officers was unfair. The four sieges of 1811 and 1812 had all been arranged with limited resources and limited time. This led to compromises that affected the chance of success and the level of casualties. There was not sufficient time at any of these sieges for formal approaches to be prepared. Complaining about the lack of troops to deliver formal approaches is not reasonable when such troops would not have had the time to make the approaches anyway.

In the archives at the British Library, there is a scrap of paper written by John Squire on 8 April 1812. You can feel the shock and exhaustion he was feeling as he wrote his brief note on the successful assault and the loss of more friends. He finishes it with 'I am a little fatigued, so you will excuse me breaking off so abruptly'. A month later, he was dead, collapsing and dying whilst travelling with General Hill.[77]

Fletcher was left at Badajoz to carry out repairs and Burgoyne accompanied Wellington with the army as it set out on the Salamanca campaign. This was an unusual arrangement, as typically the senior engineer would travel with Wellington. Whilst there has been some question about whether this was evidence of a lack of trust in Fletcher, there is no evidence to support this view. Wellington's decision was probably based on two points that would have been foremost in his mind. Firstly, that losing Badajoz again was unthinkable, so every effort had to be made to protect it. Secondly, Wellington had handed over responsibility for Ciudad Rodrigo to the Spanish only four weeks before and he had already received communications to show that little progress had been made to complete the repairs; the Spanish were asking for further help and they had already used most of the supplies left for the use of the garrison. Because of this Wellington was forced to remain in a position where he could support Ciudad Rodrigo when one of his options would have been to pursue Soult south.[78] Although it was not approved, Wellington had also asked for promotion for Fletcher after Ciudad Rodrigo.[79]

In summary, Badajoz was attacked with a second-rate siege train; the lack of sappers and miners meant that the preferred choice of attack could not be chosen; the fortress was assaulted too early; and together these factors caused the high casualties. Badajoz was taken due to the secondary attacks succeeding when all the main attacks had failed. Wellington was lucky.

However, Wellington's complaints reinforced the desire of the Board of Ordnance to progress the development of the School of Military Engineering that had just been formed on 23 April 1812 (see Appendix 5). Liverpool wrote to Wellington on 28 April, informing him that the Board of Ordnance had been working on this issue for some time and that the first troops would be with him before the end of the month.[80] Although this was unrealistic, it is true that Charles William Pasley had previously started work on training artificers. The incorrect understanding of the causes of the formation of the Royal Sappers and Miners still appears in most works. Oman[81] assumes that Wellington's letter of 7 April caused an immediate change and the formation of the corps. Fortescue seems even wider from the mark, suggesting that Wellington was 'beginning himself to train one on the spot'. Myatt does not recognise that the Board of Ordnance had been working throughout 1811 to rectify the situation.[82] Similarly, in the most recent books on sieges in the Peninsula, there appears to be a misunderstanding of the role of sappers and miners. They would undertake the specialist tasks, like sapping up to the glacis or mining, but the line infantry would still do the bulk of the 'spade work' with the trained artificers providing supervision.[83]

Whilst this siege is often seen as a breakdown in trust between Wellington and Fletcher, I am not so sure. Fletcher was wounded on 19 March but Wellington insisted on him retaining command even though he was bed-bound, visiting him each morning. Wellington could easily have sent Fletcher away, but chose to retain him even though other engineer officers, seen as his 'favourites', were present, i.e. John Burgoyne and John Jones. Whilst Jones suggested that Wellington left Fletcher to repair Badajoz as a punishment, I believe he was left there because he was not fit to travel. Fletcher only left his tent for the first time on 4 April, two days before the assault and riding was probably impossible.[84] There is plenty of correspondence to confirm Fletcher remained in charge of the engineer department for Wellington's army whilst he was at Badajoz.

As soon as order was restored, work started of repairing the fortress, Burgoyne noting on 9 April that 300 men from Power's brigade commenced filling in the trenches.

The following day, Burgoyne was dispatched to Villa Velha to be ready to take up the pontoon bridge as Marmont had started an advance into Portugal to try and distract Wellington from the siege that had just been completed. Wellington was not sure that he could get troops there before Marmont and did not want to lose the bridge or his ability to cross the Tagus. Burgoyne rode post horses to the river and there:

> found the Portuguese Captain of Engineers in charge of the bridge in great distress, having been ordered to remove the bridge [only] when the enemy arrived . . . knowing how impossible this would be . . . he determined on preparing to burn it as the French had entered Castello Branco yesterday . . . and were expected down at Villa Velha hourly. Neither General Lecor . . . nor General Baron Alten . . . would take upon themselves to give an order for removing the bridge . . . On my arrival, I had it immediately withdrawn.[85]

Burgoyne's implied criticism of the unwillingness of senior commanders to make decisions without direct instructions from Wellington is then extended by reporting that the commandant of the sick at Villa Velha, who had made arrangements to remove the sick and stores based on intelligence he received from General Lecor, was criticised for not waiting for instructions from headquarters. The French retired from Castello Branco on 14 April, presumably having heard that Badajoz had fallen. Burgoyne rode to the point where the twelve boats had been stored and noted with satisfaction that the Portuguese engineer was already working with 200–300 peasants to move the bridge back into place and it would be ready the next day. When he arrived back at Headquarters on 17 April 1812 he noted that he was now attached to headquarters, 'Colonel Fletcher and other officers of engineers to remain at Badajoz'.

Other Engineering Work in Early 1812
Away from these two major sieges, other engineer officers continued to provide support to a variety of operations. John Squire remained in the south with General Hill's detached corps and noted their advance into Spain in January 1812, a movement clearly intended to distract the French from the siege at Ciudad Rodrigo. Work continued on repairing and strengthening the various strongpoints in Portugal, Captain Wedekind reporting plans to move some of the fresh water springs around Abrantes to within the perimeter defences and also to improve the water storage capacity.[86] Lieutenant Pringle RE was working on improving the embarkation jetties

at fort St Julian near Lisbon and Captain Boteler and Lieutenant Tapp continued work on the defences to the south of the Tagus.

Lieutenant Marshall RE had been sent to carry out further work on the river Douro to allow boats to carry supplies up to the border at Barca d'Alva. This had been started in 1811 under the charge of George Ross but the first boats to try and navigate the whole length reported there were still areas where the river was too shallow to pass. The supplies still reached their destination, but had to be unloaded to pass the shallows.

In late April, Squire was sent to repair the bridge at Merida that the Allies had previously destroyed. He knew this repair was for a secret operation that was being planned and reported:

> Two arches of the formed bridge at Merida have been exploded with gunpowder and I have been desired to make the bridge passable again. The width of the opening is 66 feet 6 inches, fortunately part of the pier still remains 6 or 7 feet above the level of the river, which will assist our operation very much I have desired the Alcalde of the place to collect the necessary timbers; and I should think in a fortnight the passage of the bridge may be restored.[87]

A month later, Squire was dead, having collapsed and died at Truxillo.

In the north, the French made a reconnaissance in strength towards Almeida, inspecting the repairs and the activity of the garrison. They tried to pass over the Agueda at San Felices but the bridge, which had been previously mined by a Portuguese engineer, was blown. Having determined that there was no opportunity to re-take the fortress, they retired. The repairs at Ciudad Rodrigo were under the charge of the Spanish engineers. Burgoyne noted that Lieutenant William Reid RE who formed a good working relationship with the Spanish General D'España was given charge of part of the repairs and this had allowed greater progress to be made. Whilst these activities carried on in the background, Wellington was looking further east.

Chapter 7

1812 – Triumph and Failure

Following the successful siege of Badajoz, the army moved north at a relatively slow pace, Burgoyne saying this was to avoid tiring the troops. For the first time in months he was not busy 'being now unemployed at Headquarters'. He asked John Squire to send him the captured diary of the French siege of Badajoz for him to read during his leisure time.[1] The French were watching Wellington's advance with concern and they started evacuating their sick and stores from Salamanca. Preparations were also underway to defend the city from the advancing Allies. Burgoyne noted on 18 May 1812, a month before they arrived, that 'they are fortifying some of the convents and have pulled down 300 or 400 houses around them'.[2]

On the same day, General Hill was carrying out a daring raid on the French crossing-point over the Tagus at Almaraz, the most westerly crossing-point they held. Wellington ordered Hill to carry out the raid on 24 April and to make his preparations in great secrecy. Hill departed from Almendralejo, south of the Guadiana, and advanced to Merida, arriving on 9 May, before the bridge repairs had been completed by Squire and Lieutenant Peter Wright RE. Hill had to wait three days before he could cross the river on the repaired bridge. Hill's force also had six pontoons with them. John Squire was with Hill when he arrived in Truxillo on 15 May, but he fell ill and died two days later, leaving Lieutenant Wright unexpectedly in the position of senior engineer with Hill's force. Approaching the pass of Miravete on the 17th, Hill looked without success for a way to get his artillery into the valley of Almaraz. The following morning, Lieutenant Wright was ordered to reconnoitre the forts and the terrain but no route for the artillery could be identified. Hill now decided to attack without his guns and the troops filed through the hills, falling on the French defences at daybreak on 19 May, ejecting the garrisons from the forts and destroying the bridge. Wright was wounded in the attack and it is not clear what role he had in directing the destruction of the forts and the bridges. It is probable than Dickson would have taken charge of this. One of the artillery officers, Lieutenant Thiele from the King's German Legion artillery, was killed whilst setting off the explosives at Fort Ragusa.

Whilst this operation was under way, Wellington took the opportunity to dispatch Burgoyne to visit the Douro and clarify what appeared to be contradictory reports on its navigability. Burgoyne spent the next three weeks examining the river and making recommendation on improvements, returning just before Wellington moved on Salamanca.

On 2 May, about the same time as authorising Hill's raid on Almaraz, Wellington ordered Colonel Sturgeon of the Royal Staff Corps to proceed to the damaged bridge over the Tagus at Alcantara and determine if it could be repaired.[3] Again, secrecy was essential so that the French could not determine his strategy. Wellington needed the bridge repaired so that he could move the siege guns from Elvas for the attack on Salamanca. As described earlier, the bridge at Alcantara had been broken in May 1809, with one of the arches destroyed. The gap was about 100 feet wide with a drop of over 100 feet and there was no easy way of repairing it. With Captain Alexander Todd RSC, Sturgeon came up with an ingenious solution that was effectively a rope suspension bridge. Using material and some expertise supplied by the Royal Navy, he constructed a rope structure that could be tensioned using capstans and then have a roadway placed across it. It was pre-prepared at Elvas and transported to Alcantara where it was ready for use on 11 June.[4]

With these two operations, Wellington had significantly altered the strategic situation in central Spain. The loss of Almaraz now meant that the French had to travel further east to cross the Tagus and the repair of Alcantara reduced the distance the Allied had to travel. Wellington could now manoeuvre his forces much quicker than the enemy. Writing to Liverpool, he said:

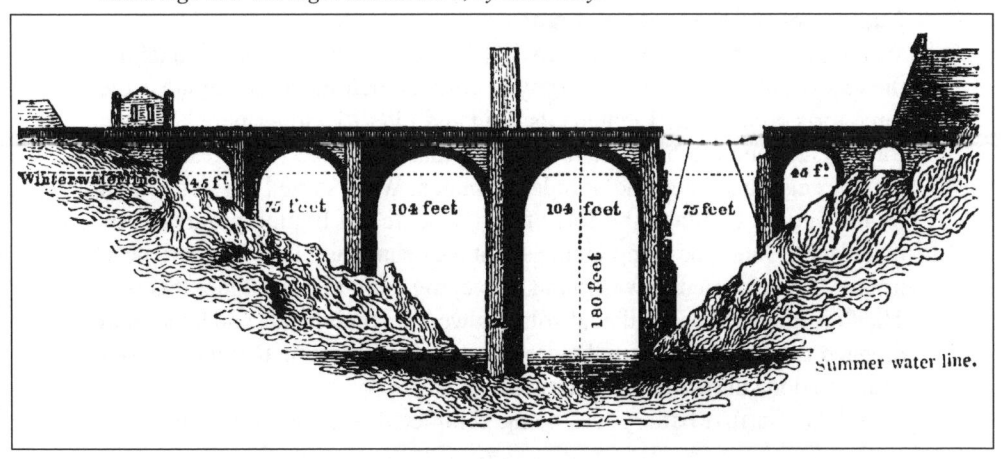

The bridge over the Tagus at Alcantara, by Leith-Hay.

The result . . . been to cut off the shortest and best communication between the army of the south [Soult] and the '*Armee de Portugal*' [Marmont] which under existing circumstances, it will be difficult, if not impossible to re-establish.[5]

Dickson was ordered to move a brigade of six 24-pounder howitzers to Alcantara, ready to cross the river Tagus. Arriving on 9 June, he had to wait two days until Sturgeon completed the repairs. He then moved on to Salamanca, arriving on the 20th. Four 18-pounder guns were also dispatched from Almeida to make up the artillery for the attacks on the forts at Salamanca. These arrived on 17 June and, as Dickson had not arrived yet, three howitzers were borrowed from a field brigade to start the attacks.

The logistical challenges of moving even such a small siege train need to be described to understand the difficulties that moving stores and equipment caused. To move the four siege guns and a small quantity of shot and spares from Almeida required fifty bullock carts each with two bullocks. Each of the siege guns required twenty bullocks, making a total of 180 animals. To move the six 24-pounder howitzers (which were effectively field pieces) and their shot required 150 bullocks.[6] Dickson noted that a further 120 bullocks joined them *en route*. To move these ten small guns needed a total of 450 bullocks! It is also worth saying more about the 24-pounder howitzer. This piece was alternatively known as a 24-pounder carronade or a 5½in howitzer. Most readers on the British army in this period will be familiar with the 5½in howitzer as a low-powered field piece which gave some high-angle capability to field batteries. As a siege piece it was nearly useless, having neither the power nor the accuracy to attack fortresses.

Capture of the Forts at Salamanca
Wellington approached Salamanca on 17 June, with the 6th Division taking the lead in the investment. Burgoyne commanded the attack against the three forts, assisted by Lieutenants Reid and Pitts RE. Jones noted that the forts were 'found to be more respectable than supposed',[7] suggesting that their strength had been badly underestimated. Work started the same night on the battery to attack the fort of San Vicente but limited progress was made, with Burgoyne complaining about the behaviour of the inexperienced troops: 'Great difficulty was found in keeping them to work under this fire. The Portuguese in particular, absolutely went on their hands and knees and dragged their baskets along the ground, It was impossible that much work could be done under these circumstances.'[8]

Whilst the first battery was being completed, an attempt was made to destroy the ditch in front of the convent. Lieutenant Reid and four miners crawled forward to attempt to construct the mine. They gave up after several attempts to approach unseen were thwarted by the presence of a dog with the defenders.

On the night of 18 June, the first battery was completed and the four 18-pounders and three 24-pounder howitzers were installed. Two additional small batteries were constructed for five other small howitzers. The next day the main battery opened and fired with some effect for three hours when it had to stop to conserve the meagre amount of ammunition available. One of the other batteries now opened with two 24-pounder howitzers. Little further damage was caused to San Vicente but the artillerymen firing the guns suffered severe casualties due to the limited protection afforded by the batteries. The stock of ammunition was now so low that an order was sent to Almeida for more.

The firing continued on San Vicente on 20 June but was suspended until more ammunition arrived and also until the intentions of Marshal Marmont, who had arrived in the vicinity, were clear. On the 23rd, the remaining ammunition was fired against the Gayetano fort in the hope that a breach could be made and enable an assault. No breach was made but Wellington ordered an assault to be made that night. Lieutenant Reid led the party forward but there was limited enthusiasm and the attempt failed. When more ammunition arrived on 26 June, the firing on Gayetano commenced, with red-hot shot also being fired against San Vicente. Trenches continued to be dug forward trying to get closer to the forts. Finally, on 27 June, a breach was formed in Gayetano and San Vicente was set on fire, leading to both being taken with little resistance.

It had taken nine days to reduce these three temporary defences. The artillery available was barely capable of breaching them and insufficient shot and shell had been available, leading to delays in taking them. There is no doubt that Wellington knew that the French were fortifying Salamanca. He admitted that he underestimated the strength of the forts, saying 'I was mistaken in my estimate of the extent of the means which would be necessary to subdue the forts'.[9] The three forts were now dismantled and Burgoyne also noted that several days later Wellington asked for further defences to be destroyed and Lieutenant Reid was dispatched for this purpose.[10] Reid's efforts during the siege were recognised in the Divisional Orders: 'The zeal and conspicuously gallant conduct of Lieutenant Reid of the Royal Engineers has not failed to attract the particular attention of the Major-General [Clinton] and he trusts they will be duly appreciated by the Commander of the Forces.'[11]

A tense stalemate now developed, with the Allied and French forces manoeuvring in the vicinity of Salamanca, each looking for an opportunity. This came on 22 July, when Marmont over-extended his troops in trying to outflank the Allied army, giving Wellington the opportunity he had been waiting for. He turned his forces on the spread-out French and comprehensively defeated them. Over the coming days the French were pursued north, Wellington entering Valladolid on 30 July. The Allies now turned towards Madrid, arriving there on 12 August. Hearing that French troops were still in the Retiro fort, Wellington sent Burgoyne to demand their surrender. The use of Burgoyne for this task reflects the level of trust in him (or possibly a lack of language skills amongst the gentry on Wellington's staff). There were several occasions in the coming months when Burgoyne carried out tasks like this for Wellington, even though other members of his staff were available. Although the French refused to surrender at Burgoyne's request, two days later, realising that resistance was hopeless, they marched out of the fort into captivity. After a couple of weeks of inactivity, Wellington now moved north, his objective being Burgos.

The Siege of Burgos
To take full advantage of his successes in the first half of 1812, Wellington had to hold his forward position, and to do this he needed to take Burgos. The Allies had taken the artillery used at Salamanca with them. These were three 18-pounder guns, one of the original four having been irreparably damaged, and five 24-pounder carronades.[12] Having acknowledged that this train was not sufficient for Salamanca, it is difficult to understand why this was all Wellington brought to Burgos. Whilst not a first-rate fortress, was strong enough to resist the attackers' guns. The defenders also had significantly more ordnance with which to resist the attack. Of even more concern to the Allies was the very limited amount of shot, shell and powder, which meant that the attackers were worried about supply levels before they had fired the first shot.

Timeline for the Siege of Burgos	
19 September 1812	Burgos invested
19 September 1812	Hornwork stormed on night of 19/20th. Work on trenches started
22 September 1812	First battery armed on night of 22/23rd
22 September 1812	Attempt to storm outer wall failed
23 September 1812	Trenches started from suburb of San Pedro on night of 23/24th

25 September 1812	Work started on first mine
27 September 1812	Work started on second mine
29 September 1812	First mine blown and second attempt to storm outer wall failed on night of 29/30th
4 October 1812	Second mine blown and third assault takes outer wall on night of 4/5th
5 October 1812	French launch sortie on Allied positions
8 October 1812	French launch second sortie on Allied positions
10 October 1812	Work started on third mine under church of San Roman
18 October 1812	Third mine blown and fourth assault fails to take French second line
20 October 1812	Siege lifted

Wellington took with him four divisions and two independent Portuguese brigades. The more experienced 3rd, 4th and Light Divisions, that had suffered most of the casualties at Ciudad Rodrigo and Badajoz earlier in the year, were not assigned to this siege, as Wellington did not expect serious resistance.

The general plan was to take the hornwork of San Miguel on the first night and establish batteries there. At the same time, trenches would be dug from the suburb of San Pedro to enable a mine to be placed under the outer wall, which would be assaulted when the mine was blown. The two sets of inner defences would then be breached using the batteries. There were only five engineer officers, Lieutenant Colonel Jones, Captain Williams and Lieutenants Pitts and Reid, commanded by John Burgoyne. Fletcher was still at Badajoz finishing its repairs. Additional support came from ten assistant engineers (five of whom had previous experience),[13] eighty-one volunteers from the line regiments and eight Royal Military Artificers.

The fortress was invested on 19 September, and the same tactics employed at Ciudad Rodrigo were used, with an immediate assault on the San Miguel hornwork that protected the preferred point of attack. It was taken with heavy casualties of seventy-one killed and 349 wounded. Oman described this as a 'vast and unnecessary loss of life'.[14] Jones privately criticised the orders that were given to support the assault: 'Luckily the assaulting columns carried the work and success glossed over this most unmilitary and inefficient mode of supporting them.'[15] On the morning of the 20th, Burgoyne had a narrow escape when he was hit on the head by a musket ball, He recorded that 'it was fortunately a distant shot and of not much consequence'.[16]

Work immediately started on two batteries, the first of which was fitted with two guns and three howitzers on the night of the 22nd/23rd.[17] Then Wellington decided to change the plan 'with a view to abridge the attack and save the troops from unnecessary fatigue'.[18] He ordered an assault on the outer line of defences the same night, but the small group of 400 volunteers failed completely, suffering 158 casualties. Lieutenant Reid led the attackers forward. For the second time in three days, Wellington had used his troops as cannon fodder without taking the time to soften the defences. He then reverted back to the original plan to mine the outer wall. The defenders kept up a continual fire of shot and shell on the attackers and the trenches were so close to the walls that the French could roll the shells down the hill into them. Captain Williams was killed on the night of the 23rd/24th whilst working in the trenches. Engineering expertise was now so limited that Lieutenant Pitts, who had broken his arm when thrown from his horse, was forced to resume duty.[19]

The Allied battery opened for the first time on 25 September. Dickson commented at the end of the first day that 'it being found from the want of precision in the [24-pounder] howitzers with round shot, a greater expenditure of ammunition would be required . . . than the limited means . . . could afford'.[20] Ten per cent of the available round shot were used in one day to discover that the guns were highly inaccurate! Dickson recorded that the soldiers were offered a bounty for every roundshot they could recover for re-use and so as not to discourage them, even roundshot of calibres which were of no use were paid for. Wellington wrote to both the Royal Navy and the nearest fortresses for additional supplies. On the same day, a mine was started to run a shaft through to the ditch. On the 29th, the a mine was declared ready and the assault planned for that night. Like the previous attempt, the assault party was small, only 300 men. The mine exploded, but the assault failed due to the forlorn hope losing their way in the dark and missing the breach. There was no engineer officer available to accompany the assault party and this probably was a contributing factor to the soldiers losing their way.[21] Jones noted that the effect of 1,000 pounds of powder in the mine did not have the impact he would have expected and this may have been because the mine was placed against old foundations rather than against the current wall.[22]

Work progressed on a second mine and a new battery close to the wall on the west side of the fortress. The French detected it before the battery had opened fire and they pounded it mercilessly, damaging two of the three guns that Wellington possessed. On the orders of Wellington, the two damaged guns were mounted on temporary carriages and fired with reduced charges (and reduced effect) for the remainder of the siege. The second mine was successfully blown on 4 October, and finally the outer wall was taken by a battalion of the 24th Foot. Casualties during the assault amounted to thirty-seven killed and 213 wounded. Among the wounded was John Jones, reducing the number of engineer officers present to three. His injuries forced him to return home, although this did give him the spare time to publish in 1814 the first edition of his comprehensive work on the British sieges of the Peninsular War. Jones' autobiography described the circumstances:

> Lord Wellington desired Colonel Jones to proceed into the trenches . . . adding however that he should not fire the [mine] till after he [Jones] had taken off his hat and the signal had been acknowledged by a similar lifting of his Lordship's beaver . . . a little after sunset Colonel Jones . . . stepped out of the parallel . . . and made the arranged signal . . . by holding up his hat; no acknowledgement followed, again and again the hat was held up . . . on the signal being . . . repeated . . . there was speedily a line of musketeers firing at him . . . at length one took effect, knocked him over and with difficulty he rolled himself over into the parallel.

Wellington later explained that Jones was not making the signal at the agreed spot, as he was trying to stay out of sight of the French garrison when he realised the agreed spot was out in the open. Eventually he moved to the agreed spot to make the signal and was shot by the defenders. Jones was upset that he was not mentioned in dispatches, Wellington remarking that he would not give praise to any officer who unnecessarily exposed himself. Jones' painful injury required his removal to Lisbon and he recorded that Wellington gave him the only sprung waggon with the army and all his remaining claret.[23] There is a touch of theatre to Jones' descriptions of events in his Autobiography. It is unlikely that he would have been mentioned in dispatches for the third time in 1812. The previous two times had resulted in brevet promotion and this had already caused resentment amongst his peers.

For the next sixteen days the siege staggered on. The Allies had neither the guns nor ammunition to make progress and the defenders had plenty of both. The situation reached its worst point on 2 October, when the whole of the working party for the night, with the exception of the Guards regiments, did not turn up. This led to a stinging rebuke from Wellington and some officers being arrested for neglect of duty. The French launched two sorties on 5 and 8 October, causing some damage but Wellington's troops had just lost heart. A third mine was started on the 10th, under the church of St Roman. Sturgeon suggested that a gallery could be run from the trenches to the castle, a distance of about 100 yards using the town fire engine to pump air, but Burgoyne thought this was not possible 'and the idea was dropped'.[24] The mine was blown with the final assault on 18 October, when 400 troops assaulted the second line. The defenders stood firm and the attack was repulsed with the loss of 160 men. After this, the siege just petered out and it was raised by Wellington two days later as the French armies finally started to threaten his position.

Analysis of the Siege
There was clearly a serious underestimation of the resources required for the siege. Burgos was not a strong place and even the smallest siege train would have caused severe damage in very little time. Jones described Burgos 'as a very insignificant fortress'.[25] Wellington must have believed that it would put up no defence and once the siege started he would not accept that there were insufficient resources to take it. According to Fortescue, Wellington had 'snatched away more than one Indian fortress by escalade, he hoped to do the like with Burgos'.[26] Fortescue summed up the result: 'At Burgos . . . he fulfilled his threat and tried East Indian methods with disastrous results'.[27]

The three attempts to assault the castle were all made by small groups of men who were heavily outnumbered by the defenders.[28] Whether this was due to Wellington's guilt about the casualties at earlier sieges is not clear, but launching troops against defences that had not been seriously weakened could have no result other than high casualties. The effort of the troops and officers was not up to the usual standard and Burgoyne particularly singled out the Portuguese units for their lack of effort. But it must have been obvious to all the troops that the resources available were insufficient. Perhaps the troops were getting sick of being used as cannon fodder? Two thousand were injured at Burgos with nothing to show for it. The retreat that followed finished 1812 with a real blow after the successes earlier in the year.

In his dispatch after the siege had been raised, Wellington made it clear that he did not hold the artillery or engineer officers to have been at fault,[29] a fairer statement than those he made after the successful siege of Badajoz. Considering the resources that they had to work with, it is difficult to see what else could have been achieved. The engineer resources were minimal. From the eighth day of the thirty-five day siege, they were down to four engineers when Captain Williams was killed and three engineers from the eighteenth day when Jones was incapacitated. Burgoyne was lucky to be alive and the two engineer lieutenants, Reid and Pitts, were also sick for part of the time. Of the ten assistant engineers, six were killed or wounded.

Three mines were dug and exploded without any trained miners being present. There were also no miners' tools and normal pickaxes had to be used.[30] Jones stated that the reason for the unplanned assault on the outer wall on 22 September was because Wellington was doubtful that the mining could succeed without trained miners.[31] Jones continued that because the second assault failed, a further five days were lost whilst the second mine was dug. The mines had varying success. The first did not do the damage expected, possibly due to encountering old foundations. The second made a large breach in the wall as expected, while the third caused extensive damage to the terrace in front of the breach but did not bring down the church, which it had been expected to do. However, the purpose of the third mine was to provide access to the upper level and this was achieved by destroying the terrace.

Overall, Jones was much more critical of the engineering effort than Wellington, although the principal thrust of his criticism was still the lack of trained sappers and miners, believing that if sufficient had been present, much more progress would have been made. The decision to mine the defences was probably made to remedy the deficiency of ordnance. The walls, as even the limited ordnance available showed, were not very strong. A proper siege train would have removed any need for mining. Jones, who became a trusted advisor to Wellington in post-Waterloo Europe, still blamed him personally for his injuries and Burgoyne, who was also well thought of by Wellington, was no less critical. Burgoyne, writing privately to Fletcher, was highly critical of the efforts of the troops and of Wellington's decision to assault with small numbers of men. Like Jones, he believed that Burgos could have been taken with the resources available. One of Burgoyne's final comments, which Wrottesley[32] did not print in his biography, was 'the last assault failed entirely due to the small number of the storming parties against a fort having 1,500 men in it – they carried the works easy but could not hold them'.[33] As on a number of other occasions, Wrottesley adjusted Burgoyne's quotes when they were especially critical of Wellington. Burgoyne's final paragraph in his private letter to Fletcher, in the version published by Wrottesley stated: 'I have heard a hint that Lord Wellington said that the engineers told him "the fort might be taken without guns". This I do not believe; first, because it is not like him to say that he went by other people's advice . . . although he occasionally listened to some project or other.'[34]

Burgoyne actually wrote:

> I have heard a hint that Lord Wellington said that the engineers told him 'the fort might be taken without guns'. This I do not believe

because it is not like him, as I believe he never pays anyone the compliment to insinuate that he took their advice, though he may perhaps in a case of failure . . . and although he occasionally listened to some foolish project or other.[35]

His personal view was not new. A year earlier, he had written:

There is an account current that his Lordship says 'if he undertakes another siege, he will be his own engineer.' Whatever faults were committed at Badajoz [in 1811], I suspect he was not aware of them, and I think it is very doubtful whether he knows them now. *This is a consequence [?] of his system of insinuating blame . . . whether deserved or not.*

The final sentence in italics is the portion of the letter criticising Wellington that Wrottesley also 'forgot' to include in his biography of Burgoyne.

There is an interesting parallel between the French attitude to the Lines of Torres Vedras and the Allied failures in front of the forts of Salamanca and at Burgos. Both forces had been told about the situation in front of them, but both chose to ignore the warnings until it was too late, with terrible results.

The engineers did what they could with very limited resources and for once the British army did not pull a victory from the jaws of defeat in spite their general's failings. Burgos was probably the biggest failure under Wellington's command in the Peninsula. Wellington seemed to go out of his way to exonerate his engineer and artillery officers from any blame, which is probably as close as he ever came to admitting a mistake. The Allied failure in front of Burgos was now to become even worse.

The Retreat from Burgos
Although Porter, the historian of the Royal Engineers, unbelievably described the retreat as 'leisurely', it was anything of the kind, being the nearest Wellington came during the war to losing his army.[36] On 20 October, the troops started their withdrawal, with the siege guns going the following night. Dickson, finding the roads too poor to move the heavy guns, destroyed them. The Allied army, with the French in close pursuit, retired towards Valladolid. On the 24th, Wellington tried to make a stand at the Carrion river near Palencia. Later that day, Burgoyne was ordered to destroy four bridges in the area at Dueñas, Tariego, Villa Muriel and Palencia. Having only two engineers with him, Lieutenants Pitts and Reid, Burgoyne also used two Assistant Engineers, Major Thomson and Lieutenant Barney.

Pitts was sent to Tariego but was incorrectly told by the Allied outposts that the French already had taken the bridge. Realising the mistake in the morning, Pitts went to the village but the French arrived before the bridge could be destroyed. Similarly at Palencia, Reid could not destroy the bridge before the French entered the town. Major Thompson succeeded in blowing one arch at Villa Muriel and Lieutenant Barney succeeded in partially destroying an arch at Dueñas with advice from Burgoyne.

Several miles to the south-west, Burgoyne blew the bridge over the Pisuerga at Cabezon. He recounted a rare difference of opinion between the engineering services where Wellington had asked Sturgeon of the Royal Staff Corps to blow the bridge and to his surprise, Sturgeon reported he needed thirty-six hours to do it. When Burgoyne was asked for an opinion he said he could do it much quicker and completed the task in five hours.[37] The command of the engineers changed on that day, with Burgoyne simply noting 'Sir Richard Fletcher arrived from Badajoz'. Every available engineer was being used to destroy bridges on the retreat to delay the French pursuit. Two bridges over the Pisuerga were put out of action near Valladolid and, further west, bridges over the Douro at Tordesillas and Toro were mined. On 29 October, bridges were mined at Zamora and Tudela. Wellington now tried to hold the French at Tordesillas and redoubts and batteries were built over the next four days. On 8 November Wellington retreated to Salamanca, building redoubts on the heights of San Christobal. Lieutenant Harry Jones RE (brother of John Jones) noted in his diary 'building three breastworks at Aldeaseca and Vilanes'.[38]

Lieutenants Pitts and Barney (Assistant Engineer) were sent to mine two more bridges over the Tormes at Congosta and Barco de Avila. Wellington managed to stay there for a week but superior French forces were concentrating before him and managed to cross the Tormes on 15 November, forcing him to retire once again towards Ciudad Rodrigo. Burgoyne noted in his diary on 16 November that he was ordered to ride for the fortress, Wellington having received information that the recently-repaired walls 'had fallen in'. Burgoyne noted with surprise that the repairs designed by Fletcher had 'not fallen in, but menacing it strongly, and [were] propped up with beams'.[39]

One can imagine that Wellington would have been very unhappy with his engineers. Having had ten months to complete the repairs, they failed just as he was in desperate need of a secure base. With a superior French army approaching, there was a very real chance that Ciudad Rodrigo could be lost again. Fortunately, the French did not press their pursuit any further and were not aware of the opportunity they had missed. Bizarrely, there did not appear to be any real urgency to correct the fault. Lieutenant Reid reporting on 17 December that he could not get enough workmen and he expected that the repairs would not be complete until mid-February 1813. It is difficult to believe that the Allies thought the fortress would be safe through the winter when it was less than a year since Wellington had taken it in exactly those circumstances.

The precipitate retreat from Burgos had led to a breakdown in order in the Allied army and many troops were lost to sickness and the French. Wellington lost 5,000 men and it would be some time before the army was re-organised and the huge numbers of sick reduced. The casualties could have been much worse or he could have even suffered a major defeat without the efforts of the engineer officers to disrupt the enemy's pursuit.

Other Engineer Activity in 1812
As with previous years, the main events, the three sieges and the Battle of Salamanca, attract most attention, but the engineer officers continued to provide more everyday but nonetheless vital services to the Allied cause. Near Lisbon, work continued on both sides of the river Tagus to maintain and improve the defences. Little new work was carried out north of Lisbon but work continued all year to complete and improve the defences south of the Tagus around Almada, and a number of engineer officers were involved through the whole period. The common problem of delays due to the slow response from the Portuguese authorities was still evident. Captain Rhodes wrote to Fletcher asking if he or Wellington would press the authorities on his request to be allowed to cut wood from the royal forests south of the Tagus.[40]

Repair of the damage to Ciudad Rodrigo and Badajoz was of vital importance to Wellington. The loss of either would again cripple his strategy and work continued on both to the end of the year. The importance Wellington put on holding these fortresses can be seen in him leaving Fletcher at Badajoz for six months to ensure the repairs were completed properly. There was also regular correspondence between the two where the details of the works were discussed and Wellington was able to give directions on the work he wanted. Similarly improvement to the defences at Abrantes continued, with Captain Wedekind from the King's German Legion engineers taking over after Captain Patton was killed at the siege of Badajoz.

In late September 1812, Lieutenant Pringle arrived at Merida to repair the broken arch on the bridge. Having inspected the bridge he proposed a temporary repair using wood. His plans were initially delayed by the lack of tools and material. The Allies had also built a crossing at Almaraz, Wellington wanting good lines of communication between himself and Hill.

1812 – Triumph and Failure   157

Lieutenant Piper RE had put a pontoon bridge across the river and had remained there as it needed constant attention due to the changing height of the river and the damage caused by the constant heavy commissary traffic. As winter approached, keeping it open became even more difficult.[41] To resolve this problem, Wellington ordered Sturgeon to repair the bridge at Almaraz using the same technique that had been used at Alcantara in June.[42] Alexander Todd RSC was sent to carry out this work. The importance of this bridge to Wellington can be seen in the numerous mentions in his dispatches in November and December 1812. He was anxious that it would be available for the movements of Allied troops but also that it could be removed if the French threatened it. As early as 10 October, Wellington was warning Hill that he might be retiring from Burgos and the bridge at Almaraz may need to be removed. One of the most ingenious aspects of Sturgeon's bridge design was that it could be removed and replaced as the needs of the service changed.

Building the rope suspension bridge at Almaraz also freed up the pontoon train and Lieutenant Piper was ordered to move it to Salamanca as soon as the replacement bridge was in place. This order looks like planning for his intended retreat from Burgos and ensuring that he had the ability to cross rivers during the movement back towards Portugal. Piper was put in command of the pontoon train, a position he held until the end of the war. The pontoon train at this time was located at Elvas and Piper had a number of challenges keeping it ready for use. On 10 December, he reported that a large number of the bullock drivers had deserted through not being paid. In the same letter he reported that the pontoons were rusting badly.

Lieutenants Hulme and Marshall spent several months working on improving the navigation of the Douro. They were working to improve both the river bed and the towing paths on the river banks.[43] Hulme reported the difficulty of keeping even the 'poorest class of peasant' employed due to the lack of money to pay them and their having to seek work elsewhere as a result.

December 1812 saw an incident which, I believe, is unique during the Peninsular War: Wellington asked for two engineer officers to be removed. Both were new to the Peninsula, having arrived earlier in the year. Captains Henderson and Slade had been assigned to complete the repairs at Badajoz. Henderson arrived first at Badajoz during the summer and Slade arrived on 5 December. A few days after Slade's arrival, Henderson wrote to Fletcher informing him that due to Lieutenant Pringle RE being too ill to stay at Merida and based on information that the enemy were advancing on that place, he had decided to go there to make arrangements to blow the bridge. This appears to have been done without reference to any authority and looks like an officer seeking his moment of glory. When his letter arrived at headquarters he was ordered to return immediately to Badajoz. Unfortunately for the two officers, Wellington happened to pass through Badajoz a few days later on his way to Cadiz and was clearly not happy, writing to Fletcher:

> I am by no means satisfied with either Captain Henderson, whom I have not seen, but who is gone to Merida to destroy the bridge without orders that I know of; or with Captain Slade, who appears to me quite incapable of executing such a trust as that of the charge of the works of this place. I beg therefore that both may be relieved from hence without loss of time, and that you will send here an officer on whose judgement and discretion you can rely to execute the trust reposed in him.[44]

Captain Slade was probably the unlucky partner in this incident. Having just arrived at the fortress, he was probably unprepared to answer the knowledgeable questions of Wellington and, in the absence of his superior officer Captain Henderson, faced Wellington's anger alone.

The winter of 1812/13 saw changes in the engineering command and some internal friction. In early December, Fletcher was granted leave to return home for a short period. His eventual successor Howard Elphinstone gossiped that he was looking for a wife and would not return to the Peninsula. Fletcher's wife had died in 1809 and his six children had been looked after by relations since then. Dickson's brother, Admiral Archibald Dickson, also commented that Fletcher was to be married to Eliza Carter on his return to England and he was 'a man in love'.[45] Elphinstone had a slightly different view based on letters from his wife claiming that Miss Carter was less enthusiastic, as marrying Fletcher would also include the care of his children.

In the meantime, Captain Henry Goldfinch was confirmed as temporary CRE on 11 December but only after Burgoyne had asked Wellington to rule on whether Corps or Brevet rank took precedence. It is surprising that Burgoyne challenged this as Fletcher had clearly identified Goldfinch for the command.[46] The timing suggests that Burgoyne waited until after Fletcher left headquarters and then directed the question on seniority to Wellington. His question should have been directed to the Board of Ordnance, not Wellington, but they would have rejected his claim out of hand and Burgoyne knew that. I believe this late change of command was because Howard Elphinstone was supposed to have taken over from Fletcher. Elphinstone had been ordered to come out in November 1812. He was at Portsmouth on 12 December but did not arrive in Lisbon until 3 February 1813. Writing a few days after his arrival in Lisbon, he told his wife he had been ordered to report to headquarters, but said he was not moving from Lisbon for several days as it was raining. Then he planned to review the lines of Torres Vedras, return to Lisbon to rest his horses and then set out to see, as he put it, 'The great man'. He did not arrive at headquarters until 4 March, over three months after he was ordered out! During the period when Elphinstone was sightseeing, Fletcher had been to England and returned, arriving back at headquarters on 13 April. Elphinstone was sent back to Lisbon the next day. I am sure this was due to displeasure at Elphinstone taking so long to arrive.

1812 had been a year of contrasts. The successes at the sieges of Ciudad Rodrigo and Badajoz followed by the Battle of Salamanca led to a feeling of hope in the Allied camp. The failure at Burgos and the disastrous retreat that followed tarnished Wellington's reputation. However, the French in the Peninsula were firmly on the back foot. Whilst Madrid was back in their hands, the siege of Cadiz had been raised and the whole of Portugal and southern Spain was now free. Wellington's difficulties were completely overshadowed by the destruction of Napoleon's army in Russia. Despite their recent setbacks, the Allies looked forward to 1813 with considerable optimism.

Chapter 8

1813 – The Road to France

Wellington, having made a trip to Cadiz to discuss his role as commander of the Spanish Army, had returned to his headquarters at Freneda to start planning his next campaign. This was going to very different from previous years, in that the Allied army would be moving into new parts of Spain. Communications, both roads and bridges, would now be extended into these new areas. The barriers of the Tagus, Douro and Guadiana were less important, as they were not now on the front line.

There was extensive correspondence through the winter about the availability and condition of pontoons, as 1813 would be the first time that Wellington would move a pontoon train with the army. On 20 December 1812, he wrote to Lieutenant Piper RE asking him to obtain details of the number of pontoons and carriages at Lisbon and also to do the same with the equipment at Elvas, and for Piper's report to be ready in ten days' time.[1] Following receipt of the report, Wellington ordered Dickson to organise the large pontoon train at Lisbon 'until the arrival of Mr Pakenham' the Bridge Master.[2] Once the pontoon train was complete, the intention was to ship it up to Abrantes, and on 28 January 1813 Dickson applied for twenty-five large river boats to be made available to ship the thirty-four pontoons, carriages and equipment.[3]

Planning continued through the early weeks of 1813. A unit of Portuguese seamen was attached to the pontoon train in Lisbon and two companies of Portuguese artificers, with their engineer officers, were attached to the army.[4] A small siege train of 18-pounders was also put together to travel with the army, there being a number of larger siege guns available at Almeida and Elvas if required.[5] Orders were also issued to put the rope bridge back in place at Almaraz.[6] Lieutenant Wright RE was ordered to fully destroy Fort Napoleon and the fort at Miravette near Almaraz and was then sent to build a bridge over the Alagon at Galisteo.

On 27 April, Lieutenant Harry Jones, who was attached to the 5th Division, was ordered by Murray, the QMG, to report on the means of passing 'troops, horses or artillery' over the Douro at Peso da Regua 'and what can be done towards increasing the means of passing the river'. Jones reported back two days later that 13,000 troops could cross in ten hours, a brigade of artillery in five hours and 1,000 dragoons in the same time. He went on to describe in some detail the work required to collect the boats and prepare the river banks, also commenting on the impact of the river level rising and proposing alternative crossing-points. When the 5th Division crossed the river at this point on 14 May, Harry Jones crossed with them and two days later was employed repairing the roads to make them passable for the divisional artillery.[7] Jones remained with the artillery for the next few days, working with the artillery officers to get the guns up and down the steep inclines. About the same time as Jones received his orders to report on the crossing-point for the 5th Division, Burgoyne received a similar order to do the same for the 3rd Division. Travelling with Lieutenant Hulme RE, they prepared crossing-points at Collegio and Villarinho. Part of the 3rd Division crossed here on 18 May.

In early May, Wellington wrote to Colonel Fisher, commanding the Royal Artillery, informing him that 264 horses were to be taken from Cairns' artillery brigade and from the reserve artillery to equip the pontoon train that was made up of forty-four pontoons. This will have been extremely unpopular with the artillery but Wellington clearly wanted the pontoon train to be as mobile as possible and felt it necessary to swap the bullocks for horses.[8] It will have been some consolation that this was a temporary measure until replacement horses arrived from Lisbon. Cairnes commented that 'Although perhaps considered necessary by his Lordship unavoidable and essential to the service, [it] has mortified and vexed me beyond all possible expression . . . His Lordship was. I hear, pleased to express his regret at knocking up my Brigade.'[9] Cairns went down to deliver the horses personally and remarked that he was unconvinced that the replacement of the oxen would improve the poor progress made by the pontoon train. His view was that the carriages were too light and unwieldy and the substitution of horses would make the situation worse as 'nothing but the slow steady pull of the ox prevents it either from upsetting or breaking something'.[10]

Wellington's plans for the campaign were delayed due to the difficulties in getting the pontoon train to the army. He wrote to Bathurst on 11 May informing him of his plans to establish a bridge over the Douro near Zamora but the pontoon carriages had suffered many breakages on the way and this had slowed its progress. On the 14th, Wellington rode to inspect the pontoon train himself. Writing to Fletcher, he said it would be two days before it would be ready to move and that he had asked for twenty pairs of wheels to be supplied by the Royal Artillery, making it clear that the pontoon train's needs were in his opinion greater than those of the artillery. Wellington had asked Fletcher to personally check the road that was planned to be used by the pontoon train and make sure it was passable.[11] A few days later, Wellington wrote to Bathurst enclosing a report from Fletcher on the condition of the pontoon train and asking that 'good carriages constructed as proposed by Lieutenant Colonel Sir R Fletcher' were sent out to Corunna (see Appendix 4 on military bridging for more details).

By mid-May nearly everything was ready for the advance. Essentially, the plan was for the Allied army to move in two columns, one up the main road to Salamanca and the other to sweep round the French flank to the north. In Wellington's instructions for movement, issued to Sir Thomas Graham on 18 May, he informed him that 'Captain Mitchell [QMG Department] is now employed in the examination of the fords and other passages of the Esla'. He also informed him that he intended to

> lay the bridge of pontoons at the Barca de Villal Campo, about a mile below the junction of the Esla with the Douro, where it is expected to arrive on the 30th . . . the object of these movements is first to turn the enemy's positions on the Douro and next to secure the junction of the right of the army with the left, as far up the river as may be practicable.[12]

If all went to plan, around 30 May the two wings of the Allied army would arrive at the junction of the Esla and the Douro on the same day that the pontoon train arrived to connect the two forces. The first of the Allied columns set off on 20 May, with Wellington leaving his headquarters at Freneda two days later. Concerned that the two wings of the army could be vulnerable to a French attack, having a river between them, he decided to split the pontoon train and make an earlier crossing at Espadacintra until the main crossing-point on the Douro/Esla was established. Whilst there were some delays, the Allies moved forward, with Hill's corps nearly catching the French at Salamanca as they delayed their retreat, trying to obtain accurate information on the forces moving against them. The bridge at Alba de Tormes was captured intact, Lieutenant Wright RE describing the French repairs to the bridge a few days later.[13]

Orders to lay the pontoon bridge over the Douro at Barco de Villal Campo were given on 28 May 1813 but two days later Wellington wrote to Hill saying the order had been countermanded as he needed the pontoon bridge over the Elsa, where the river had risen and the fords become impassable, Harry Jones noting 'I attempted to cross on horseback, but was very near being carried away; water above horse's chest.' This sudden rise in the water level caused a day's delay until the pontoon bridge was put in place.

Initially the French believed that Hill's force was the only one advancing and it was several days later before they realised their mistake. The French had to hurriedly evacuate Zamora and retire towards Burgos, Wellington leaving a small Spanish garrison and Lieutenant Hulme to repair the defences there. Anticipating the French retreat, Wellington continued his flanking movement and Burgos was also evacuated on 13 June, the French destroying the fortress that he had failed to take the previous year. Fletcher and Dickson examined the damage the same day, even though the French were still close by, and following their report Wellington believed that he thought 'it was possible to put in a state of repair for a reasonable expense'.[14]

Wellington's flanking manoeuvre continued to be successful and the French retired again, their forces concentrating at Vitoria from 19 June to protect the retreating baggage train containing the fruits of six years of plunder. Wellington, following closely, realised that he was stronger than the French and launched a co-ordinated assault on the morning of the 21st. Overwhelmed and outflanked, the French were comprehensively defeated and King Joseph's army disintegrated and fled to the north. Following a trend of bad behaviour that had been growing throughout the war, the Allied army now also degenerated into a mob looting the French baggage train, any though of pursuing the French lost amongst the riches to be gained. Officers were as guilty as the rank and file. It was the following morning before an organised pursuit began, but the French had a head start and, with some skirmishing, retired across the Bidassoa, leaving garrisons in the major fortresses at Pamplona and San Sebastian and the minor fortress of Pancorbo. The Spanish General O'Donnell was ordered to take the latter and Lieutenant Stanway was ordered to assist him. Pancorbo was invested on 25 June, the lower fort was stormed on the 28th and the place surrendered two days later, although this was more due to lack of water than the threat of assault.

Wellington, with the bulk of the army, continued to press the French and Fletcher remained with him. Hill was dispatched to Pamplona with Henry Goldfinch RE in attendance and Graham was sent to San Sebastian with Charles Smith RE. Wellington needed to take these fortresses to capitalise on his success. The French had retreated into the Pyrenees and if Wellington could take the fortresses, he had a much better chance of holding the line of the mountains against any future French advance.

The Blockade of Pamplona

Four days after the Battle of Vitoria, Lieutenant General Hill closely blockaded Pamplona, the original intention being to lay siege to the place. Wellington ordered Major Augustus Frazer RA to ride to Santander and divert to Deba the siege train that was waiting in transports on the north coast of Spain. He also made arrangements for twenty-four 12-pounders captured from the French to be sent there. On 28 June, Wellington wrote to Hill ordering a close blockade of the place and Hill reported that 'I shall do my utmost to fulfil your Lordship's wishes relative to the blockade of Pamplona. Major Goldfinch is now out examining the place, with the view of carrying into effect your instructions.'[15] Two days later, Hill sent Wellington Goldfinch's report on the defences, and on the same day, Frazer reported that the siege train was at Deba and unloading had started. Wellington's original plan had been to attack Pamplona, but he now decided to attack the weaker fortress of San Sebastian and blockade Pamplona into submission. This also gave Wellington the advantage of shorter distances for the siege train to travel from the northern coast. John Jones suggested that this decision was based on a reconnaissance by Wellington and Fletcher on 1 July where they realised that Pamplona was too strong to take with the resources at hand,[16] but this does not appear to match Wellington's correspondence. Writing to Graham on 26 June, he said 'I therefore propose to blockade the place rather than lay siege to it. We shall get the place at a later period.'[17] Wellington ordered the blockade to be taken over by the 6th and 7th Divisions under Lord Dalhousie until O'Donnell's Spanish army arrived, and for nine redoubts to be built to surround the fortress. Fletcher remained to oversee the construction of these with other engineer officers including Goldfinch, Burgoyne and Pitts. Writing to Dalhousie on 2 July, Wellington said:

> I am anxious to establish a strict and close blockade of Pamplona . . . and to arrange the details with Colonel Fletcher, who has received my instructions on the subject . . . redoubts should be constructed on certain favourable spots which Colonel Sir R Fletcher will point out, at a distance of 1,000 and 1,200 yards from the place.[18]

The strict blockade also included cutting off the water supply, shooting at anyone approaching the river, and removing or destroying any crops in the fields in the vicinity of the fortress. The redoubts were built by Spanish peasants under the direction of the engineer officers and a small number of artificers. Lieutenant Thomas Pitts RE remarked 'Pasley's sappers are most valuable and generally extremely zealous'. These will have been some of the first 'trained' artificers to have gone through Pasley's School of Military Engineering at Chatham. The redoubts were armed with French field guns captured at Vitoria. Over the coming weeks a number of buildings were turned into strongpoints and a signalling system was set up to provide rapid communication between the redoubts.

On 11 July, Fletcher reported his progress to Wellington: 'I am sorry to say that having found much stone or rock in the ditches of the redoubts, their completion will necessarily be delayed somewhat beyond the time I had mentioned.'[19] Three days later, Fletcher and Burgoyne set of for San Sebastian where the siege was just starting. Despite a belief that the garrison was desperately short of food, Pamplona held out until 31 October.

The First Siege of San Sebastian
After San Sebastian was invested on 11 July 1813, Wellington, Major Charles Smith RE[20] and Dickson rode around the fortress, and at the suggestion of Smith,[21] the same basic plan of attack was proposed as had previously been used by the Duke of Berwick in 1719. The plan was to breach the wall on the eastern side where it was fully visible, due to the sea going right up to the base of the wall at high tide and preventing any other form of defence in front of it. At low tide it was possible for troops to cross the tidal estuary of the river Urumea and storm any breach. It would also be necessary to take some of the outworks on the land side to reduce the fire that could be brought to bear on any attack across the estuary and also to give access to the foot of the eastern wall. With this aim in mind, the convent of San Bartolomeo was to be captured and trenches thrown forward to allow the defences to be silenced and for enfilade fire on the proposed breaches.

By the time Fletcher arrived at San Sebastian the plan of attack had been agreed. It is not clear if Fletcher agreed with the plan. Burgoyne certainly did not, but the matter was decided before he had a chance to influence the decision. Graham writing to Wellington reported that Fletcher was concerned about the protection of the troops during an assault and recommended a second breach. Graham later, also made the comment 'It is evident, however, that Major Smith thought too lightly of the strength of the place.'[22]

Timeline for the First Siege of San Sebastian	
11 July 1813	Batteries started against San Bartolomeo on night of 11/12 July
13 July 1813	Work started on batteries against eastern wall
14 July 1813	Fire opened on convent of San Bartolomeo
17 July 1813	Convent of San Bartolomeo taken
20 July 1813	Fire opened on fortress
21 July 1813	Governor rejects summons
23 July 1813	Main breach practicable, second breach started
24 July 1813	Assault postponed due to fires in town
25 July 1813	Assault fails
26 July 1813	Siege guns removed but blockade maintained on fortress

As at the siege of Ciudad Rodrigo, Wellington had effective siege guns available. A new siege train had been sent out to the Peninsula for use in northern Spain and with the six 18-pounders that travelled with the army and six 24-pounders supplied by the Royal Navy, from HMS *Surveillante*, Wellington had a siege train of forty guns made up of:

- Twenty 24-pounders including six naval pieces.
- Six 18-pounders.
- Four 68-pounder carronades (short-barrelled and not accurate but useful for spraying the breaches with canister).
- Six 8in howitzers.
- Four 10in mortars.

Whilst at first glance this looked like a substantial siege train, it was not for a fortress on the scale of San Sebastian. There were only twenty-six guns to batter the walls, of which six were the smaller 18-pounders which had significantly less battering effect. Of the larger 24-pounders, the six naval guns had shorter barrels, which reduced the accuracy that was vital for bringing down walls. Dickson noted in his journal that 'Fletcher thought this scanty for such a fortress and it certainly is so, at least in heavy guns'.[23]

The engineering personnel commanded by Fletcher included seventeen officers and over 300 rank and file from the Royal Sappers and Miners.[24] This was the first siege at which there were a significant number of them present. Although John Jones' published Journal does not record the employment of assistant engineers (officers volunteering from the army to assist), both Burgoyne and Fletcher mention that a number were used on the left attack.[25] In addition there was a party of fifty Portuguese artificers and engineers. Overall command of the siege was given to Sir Thomas Graham, Wellington staying with the army to monitor the activities of the French forces under Marshal Soult.

The initial attack was made against the convent of San Bartolomeo. Two batteries were constructed and they opened fire on 14 July. The following day, a force of Portuguese infantry was sent forward, but they encountered strong resistance and retired. The guns continued firing on the convent for two more days, and it was taken on the 17th, though not without considerable loss thanks to an undisciplined charge by British infantry against the main French positions. Two new batteries were started near the convent and the plan was to dig a parallel right across the isthmus.

The batteries against the eastern wall opened on the morning of 20 July and once the French realised where the main point of attack was going to be, they began establishing defences behind the wall being breached. The same night, the attackers started work on the main parallel across the isthmus, but due to the poor weather the majority of the Portuguese troops allocated for the work did not turn up and only a third of the planned work was completed. The following night, whilst completing this parallel, a large drain was found which had supplied water into the town until the supply was cut off. This was explored by Lieutenant Reid RE, who found it went up to the western side of the hornwork and it was decided to place a mine at the end of the drain with the intention of breaching the hornwork.

Burgoyne was sent by Graham with the first summons on 21 July, which was refused.[26] Burgoyne regularly was used in this sort of role, a task that you would expect would be given to permanent members of a general's staff. Clearly he possessed some skills that were judged useful in these situations. It may have been his language skills but I think it more likely that it was an opportunity to get a close-up, professional view of the defences.

The breach in the eastern wall appeared practicable on the 22nd, but the French were making great efforts to clear away the debris despite the Allies continually sweeping the breach with grapeshot and shells. On the following day, the breach was declared practicable and the guns were directed to make a second breach in the wall at a location that locals had suggested was particularly weak. This second breach was ready that night, although the continuous shelling had started numerous fires in the houses behind the two breaches. Graham ordered the assault for the 24th, but in the morning it was cancelled as it was thought the fires that were still raging would impede the troops.[27] This delay gave the French an extra twenty-four hours to improve the defences, although they were working under a continuous bombardment from the attackers.

The plan of attack was for troops from the 5th Division to assault the two breaches, starting from the right (eastern) end of the parallel across the isthmus and skirting the foot of the wall until they reached the breaches, the siege batteries providing heavy covering fire from across the bay. The plan was dependent upon the time of low time and daybreak, which were both expected to be around 5 a.m. The signal for the start of the assault would be the blowing of the mine in the drain by the hornwork.

On the morning of the 25th, the mine was blown before daylight and the assault commenced. Filing out of the parallel was very slow and the first troops arrived at the breach only in small numbers. Although initially successful, there were not sufficient men present and they were quickly driven back, having been stopped by a twenty-foot drop from the breach into the town itself. In doing so, they became mixed up with the group who were tasked with assaulting the secondary breach and all retired in some disorder. The assault had failed completely before there was enough daylight for the artillery across the bay to provide any support, casualties amounting to 570 killed and wounded. There were five engineer casualties during the assault. Lieutenant Colonel Richard Fletcher, Lieutenants Harry Jones and Reid were wounded, Captain Lewis lost a leg and Lieutenant Machell was killed. Another officer, Lieutenant Hammond Tapp, had been severely wounded earlier in the siege on 13 July.

When Wellington heard about the failure of the assault, he rode over from his headquarters determined to continue the siege. However, he accepted that it would have to be postponed temporarily as powder and shot were running low and new supplies needed to be delivered. In the meantime, as Soult was still threatening to attack, Wellington ordered most of the siege guns to be removed and returned to the boats where they would be safe until further ammunition was available. He ordered a tight blockade to be kept in place.

Analysis of the First Siege
Both contemporary and more recent writers have criticised the performance of the engineers in a number of areas. Fortescue[28] leads the attack with an unjustifiable apportioning of blame for the failures at San Sebastian, while Oman[29] only holds the engineers partially to blame but identifies them as the primary culprit. Their assessments in both cases appear to be led by the opinions of one particular army officer who clearly had a dislike for the 'scientific soldiers'. The analysis below will look at the criticisms and compare them with to the available facts.

Oman, and more recently Myatt,[30] criticised Major Smith's proposal to follow the Duke of Berwick's plan of attack of 1719. Oman wrote that Graham, Wellington, Fletcher, Dickson (commanding the Royal Artillery) and Frazer (commanding the siege batteries) all agreed with the plan and they 'forgot' that the Duke of Berwick did not have to assault the fortress.[31] It is inconceivable, even excluding the other officers, that Wellington 'forgot' about the possibility of another costly assault. The strength of the fortress was directed against the land approaches for obvious reasons and once again the view was that there would be insufficient time to formally approach from the land side. Fletcher's view on the proposed attack on the eastern side was that 'it would certainly save much *time* [my italics] . . . compared with a regular siege of the very powerful defences crossing the isthmus'. An attack on the land front would be a 'work of great difficulty' requiring a larger battering train and thirty to thirty-five days' effort.[32] Burgoyne initially supported the proposed plan, although with the benefit of hindsight he thought that finding the drain tipped the balance in favour of an attack across the isthmus. He did, however, acknowledge that this would have taken more time. Oman and Fortescue both wrote that when Wellington arrived after the assault he was insistent that the siege would continue and required the engineers to come up with a plan for a formal attack from the land side. Burgoyne and Frazer indicate that an alternative plan of attack was discussed at the meeting with Wellington on 25 July. Jones, in his diary entry for that day, noted that 'after some consideration, it was decided to persevere in the same plan of attack'.[33] Fletcher also wrote to Wellington on the 27th noting that Wellington's opinion was for an extended attack using the original plan.[34] Lack of ammunition prevented any progress in the short term. By the time the new supplies had arrived, the plan, as Jones noted, remained the same as before, with an attack on the east-facing sea walls. Any thoughts of using a different plan were clearly put aside very quickly.

Oman's narrative stated that when the mine was blown, the hornwork was to be assaulted by Portuguese troops from the parallel on the isthmus. He continued that the engineers were unsure how much damage would be caused by the mine and because of this no concrete proposals were made to make use of the explosion. He noted that for the attack on the 25th, 'a little more attention, but not nearly enough, was given', but overall described the engineers' plans as 'half-hearted'.[35] Burgoyne clearly understood that the mine was to be used 'as a signal only and with the chance of alarming them [the French defenders]'.[36] Jones makes no mention of an assault on the hornwork. Dickson's view before the assault was that blowing the mine would 'create such an alarm as may make them evacuate . . . and so produce a favourable diversion', a view shared by Lieutenant Harry Jones.[37] After the assault, Dickson noted, 'A party of Caçadores [Portuguese Light Infantry] availing themselves of the consternation produced amongst the enemy . . . made . . . their way into the ditch . . . but the defenders . . . commenced a fire . . . which obliged them to make . . . their way back'.[38] It would appear that Oman based his suppositions on the comment above from Dickson, which does not give any real indication that it was a pre-meditated action. There does not appear to be any evidence to back up his claim that an attack on the hornwork was planned and that it was badly organised by the engineers. It should also be noted that it was not the engineers' responsibility to organise the troops for any attack, but that of the commander of the troops, so any blame should have been directed at Graham, not the engineers.

There are a number of criticisms of the delay between the first breach being practicable and the assault, thereby giving time for the defenders to reinforce the damaged areas. These criticisms are not helped by some confusion amongst the Ordnance officers themselves. Frazer complained in his letter of 23 July that 'after [making] this excellent breach, they hesitate about using it . . . I am now ordered to make another breach . . . by which time the original breach will be entrenched'. His view was clearly that the failure of the assault was caused by 'delay and indecision'.[39] According to John Jones, the general plan as had been used in previous sieges was to open a second breach at the last minute to stretch the defenders. Frazer did not appear to be aware of this, perhaps because this was the first siege at which he was present. Oman and Fortescue both criticise the two-day delay between the first breach being ready and the assault. Fortescue in particular seized on Burgoyne's remarks after the first siege where Burgoyne commented that the 'whole of the batteries . . . were constructed on the right bank . . . giving them immediate insight into the nature of the attack ... and the breach was practicable two days before the trenches'.[40] Careful review of the dates shows that the trenches were ready on the morning of the 23rd,[41] the breach was declared practicable the same morning and the assault was planned for the following morning. The two-day delay is calculated because the assault was then delayed for twenty-four hours due to the fires behind the breach. This delay may have been unfortunate and significant, but it was not due to the trenches not being ready. It is difficult to see how the work on the breaching batteries could have been delayed to hide the point of attack. They were started on the 13th, which was four days before the convent of San Bartolemeo was taken. It is unlikely that they would have all been ready on the 20th, if they were not started until the 17th, and this would then have lengthened the siege. In every siege in the Peninsular War, time was a critical factor. San Sebastian was no different and the decisions taken were to save time. Graham wrote to Wellington on 24 July, pointing out that the artillery had nearly run out of 24-pounder shot. If the assault had not gone in on the morning of the next day, the siege would have had to revert to a blockade, as there was insufficient ammunition to continue.[42] One other factor that must be taken into account is the problems with working parties. The working parties absenting themselves on the night of 20 July cost the attackers twenty-four hours. They should have been ready on the morning of the 22nd, which would have been the day before the breaches were declared practicable.[43]

There were a number of criticisms around the assault on the morning of the 25th itself. The plan required daylight so that artillery support could be given to the assault. Dickson had told Graham that the artillery would be able to suppress the defenders' fire during the assault. Graham's official report stated that the attack took place 'soon after daylight', and Fletcher stated that the assault was given at daylight . . . the mine having been previously sprung'.[44] However, the artillery officers recorded that the assault had failed before there was sufficient light for them to determine what was happening. Dickson stated 'the column of attack certainly moved forward too early, either from a mistake . . . or from over anxiety on the part of the directors'.[45] Frazer was more forthright, writing 'The assault was . . . made . . . stupidly an hour before, instead of after daybreak'.[46] It is almost certain that the mine was blown before 5 a.m. as Graham's letter to Wellington informing him of the failure of the assault was written at 5:30 a.m.[47] In his biography of Sir Thomas Graham, Aspinal-Oglander strongly refutes the claim that the attack commenced before daylight, but seems to base his argument on the fact that Graham's dispatch reported it was in daylight.[48] While no account clearly stated who gave the order to start the assault, it is likely that Graham did. Even if he did not, he must, as commanding officer, still take responsibility for the failure.

General Oswald, the commander of the 5th Division, did not plan the actual attack well. Campbell of the 9th Foot was of the opinion that the troops were too extended during the assault and thought that if a compact mass had arrived at the breach they 'would have bodily forced through all opposition'.[49] He may have had a point about the organisation of the troops, but his approach would not have worked against the twenty-foot drop that the attackers were faced with in the main breach. Oswald's plan, bearing in mind the concerns about the narrow area in which the assault had to take place, organised his troops so that those heading for the nearest breach went first followed by those who needed to pass the first breach to go to the second breach. With the failure of the assault on the first breach, the troops destined for the second breach could not get past the retiring troops and were swept back into the trenches with them.

A more contentious issue is the view expressed at the time that the 5th Division had not tried very hard. Oman called this a 'monstrous injustice' writing 'everything that mismanagement could accomplish had been done to discourage them'.[50] He quoted statements from Frazer and Larpent (Judge Advocate General and part of Wellington's headquarters) who are generally respected commentators, but pointed out that neither was present at the assault. Burgoyne, recognised by Oman as one of the authorities on the siege, also recorded that the officers 'could not get the men to follow them'.[51] Jones wrote that the attack was not pressed energetically, but finished cryptically by noting although many officers thought so, it could not be true as the 'highest authority', Graham, had stated in his dispatch that the troops had done their best.[52] One authority not used by Oman was Lieutenant Harry Jones RE, who led the column to the main breach and was captured there after being wounded. He commented:

> Finding the descent [from the breach into the town] too great on the inside, I returned for the ladders . . . but upon reaching the foot of the breach everybody was running back with their heads between their legs as hard as they could. At the foot I waited, expecting them to rally and come on immediately, which not being the case, the enemy's Grenadiers jumped into the breach sword in hand and made prisoners all who were able to crawl.[53]

Oman's comment about the mismanagement has some validity, but this, sadly, was true of every other siege and the troops usually did their best despite the mismanagement of their superiors. Whether the criticism of the 5th Division was fair or not, this was a view held at the time and Wellington was clearly concerned enough to ask for volunteers from the other divisions, which the 5th Division took as a clear insult.

A figure that appears to have generated much of the criticism of the engineers was Lieutenant-Colonel William Gomm, who was with the Quarter Master-General's department attached to the 5th Division and also an officer of the 9th Foot, one of the regiments involved in the failed assault. Gomm's criticisms are extensively used by Oman, Fortescue and Myatt with variants of:

> The successes [at Ciudad Rodrigo and the third siege of Badajoz were] . . . owing to the almost miraculous efforts of our troops has checked the progress of science among our engineers . . . the

artillery have become as summary in their proceedings as our engineers . . . providing they can make a hole in the wall . . . they care not about destroying its defences.[54]

Of the above writers, only Fortescue uses the portion of Gomm's letter that reads : 'had we . . . attended to the niceties of the art in the attack of Ciudad Rodrigo or of [the third siege of] Badajoz it is possible we should have taken neither'. Gomm appeared to recognise that the sieges were being undertaken using methods that were not typical, and commented in the same letter that in his opinion there were sufficient resources to attack according to the normal rules of siege warfare. This was clearly not a view shared by Wellington, the artillery officers or the engineers. Gomm's scathing comments continue in his subsequent letters with phrases such as: 'escaping from the hands of those Philistines, the engineers' and 'when we commence [the siege] again, I dare say we shall do it a little less *en charlatan* and more *en regle*'.[55] In this same letter he also notes that 'the enemy made a sortie this morning upon our lines, and, as we did not expect them, gave us more trouble than was necessary'. Perhaps the army officers should have been paying more attention to their own duties before criticising other branches of the military. Gomm was not untypical of the ambitious, confident officer who had a view on everything, which sometimes did not match the views of their superiors or the actual circumstances. A number of the engineer officers would also fall into this category from their private letters.[56] They may be entertaining to read but that does not make them accurate. It is a little more surprising that Gomm is so outspoken about scientific soldiers, because he was one of them, having attended the Royal Military College in 1805. It is possible that there was an element of professional jealousy in his opinions.

One final puzzling fact from the first siege of San Sebastian is the complete lack of comment on the presence of a large body of the Royal Sappers and Miners for the first time. Connolly's history of the corps details their efforts in the siege and the assault,[57] but there is no mention of them by either engineer or army officers

Roncesvalles and Sorauren
Soult was determined to try and relieve the invested French fortresses. On 25 July, the same day as the first assault on San Sebastian, he launched two attacks on the Allied positions at Maya and Roncesvalles. Although the 3rd and 4th Divisions were initially surprised and pushed back, the Allies regrouped and then held their ground over the next few days until Soult realised that his attack had failed. He had got within a few miles of

Pamplona but could not break through. Lieutenant Wright RE, who was with the Allied troops, reported trying to warn General Byng, brigade commander in the 2nd Division, of the danger to his left flank 'but in vain; I had not an opportunity of doing so to General Hill until the day it happened. General Hill then became very anxious about that point, but before any order could be sent the attack took place'. Wright remained with Hill until 28 July, working on repairing roads in the area and then asked for permission to return to San Sebastian. Hill ordered Wright to stay and later he was ordered to fortify the ground around Roncesvalles. He remarked 'I have never had so much work in my life.'[58] Wellington realised that Soult's attack had nearly succeeded and, writing to Fletcher, said: 'A great deal can be done to strengthen the positions on the right; but engineer officers and intrenching [sic] tools will be required. I beg to know where the field equipments [sic] of intrenching tools are, and what officers can be sent on this service, without loss of time.'[59]

In the period between the two sieges, whilst the Allies waited for new supplies of ammunition to arrive, Wellington made use of the pause by ordering an engineer officer to the port of Guetaria, as he wanted to provide the maximum number of safe anchorages for Allied shipping, particularly as winter was approaching. He asked for an investigation into 'the time and expense would be required to construct wells' as well as an estimate of the size of the garrison required. If wells could not be dug, then water would need to be supplied in casks. Captain Stanway was given this task and Graham reported back to Wellington on 14 August that Stanway thought 'the making of the wells would be tedious'.[60] The following day, after receiving an update from Beresford, Wellington gave up on the idea and ordered the engineers to destroy the place.

The Second Siege of San Sebastian
Whilst Wellington was busy repelling Soult's attacks at the end of July, Graham remained at San Sebastian with sufficient troops to maintain the blockade and keep the French from recovering any of the ground that had been taken. It was not possible to stop them making repairs in the town but there was only a limited amount that they could achieve.

Timeline for the Second Siege of San Sebastian	
19 August 1813	Supply ships arrive from England
21 August 1813	Remaining supply ships arrive from England
24 August 1813	Work on batteries resumes
26 August 1813	Guns open on fortress

1813 – The Road to France 175

26 August 1813	Island of Santa Clara seized on night of 26/27th
31 August 1813	Town stormed successfully, French retire to castle
1 September 1813	Bombardment starts on castle
3 September 1813	Governor refused second summons to surrender
8 September 1813	French surrender

Following Wellington's orders, the siege guns were returned to the transports until it was judged safe to land them again. Everything was on hold, waiting for the additional guns and ammunition from England. Four transports arrived on 19 August containing two full siege trains and a further full siege train arrived on the 21st. There was now sufficient roundshot to consider restarting the siege. For the first time in the Peninsular War, the Allied army had more heavy guns than it could use.

All the guns were back in place and fifty-seven guns opened fire on the morning of 26 August. The plan, as mentioned above, was similar to that used in the first siege. The larger number of guns on the eastern attack would attempt to destroy the whole south-eastern corner of the fortress. There were fewer guns used on the attack on the left (isthmus) and they made poor progress due to the distance from the walls. Graham complained about this on the 26th and 28th,[61] and Wellington ordered a new battery to be constructed. Frazer noted that 'Wellington wisely ordered another and more advanced battery'.[62] This battery had an immediate impact on the wall of the fortress when it opened fire.

A false attack was made on the night of the 29th, to try to get the French to blow any mines they had placed in the defences of the town, but they were not taken in. By the next day, the damage caused by the batteries formed one continuous breach in the walls, and many of the guns were turned to attacking any remaining defensive armament, the intention being to assault the town the following morning at low tide.

The assault was scheduled for 11 a.m. on 30 August. The situation with regard to the perceived lack of effort from the 5th Division in the first assault was resolved to no-one's satisfaction. General Leith, who had returned as commander of the 5th Division on the 27th, refused to have the volunteers lead the assault and they were to be held in reserve, with the 5th Division making the attack. The attack started on time and once again the troops could not get through the breaches due to the fire and defences of the French. The volunteer reserves were also thrown in without effect. An attack was also made across the estuary by the Portuguese but they did not make any better progress. After about an hour, Graham gave the risky order for the siege guns to open fire and sweep the walls and defences of the town over the heads of the attacking troops. Twenty minutes later, when the guns ceased firing, the assault had finally made some progress with the French retreating into the castle. By 2 p.m., the town was in Allied hands, but it was also in ruins and large parts of it were on fire due to the shelling. Following what was now becoming the norm, many of the troops dispersed in an orgy of looting and destruction that took two full days to settle down. During this period, Graham and Wellington were genuinely concerned that if the French made a sortie from the castle, the Allies would be hard-pressed to hold the town. Fortunately, the French were in no fit state to do so.

The Allied guns were now turned on the castle. Beginning on 1 September, they bombarded it for the next six days during which time fires continued to rage through the town. The French governor, Rey, refused another summons on the 3rd, and new batteries were prepared to attack the castle. At 10 a.m. on 8 September, fifty-six guns opened on the castle, which had no shelters for the French or their prisoners. Rey finally accepted the inevitable and raised the white flag around noon.

Casualties during the siege and assault were high, with nearly 2,400 killed and wounded. Engineer casualties were three killed, including Fletcher, and three wounded, including Burgoyne,[63] but his wound was not serious and he temporarily took command of the engineers.[64] Across both sieges, of the eighteen engineer officers present, four were killed and seven were wounded. Captain Stanway was left to repair the fortress with a company of Royal Sappers and Miners, work continuing until six months after the end of the war.

Analysis of the Second Siege of San Sebastian
During both sieges, Wellington was again pushed for time due to the very real threat from Soult, who made two determined attempts to disrupt the siege and the blockade of Pamplona. There is no doubt that there would have been fewer casualties had San Sebastian been besieged according to the established rules, but, as Fletcher pointed out, this would have taken much longer. In both sieges, the time from opening fire to the assault on the town was five days, which only allowed the walls to be breached and did not allow sufficient time to destroy the defenders' artillery and reduce the garrison both physically and morally. Ironically, Wellington had given orders to limit the amount of shellfire so as to reduce the damage to the town, with a consequent reduction in damage to the defenders. Unfortunately the town was pretty much destroyed by fire anyway and Wellington was accused by the Spanish

of deliberately burning the town to the ground as a punishment for the Francophile tendencies of its population. Like the previous three sieges at Ciudad Rodrigo, Badajoz and Burgos, Wellington cut corners to reduce the time required due to external pressures. The impact of the time reduction was measured in the increase in casualties that occurred.

The biggest single criticism of the siege concerned the strategy selected for the attack. It is inconceivable that Wellington was not aware of the risk and costs associated with the plan selected. He wanted the fortress taken quickly to avoid the very real chance that Soult would relieve it. Blaming the engineers for the plan is unreasonable since they were producing plans that met the requirements given to them by Wellington. With hindsight, it may have been better to go for the formal attack, as the twin sieges took nearly two months in total, but that was not known or expected when the first one began. However, the plan agreed by Wellington was to continue the same basic plan of attack for the second siege.[65] The criticism of the engineers, and to a lesser extent the artillery, suggesting that they were indifferent to the casualties in the army, is unfair and ignores the fact that it was usually an engineer officer who was leading these desperate attacks and their casualties reflect this. The high casualties in the besieging army were caused by rushing the sieges and the responsibility for that rests with the commander. This was compounded on the first assault by it taking place before daylight, an action that Wellington had strongly discouraged.

In terms of the operations of the engineers, both sieges were managed reasonably well. There were some problems with the use of short naval 24-pounders (accuracy), the supply of working parties and the distant positioning of some batteries, but nonetheless the breaches were still made very quickly. Neither assault would have been quicker if these events had not occurred, as there were other tasks that had to be completed before the assault could happen. The siege was under the control of Sir Thomas Graham, who corresponded with Wellington daily. In some of these letters, Wellington was personally critical of Fletcher and Dickson, particularly of their demands for working parties.[66] Such criticism must have undermined the credibility of these officers with Graham. Wellington knew Dickson and Fletcher well, trusted them and had worked with them for a number of years, but Graham did not know them and such criticism must have affected his view of their competence. Graham had no experience of commanding at a major siege and his lack of experience cannot have helped the situation.

The availability for the first time of significant numbers of troops from the Royal Sappers and Miners does not appear to have had any material effect. There is a surprising lack of comment on their presence by both engineer and army officers. Harry Jones makes one comment about the lack of training – 'sappers and miners who have never seen a gabion made!'[67] – but this is in a letter complaining about the number of engineer and sappers present at the siege, which is full of errors. Neither John Jones nor Burgoyne made any comment at the time, but it is telling that when Burgoyne was asked to carry out some mining activities between the sieges, he requested volunteers from the line regiments.[68] Though most of the sappers present were troops who had been in the Peninsula for some time, the company that arrived on 15 August was the first to have been through Pasley's School of Military Engineering. Unfortunately, the company did not initially live up to expectations. Writing several weeks later Burgoyne reported:

> On the subject of the Sappers, my complaint lies not to their want of ability but, I am sorry to say, to their irregularities and insubordination . . . Many of them, as individuals, showed ability, spirit and regularity as was highly useful and creditable. They commenced [the second siege of San Sebastian] however by such insubordination, almost amounting to mutiny, and proved in many instances so little trustworthy, disappointing us in the execution of important services, that although many, and perhaps most of them, were very good men, we lost all confidence in them and did not therefore reap much benefit from their employment. . . . I have, since the siege, given the command of this company to Captain Pitts, an active officer who, having them with him, attached to repress their irregularities, and I fully expect that at the next siege they will render us good service and enable the Commanding Engineer to give a more favourable account of them than I feel myself justified doing on this occasion.[69]

A few weeks later, Burgoyne was able to give a more positive report

> I send a further note from Pitts on the latest company from you. I learn from him that they are 'excellent, able, useful and steady', in short, he now has a good military view of them which was all they wanted and he is delighted with them.[70]

The first assault on San Sebastian was a very poor attempt that was never going to succeed, mainly thanks to the bad planning on the day of the assault. The second assault on the town barely succeeded and could very easily have failed also. The pinpoint artillery fire during the second assault just tipped the edge in the attackers' favour. It could easily have gone either way. Again, Wellington was lucky.

The Death of Fletcher

Wrottesley, the biographer of John Burgoyne, recounted a story that Wellington wanted to retain Burgoyne and that was why he did not recall Elphinstone from Lisbon after Fletcher's death.[71] I also think it is likely that Wellington was perfectly happy with Burgoyne commanding the Engineers and was in no hurry for Elphinstone to come up. On 10 September, Burgoyne sent his account of the siege direct to London saying 'which I transmit to you direct to avoid any circuitous route by Lisbon through Lieutenant Colonel Elphinstone, which I trust will meet with your approbation'.[72] Elphinstone would have been extremely unhappy about this. Fletcher had led the Royal Engineers for most of the war but he never managed to create any real sense of loyalty in his subordinates. John Jones wrote:

> Sir Richard Fletcher possessed in an unusual degree, the knowledge and accomplishments of a finished soldier . . . but these valuable qualities were . . . almost paralysed, by what in military language is called a deficiency of moral courage, or in other words, being too sensitive to the awful responsibility of risking human life, and being . . . distrustful of his own judgement to plan or direct any unusually bold or hazardous enterprise. He also had the military weakness of being far too honest and conscientious to support or advise any . . . undertaking of his chief, which his military judgement did not approve.[73]

He went on to say he believed Wellington blamed Fletcher for the heavy casualties at the third siege of Badajoz due to him recommending a day's delay in the assault. He also said that Fletcher was strongly opposed to the plan for the siege of San Sebastian and arguing against it further set Wellington against him. Elphinstone, not the most reliable of sources, writing in 1813 stated that three of the senior engineers 'Goldfinch, Burgoyne and Boteler do not speak to Fletcher',[74] and Burgoyne, writing after Fletcher's death, said: 'Poor Sir Richard had no arrangement whatever, any system or improvement recommended to him, he would highly approve of, but never acted upon it.'[75]

Burgoyne had not been mentioned in Wellington's dispatch after the siege of Ciudad Rodrigo, an error which led to him not receiving brevet promotion, while two junior engineer officers did. In the nineteenth century there was nowhere to get news other than the official dispatches. If you were not mentioned then you had done nothing remarkable. Even worse in this case, two of Burgoyne's juniors were mentioned, so people might have thought that Burgoyne was being deliberately snubbed due to some failure. It was corrected a few months later but Burgoyne was very angry about it.

Whilst there was some criticism of Fletcher, I believe that Wellington was not unhappy with him. When compared with the way he treated the senior artillery officers during this period it is safe to assume that Wellington could have made life very difficult for Fletcher if he did not want him. Whilst not a dynamic leader, Fletcher showed great competence in co-ordinating the various wide-spread activities of his officers and managing the difficult boundary between the Army and the Ordnance. Wellington's anger and frustration at the sieges clearly boiled over into highly critical letters home, but that is different from believing the engineer officers with him were at fault. As Wellington was to find out, Fletcher's successor was not an improvement.

Elphinstone arrived unannounced at headquarters at Vera on 13 October, 'so that they were rather surprised at seeing me' he said.[76] The following day he dined with Wellington and wrote:

> The dinner went off exceedingly well and I now consider myself completely fixed. I therefore send you a list of articles for the canteen. I must keep a table, therefore it is nonsense buying trumpery articles. Indeed considering my pay and station it would be mean and paltry not to do so.

Two days later, he wrote to his wife:

> The conduct of the officers of the Corps has been most gratifying to me, indeed Burgoyne wrote to me to say that if Wellington attempted to give him the command, upon his present commission, he would refuse it . . . My coming up will I fancy make some little bustle at Woolwich, as Ld W. has sent away two Lt. Col's and put Dickens [sic – Dickson] in command upon his brevet rank over the heads of four senior officers in the country, all of whom are mean enough to remain and serve under him.[77]

Elphinstone was of course referring to the ongoing controversy over the appointment of Dickson to command the artillery. Wellington had made life so difficult for Dickson's superiors that one after another they had resigned. There were still artillery officers senior to Dickson in the Peninsula, but Wellington made sure they did not come anywhere near his army. Elphinstone half expected that he was going to receive the same treatment to allow Burgoyne to continue in command with Wellington's forces.

Howard Elphinstone, like Fletcher, had operational experience that equipped him for this role. The son of Admiral John Elphinstone, he had been commissioned in October 1793. His first active service was at the capture of the Cape of Good Hope in 1795 after which he served in India for the next five years. In 1801 he accompanied the division sent from India to Egypt under Sir David Baird, arriving in Egypt in August 1801 after which he returned to the UK serving at Plymouth. In 1806 Captain Elphinstone was attached to Lord Rosslyn and General Simcoe's special mission to Portugal, to advise the Portuguese government on the defence of Lisbon. In early 1807 he accompanied Major-General Whitelocke to South America as Commanding Royal Engineer, but he never landed in South America, arriving after the expedition had failed. By the time he landed back in the UK he had spent a year on board the fleet. He was then assigned to command the proposed South American expedition under Sir Arthur Wellesley, and when this was diverted to the Peninsula, he travelled with it.

Clearly Elphinstone knew that his coming to HQ was not going to be universally welcomed. It is also clear where his priorities were. Most of his letters home during this period focus on getting the appropriate uniform, stable and canteen for an officer of his station. What is interesting is that there is almost no correspondence between Elphinstone and his subordinates, the Army and the Ordnance. Apart from his letters to his wife, it is as if he never existed. The few letters home are complaints about allowances, refusal to appoint a bridge master and engineer officers not getting medals when he thought they should (including himself). He even records being officially 'encouraged' to write home more but making it clear he had no intention of.

The impact of the change of command quickly became apparent. Captain Stanway, who had been left to repair San Sebastian, wrote to Burgoyne two weeks after Elphinstone's arrival saying: 'I can get nothing from Colonel Elphinstone neither men nor authorities for the Alcades, so that I shall give it up as a hopeless job . . . If you have any interest with Col. E. pray get him to represent my want of men.'[78] Other engineer officers were making similar comments: 'Now that Sir Richard is dead we have found out his value and I fear we shall not soon see his place as ably filled.'[79]

Elphinstone seemed to delight in fighting with everyone, including the Board of Ordnance, his fellow officers and even Wellington. Whilst there was friction between the generals and some Ordnance officers, there was generally a good working relationship between engineer officers and the senior commanders. One example is demonstrated by a request from Burgoyne to General Cole to write a testimonial for Lieutenant Pitts after the siege was completed. Cole responded:

I enclose a letter you required respecting your friend Pitts . . . and have done it so as to appear as if it came from myself without the suggestion of others. Independent of my regard for Pitts, I shall feel great pleasure at all times in doing justice to a corps throughout the younger branches of which there is a spirit that no other corps I know of possesses to the same degree.[80]

Actions on the French Border
Whilst the siege of San Sebastian was still underway, Wellington was looking ahead to the next steps. Following Soult's failed attacks at Maya, Roncesvalles and Sorauren, he considered pursuing the French straight across the Bidassoa. On 1 August 1813, Wellington asked Graham to bring up the pontoon train and prepare for the crossing of the Bidassoa.[81] But he quickly went off the idea when he took stock of his losses and the condition of his troops and equipment. Explaining his decision to Bathurst, he wrote:

> It is a very common error, among those unacquainted with military affairs . . . that we shall immediately invade France; and some even here expect that we shall be in Paris in a month . . . the enemy still possesses all the strongholds within Spain [the border fortresses] . . . Then in France . . . there are other strongholds . . . [The] army . . . is much deteriorated . . . the equipment, ammunition, shoes etc. require renewal. I entertain no doubt that I could tomorrow enter France and establish the army on the Adour, but I could go no further.[82]

Wellington realised that securing his current position should be his priority. Major Charles Smith RE was ordered to Irun to make proposals for fortifying the place. Captain Todd RSC was similarly ordered to the area to survey the terrain. Wellington wrote to Graham on 15 August, in response to his recommendation to start a second line of defences behind the Bidassoa, remarking 'we cannot make the position between Oyarzun and the Bidassoa too strong . . . no time should be lost in commencing the works'. On 21 August, Wellington wrote a detailed memo to Fletcher detailing the defensive works he wanted constructing around Irun. The first line would cover the site of the bridge at Irun through to the convent at San Marcial. It comprised three redoubts and 'breastworks, abatis and musketry posts which the troops on the ground can construct'. Wellington said Captain Todd RSC would point out the locations. A second line would also be prepared overlooking the Bidassoa, which Major Smith RE could point out the locations for. Between Irun and Funterrabia, a third set of defences was to be constructed with a fourth set in the valley of the Bidassoa between Irun and Oyarzun.[83] Wellington asked Fletcher to mark out the works and estimate the number of workers he would require. The following day Fletcher received a similarly detailed letter from George Murray, the QMG, confirming that the instructions were based on Wellington riding over part of the terrain with Captain Todd and also from the surveys carried out by Major Smith. Murray asked Fletcher if he could ride over the terrain and 'exercise your judgement both as to the situation and the form of the works to be constructed'. He expressed the concern that this might not be possible owing to the wound Fletcher had recently received during the first assault at San Sebastian. Murray clarified the purpose of the defences in his final paragraph:

> Our first object by these works is present security, until we can get possession of San Sebastian and Pamplona, But besides that, we should look forward to rendering a part of our force disposable for operations more to the eastward, if necessary; also securing tranquillity in the winter and even to something of permanent utility to the Spanish frontier. Our offensive operations have turned out very well, but we have not yet such firm hold of our conquests as we ought to have.[84]

Significant defensive works were also being constructed in the passes to the east. Lieutenant Pitts RE, who was present with the 4th Division during the French attacks at the end of July, was ordered to construct a number of redoubts and breastworks around Maya. Writing to Burgoyne on 25 August, he reported that Wellington had sent for him and asked him to make some changes to the defences that he had already completed.[85] As mentioned earlier, Lieutenant Wright RE was ordered to construct similar defences at Roncesvalles. Work on improving the defences in this area continued through to October 1813.

By the end of August, the Allied army's situation had improved significantly. San Sebastian had finally fallen. A final desperate attack by Soult at San Marcial on the 31st failed, in part due to the substantial defensive works that had been prepared over the last few weeks. Pamplona still held out, but the Allies were getting information on its state of supplies and knew the fortress could not last much longer. Wellington was sure that the French were unable to breach his defences and could look to his next move.

On 9 September, the day the castle at San Sebastian surrendered, he wrote to Graham ordering the officer in charge of the engineer department to do two things:

> The pontoon train must be got together, with the exception of those boats absolutely necessary for the communication with San Sebastian, and the train should be assembled somewhere near Oyarzun.
>
> He must immediately take measures for securing the place [San Sebastian] against a *coup de main*, by clearing the rubbish and blocking the breaches and he must let me have without loss of time, a plan and estimate for the repair of the place.[86]

Wellington mentions Dickson, the commander of the artillery, by name in the letter but refers to 'the officer in charge of the engineer department'. Wellington was fully aware that Burgoyne was the senior engineer so the omission of his name is odd in the context of what happened next. On 17 September, Wellington, with great anger, complained to Graham that:

> Lieutenant-Colonel Burgoyne is really too bad: this is the eighth day since he received the orders to collect the pontoon train on the high road and he is not now certain that the orders he sent have reached the officers in charge of them, and he has taken no measures to repeat them.[87]

On the same day, Burgoyne received a letter from the Adjutant General asking for an immediate detailed explanation of how he sent his orders for the movement of the pontoon train and asking for an officer to ride post to Vitoria to order the pontoon train forward. Two days later, Wellington was still angry, telling Bathurst that he had intended to move the army across the Bidassoa immediately after the fall of San Sebastian but it had 'been delayed by a mistake made by the officer of engineers in transmitting the orders for the collection of the pontoon train'. He continued saying 'But I acknowledge I feel a great disinclination to enter the French territory under existing circumstances'.[88]

Wellington's letters around this time have an even greater level of sharpness than was usual for him. One wonders if the pressure was beginning to tell. He was trying to deal with a number of events that could or were impacting on his operations. These included:

- The failure of Royal Navy to blockade the northern coast leading to difficulties for his supplies and the regular supply of the French forces.
- The continued resistance of the French in Pamplona and San Sebastian.
- Murray's mismanagement at Tarragona.
- The delays in the Board of Ordnance supplying additional siege guns.
- The continued issues with the Spanish government over command of their army.

- Concern about the reaction of the French population when he invaded France.
- Concern about how the Portuguese and Spanish troops would treat the French population.
- Concern about what the European powers were planning around the invasion of France.

Wellington's complaint about Burgoyne does not ring true. Nothing done by that officer before or after this incident fits the unprofessional picture painted by Wellington. Burgoyne's diary is strangely silent from 10 September, when the castle at San Sebastian surrendered, until the 27th. The inference is that he was working on the damage at San Sebastian as his diary entry for the 27th notes him completing his report on the repairs of San Sebastian and setting off for headquarters.[89] Wellington must have had some knowledge that the pontoon train could not be moved immediately as he noted in a letter to his brother on 12 September, 'I am waiting here till the animals of the pontoon train will be relieved from the work consequent on the siege, when I shall cross the Bidassoa'.[90] Again, on 15 September, he asked Graham to let him know when the pontoon train was likely to be on the road with its equipment. Looking at Wellington's original letter of 9 September, the priority of repairing San Sebastian is clear, the movement of the pontoon train less so.

On 15 September, Captain Stanway RE delivered a report on the options for crossing the river Bidassoa in front of the height of San Marcial. The same day Wellington rode over the area with an engineer officer (Stanway, I assume) pointing out where he wanted further redoubts building to support the planned crossing. Wellington was planning on the initial advance being carried out by infantry fording the mouth of the Bidassoa. This was only possible at the lowest tides which were around 23 September. Finding the pontoon train was not going to arrive in time for the fording of the river probably led to his show of impatience.

I expect that Burgoyne got distracted working to make San Sebastian defensible and, having passed the order for the pontoon train to move, lost sight of what appeared to be a secondary task. It is also clear that Graham had done nothing to check on the situation even though the orders had been sent to him. Everyone had taken their eye off the ball. It unlike Wellington to miss an important detail like this. Perhaps, it suited him to have someone to blame for the delay in entering France? The next low tide was around 9 October 1813 and Wellington planned to be ready.[91]

Chapter 9

1813–14 – Into France

In the days leading up to 7 October 1813, Wellington tried with evident success to convince the French that his attack, when it came, would be inland, probably around Maya. Soult therefore placed the bulk of his troops in this area, leaving the mouth of the Bidassoa virtually undefended, believing that the river was not fordable. Unfortunately for the French, Wellington knew that it was, thanks to the help of local fishermen. The French had heavily fortified the right bank of the river and their troops were spread over many miles, manning various redoubt and forts. The defences looked impressive but Wellington was confident they could be taken, saying to Captain Harry Smith of the 95th Foot 'These fellows think themselves invulnerable, but I will beat them out with great ease'.[1] He went on to explain that they did not have enough troops to hold their position. On the morning of 7 October, the attacks were launched. The two main attacks were at the mouth of the Bidassoa and against Vera. Captain Todd RSC, who had been surveying the area for some weeks, was with the attackers fording the river, no doubt guiding them to the fords. Other RSC officers carried out similar roles at the several fords used to get the troops across. As predicted, Wellington was able to outflank and overwhelm the enemy.

Two days later the whole area was in Allied hands and Soult had withdrawn his demoralised troops across the next barrier, the river Nivelle. As soon as the right bank was secured, work started on laying the bridges. Wellington's orders for the attack stated:

> A pontoon bridge is to be thrown across the river near the ruined bridge [at Irun] as soon as it is possible to establish it. To cover its construction and the passage of the troops, the 18-pounder battery and two other batteries are to be placed on the San Marcial heights.[2]

Apart from the number of guns, the 18-pounders would have greater range than anything the French could bring up to try and disrupt the operation. Wellington's orders also specified a second pontoon bridge further up the river. Burgoyne noted 'we commenced throwing bridges of trestles, boats, pontoons, etc. over the Bidassoa'.[3] Frazer also wrote that by 10 October there were two pontoon bridges and a third bridge of boats in place. As well as the bridges, new redoubts were started on the right bank. This was the first occasion where a substantial number of Pasley's trained Royal Sappers and Miners (RSM) were present. Some worked under Lieutenant Piper RE to throw the pontoon bridges across the river at Irun, while another company under Captain Dickens RE built a trestle bridge further upstream. Although these bridges were washed away by the strong current, they were speedily restored. Captain Wells RE was building defences on the Bidassoa, General Hope reporting that working parties had been assigned to him and asked if Burgoyne could look at the ground around the pontoon bridge as he thought 'that several considerable works may be necessary'.[4] Further east, Captain Pitts RE with another company of RSM quickly erected breastworks at Vera and then proceeded to build several redoubts around La Rhune. Further east again, Lieutenant Wright RE was erecting defences around Roncesvalles. The work done by the Royal Engineers, Royal Staff Corps and Royal Sappers and Miners is often difficult to identify, but these corps made a significant contribution to strengthening the defences to resist French attacks, then in getting the army across the Bidassoa and then building further defences to allow Wellington to retain his toe-hold in France.

For the first time in the Peninsular War there were now sufficient artificers from the RSM to attach companies to divisions in the army. For the next few months they lived and fought with the soldiers and after a shaky start, appreciation of their value grew, Reid, who commanded the company with the Light Division, remarking 'the arrangement seems to answer. My Company was taken away the other day, which put all the division in a rage. Sappers are thought absolutely necessary now.' A few weeks later, Reid commented again, that 'Baron Alten got in a rage and wanted to write to Wellington' when the divisional entrenching tools were taken away.[5]

For the next few weeks Wellington waited for the surrender of Pamplona and for news from northern Europe. Following a request from Sir John Hope, Captain Todd RSC was employed to improve the roads around Vera to aid troop movements. As mentioned earlier, there was change of command in the Royal Engineers. Elphinstone returned to headquarters on 13 October and Burgoyne was speedily reassigned to Sir John Hope's force. Elphinstone, having arrived by sea, needed to settle himself in. Writing to his wife he said:

Hitherto I get on famously with Lord W., but he is said to be so violent and capricious that it is impossible for any one to say how long the civility may continue. It was decidedly his wish that I should come up [I do not believe this is true] and I think he is pleased with my coming up as I have done without any regard to my personal comfort . . . I have purchased a mare . . . for the enormous price of 80 guineas . . . In England I should not have paid above 40 for her. I have also purchased a mule for 130 dollars . . . Ellicombe and myself dine with each other alternately, each party bringing their own plates, knives and forks, as always living with Fletcher he is as badly of for canteen, cook etc. as myself. I shall be very glad to get my new canteens . . . I am told my coming up is already making a row in the artillery – there certainly will be a breeze, whether I shall stand the squall or not remains to be proved. I heard rather a moderate man say he thought if any officer senior to Dixon [*sic*, Dickens] remained to serve under him after my coming up they ought to be sent to Coventry by the regiment.[6]

Following the surrender of Pamplona on 31 October, Wellington was free to act. The Allies had superiority in numbers and probably also in the quality of their troops. The next challenge was to pass the river Nivelle. Following the French withdrawal, Soult has set his troops to work building a set of defences on the banks of that river, similar to those that had failed to work on the Bidassoa. The natural defences of the area also assisted the French. Heavy rain and snow now fell and the river levels rose, making crossing difficult, if not impossible. Hope was concerned that the bridges across the Bidassoa could be lost. He wrote to Wellington on 1 November:

> We have had torrents of rain last night and it has just been reported to me that the upper bridge, constructed, I believe, by the Portuguese, has been carried away, and that they are in some apprehension the coming down of the materials and other matters carried by the river may injure the Spanish bridge. Burgoyne and Todd are, however, doing what they can to secure it, as well as our pontoon bridge.

Writing again the next morning, he reported 'I found that a premature report had been made respecting the trestle bridge above Biriatou, which, though in danger, was not carried away.'[7] There are a number of interesting points in this letter. Firstly, the Royal Engineers and Royal Staff Corps are once again mixing roles as circumstances required. Secondly, Hope mentions both the Portuguese and Spanish as having a role in the construction of the bridges. Burgoyne had mentioned some weeks earlier that there was a company of Portuguese artificers with engineer officers at San Sebastian. The same day that Hope wrote the letter above, Wellington remarked that 'Hill, however, being up to his knees in snow, it is absolutely necessary to defer our movement for a day or two'. The weather continued poor and Wellington had to postpone an attack that was planned for 8 November, which was re-scheduled for the 10th. Hope carried out feint attacks around the mouth of the Nivelle at St Jean de Luz, Hill similarly demonstrated around Ainhoue and Beresford made the main attack around Sarre.

The outnumbered and demoralised French put up only limited resistance before once again retiring to the next barrier, the river Nive, and the city of Bayonne. As the French retired from St Jean de Luz on the morning of 11 November, the Allies quickly moved into the town, Burgoyne recording that 'the bridges . . . were burning but saved them before much mischief was done'.[8] Hope reported the next day that Captain Todd was repairing the bridges at St Jean de Luz and having moved forward to Guethary, noted on the 13th that 'a pontoon bridge has been established across the stream of Bidart'.[9] As Burgoyne was with him, it is likely that he was involved in its construction. Wellington agreed with the need to have the pontoon bridge because a means to move artillery across the river would be the 'best defence for our posts towards the Nive', but cautioned that the bridge should be able to be quickly removed.[10] A third bridge had been built across the Nivelle at Sarre by the company of RSM under Captain Pitts. The trestle bridge had been constructed using material taken from a local farmhouse.[11] Pitts, describing the action around Sarre, mentions around thirty redoubts built by the French to defend the area.[12] Elphinstone also recorded the events of the last few days in a letter to his wife:

> Good news and I am quite safe and well. Having stated above what is of most consequence to you I shall now add an outline of our proceedings, that is such part of them that I happened to see. On the 10th at 3am I left Vera and went to the advance post where I knew the attack was to commence. Lord Wellington arrived soon after and as soon as it was light, a cannonade commenced on the advance redoubt of the enemy . . . the gentlemen not approving much of the effects of our artillery, saved us the trouble by taking to their heels . . . The works were also deserted one after another except one which was the largest and most formidable. This Lord Wellington continued to surround most completely that an officer was sent to advise them to lay down their arms . . . They then retreated across the Nivelle in such a hurry that they had not time to destroy the

bridges. Our people followed them and got into the village of St Pé ... It was at this place that I regret to say Mr Power [Lieutenant Robert Power RE] was killed ... It is the only casualty in the Corps ... we set off to return to Vera at least 3 leagues off, and where we arrived at half past eight o'clock. The ride home was altogether the worst part of the day. It was so dark that they rode with a torch before Lord Wellington to show him the way and we were obliged to follow trusting entirely to our horses ... Except a few shots from the first redoubt, the Head Quarters party were never nearer than a mile to the enemy, so that it was nothing more than being at a review. I took out plenty of toast and hard eggs so that I had nothing to do but munch all day. What a fortunate thing it has now been my coming round by water.[13]

I am sure his engineer officers would have been happy to have nothing to do but munch all day! The Allied army's communications were now divided by two major rivers and the next few weeks was a constant battle to keeping the bridges in place as the winter torrents battered them and trying to move bulky pontoon trains on near-impassable roads.

Once again the Allied army settled themselves in to guarding the crossing-points over the Nivelle. The French destroyed their bridge and *tête du pont* at Cambo on 17 November and Colville reported that he had ordered Captain Henderson RE to strengthen his piquet defences around Ustaritz to be able to withstand field artillery. Whilst Wellington was keen to press on, the weather made any rapid movement impossible and there was a lull as all the equipment and material was moved into place.

The final action of 1813 was the passage of the river Nive. Wellington wanted to expand the area his troops occupied but also restrict the ability of the French to supply Bayonne. If he could place his troops on the left bank of the Adour, the French could not use the river to bring in supplies. Once again, Wellington decided on three simultaneous attacks. The first column under Hope was to advance up the coast from St Jean de Luz. As part of his advance, Hope was asked to push on to the mouth of the Adour to reconnoitre for the 'possibility of a bridge being thrown over the river there in some future operations of the army'.[14] Inland, Beresford was to attack in the centre at Ustaritz where the plan was to capture the bridges and if required to thrown pontoon bridges across. Further east, Hill was to attack at Cambo, again with the intention of throwing a bridge across. Detachments of Royal Sappers and Miners and Royal Staff Corps were attached to each of these columns.

The pontoon train was moved up and a pontoon bridge thrown across the Nive at Ustaritz in the early hours of 9 December. Burgoyne, describing the situation a few days' earlier, wrote:

> Five pontoons have been ordered to Ustaritz, to throw a bridge across the Nive, where an island to which we have access, makes it very narrow ... There is great difficulty however to get pontoons to the spot, on account of the state of the roads and the heavy rains that have now recommenced; two days of them will probably increase the Nive and stop the operation.[15]

Early that night, the pontoon train was laid from the left bank to the island and in the morning the troops forded the river to the right bank. Once secure, the final part of the bridge from the island to the right bank was completed.

At the same time, Hill forded the river at Cambo with the intention of re-establishing the bridge once the right bank was secure. Burgoyne praised the inventiveness of Sub-Lieutenant Calder RSM:

> A bridge was to be made over the Nive above Cambo. It was there 90 feet wide with low banks frequently inundated. – Goldfinch asked Mr Calder if he would undertake it with a few Sappers and some rough carpenters tools only – he said he would – well how will you do it? – why, I'll cut a large mallet and drive a few piles.[16]

Both these crossing were achieved with surprisingly little opposition. Wellington's army was now split on both sides of the river Nive with lengthy communications between them. This appears to be what Soult had hoped for, and on successive days he attacked each formation separately. The first attack against Hope seems to have been unexpected and there was hard fighting before the French retreated. The following day, Soult moved his forces back through Bayonne and attacked Hill on the right bank of the Nive. Soult's superior forces came very close to defeating Hill before reinforcements could arrive. The Allied situation was made more critical by the pontoon bridge at Villefranque being washed away and it was after noon on that day before it was repaired and reinforcements could move to support Hill.

Whilst these actions were taking place, the engineering services raced to stabilise the crossings across the river. Beresford reported to Wellington on 11 November that the pontoon bridge had not been completed the previous night and was still liable to be swamped by the rising river. Consequently, the bridge of boats that had also been thrown across the river could not be moved downstream to the preferred position at Villefranque.

This work was under the command of Captain Henderson who had been in the area for a number of weeks and consequently knew it well. Henderson had recovered his reputation with Wellington after being removed from the repairs at Badajoz in late 1812, partly through his conspicuous gallantry at the siege of San Sebastian. The following day, Beresford was more confident but reported the bridges were still not exactly where he wanted them due to a lack of materials and anchors (to hold the pontoons in place against the fast-flowing rivers). He expected to improve them in the following days. Wellington was keen to get the main bridge at Ustaritz repaired as soon as possible so that these pontoons could be removed and placed in reserve for any new opportunity. Burgoyne recorded on 12 December that three bridges were in place at Herraritz, Ustaritz and Cambo. Anton, who served with the 42nd Foot, noted that 'our artificers lost no time in making the necessary repairs [to the wooden bridge] for the passage of troops and stores'.[17] Frazer also noted that 'troops were filing over' the bridge at Cambo 'which had been hastily and inexpertly repaired'.[18]

As before, once the situation stabilised, the Allied troops dug in. Cole was ordered to dam some tributaries on the Nive and construct breastworks and redoubts to strengthen his front, the main works to be at Garat's House.[19] The QMG also noted when issuing the orders that Cole would have to do his best as his company of RSM had been removed to work on the bridges. Other engineer officers continued to serve on the general's staff, Lieutenant Peter Wright noting that 'he had been drawing all day for Sir Rowland [Hill]'.[20]

Following these engagements, the army went into cantonments through the worst of the winter, but the work of the engineers continued. Elphinstone was engaged in fortifying the area around the mouth of the Bidassoa as the river was to be used to supply the army and more importantly to deny it to the French. Keeping the various bridges in place was a constant challenge due to the bad weather and the torrents coming down the rivers, Frazer noting on 23 December that all the bridges across the Nive had been washed away but would soon be restored. Captain Wells RE had also been dispatched to Santona to assist the Spanish forces that were blockading the port.

Writing to his brother, Lieutenant Harry Jones gave some idea of the internal politics of the Corps under its new commander:

> Oh what a difference in the spirit of our undertaking compared with the time of your Sir R. Fletcher. At the present while my division is busy strengthening its front by field works, he [Fletcher] would have been constantly moving about and giving every assistance

required; whereas I suppose Col. Elphinstone does not go around the line once in a fortnight and when he does he is so much in a hurry and is so near sighted that he retains very little more than when he left his house. Ellicombe, upon the strength of Lord Wellington's answer to Sir R. Fletcher when he recommended him for Brigade Major; still keeps the situation, very much to the annoyance of E————e who wishes to have Boteler and is always complaining of it. Ellicombe told him; unless he ordered him to give up the situation he should not do it.[21]

Elphinstone himself had little good to say about anyone. He had waited anxiously to see if he would be mentioned in dispatches for the crossing of the Nive and was disappointed when he was not:

I am not seriously disappointed at not being mentioned, but he mentions the bridges and the attack on the Chateau D'Arcangues – therefore according to the old proverb he might have praised the bridge that carried him over . . . I send home by this pacquet a very fine military sketch of the position, to General Mann, but [I am] afraid it will be putting pearls before swine.

Having had a bit more time to think about it, he wrote home again:

I am not aware upon what occasion Lord Wellington can have said anything in my favour, but I assure you that he is so uncertain and violent with everybody that you are not certain for five minutes of retaining his good opinion. The only person I know of to compare him to in character is Dfezzan Pasha who had always his ante-room filled with people without noses or ears whom he called his marked men. I firmly believe that he sighs for the same power – a peace is necessary if it is only to put an end to his over grown power and dissolve this army, which is a complete mass of corruption.[22]

Probably his most unpleasant comment was to his wife in January 1814, when he wrote: 'Don't you set fire to yourself as poor Dickson's wife has done – though I don't know that he would have been very sorry if it had not been put out. It is not being very charitable you will say.' The only good point about this uncharitable comment is that for the first time he spells Dickson's name correctly. Dickson's wife had been involved in an accident in December 1813 and Dickson was receiving updates from the Royal Artillery headquarters on her condition and the care of his children.[23]

In the days leading up to the crossing of the Adour, Elphinstone described his relationship with Wellington and his position in the army:

> I assure you I now fair sumptuously every day, and as it happens at present that I am obliged to see a great many people having even Naval officers under my orders; my splendour has its effect. I have had two or three most extraordinary rows with the Peer [i.e. Wellington], but I believe I have come off the victor. The first arose from his being obliged to dismount his artillery to furnish horses for the pontoon train. He was perfectly furious and like a mad man; however I gave up no one point to him, and he personally asked me to dine with him the next day. The next day following he sent for me and took all the platforms we had, to make a bridge across the Adour by the Staff Corps. However, two days after, I received a letter from General Murray to desire I would make the bridge and that the Staff Corps were to be under my orders. Now that he finds he cannot get the better of me by argument he makes me report to him twice a day the progress of the work. It is really quite ridiculous to see us together; he tries all he can to get me to make him promises as to time and I as resolutely refuse it. I told him plainly yesterday [12 February 1813] I would not deceive him, and that I had no one ground upon which I could say when our preparations would be ready. You may depend upon it I am doing right.

Whether he was right or wrong, his behaviour would not have been appreciated by Wellington. Bridges and pontoons would remain a source of tension until the end of the war.

The Bridging of the Adour
The campaign of 1814 began in February with Wellington pushing east and forcing the French defenders back from the rivers Bidouse and Saisson to the Gave D'Oloron. He left Elphinstone and Burgoyne at Bayonne to organise the blockade and siege, taking Lieutenant Colonel Goldfinch with him. Having firmly attracted Soult's attention to his left, Hope now started the crossing of the mouth of the Adour on Soult's right on 23 February. The plan was to put a pontoon bridge in place as a temporary measure, whilst much larger coastal vessels were moved into place to form a more substantial bridge.

However, on the morning of the 23rd it was discovered that it was impossible to move the heavy pontoon carriages over the sand on the banks of the Adour. Larpent recalled that 'Elphinstone had been quite in despair;

the pontoon car sunk so much in the sand, that at last thirty horses would not move them, and for the last five hundred yards they were conveyed on the shoulders of Guardsmen, twenty-six men to a pontoon.'[24]

Even more worryingly, the Navy reported that they could not get their vessels up the river due to the turbulent water over the bar at its mouth. A small number of troops were ferried across in boats, which, due to the speed and ferocity of the current, was slow and very dangerous, Hope writing to Wellington recognised the risk he was taking in leaving his troops open to a counter-attack but thought 'as the object is desirable, I have determined to persevere'.[25] Fortunately for Hope, there was no serious attempt by the French to resist the crossing. Even the following day it was found that the ferries could only be used when the tidal flow was at its lowest, but by the end of the day the bridgehead was large enough to defend itself. Writing that evening, Admiral Penrose reported that attempts earlier that day to cross the sandbar had failed. However, understanding the urgency, he pushed for attempts to continue and by the evening most of the boats were across but not without the loss of several of them.[26] To keep the French off, both troops and gunboats, four Allied gunboats had managed to get across the sandbar and Wellington's 18-pounder battery was also in place at the bridgehead. By 25 February, Hope had 5,000 troops across and moved off towards the suburbs of Bayonne to keep the French away. He reported to Wellington that 'every preparation is making for laying down the bridge, and boom, and the former it is hoped will be ready by tomorrow night. It is impossible for me to express adequately my sense of the exertions of the officers of the navy on this occasion.'[27] Amazingly, this large construction was complete and passing troops on the morning of the 27th. The crossing of the Adour was a major engineering challenge.

It was also a rare example of good inter-service co-operation, involving Army, Engineer, Staff Corps, Navy and civilian personnel. Wellington had written to Admiral Penrose, the commander of the Royal Navy squadron off the mouth of the Adour on 7 February, informing him of his plan and asking for his support to collect the necessary boats which he described as being 'from 15 to 30 tons, two masted . . . to be anchored by head and stern . . . I propose to lay cables across these vessels from bank to bank'.[28] Wellington asked for forty boats to be collected. The letter was hand delivered by Captain Todd RSC 'who will explain to you the want of a few blocks'. By blocks, Wellington meant pulleys and capstans to tighten up the cables. The boom mentioned above was to protect the bridge from anything that the French might send down the river to try and cause damage. Each boat used in the bridge had modifications made to allow the passing of the five cables across the decks. On one bank of the Adour, the cables were

The bridge over the Adour, by Batty.

fastened by affixing them to several large siege cannon, while on the other bank, the cables were tensioned using a pulley system. There is little doubt that the bridge design came from Henry Sturgeon of the RSC, there being similarities with his innovative designs used to repair the bridges at Alcantara and Almaraz in 1812. There is also no doubt that Captain Todd RSC was present in the background through the planning and construction.

Several engineer officers were engaged in placing the boat bridge. Captain Slade and Lieutenants Savage, West, Robe and Rivers commanded each division of boats. Lieutenant Reid secured the ropes on one bank and Lieutenant Melhuish secured and tightened them on the other. Admiral Penrose recognised their contribution:

> That so many Chasse-Marées ventured the experiment [passing the sandbar] I attribute to there being one of more Sappers being placed in each of them, and a Captain and eight Lieutenants of engineers commanding them in divisions. The zeal and science of these officers triumphed over the difficulties of the navigation.[29]

General Graham, reporting the successful bridging operation, wrote: 'I am bound to mention to your lordship Lieutenant-Colonel Elphinstone for the arrangements he made, and Lieutenant-Colonels Burgoyne and Sturgeon, and the officers employed under them, for the zeal with which they executed his orders.' Burgoyne also made special mention in his reports of the efforts of Lieutenant Tapp and a company of Portuguese pontooneers who had been with the pontoon train for many months. The bridge of boats remained in place until the end of the war. Jones noting that 'it was never broken or injured by the action of the water. It however met with several accidents from vessels but which by the activity of Major Todd, who was left in charge of the infrastructure, were instantaneously remedied.'[30]

Holding both sides of the river Adour now allowed a complete blockade of Bayonne and this allowed Elphinstone's engineers to start preparations for the siege. On 25 February Wellington had ordered a survey to be made of the Citadel at Bayonne 'with a view to an attack upon it'. He also asked for two redoubts to be constructed immediately to cover the exit from the entrenched works around the city. Elphinstone's initial report did not satisfy Wellington, who wrote 'it does not give much information, It is desirable to know what quantity of ordnance he will require, and of what description, and to have a general plan according to which he proposed that this place should be attacked.'[31] An updated report was sent to him on 4 March.[32] We will come back to Bayonne shortly.

Wellington now ordered Marshal Beresford to push north towards Bordeaux, having received a deputation saying the town was willing to surrender. Beresford arrived on 12 March and the town declared for the French King. Unfortunately, the Allies could not access the port or the river Garonne as troops loyal to Napoleon continued to hold the forts at the mouth of the river. On 24 February, Wellington continued his push east across the Gave d'Oloron. Whilst frontal attacks by Beresford and Picton kept the French busy, Hill constructed a pontoon bridge at Viellanave and once again outflanked the French, who retired towards Orthez. Another promising engineer officer, Captain Thomas Pitts, was killed the day before whilst reconnoitring the place to build the pontoon bridge.[33] On the 25th, Wellington asked for boats to be sent up the river Adour to make a bridge at Port de Lanne, mid-way between Bayonne and Orthez, to improve his communications as he moved east. The next day he also asked for the twelve pontoons with Hope to be moved to the same place 'as now that your bridge is laid . . . you have probably no further use for them'. The pontoon train was again in action a few days later, placing a bridge across the Gave de Pau at Berenx, north-west of Orthez. Other pontoons were with Hill in case they were needed.

Another close-fought battle on 27 February at Orthez saw Soult pushed back, but only after inflicting serious losses on Wellington. The engineers suffered another loss to their numbers when Captain Edward Parker was killed whilst acting as an extra ADC to General Picton during the battle. Picton recorded that he was 'killed by a cannon shot within a few yards of me'.[34] Both sides now halted to regroup, with the French holding the line of the Adour at St Sever for several days. It was raining heavily in the first few days of March and Soult had destroyed all the bridges. Wellington told Bathurst that 'that the river is so rapid that the pontoons cannot be laid across it'.[35] Several days later he says the rise in the rivers had made repair of the bridges nearly impossible and as the various columns of his army could not communicate easily, he remained where he was.

The weather having improved, on 18 March Wellington moved east again and came into contact with the French at Tarbes, who fought a rearguard action to allow the bulk of their forces to retreat, and then headed towards the great French city of Toulouse. Wellington followed slowly, reporting on 26 March that he was two leagues from the city. He was still concerned about the state of the rivers, remarking that 'the Garonne is too full and large for our bridge'.[36]

On 27 March, an attempt was made to cross the Garonne near Portet, which failed immediately as the pontoons available were not long enough to cross the rain-swollen river. This event does not appear in Wellington's dispatches and is the more remarkable as it was only the previous day that he had told Hope that his pontoon train was not large enough. However, there were witnesses, Larpent writing that 'the 2nd Division that had left this village at ten, was just returning . . . owing to the bridge of boats having been too short last night . . . with five more pontoons the whole world would have been affected.'[37] Larpent went on to say that the bridge was half-constructed when it was discovered the river was twenty yards wider than thought. He did note that the width should have been checked before the operation started but thought that maybe there was no 'close observation for fear of exciting [the] suspicion' of the French. Napier commented that 'he never saw him [Wellington] in such a rage, and no wonder'. Larpent finished his story saying that 'it would be a triumph to Elphinstone, though I am sure he will not feel it much . . . for once [he has] suffered for not attending to the counsel of his more steady and regularly-bred scientific advisors'. Elphinstone had told Wellington he was not taking enough pontoons but was overruled. The story has a ring of truth about it as Elphinstone and Larpent had become friends at headquarters and dined together often. It is also hinted at by Frazer who commented on 30 March that 'a want of boats in sufficient number to form a bridge has prevented us getting over sooner'.[38] Lieutenant Peter Wright RE, who was present that night, sent a detailed description to Burgoyne:

> [Captain] English's pontoons marched from this place, yesterday, around 8 o'clock pm and arrived at Portet at 10 o'clock pm. It was fortunately a fine night and I was in hopes everything would have gone on well. The following arrangements were made. I was to pass with about 400 men and occupy some houses on the opposite side and cover the crossing . . . English was to have gone on making the bridge in the meantime. The whole of this plan was very shortly knocked on the head. English first sent his jolly boat with the sheer line, whether from mismanagement or from the rapidity of the current the boat went down the river and was about an hour before it could be brought up again; they then tried the thing over again and with the same success. It was then though wise to go higher up the river and at last they fastened it to the other bank. Unfortunately, the rope instead of swimming[?] down the river stuck so fast at the bottom, that it was a full hour before they could get it loose and then it immediately stuck <u>again</u> in the same kind of way. When it first got fast at the bottom, I tried to persuade English to place two or three pontoons under it, some distance apart in order that the rope might be floated; however, they were afraid the pontoons might be lost in so rapid a current; at last after sticking at it for two or three hours more they tried this plan and succeeded in stretching the sheer line across, after <u>five hours</u> hard labour. My people were stopt [*sic*] until they had ascertained the width of the river. That could not be done until our sheer line was across; at length when they were preparing to measure it, three of four shots from the opposite bank were fired at the boat and obliged them to return; we then sent two boat loads to cover the operation and we could not discover anything on the other side and after having ascertained that the river was 159 yards wide and that we only had 133 yards of bridge the thing was given up and everything taken up. The people who fired at us were two of their cavalry videttes, I think, and who rode away without cutting the sheer line when there was nothing to prevent them. Thus ended this [bungling?] affair; besides a little mismanagement, the darkness of the night and unexpected difficulties greatly contributed to make it so. It is not yet known how we are to cross; Lord W. was not very much displeased but has ordered us to make rafts sufficient to complete the bridge.[39]

Another pontoon bridge was laid on 1 April at Cintegabelle over the river Arriège and Hill explored north towards Toulouse. Finding the roads impassable, Hill retired and the bridge was withdrawn. Wright again takes up the story:

> On 31 March, Lord Wellington determined to make a second attempt to cross the Garonne . . . English commenced his bridge immediately after dark, but from the rapidity of the current, the clumsiness of the workmen . . . the bridge was not completed until daylight. Sir Rowland Hill's corps immediately crossed and . . . found the roads so excessively bad from the late rains that Lord Wellington was obliged to order the corps back again.[40]

A few days later, Wellington commented, rather tamely, that 'all endeavours to lay the bridge below the town have been frustrated'. Lieutenant Colonel Goldfinch, writing to Elphinstone on 2 April 1814, reported:

> Below Toulouse, the Garonne is so much wider, that the 18 pontoons English has brought with him cannot reach across with all the assistance we can muster . . . I believe that Lord Wellington is now decided not to make any further attempts above the town. Wright is making a reconnaissance of the river below, but has not yet returned.[41]

In the letter, Goldfinch also expressed concern that Dickson had appointed an artillery officer to look after the artillery horses that were with the pontoon train, this artillery officer, Captain Green, being senior to Captain English who commanded the pontoon train. Goldfinch, believed the move was deliberate to bring the pontoon train under the command of the artillery. We will come back to this.

Wright continues the story:

> [Lord Wellington] desired me to reconnoitre the Garonne in the neighbourhood of Grenade and Verdun, fortunately the ground was very favourable about ½ a league from Grenade on the road to Toulouse; Lord Wellington was much pleased with the spot and determined to force the passage there; I proposed to him to do it in daylight under cover of forty or fifty pieces of artillery, because the enemy would be just the same time collecting his people to oppose us and we should be able to complete the bridge in two or three hours less time. As it was impossible to throw over the bridge

undiscovered and the ground being so extremely favourable for our artillery, Lord W determined to commence at daylight although he had a long battle with Marshal Beresford who was much against it.[42]

How much Lieutenant Wright had to do with the final decision we do not know, but the plan adopted appears to match what he wrote. Wright drew a sketch of the crossing-point a few days later and it that shows the artillery on the hill overlooking the river. On 3 April, Wellington issued orders for the pontoon bridge to be constructed the following morning. Wright was in charge of laying the bridge, with Lieutenant Colonel Goldfinch RE in overall command of the operations. The bridge was laid where Wright had suggested, north of the city. During the day, about 19,000 of Beresford's troops were transferred across, but a sharp rise in the level of the river threatened to wash the bridge away and the planks were taken up that night. The following morning, there being concern that items being washed down the river due to the floods could damage the bridge, the pontoons were taken out of the river, cutting the advance guard off completely. Orders were issued for the stranded detachment to post strong pickets, to hold all the high ground in the vicinity and to stop locals approaching Toulouse to try and ensure the French did not find out about the problem.[43] It was three frustrating and worrying days before the bridge was back in place. Wright now completes the story:

> On the 4th at daylight we began and completed the bridge in something less than four hours, the river was 125 yards wide, the stream rapid, and the approach to it with our pontoons difficult. The enemy did not attempt to interrupt us and not a shot was fired on either side; the 4th, 6th and 3rd Divisions immediately passed over with their artillery and some cavalry; General Freyre's [sic] Spaniards and the Light Division were obliged to halt, the bridge becoming impassable from the swelling of the river and the rapidity of the current; English thought it best to take up everything except the pontoons, which were secured by their lines. The bad weather now appeared to have set in; and on the 5th, the river still continuing to swell, English took away four or five pontoons from the centre, the sheer lines immediately fell in the water and one pontoon was sunk by the weight of the sheer line. Lord W who was on the spot ordered the whole to be taken up; thus Marshal Beresford with three divisions was without any communication with the rest of the army for three days. Everyone was surprised Soult did not attack him. Even Lord W expressed his surprise, but

he put a very good face on it, said we must have patience and did not appear to be at all alarmed about it. On the 8th, in the morning the bridge was re-established and Freyre's Spaniards passed over. Lord W then ordered the bridge to be placed higher up the river near Aussonne to render the communication shorter with Sir Rowland Hill. He expected to have it ready by 9 o'clock in the morning of the 9th, to pass over the light division and to attack the enemy in this position. English was the whole night taking up his bridge and did not reach the spot approved until half past nine. Lord W was in a most violent rage, told English that he had [failed?] his duty, and put him and the whole train under the orders of Captain Green of the artillery, who had previously been placed there to take charge of the artillery horses. English unfortunately had left the jolly boat and sheer line until last, and they unfortunately lost their road and did not arrive until 12 o'clock; the bridge in consequence was not completed until three. The movement of the army was thus stopped until the day following.[44]

The lack of complaint by Wright about Wellington's treatment of English in what was essentially a private letter to Burgoyne, would suggest that he thought Wellington was correct. The replacement of Captain English by Captain Green, exactly as Goldfinch had predicted, would have caused Elphinstone great concern. Wright appears to have been liked by Wellington, saying ' he used to send for me almost every day and he always appeared to me a very reasonable kind of man; he was never violent except when I think he ought to have been'.[45]

Once more, Wellington was lucky. The French made no serious attempt to attack his exposed force before the bridge was replaced. The bridging attempts over the past two weeks all appear rushed and took great risks that a force could be stranded without support. Soult was close by and could rapidly descend on any isolated forces. Operationally, it is difficult to see what the hurry was and Wellington tended to be cautious. One wonders whether there was a political element to his manoeuvring in that he wanted southern France under his control to exert more pressure on Napoleon and strengthen the bargaining position of the British government?

Having got his whole army across, Wellington immediately moved on Toulouse where the final battle of the Peninsular War was fought on 10 April. The following day, earthworks were started round the city to closely blockade it, Lieutenant Reid remarking that he had been ordered to build several redoubts, the troops being given 'positive orders never to abandon them'.[46] On 12 April, Wellington entered Toulouse, Soult having withdrawn the night before. News of Napoleon's abdication arrived that night. The account of the final military action of the war now needs to be completed.

The Blockade of Bayonne
Whilst the bridge of boats across the Adour was being completed, Hope realised that the French were building extensive field works around the citadel on the northern bank and after a sharp struggle pushed them back into the fortress. As described above, Wellington had asked for plans to besiege and attack the citadel. Having received the updated plan from Elphinstone on 4 March 1814, he now issued his typically detailed orders for collecting the stores for the siege. He planned to use St Jean de Luz and the river Adour to bring up the engineering stores.

Wellington continued to complain to Hope that Elphinstone's estimates for the men required were excessive. He had asked for 15,000 men to be made available. The working party was to be 3,000 strong with a further 2,000 for the covering party with three shift changes a day. Wellington asked Hope to 'converse' with Elphinstone, adding 'if we are to have 15,000 men for the attack of the Citadel, I am apprehensive that we must give up our plan'.[47] Writing a few days later, he said 'Elphinstone, like other engineers, has called for more men than he wants, or can employ, and the loss would be enormous if so many men were placed in such a small place'.[48] Wellington then added a detailed breakdown of his estimation of how many troops would be required, it being about half of Elphinstone's estimate. To be fair, Elphinstone's breakdown clearly stated where the troops were to be used and it covered all possibilities. In most cases, where Wellington reduced the number, Elphinstone would have done the same once he received clarification of the scope of the task, one example being the provision of troops to unload the supply boats, which Wellington struck out because he would expect that to be dealt with by others. This was the first siege Elphinstone had worked on and he would have been less familiar with the working practices that had developed over the past three years.

Seventy guns were selected for the attack and these with the necessary ammunition were slowly moved forward using 700 artillery horses. Hope seemed to be in no hurry to start the siege, however, being content to continue blockading the place. By 13 April, the artillery, ammunition and 670 gunners were in the artillery park in front of the Citadel. The French garrison, which was both strong and well-supplied, launched an attack on the morning of the 14th and caught the Allies unprepared. Sappers who were with the French attack immediately started filling in the trenches. In the confusion General Hay was killed and Sir John Hope captured and there were several hundred casualties on each side. This attack was completely unnecessary as both the Allies and the French had received word of the abdication of Napoleon. On 28 April, Elphinstone reported to his wife 'that the white flag was hoisted at noon in Bayonne'. With this action, the Peninsular War came to an end.

Disappointingly, the final months of the war did little to enhance the reputation of the Corps of Royal Engineers with Wellington. Elphinstone did nothing to build a relationship with his commander, and the problems crossing various rivers including the Garonne could have been catastrophic. There is a little twist in the tale of Commanding Royal Engineers in the war in that on 4 March 1814, the Board of Ordnance awarded command pay to Burgoyne as CRE of the separate corps under Sir John Hope, Elphinstone being with Headquarters to the right.[49] Today, it is not clear what they thought Elphinstone was doing. Burgoyne, was also strangely silent on the matter.

It is difficult to understand why Wellington tolerated Elphinstone's behaviour. I can only assume that he felt the war was pretty much over by the time he arrived on the scene. It was the right decision to leave Elphinstone for the siege of Bayonne as strategically this is where the engineers could do the most good. With the end of the war, Elphinstone went home as soon as he could, never to venture abroad again. The commanding engineers for the American and Waterloo campaigns were both junior to Elphinstone and both had served in the Peninsula under Wellington.

Conclusion

When you started reading this book, you might have thought that Wellington did not really need many engineers, as they were only used for sieges and there were not many those in the campaign. Whilst this book is primarily about the Royal Engineers, it is actually about the rise of 'Scientific Soldiers' and the military's recognition that they were needed. The establishment of the Royal Military Academy in the eighteenth century and the Royal Military College at the beginning of the nineteenth century began the trend that led to the professional military that we expect today. The basic skills that were taught to the Ordnance officers were not very different from what was taught to staff officers during the Napoleonic Wars.

You will have a better insight now into how well embedded the 'Scientific Soldiers' were into almost every aspect of military operations. When you read a book that says General X advanced to Y, think again. Before General X could make that decision, someone had prepared a map and someone else had probably made a reconnaissance up the road to town Y. When the book says General X threw a bridge across the river, think about the planning to get the bridge there, the surveying of the selected location, the consideration of the weather conditions and the building of the bridge. When General X starts his siege with numerous siege guns, who has done the planning to move hundreds of tons of equipment to the selected location? Behind every great general there is a great backroom team.

The British army in the early nineteenth century was still not convinced of the need for 'Scientific Soldiers'. It had managed for many years just hiring expertise when it needed it. An army officer learnt his trade 'on the job', which could be a brutal, Darwinian process. What he learnt was very dependent on the interests of his commanding officer. The Board of Ordnance had realised in the middle of the eighteenth century that artillery and, subsequently, engineer officers needed a proper military education. The army was slowly following. The British army started the Peninsular War with specialist services spread across two separate Corps in the Board of Ordnance (RE and RSM), a third in the Army (RSC) and a miscellaneous assortment of groups in the QMG's Department (Guides, Exploring Officers, Mounted Staff Corps as well as the official staff of the QMG). What is surprising is that it worked at all.

In the early years of the war, the role of the engineers was only visible in static operations like the Lines of Torres Vedras and the sieges. By the campaigns of 1813 and 1814, however, the army would have struggled to operate without the presence of engineers and artificers. In these campaigns, pontoons were essential. This sometimes caused problems due to transport, or more accurately, the lack of it and often dictated the speed of operations. This was a huge challenge for the Ordnance as there was never enough transport available to move either guns or pontoons. The final campaign of 1814 saw engineers and artificers embedded in army units for the first time and the army discovered they were useful.

So how do we summarise the role of the Royal Engineers during the Peninsular War? The CRE faced the constant challenge of too few of officers and sappers for the work required. This meant that delivering the service was a constant compromise and on occasions it did directly impact on operations. The lack of resources sometimes caused resentment in the army, when the soldiers and officers felt the demands on them were unreasonable. Sieges were always unpopular, being an inglorious way to die. This led to a lack of enthusiasm among the troops and greater exposure for the engineer officers in leading by example.

Advising Wellington was never easy, but, apart from a small number of high-profile issues, he generally appeared satisfied with the support he was getting. The constant lack of engineering resources must, on occasions, have made audiences with Wellington very uncomfortable. Fletcher reported to Wellington from 1809 up to his death in 1813. There are a number of occasions where it could have been possible to replace him, but Wellington chose not to. Wellington did write some very critical letters home but then again he did that about his army, his generals, the commissary, the British, Portuguese and Spanish governments, the Portuguese and Spanish armies and the Royal Navy.

Even though, on occasions, he was not happy with the engineers' performance, he did trust them and fought for them. There were occasions where he directly supported Fletcher, Chapman, Squire, Burgoyne and Jones. I am less sure what Wellington's opinion of Elphinstone was. Examples include asking for John Squire not to be recalled after his argument with Craufurd in 1810; supporting John Jones when the Board of Ordnance wanted to put him on half pay immediately after the war, and then employing him for the next three years; and writing in support of Fletcher's family after his death.

One thing which is very apparent is that there was a big difference between Wellington's relationship with the artillery and with the engineers. Whilst there is no evidence of Wellington complaining about Fletcher, there is no doubt that he manoeuvred Dickson into the senior artillery role. He made life so uncomfortable for Dickson's superiors that they felt they had no alternative but to go home. Wellington could have done the same with Fletcher. I do not believe that he had concerns about Fletcher, I am less sure about Elphinstone. In the end Wellington made no attempt to interfere with engineer seniority in the same way he did with the artillery.

The relationship between the Army and Ordnance at command level improved during the war. The friction caused by the lack of trained artificers soured relations in 1811–12 but once there were more these troops it stopped being an issue. Similarly, after criticising Wellington for asking for more engineers in July 1809, the Board of Ordnance increased the number of engineers every year. Almost all the increase in officer numbers was allocated to the Peninsula. By the end of the war, the Master-General, in approving a request for more engineer officers to be sent out, said 'that it is highly important in the present urgent crisis, not to fall short of the demands of the Marquis of Wellington, as he has important fortresses to repair and improve, and may at an early period have new sieges to carry on'. A similar request from Elphinstone, which earned him a rebuke for not following the correct process, was still approved.

Operationally, there is no evidence of significant friction between the engineers, Staff Corps and QMG's department. In the theatre, the officers got on with what needed to be done and the 'professional boundaries of responsibility' were frequently overlooked to get the job done. There was also evidence of officers in the different departments sharing information on best practice to enable them all to improve their effectiveness.

So, why were the engineers so useful? Part of the reason was that army officers received no formal basic training and there were very few officers who had been to Staff College. Ordnance officers would have been a significant proportion of the 'Scientific Soldiers' with the army. Was the lack of trained army officers available for staff duties being masked by the availability of Ordnance officers (usually engineers) to carry out these roles in an unofficial capacity? Engineer officers fitted smoothly into the command structure of the army and were always seen as welcome additions to a general's 'family'. There are no instances of an engineer officer being removed from a general's staff group. Even General Robert Craufurd, who had a major row with John Squire, had an engineer officer on his staff most of the time. The senior officers, like Fletcher and Burgoyne, were often used for non-engineering tasks where their experience and sense could be relied on. When one considers the trust that Wellington placed in officers like Dickson, Burgoyne, Sturgeon and Jones, it shows that he greatly valued the contribution of the 'Scientific Soldiers' although he never really accepted that formal military education was required before an officer received his first commission.

Wellington's strategy from the very start of the war was to fight the numerically superior French when the opportunity arose. He also needed strongholds to which he could retire when he was threatened. Whilst Torres Vedras was the most visible sign of this, it also included the major fortresses of Elvas, Badajoz, Almeida and Ciudad Rodrigo and the minor defences at Abrantes, Peniche and Setubal. In conjunction with the strongholds at Gibraltar and Cadiz, the French were never able to concentrate enough troops to overwhelm Wellington. The engineers played their pivotal role in capturing and/or fortifying these places and ensuring that the Allied forces always had a place of safety.

Along with their work in reconnaissance, and in improvements to the road and river communications in the Peninsula, they played an unsung but vital role in the defeat of Napoleon and the key to this success were some very junior officers who took huge responsibilities on their own shoulders and generally made it happen.

Appendix 1

Commanding Royal Engineers (CRE) with Wellington's Army, 1808–14

Name	From	To	Duration
Howard Elphinstone	1 Aug 1808	17 Aug 1808	16 days
George Landmann	17 Aug 1808	21 Aug 1808	4 days
Richard Fletcher (see Note 1)	22 Aug 1808	5 Dec 1812	52 months
Henry Goldfinch (see Note 2)	5 Dec 1812	4 Mar 1813	3 months
Howard Elphinstone	4 Mar 1813	13 Apr 1813	6 weeks
Richard Fletcher	14 Apr 1813	31 Aug 1813	4 months
John Burgoyne (see Note 3)	31 Aug 1813	13 Oct 1813	6 weeks
Howard Elphinstone	13 Oct 1813	End of war	9 months

Note 1. Fletcher was absent from the Peninsula from January to April 1809 following the Corunna campaign. The senior Engineer officer in Lisbon was Captain Peter Patton who remained there when Moore's army advanced in October 1808. There was a temporary internal quarrel in late 1808 when George Landmann tried to claim seniority in Portugal. This was rejected by both the army commander, Sir John Craddock, and the Board of Ordnance. Landmann was part of the Gibraltar garrison and had been ordered back there. He managed to avoid doing so for several months, a skill he demonstrated several times throughout the war. Patton was superseded by Captain Stephen Chapman on 4 March 1809 on his arrival from England.

Note 2. I believe that Elphinstone was supposed to take over command from Fletcher. He should have sailed for the Peninsula in December 1812 and Fletcher did not arrive in England until the first week of January 1813. Elphinstone did not arrive in Portugal until early February and did not arrive at HQ until 4 March 1813. Fletcher returned six weeks later and Elphinstone was immediately sent back to Lisbon.

Note 3. Technically, Elphinstone was in command, but Burgoyne was with Wellington's army until Elphinstone arrived at HQ. Wellington had effectively kept a succession of senior artillery officers in Lisbon to allow Dickson to retain command with the army.

Appendix 2

Engineer Officers who Served in the Iberian Peninsula

This includes officers who served in the east coast campaigns. It does not include officers who served in the Mediterranean.

Name	From Month Year	To Month Year	Location
Barou, Richard John	Feb 1813	Sep 1814	Peninsula
Barry, Philip	Sep 1812	Aug 1813	Peninsula
Birch, James	Jan 1813	Apr 1814	Spain – East Coast
Birch, John Francis	Sep 1808	Jan 1809	Peninsula
Blanshard, Thomas	Mar 1814	Apr 1814	Peninsula
Bolton, Daniel	Dec 1813	Aug 1814	Peninsula
Boothby, Charles	Aug 1808	Jan 1809	Peninsula
	Apr 1809	Jul 1809	Peninsula
Boteler, Richard	Jul 1808	Jan 1809	Peninsula
	Mar 1811	Jul 1814	Peninsula
Burgoyne, John Fox	Aug 1808	Jan 1809	Peninsula
	Apr 1809	Jun 1814	Peninsula
By, John	Apr 1811	Aug 1811	Peninsula
Chapman, Stephen Remnant	Mar 1809	Nov 1810	Peninsula
Cheyne, Alexander	Oct 1808	Jan 1809	Peninsula
	Apr 1812	Jul 1812	Peninsula
	Aug 1812	Dec 1813	Spain – East Coast
Collyer, George	Aug 1813	Aug 1813	Peninsula
Davy, Henry	Oct 1808	Jan 1809	Peninsula

De Salaberry, Edward	Jun	1811	Apr	1812	Peninsula
Dickens, Thomas Mark	Sep	1813	Apr	1814	Peninsula
Dickenson, Sebastian	Mar	1810	May	1811	Peninsula
Ellicombe, Charles Grene	Dec	1811	Jul	1814	Peninsula
Elliot, Theodore Henry	Jul	1811	Jul	1812	Peninsula
	Aug	1812	Aug	1813	Spain – East Coast
Elphinstone, Howard	Jul	1808	Aug	1808	Peninsula
	Feb	1813	Jul	1814	Peninsula
Elton, Isaac Marmaduke	Jul	1813	Jun	1814	Peninsula
Emmett, Anthony	Mar	1809	Nov	1809	Peninsula
	Dec	1809	Oct	1810	Peninsula
	Nov	1810	Jun	1812	Peninsula
	Nov	1813	Jun	1814	Peninsula
English, Frederick	Aug	1808	Jan	1809	Peninsula
	Dec	1813	Jun	1814	Peninsula
Fanshaw, Edward	Aug	1808	Oct	1808	Peninsula
	Jan	1809	Jan	1809	Peninsula
Fletcher, Richard	Aug	1808	Jan	1809	Peninsula
	Apr	1809	Dec	1812	Peninsula
	Apr	1813	Aug	1813	Peninsula
Forster, William Frederick	Apr	1808	Jan	1809	Peninsula
	Jun	1809	Jun	1811	Peninsula
Fyers, Thomas	Oct	1808	Jan	1809	Peninsula
Fyers, Edward	Mar	1809	Sep	1809	Peninsula
Gilbert, Francis Yarde	Dec	1812	Jun	1814	Peninsula
Gipps, George	May	1811	Jul	1812	Peninsula
	Aug	1812	Feb	1814	Spain – East Coast
	Mar	1814	Jun	1814	Peninsula
Goldfinch, Henry	May	1809	Jan	1812	Peninsula
	Jul	1812	May	1814	Peninsula
Grierson, Crighton	Jul	1813	Apr	1814	Spain – East Coast
Hamilton, George	Apr	1809	Jul	1809	Peninsula
Harding, George Judd	Jun	1812	May	1814	Spain – East Coast
Henderson, George H.	Sep	1812	May	1814	Peninsula
Holloway, William Cuthbert	Mar	1810	Apr	1812	Peninsula
Hulme, John Lyon	Apr	1810	Jun	1814	Peninsula

Appendix 2 213

Hunt, Richard	Mar	1811	Jun	1811	Peninsula
Hustler, Robert Samuel	Jun	1810	Aug	1810	Spain – East Coast
	Aug	1812	Apr	1814	Spain – East Coast
Hutchinson, Thomas Kitchingham	Oct	1808	Jan	1809	Peninsula
Jones, Harry David	Mar	1812	Jun	1814	Peninsula
Jones, John Thomas	Sep	1808	Jan	1809	Peninsula
	Apr	1810	Feb	1813	Peninsula
Jones, Rice	Mar	1809	Feb	1812	Peninsula
Landmann, George Thomas	Aug	1808	Feb	1809	Peninsula
	Dec	1810	Mar	1812	Peninsula
Lascelles, Thomas	Jul	1811	Apr	1812	Peninsula
Lefebure, Charles	Aug	1808	Jan	1809	Peninsula
Lewis, Griffith George	Feb	1813	Jul	1813	Peninsula
Macaulay, John Simcoe	Jun	1812	Dec	1812	Spain – East Coast
MacCulloch, William	Jun	1811	May	1812	Peninsula
Machell, Lancelot	Dec	1812	Jul	1813	Peninsula
Macleod, George Francis	Apr	1811	Apr	1812	Peninsula
Marshall, Anthony	Mar	1811	Oct	1813	Peninsula
Matson, Edward	Dec	1812	Dec	1813	Peninsula
	Mar	1814	Jun	1814	Peninsula
Melhuish, Samuel Camplin	Jun	1811	Apr	1814	Peninsula
Melville, David	Mar	1811	May	1811	Peninsula
Mercer, Cavalier Shorthouse	Jul	1808	Oct	1808	Peninsula
Mudge, Richard Zachary	Mar	1809	May	1810	Peninsula
Mulcaster, Edmund Robert	Jul	1808	Jan	1809	Peninsula
	Apr	1809	Mar	1812	Peninsula
Nicholas, William	Mar	1812	Apr	1812	Peninsula
Ord, William Redman	Jan	1812	Sep	1814	Spain – East Coast
Parker, Edward	Dec	1812	Feb	1814	Peninsula
Pasley, Charles William	Oct	1808	Jan	1809	Peninsula
Patton, Peter	Aug	1808	Jun	1811	Peninsula
Piper, Robert Sloper	Mar	1810	Jun	1814	Peninsula
Pitts, Thomas James Heblethwayt	Mar	1812	Feb	1814	Peninsula
Power, Robert	Jan	1813	Nov	1813	Peninsula

214 Wellington's Engineers

Pringle, John Watson	Mar	1811	Jun	1814	Peninsula
Reid, William	Mar	1810	Jun	1814	Peninsula
Rhodes, Charles Steech	Sep	1812	Aug	1813	Peninsula
Rivers, Charles	Dec	1813	Jun	1814	Peninsula
Robe, Alexander Watt	Dec	1813	Jun	1814	Peninsula
Roberts, Thomas	Jan	1812	Mar	1814	Spain – East Coast
Ross, George Charles	Aug	1809	Jan	1812	Peninsula
Savage, Henry John	Jan	1814	Jun	1814	Peninsula
Scott, Richard Evans	Aug	1812	Apr	1814	Spain – East Coast
Skelton, Thomas	Jan	1811	Jan	1812	Peninsula
Slade, William Henry	Apr	1812	Aug	1814	Peninsula
Smith, Charles Felix	Mar	1813	Aug	1813	Peninsula
Smith, Henry Nelson	Mar	1813	Apr	1814	Spain – East Coast
Smith, William Davies	Aug	1808	Jan	1809	Peninsula
Smyth, James Carmichael	Oct	1808	Jan	1809	Peninsula
Squire, John	Jul	1808	Jan	1809	Peninsula
	Mar	1810	May	1812	Peninsula
Stanway, Frank	Aug	1808	Aug	1814	Peninsula
Tapp, Hammond Astley	Mar	1810	Jun	1814	Peninsula
Thackeray, Frederick Rennell	Aug	1812	Mar	1814	Spain – East Coast
Thomson, Alexander	Mar	1809	May	1812	Peninsula
Tinling, George Vaughan	Dec	1813	Jun	1814	Peninsula
Trench, Samuel	Mar	1810	Jun	1811	Peninsula
Vetch, James	Mar	1812	Apr	1812	Peninsula
Victor, James Conway	Feb	1813	Jun	1814	Peninsula
Ward, William Cuthbert	Jul	1812	Sep	1813	Spain – East Coast
Wells, John Neave	Aug	1808	Jan	1809	Peninsula
	Jan	1812	Apr	1812	Spain – East Coast
	Sep	1813	Jun	1814	Peninsula
West, George Innes Perry	Dec	1812	May	1814	Peninsula
Williams, John Archer	Jul	1808	Sep	1812	Peninsula
Wortham, Hale Young	Aug	1813	Jun	1814	Peninsula
Wright, Peter	Mar	1811	Jun	1814	Peninsula
York, Frederick August	Oct	1808	Jan	1809	Peninsula

Name	From Month Year	To Month Year	Location
King's German Legion Engineer Officers who served in the Iberian Peninsula 1808–14			
Meineke, George Frederick	Mar 1810	May 1814	Peninsula
Unger, William	Dec 1811	Sep 1814	Peninsula
Wedekind, Charles	Aug 1808	May 1814	Peninsula

Appendix 3

Military Reconnaissance and Surveying

Whilst the Peninsular War was won on the battlefield, we must not forget the less visible work that allowed the army to arrive at it. One key component was the logistics that delivered food and ammunition to the army on the move, but another equally important but almost unseen task was the work that went into mapping the country in which Wellington fought. From the first days of 1808 up until 1814, officers were dispatched far and wide, producing detailed and accurate maps of Portugal and Spain. This was something that the French were never able to do other than in the small areas that they held in strength. A British officer could ride alone through most of the Iberian Peninsula, knowing that he was unlikely to be molested by the locals, often being hidden and fed by them when the need arose. A French officer attempting to do the same was more likely to come to an unpleasant end.

One of the key differences between the Allied and French armies was that Wellington had better maps than the French. This is a little surprising, particularly as the French had free access to the whole of the Iberian Peninsula throughout much of 1807 and 1808. When the French commander Junot arrived in Lisbon in 1807, he ordered his Chief Engineer, Vincent, to complete surveys of the surrounding area and then across the rest of Portugal using Portuguese army engineers. Raeuber[1] said that the Portuguese did not have large-scale maps of their own territory at this time. Whilst that would appear surprising, it is probably even more surprising that England did not either! It was the threat of a French invasion that forced the British government to rectify the failure and accurately map the south coast of England. This omission was being dealt with as a matter of urgency in the early years of the nineteenth century. There was no decent mapping of Ireland for another twenty-five years and parts of Scotland had only been mapped as a result of the 1745 rebellion.[2] The first posting for newly-commissioned Royal Engineer officers was to spend six months working on the Ordnance Survey to develop some basic skills before their first official posting.

The results of Junot's order included the publication of probably the first modern map of Portugal, the *Carta militar das principaes estradas de Portugal*, which was produced by the Portuguese engineer Lourenço Homem da Cunha d'Eca and published in 1808. When Junot evacuated Portugal after the Convention of Cintra, the Portuguese map was shipped back to France, but incredibly was not given to Masséna for the third invasion in 1810. Raeuber suggested the likely reasons were that there was not time to make copies or they were too valuable to give to Masséna.[3] I find both of these reasons difficult to accept. The French had two years to make copies and the whole point of the French military archives was to make information available to their forces. Having said that, it is difficult to come up with a plausible alternative. Surely Junot must have told Masséna that he had good maps made! Or maybe he didn't? Raeuber argues more convincingly that Masséna was 'feeling' his way forward when he advanced into Portugal. He was reported to be reliant on the map of Spain and Portugal created by Lopez. This map was not produced by topographical survey but by sending questionnaires out to priests and civil servants, asking them to describe the immediate vicinity to their town or parish. Lopez then constructed his map based on their responses.[4] The result was a map that, whilst beautifully printed, was very inaccurate. The whole campaign could have ended very differently if Masséna had taken the best road when he invaded Portugal rather than the worst.

The start of the Peninsular War saw the Allies in no better position that the French. Before Richard Fletcher returned to the Peninsula in April 1809 he asked for the following maps:

> The map of the Pyrenees about to be published by Arrowsmith which will include the provinces of Aragon, Catalonia, Navarre and Biscay. The map of Portugal by Lopez and [the] Mentelle map of Spain. The best plan extant of Cartagena and Barcelona and also that of Cadiz by Faden.

Mr Faden himself replied:

> Herewith you receive all the maps contained in your order which can be procured. Lopez's maps of Portugal have been sold off some time. I have the one by Jefferey in 6 sheets.[5] The plans of Cartagena are likewise all sold. I am engraving it at this time – Barcelona has not yet been published at Madrid.

So, the Royal Engineers entered the war with very few maps and even the ones they had were of doubtful quality. It would seem that the Army was in no better situation. An internal letter in the Ordnance in March 1809 noted that 'the Portuguese maps of Memoire[?] are with the Quarter Master-General's Department by the Master-General's permission, and when returned to us shall be immediately forwarded to you'.[6]

Once the officers were in the field, they realised that some of the published maps were poor. Captain John Squire RE complained, perhaps unfairly:

> All the maps of Portugal, particularly in this part of the country are extremely incorrect – Faden's last map . . . is as bad as any of them. The Carta Militar published at Lisbon can never be depended upon – To form a good judgement, it is necessary to actually visit every part of the frontier.[7]

And this is exactly what many engineers, including Squire, found themselves doing in the early part of the war. Captain George Ross RE commented in a similar fashion on the book and map published by fellow Ordnance officer, William Granville Eliot RA:

> As to Captain Elliot's [sic] book I have seen nothing of it but the maps – at least a thing which was taken out of the book by a General here to travel by and I confess it appears to me to be as little entitled to the name as any thing I ever saw – Capt E. seems to have made a bad copy, no I ought not to say a copy – it is so much worse than the Carta Militaire [sic] – He scratched some hills at random to make it pass as a drawing of his own.[8]

Commenting on his first campaign and the period immediately after the Battle of Roliça in 1808, Wellington wrote:

> I should have pushed the advanced guard as far as the heights of Mafra, and should have halted the main body about four or five miles from that place. By this movement the enemy's position at Torres Vedras would have been turned and I should have brought the army into a country of which I had an excellent map and topographical accounts, which had been drawn up for the use of the late Sir Charles Stewart; and the battle which it was evident would be fought in a few days would have had for its field a county of which we had a knowledge.[9]

Resolving the issue of maps was a high priority for Wellington and he utilised all available resources.

Both the Ordnance and the QMG's Department issued comprehensive instructions to their officers on what they expected. The original instructions to the officers of the QMG Department started 'One of the first duties of the officers of the QMG's Department is to acquire a knowledge of the country, which is the theatre of the operations of the army'.[10] The wording below comes from the 'Instructions for officers of the Corps of Royal Engineers when attached to columns, or moving through the Country'. The wording in the QMG's printed instructions is almost identical:

> The Engineer when moving with a column or otherwise will observe the general features of the country through which they pass, whether hilly, level, woody, open, or enclosed, the state and breadth of the roads, whether they are practicable for Artillery, their bearings by compass, and the passes and positions on the route. Such parts of the country as may be sufficiently open and level to enable cavalry to act with advantage should be remarked. The rivers should particularly be attended to, every breadth and depth at the time and place of passing, and as far as can be ascertained by enquiry their state at other seasons of the year . . .[11]

The diaries of engineer officers are full of descriptions of the roads, hills and rivers they passed. Portuguese Engineers were also used, e.g. General Mackenzie reporting they were active 'in upper Beira where almost all the best Portuguese Engineers are now employed on surveys'.[12] Most reports by Royal Engineer officers were textual, sometimes accompanied by a drawing. The QMG's Department tended to use a standard template for their reports (see below).

The Royal Engineer officers appeared more active on survey and reconnaissance work in the early years of the war. In 1808 engineer officers were surveying all the main routes between Portugal and Spain and also travelled with Moore's army. They were also very active in 1809 and 1810 whilst Wellington was still very much on the defensive and operated in or near Portugal. They seemed to do less surveying as the war went on. Royal Engineer reports tended to be more detailed and take more notice of the terrain they were passing through. There was also a greater emphasis on collecting details of any fortifications and the ability to move artillery. The greater accuracy, however, required much greater time to prepare. Murray, the QMG, was less interested in the detail and more interested in the rapid collection of data. He strongly favoured a quick approach to sketching and a focus on roads and accommodation for the troops.

Whilst the engineers contributed in an *ad hoc* way to the knowledge of the theatre of operations, officers of the Quarter Master-General's Department and the Royal Staff Corps did the bulk of the mapping. Officers were dispatched across the whole of Portugal with orders to produce maps at a standard scale of 4 miles to the inch (1:250,000). A number of names come up again and again in correspondence including Sturgeon, Todd, Colleton and Staveley from the Royal Staff Corps and Broke, Bainbrigge, Pierrepoint, Bell, Balck and Mitchell from the QMG's Department. Mitchell[13] was retained after the war to revisit the main scenes of actions and accurately map them. These maps eventually were published in the rare and beautiful *Wyld's Atlas*.

The main interest of the QMG was the movement of troops so the focus was primarily on the roads and the villages they passed through. A standard template was used to collect the information that was required with a simple style of drawing to illustrate the route. There are some examples of Royal Engineers also using the standard template e.g. In the National Archives, there is a report by John Burgoyne of the route from Alcantara to Ciudad Rodrigo. Burgoyne also noted on the report that it was copied from the original of Captain Godby RA.[14]

QMG – Report template

Sketch of the road	Places on or near Road	Distances	Accommodation					Notes
			No. of Houses	Permanent quarters		On the march		
		Leagues		Inf.	Cav.	Inf.	Cav.	

The extensive mapping work carried out under the orders of Murray led to Wellington having significantly better understanding of the terrain in which he was operating, and this often gave him the edge when manoeuvring his forces.

Along with the extensive mapping work, from the start of the Peninsular

War Wellington recognised the value in having people with local knowledge attached to the army. The practice used by both sides of asking locals to direct the routes were fraught with danger because their knowledge was often very limited. The Corps of Guides was formed in 1808/9 under George Scovell. Wellington explained their purpose as being:

> To make enquiries, and have a knowledge of roads, but to have a class of person in the army who shall march with the heads of columns, and interpret between the officers commanding them, and the people of the country guiding them.[15]

The initial establishment was for one sergeant, one corporal and eighteen privates.[16] Wellington described the Corps as made up of 'foreign deserters', which seems an odd use of such people. The Corps was clearly found to be useful, as it remained in existence throughout the war. By May 1809 it had grown to four lieutenants, four cornets, six sergeants, six corporals, two farriers, and twenty privates. Its numbers continued to grow, and by November 1810 there were fifty privates; by September 1811 there were eighty, finally reaching 150 in December 1812.[17] Apart from their duties as guides, some of them were used for surveying and mapping. There are a number of maps in the National Archives drawn by Lieutenant Agostino Albano da Silvera.

Wellington's superiority in mapping became less effective in the later stages of the war when he approached and crossed the Spanish frontier. His maps and his ability to create them would have been more restricted, just when he needed them most to operate over the terrain in southern France with its numerous rivers and difficult crossings.

The efforts of Wellington's map-makers are another example of the behind-the-scenes activities that contributed silently to the effectiveness of Wellington's campaigning and in their small way helped him to his victory against the French in Portugal and Spain.

Appendix 4

Military Bridging

The Iberian Peninsula was a hostile environment for Napoleonic armies. Much of the country was covered with mountains, making traversing it difficult, if not impossible. In between the mountain ranges flowed wide and fast-moving rivers that could only be crossed by bridges or boats. Rain or snow in the mountains could raise the level of rivers by several feet overnight and sweep away any crossing-points. These rivers intersected the country and without a crossing-point an army could be faced with long marches to get from one side to the other. Where there were no mountains or rivers, there were plains; barren in the winter and baking hot in the summer. Roads were rarely better than rough tracks. The royal roads between major towns might be fully cobbled but these were very rare. The best normal road might have two lines of paving stones for wagon wheels but did not allow for passing. Most roads would be hard-packed earth, passable in summer but muddy in the winter. In all cases, maintenance was minimal. It was the geography as much as anything else that defeated Napoleon's troops in Spain.

For nearly 2,000 years the Spanish had dealt with the major rivers by building strong bridges and knowing every crossing-point at the different seasons of the year. Several bridges built by the Romans still stood proud, such as those at Almaraz, Alcantara and Salamanca. Every campaign during the war relied to some extent on controlling, constructing or destroying bridges.

One of the Allies' first tasks in 1808 was to establish crossing-points on the river Tagus in Portugal to allow rapid movement between the north and south of the country. Initially this was achieved through floating bridges (ferries) but later they were replaced by pontoon bridges. The boat bridges at Abrantes, Punhete and Villa Velha remained key crossing-points in all operations for the remainder of the war. These were carefully guarded and taken down whenever there was a threat from the enemy. Keeping these in place required constant attention and maintenance, as they were large structures. Lieutenant Harry Jones RE described the boat bridge at Villa Velha when he passed in December 1812. The breadth of river was 140 paces (105m); distance of boat to boat (centre), ten paces (8m). It was made up of twelve large and two smaller boats, each having two anchors. To ensure there was no interruption in its availability, ten boats were kept in reserve.[1] He similarly described the bridge at Punhete that was made of short, stout pontoons. The length of the bridge was 160 yards (150m), made up of twenty-one pontoons. The distance from centre to centre of the boats was eight yards (8m). These pontoons only needed one anchor, as the river was less rapid. Each of these had a permanent engineering presence and a guard.

As well as strategic crossing-points, bridging featured in operational campaigns. Moore's retreat to Corunna in 1808/9 included the destruction of several bridges to delay the advance of the French. The destruction of the bridge at Castro Gonzalo (Benevente) led the repulse of the pursuing French cavalry and to a respite for the Allies. Several engineer officers were involved in destroying bridges and one, Lieutenant Davy, lost his life by misjudging his fuse. There was widespread concern in the Royal Engineers about the limited success in blowing-up bridges.

Wellington's first success in 1809 was when he ejected Marshal Soult from the Portuguese city of Oporto. The French had destroyed the bridge there and to pursue them required a boat bridge to be rapidly built to allow the bulk of the pursuing Allied troops to cross. This was done using the numerous local boats that were employed in the wine trade. The 1809 Talavera campaign relied on control of bridges further up the Tagus at Alcantara and Almaraz, and by the end of the year both of these bridges had been made impassable and the nearest intact crossing-point was at Arzobispo, which is much nearer to Madrid than Lisbon. The French constructed a boat bridge at Almaraz but this was not possible at Alcantara due to the steepness of the valley and the speed of the river. The Royal Staff Corps built an additional temporary bridge over the river Tietar for the passage of Wellington's army. The river was about 150 feet (50m) wide, which contained a deep channel about 70 feet (20m) wide. There were no pontoons or boats available in the vicinity:

> The only material at hand was the timber from a large inn at about half a mile from the place . . . which was unroofed . . . a party of 500 men [taken from the line regiments] with saws and axes was sent to a distance of three miles to procure young pines to make [twenty] stakes.[2]

The main roof beams from the inn, 20 feet long and two feet square, were floated in the deep channel. Piles were then driven into the shallow part of the river using 'large wooden mallets made on the spot'. The rafters and flooring from the inn provided enough decking to complete the bridge the whole held in place with ropes. This bridge was constructed in one day.

Whilst the major campaigns of 1809 to 1811 focussed on access to the major *strategic* bridges over the Tagus, smaller bridges were also used and discarded in the various *operational* campaigns. Wellington destroyed several bridges as the French army advanced through Spain into Portugal in 1810 as he retired into the Lines of Torres Vedras. Masséna did the same when he retreated the following March. As Wellington pursued him north he was faced with a number of obstacles. First the bridge over the Alva at Ponte de Murcella needed to be repaired. The Royal Staff Corps built a floating bridge as there was insufficient material to construct a full bridge. A few weeks later, Wellington needed a further crossing-point over the Coa near Almeida, Masséna having also destroyed this bridge. The Royal Staff corps, once again, made the bridge usable, using locally-sourced wood to fill the gap.

1811 saw major problems as the Allies now began to take the offensive. The focus of the operations moved further south and the crossing-points over the Guadiana now became more important, the only two major ones being under the castle at Badajoz and at Merida. The Allied sieges of Badajoz were seriously impeded due to the lack of a pontoon train and the

The bridge over the Coa at Fuentes d'Oñoro.

difficulty in keeping the temporary bridges made from trestles, wine casks and pontoons in place in the changeable weather. Further north, when Wellington was threatened by a superior French army at the Battle of Fuentes del Oñoro, he arranged to have a temporary bridge built across the river Coa in case he needed to retreat.

January 1812 saw a trestle bridge built across the river Agueda by the Royal Staff Corps to enable Allied troops to approach and besiege Ciudad Rodrigo. Wellington had recognised that a proper bridge was essential and that it would have to be very strong to survive the torrents of water that flowed during the winter. There was no way a pontoon bridge would survive these conditions so the decision was made to construct a trestle bridge. Large amounts of timber were required as the river was about 400 feet (125m) wide. Henry Sturgeon RSC was ordered to prepare the bridge and work started in October 1811. The foot of each trestle was tapered and weigh down with rocks to resist the water flow. This bridge was constructed in appalling winter weather and remained in place throughout the siege. It was then dismantled and stored in Almeida in case it was needed again.

As in the previous year, the third siege of the fortress of Badajoz was hampered by the problems in keeping a pontoon bridge across the river Guadiana. 1812 also saw the Allied lines of communication significantly improved through an innovative repair to Trajan's Roman bridge at Alcantara. At the same time, Wellington ordered a raid to destroy the French pontoon bridge at Almaraz. Combined, these two actions meant that Wellington could manoeuvre his troops much faster than the French. Following the siege at Burgos, the engineering services played a major role in slowing the French pursuit by destroying bridges

1813 was the first time a pontoon train travelled with the army. It was used a number of times during the Allied advance that led to the successful battle at Vitoria. Later in the year a range of methods were used to cross the rivers Bidassoa, Nivelle and Nive around the French border. 1814 started with the daring crossing of the fast-flowing and tidal river Adour where the wide river was bridged using local boats held in place with five massive cables. Around twenty-five were used with several being held in reserve.

Wellington had to use pontoons to cross numerous rivers as he pushed the retreating French army further east. He was close to disaster at Toulouse when the pontoon bridge over the river Garonne was swept, away leaving part of the Allied army stranded on the wrong side of the river for three days.

The quick summary above shows that river crossing was an essential component of Wellington's strategy throughout the war. Whilst these were the key events, officers from the Royal Engineers and Royal Staff Corps

226 Wellington's Engineers

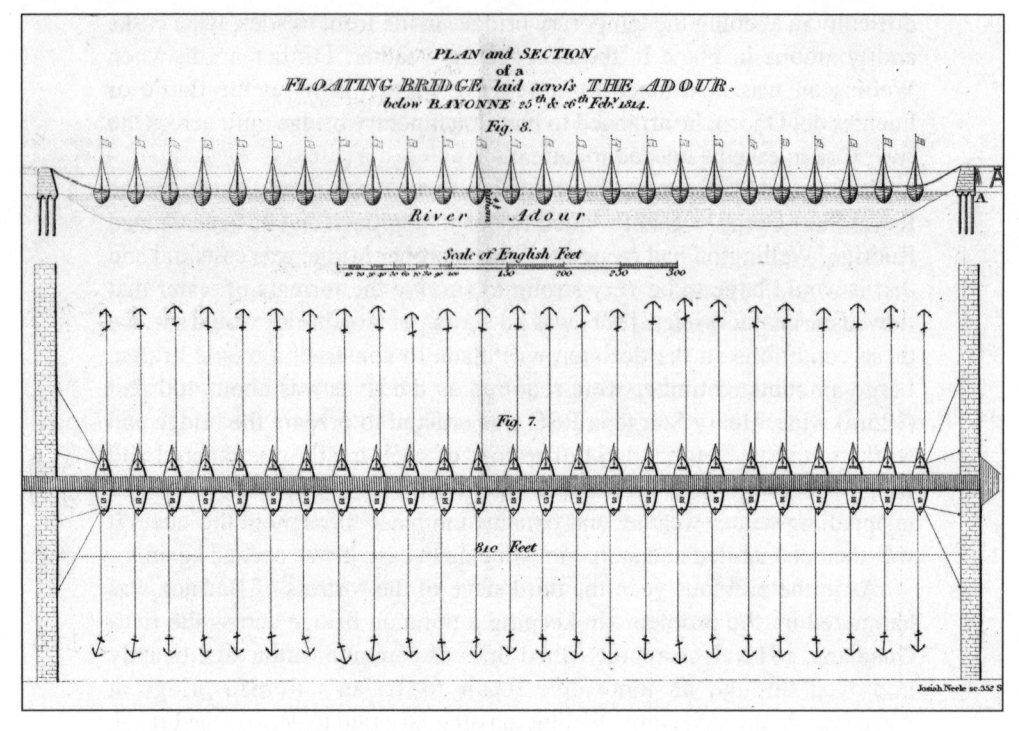

The bridge over the Adour, from Douglas.

along with their Portuguese, Spanish and Hanoverian counterparts laboured throughout the war to keep a myriad of smaller river crossings operational.

As discussed earlier, there were three British engineering units present, the Royal Engineers, the Royal Military Artificers (the Royal Sappers and Miners from 1812) and the Royal Staff Corps. Theoretically there was a distinction, in that the role of the Royal Engineers was for static defences i.e. the attack and defence of fortresses whilst mobile work was the responsibility of the Royal Staff Corps i.e. field works and bridging. There is still a debate going on about bridging, as the perceived view is that it was primarily done by the RSC. My research indicates that the Royal Engineers did most bridging work. There is a difference in that the Royal Engineers tending to do most destruction whilst the Royal Staff Corps were more involved in construction. What is apparent is that the officers from the different corps did share information and experience for the benefit of all. The picture on page 86 of the bridge at Ponte de Murcella comes from Douglas' book on military bridging. Identical pictures are in the contemporary notebooks of Engineer and Staff Corps officers (Burgoyne, Scott and West).

What all the engineer officers faced was a lack of resources, both in men and materials. This meant that river crossings often had to be made with whatever material was available. At its simplest this could be preparing the banks and bed of a river for fording. For smaller rivers and smaller loads, pontoons or boats could be rowed across, sometimes with lines to keep them in place.

The real challenge came when large bodies of troops or heavy loads needed to cross big rivers. Here the nature of the river determined the bridging methods that could be used. Flying bridges, trestles, local boats, wine casks and pontoons were all used at different times. The most frequent method was probably the repair of an existing bridge. More often than not, temporary repairs were carried out using locally-sourced wood. There are many examples where the material obtained either from nearby woods or by dismantling buildings. The two most impressive examples of this during the war were the repair to the stone bridge at Alcantara in 1812 and the crossing of the Adour in 1814. The repairs to the bridge at Alcantara (and also Almaraz) were designed by Henry Sturgeon and Alexander Todd of the Royal Staff Corps. The design is described by Andrew Leith-Hay:

> The arch destroyed was of so extensive a span, and the parapet of the bridge so great a height from the bed of the river, that no repair by using timber was practicable; the gap to be passed over being ninety feet wide, and the height of the bridge, one hundred and eighty from the bed of the river . . . The work was commenced by placing two beams on supporters four feet high and ninety feet asunder. These were secured to the side and end walls of the building by braces and tackles, to prevent their approximating by the straining of the ropes. Eighteen cables were then stretched round them, extending from end to end; eight pieces of timber, six inches square, at equal distances, were placed upon the ropes, with notches, one foot asunder, cut on their surface to secure them; these notches were seared with hot irons to prevent the ropes from chafing. The cables were then lashed to the beams; they were netted together by rope-yarn, and chains of sleepers were bolted and laid on the network, and secured to the two beams originally placed at the extremities of the work. Planks were cut and prepared for being laid across, bored at the ends so as receive a line destined to secure them to the sleepers and to each other . . . The next point was to prepare the edge of the fractured part of the bridge, and to cut channels in the masonry for

the reception of the purchases. When arrived on the spot, four strong ropes were stretched from side to side, as conductors, for passing the cable-bridge across, the beam on the south side having been previously sunk into the masonry; the whole was then stretched by windlass erected on the opposite pier, by which means it was so tightly drawn as to prevent any great sinking, or the vibration which might render it insecure and dangerous, even when heavy weights were passed over.[3]

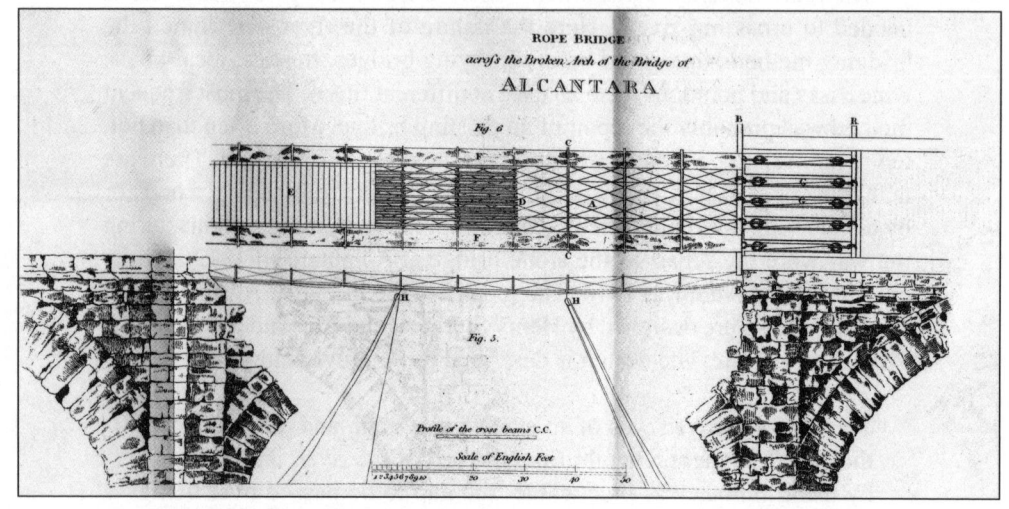

The rope bridge at Alcantara.

Crossing the river Adour in February 1814 required the construction of the largest boat bridge of the war. Over forty large local boats were used, held in place by five 13in cables. These were secured at one end by connecting them to a number of siege gun barrels and tightened using a capstan and pulley arrangement on the other bank. The design of this bridge bears striking similarities to the ones at Alcantara and Almaraz and must be attributed to Sturgeon and Todd.

Pontoon Trains
For the first part of the war, the Allies had very little mobile bridging equipment. Their only pontoon train was lost to the French when Badajoz was captured in March 1811. It is unlikely to be coincidence that Wellington wrote home on 31 March asking for a full pontoon train to be shipped out to the Peninsula. He was now commanding forces operating in two different theatres and it was essential that reliable communications were maintained

BRIDGE OVER THE TAGUS AT ALMARAZ.

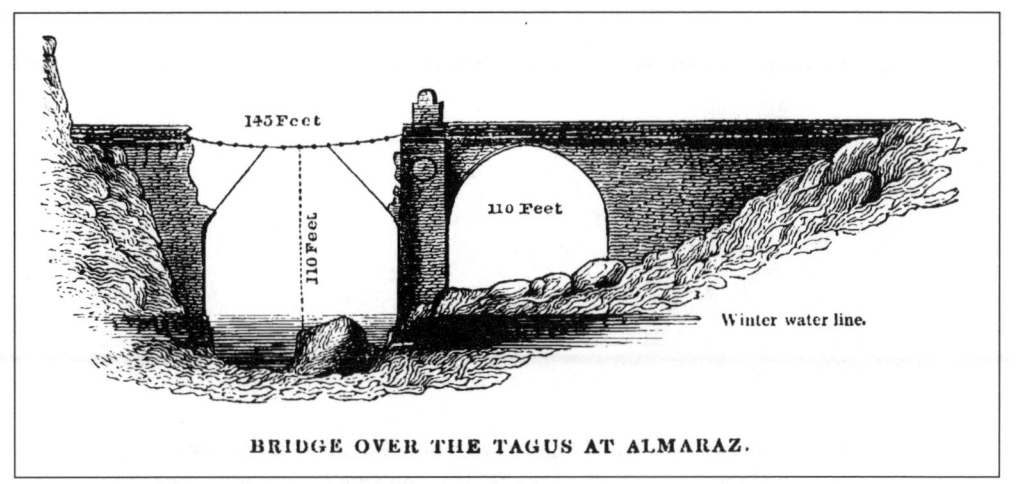

The bridge over the Tagus at Almaraz, by Leith-Hay.

between these two forces. Probably based on their excellent work over the past few weeks, on 18 April Wellington asked for two more companies of Royal Staff Corps to be sent out and noting that as 'there are no people of the description of pontooneers belonging to the service, I beg that ten warrant artificers may be sent with the pontoons . . . who will be employed to superintend the persons who must be hired in Portugal to attend them [the pontoons]'.[4]

The experience of crossing the Guadiana in May 1811 reinforced the need to have an effective pontoon train with the army. The first of the pontoons from England did not arrive until June 1811, by which time most of the campaigning for the year was over. In October, Fletcher asked for a 'person well acquainted with the construction of pontoons, the various articles belonging to them and the method of applying them would be extremely useful in this country as foreman of pontoon bridges'.[5]

British pontoons came in two sizes; small, approximately 16ft x 4ft (4.9m x 1.2m) and large, approximately 21ft x 5ft (6.4m x 1.5m). They were made of tin-plated iron and, with all their equipment, weighed over 1.5 tons.

Pontoon Weights[6]	Large Pontoon (kg)	Small Pontoon (kg)
Boat	500	350
Carriage	650	600
Equipment	650	450
Total weight	1,800	1,400

A British pontoon.

A pontoon carriage needed eight horses and, I assume, a greater number oxen to move them even on good roads. Transporting the pontoon train was a massive undertaking as its components were very large, very unstable and very fragile. There was also no clear responsibility. A Royal Engineer officer was usually in overall charge, with the Royal Artillery responsible for the horses. No one took responsibility for the drivers whether they were hired locally, seamen or from the Corps of Drivers.

Lieutenant Piper RE, who commanded the pontoon train in 1812, reported that Portuguese seamen who had been attached to the pontoon train had no rations supplied to them. He also reported in December that year that most of the bullock drivers deserted through not being paid, Piper not saying if they took their bullocks with them. In the same letter he reported that the pontoons were rusting badly. A second pontoon train joined the army at the start of 1813. Writing in May 1813, Harry Jones reported the delays in its progress:

> Piper was ... left to himself without any assistance to be found ... or any provision made against desertions of cattle, [i.e., the bullocks to pull the pontoon train] which unquestionably would be great from non-payment; so we are doomed always to labour under the greatest disadvantages of service and want of exertion on the part of those whose duty it is to provide us, or do their best, with everything that we may require.[7]

In a return of May 1813, Fletcher described the pontoon train that was moving up for the Vitoria campaign. It comprised 48 wagons with 350 men, 520 oxen and 310 horses. He also recorded the breakages it suffered over a three-week period:[8]

Appendix 4 231

Problem	Numbe
Axle bed broken/repaired/replaced	40
Draft poles repaired/replaced	25
Carriage wheels repaired/replaced	64
Carriage/boat upset	14
Pontoon boats repaired	3
Total breakages	146

The pontoons continued to be a problem when they were in use. The poor design of the English pontoon, with a square bow, shallow draft and an open top, led to predictable results; they were prone to sinking. This happened spectacularly in early 1812 during the third siege of Badajoz. Several were recovered from the bottom of the river but some were lost. A new enclosed design was approved in 1814, but they were too late for service in the Peninsular War.

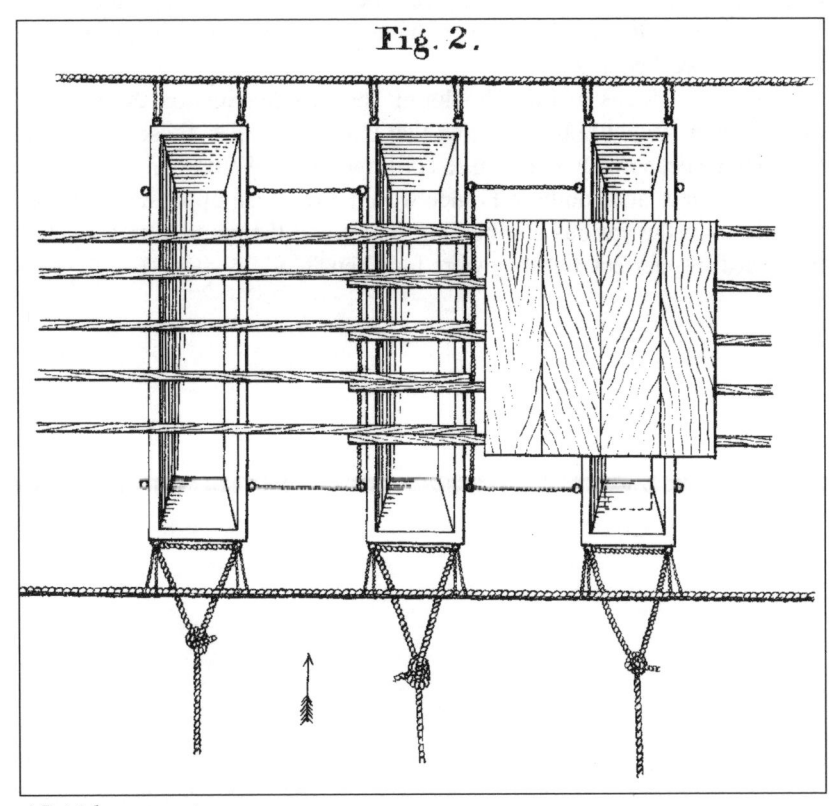

A British pontoon in use.

The final campaigns of the war saw the greatest need for military bridging and also the greatest difficulties. December 1813 saw the great rivers of the Bidassoa, Nivelle and Nive being crossed. The winter weather in the Pyrenees made working difficult, the rivers being invariably rapid and the level could rise by several feet with almost no warning. Keeping bridges in place was a constant challenge.

February 1814 saw the audacious crossing of the river Adour, as described above. Wellington took a small pontoon train east with his forces which was sufficient for most of the rivers he crossed but failed spectacularly around Toulouse, where one attempt had to be abandoned as the bridge was too short and the main crossing was held up for three days.

Considering the strategic importance of bridging in the Peninsula, it is surprising that more attention was not paid to it. Typically, the bridging train was commanded by a junior engineer, with the Royal Artillery responsible for much of the motive power, be that horses or oxen. The boatmen were provided by the Portuguese Navy. There were several civilian commissary staff and wagons attached and the drivers could come from the Royal Corps of Drivers, Royal Artillery or be hired locally. As previously mentioned, locally-hired mules and their owners were rarely paid or fed. It is surprising the system worked at all!

Whilst the focus of most books on the war remains on the military operations, it must not be forgotten that without bridges, those operations would have been much more limited or impossible. Wellington's campaign in the Pyrenees and southern France would have been impossible without the efforts of the various engineering forces and the pontoon trains. They were far from perfect, but they were indispensible.

Appendix 5

Military Education

The need for trained specialists had been recognised in the English army since the invention of gunpowder. Artillery specialists had always been present in very small numbers, but there was no recognition that training was required for army officers prior to them receiving their first commissions. The chapter on tactics in the first monthly edition of the *Royal Military Chronicle* in 1810, began with: 'It is often mentioned . . . [by] foreigners who have travelled in England, as a subject of reasonable astonishment, that we are totally without any general school for military instruction'.[1] Contradicting the views of many of the most senior officers of the day, including Wellington, the article went on to argue against the 'very shallow' objections to the study of military science to allow an infantry officer to perform his role effectively.

The eighteenth century saw the formation of the first school in England to specifically address military education. The opening of the Royal Military Academy by the Board of Ordnance in 1741 recognised the need for consistent training for artillery and engineer specialists to meet the growing demand for officers. The Army would not recognise the need for 'scientific soldiers' for another fifty years.

The question of effective provision of training and resources to the Royal Engineers is an important one. Their activities during the Peninsular War have been heavily criticised by many authors and it is time for a re-evaluation of their performance based on the availability of new primary materials and a greater understanding of the logistical and political challenges that they faced.

The Royal Military Academy and its Role in the Training of Officers
The Royal Military Academy was created in 1741 to meet the need for better-trained officers for the Ordnance Department, primarily for the Royal Artillery. At this time the Royal Engineers did not exist as a distinct corps, although the Ordnance Department retained some officers trained as engineers. The Royal Warrant of 30 April 1741 stated 'that it would conduce to the good of our service if an Academy . . . was instituted . . . for instructing

the ... people belonging to the Military branch of this office, ... to qualify them for the service of the artillery, and the business of engineers'.[2]

The rules and procedures that were drafted made it clear that the original intention was wider than the training of new cadets. The *Rules and Orders*, with the associated *Directions for the Teaching of Theory and Practice*, made it clear that the lectures should be attended by 'Engineers, Officers, Sergeants, Corporals and Cadets' of the Royal Artillery, and also all such ... as have a capacity and inclination'.[3] The word 'inclination' suggests that the various officers and soldiers mentioned had some choice in their attendance, and it should be noted that there was no greater onus on the cadets' attendance than there was on the others.

The Governor of the Academy was the Master-General himself, who delegated its day-to-day command to the Commanding Royal Engineer at Woolwich. In 1744, it was decided that the cadets would be withdrawn from the artillery companies and formed into 'The Company of Gentlemen Cadets' with an original establishment of forty.[4] Apart from attending for lectures and parades, the cadets were left to themselves, which did not appear to have done much for discipline or their studies. In many cases these cadets were young children, possibly away from home or some form of control for the first time in their lives.

In 1764 a Lieutenant Governor was appointed with direct responsibility for the day-to-day running of the Academy and in 1772, the first Inspector of the Royal Military Academy was appointed. Through their efforts, the teaching standards and the behaviour of both cadets and masters improved.[5]

\multicolumn{4}{c}{Size of the Royal Military Academy.}
Year	Number of Cadets	Year	Number of Cadets
1744	40	1810	200 (0 for EIC)
1746	48	1816	188
1782	60	1819	150
1793	90	1820	100
1798	100 (40 for EIC)	1828	60
1803	180 (60 for EIC)	1831	90
1806	248 (60 for EIC)	1839	100
1807	259 (45 for EIC)[6]		

In 1798, the number of cadets was increased to 100, although this was actually a decrease due to an agreement with the East India Company (EIC) that allowed forty of its engineer cadets to be trained. To make up the numbers for the Ordnance Department, 'extra cadets' were placed in local schools around Woolwich. In 1803, numbers were increased again to 180, of which sixty were for the East India Company. One hundred of these were at Woolwich and eighty were placed at the new Royal Military College at Great Marlow.[7] In 1810, the East India Company opened its own college at Addiscombe, and the Ordnance cadets were all moved back to Woolwich.[8]

From 1741 to 1774 all requests for entry to the Royal Military Academy were made directly to the Master-General. At this time there was no entrance examination. The newly-appointed Lieutenant Governor found on his arrival that many cadets on the muster-roll were not present at the Academy. On ordering them to report, he found the youngest was not yet ten years old. In 1774, the Master-General approved the use of an entrance examination based on the 'the first four rules of arithmetic with a competent knowledge of the rule of three and the elements of Latin grammar'.[9] This was seen as essential to improve entry standards.

In 1782 the minimum age of entry was raised to fourteen.[10] The general requirements were 'to be well grounded in arithmetic, including vulgar fractions, write a very good hand, and be perfectly the master of the English and Latin grammars'. In 1813, the Lieutenant-Governor, Colonel Mudge, persuaded the Master-General to further tighten the entry qualifications for the admission of Gentleman Cadets:[11]

> No candidate can be admitted under 14 or over 16 years. Must be possessed of (at 14) decimal fractions, duodecimals, or cross multiplication, Involution, Extraction of the square root, notation and the first four rules of Algebra, Definitions in Plane Geometry, English Grammar and Parsing, French Grammar. At 16 add, remainder of Algebra except cubic equations, the first two books of Euclid's 'Elements of Geometry' or the first 65 theorems of Dr Hutton's course of Mathematics, construing and parsing the French language.[12]

It is likely that part of the reason for tightening up the entrance requirements was to reduce the time the cadets would take to complete their studies and therefore to be able to turn out officers faster. The length of study at the Academy varied from one month to the maximum of five years. The duration depended primarily on the prior education, intelligence and application of the cadet, but also on the demand for officers by the

Ordnance.[13] In 1810, the entry fee for the Royal Military Academy was twenty guineas (£21). This amount was very small compared with the cost of buying a commission, which was around £400 in a line regiment and £900 in the Guards.[14]

In the period immediately after the foundation of the Academy, 'the cadets were under no discipline worthy of the name; they wore no uniform, and were so outrageous in study, that one of the occupations of the officer on duty . . . was [to] prevent the Masters from being ill-used, and even pelted.'[15] Discipline was a major problem through the whole period and there were many documented cases of bullying for the purpose of stopping the studious cadet from embarrassing his less industrious peers.[16] Many cadets were dismissed for their behaviour. The attitude to study was seriously affected by the demand for cadets. Throughout the Napoleonic wars the demand far outstripped the supply. This had two effects. Firstly there was pressure on the Academy to speed up the education process, which led to pressure to reduce the examination requirements. Secondly, the cadets knew the situation and on occasions had seen cadets commissioned without having to take the examinations, which had been first introduced in 1764 and were held annually, attended by senior officers of the Ordnance.[17] At that time, the gentlemen cadets had to be:

> examined and found to be qualified in Arithmetic and logarithms; Algebra as far as Quadratic equations; the first four books of Euclid; Mensuration including trigonometry and heights and distances; practical geometry; the general principles of fortification the construction of the three systems of Vauban the definition and explanation of artillery in general and the construction of a piece of ordnance, illustrated by 24 drawings; they must also be able to read and translate French.[18]

The Napoleonic Wars made demands on the supply of officers that the Academy could not meet. From 1794 to 1811, the public examination of cadets was suspended and the syllabus of the examinations varied as the demand rose and fell. The demand for officers was so great that on occasions exams were held on an individual basis as soon as a cadet felt himself competent. In 1795, the inspector was asked to recommend without examination, those cadets 'who may appear likely to prove useful at this moment as officers'.[19]

> I am directed to inform you, . . . that the . . . service requires an immediate supply of officers from the Royal Military Academy; his

> lordship therefore desires that . . . you will recommend to him for promotion such of the cadets . . . as may appear likely to prove useful at this moment as officers . . . However as the persons you are now required to propose are wanted for immediate service, a certain degree of height and manliness will be indispensably necessary, and you are not to recommend any one . . . who has not attained the height of five foot four inches.[20]

In June 1798, a change was made to the way commissions were awarded. Previously, all commissions were awarded into the Royal Artillery, with officers stating their preference to be transferred to the Royal Engineers:

> The Master-General . . . thinks it more advisable that a limited number of such cadets as may be found to have a turn for the profession should (after being duly qualified at the Academy) be sent to some station where they may improve themselves . . . by acting as Assistant-Engineers until vacancies occur for them in the Corps.[21]

The custom was that cadets wishing to join the Royal Engineers would remain at the Academy for a further six months to improve their knowledge. On 1 March 1803, the Lieutenant-Governor proposed that candidates for the Royal Engineers 'instead of remaining at the Academy an extra six months . . . were to be sent to the Royal Military Surveyors under the direction of Major Mudge, to be instructed in surveying'.[22] This had the dual benefit of getting the junior engineers some practical experience, while also providing a trained resource for the urgent task of mapping the southern shores of England, threatened by a French invasion.

The Royal Engineer officers who served in operational theatres throughout the Napoleonic Wars were the officers who passed through the Royal Military Academy during the period when public examinations were stopped and private examination requirements were variable. The most senior officer who served in the Peninsula, Richard Fletcher, was commissioned in 1790, at the start of this period. The other senior officers who served in the Peninsula were commissioned between 1793 and 1800, and all the captains by 1804.[23]

There is no doubt that the Royal Military Academy was concerned about the level of education that was being given to the cadets. There is no doubt that demand outstripped supply throughout the period, but there is also no doubt that even the partial training of an Ordnance officer at the Academy was far in excess of anything that was given to a regular army officer at that time. Until the Royal Military College started producing its first recruits after 1800, there was no other source of officers with some education and technical training.

The Royal Military Artificers, and the School of Military Engineering
The formation of the Royal Military Artificers (RMA) was discussed earlier in the book. By the start of the nineteenth century it was recognised by some that garrison-based staff did not meet the Army's requirements. This was one of the reasons why the Royal Staff Corps was formed. The intention behind the formation of the RMA was to provide skilled workmen at the main Ordnance locations around Britain, Europe and eventually the globe. There was never an intention that these troops would be mobile and available to travel in significant numbers with an army. Lacking their own officers, they were never properly managed and were allowed levels of freedom which should never have been tolerated in any military organisation. Captain Charles William Pasley commented on the soldiers 'going grey' in the corps, while stagnating in the same location.

When Pasley took command of the Plymouth Company in 1811, not one of the RMA companies had been employed as a unit on active service. In a letter to a fellow officer, he wrote:

> The command of the Company here gives me a greater insight into the nature of our establishment . . . There is no guard except of a Sunday at the Barrack gates, which breaks up at eleven o'clock . . . The . . . backward spirit amongst the Non Commissioned Officers is very great, and their ideas of subordination are exceedingly lax . . . I think these companies will not be worth much till they are changed every two or three years, and go upon actual service bodily, not by detachments.[24]

Pasley's role in the advancement of the RMA will be described further below. Another famous engineer from the period, John Thomas Jones, wrote:

> After . . . observing how very much the want of Sappers and Miners prejudiced every siege operation in Spain, it will be learnt with surprise that, . . . England paid, fed, clothed, and lodged a very large body of engineer troops, . . . These . . . composed chiefly of mechanics, were considered as more intimately intended for permanent works; and the most limited number were reluctantly

spared for field service, it being difficult to make it understood how mechanics could be required in any great number with an army.[25]

Although it had been known for some years that the Ordnance could not easily put together troops for active operations, the start of the Peninsular War highlighted this serious inadequacy both in the numbers available and the quality of the soldiers' training. Throughout the early years of the war, the Corps struggled and the sieges of 1811 brought home the fact that the current situation could not continue.

The problem had been recognised at home. Steps were being taken, but they would not bring immediate changes. One significant step was taken in May 1811 when the size of the RMA was increased to four battalions of eight companies, with a total strength of over 2,800 men. At the same time it was decided that in future the RMA companies would be rotated around the locations and would move as a whole body rather than in small detachments.[26]

The deficiency in the field was known to many of the engineers and Jones made reference in his diary in April 1811 to 'an arrangement made for instructing the RMA and the younger officers in the manner of forming a sap'.[27] A group of RMA artificers had just arrived at Elvas, under the command of Captain Ross, and since they had no previous training in operational activities, it was decided to begin training them.[28] Over the following days, Jones' diary noted that the General Order allocated 100 men from the ranks who had artificer skills, being brigaded with the RMA and being trained in siege works. The instructions they received included physically digging a sap to learn what was required. Clearly, all this preparation was for the first siege of Badajoz, and occurred before the training referred to above by Burgoyne.[29] This method of training troops from the ranks was tried during the first and second sieges of Badajoz, but with very limited success. Training troops from the line regiments at the point of need was not going to provide the skills and dedication that was required. The training also required the continuous involvement of the engineers and the troops, both of which proved very difficult. Although Burgoyne was first asked to train troops in July 1811, the order was repeated in November that year,[30] showing how difficult it was to provide any consistent form of training due to interruptions caused by operational movements. Burgoyne's diary through this period, makes almost no mention of the instruction of troops, but makes frequent mention of part or all of the 3rd Division being moved. There is no mention of instruction between the first entry on 15 August 1811 and the repeat order in November, this period of course being when Marmont was manoeuvring in front of Ciudad

Rodrigo. There is then no further mention in Burgoyne's diary up to the end of the year. It is very unusual that Burgoyne did not mention the training in his diary if it was happening, some comment, whether positive or negative, would be expected. Burgoyne does not mention the training in any of his letters before his long letter criticising the siege of Ciudad Rodrigo, dated 12 February 1812. This lack of comment suggests that little training was in fact carried out.

John Squire wrote to Pasley in March 1812:

> Every event in this country proves more and more the necessity of our having an establishment of Sappers and Miners . . . Lately at Ciudad Rodrigo we succeeded in taking the place more from its own weakness, than from any means we possessed of approaching nearer with success. I really should dread to attack a regular fortress : – we have no men fit for the operation, and if we attack Badajoz again, which is something like a regular place, depend upon it, that our loss in officers will be severe: – it must be so, until we have men drilled to this particular service. Your efforts at Plymouth do you the greatest credit . . . However, persevere in the noble work you have begun, and it is probable that their eyes may be opened, and they may be convinced.[31]

The noble work referred to by Squire, was Pasley's proposal to form a school to train soldiers in military engineering, who could effectively support the Royal Engineer officers in the field.

The Formation of the School of Military Engineering
The start of the nineteenth century saw the emergence of a new breed of engineer who faced challenges that British engineers had never done before. These engineers cut their teeth in sieges in Egypt, Turkey, South America and the Low Countries. They had seen first-hand the consequences of not having trained specialists to help with the attack and defence of places and had started calling for this situation to be rectified. Initially, these comments were addressed to each other, but the more forward-thinking, and in some respects, braver, officers started writing to their superiors making suggestions on how the corps could be made more effective. Their views did not always receive a good reception from some of the senior officers in the corps. 'Some of the old officers such as General Mercer; who objected that they could not see why this innovation should be introduced, since they themselves experienced no difficulties in the American War.'[32] General Morse, the Inspector-General of

Fortifications 'threw cold water on it [the proposals] from the first in all its stages'.[33]

The need to make changes became more public, primarily due to the actions of two men. The first was the Duke of Wellington, who suffered through four sieges in 1811 and early 1812, and wrote home on a number of occasions expressing his view that changes in the engineering service were required. On 11 February 1812, Wellington wrote to Lord Liverpool:

> I would beg to suggest to your Lordship the expediency of adding to the Engineer establishment a corps of Sappers and Miners. It is inconceivable with what disadvantage we undertake anything like a siege for want of assistance of this description . . . we are obliged to depend . . . upon the regiments of the line; and although the men are brave and willing, they want the knowledge and training which are necessary. Many casualties among them consequently occur, and much valuable time is lost at the most critical period of the siege.[34]

Wellington's letter after the third siege of Badajoz, in April 1812, made his views explicit and could not be ignored any longer. This letter, which was addressed privately to the Earl of Liverpool was lost for many years and was not printed in Wellington's dispatches. It was found in 1889, amongst Liverpool's papers:

> My dispatches of this date will convey the account of the capture of Badajoz, which affords as strong an instance of the gallantry of our troops as has ever been displayed. But I anxiously hope I shall never again be the instrument of putting them to such a test as that to which they were put last night. I assure your lordship that it is quite impossible to expect to carry fortified places by vive force without incurring great loss and being exposed to the chance of failure, unless the army should be provided with a regular trained corps of sappers and miners. I never yet knew a head of a military establishment or of an army undertaking a siege without the aid of such a corps, excepting the British Army . . . I earnestly recommend to your lordship to have a corps of Sappers and Miners formed without loss of time.[35]

Writing the day after Wellington, John Squire, who was one of the senior engineers at the siege, said nearly the same: 'This siege has served to confirm an opinion, which I have long since entertained – that constituted as our Corps is – we are decidedly not equal to the attack of a place . . .

Sappers and Miners are as necessary to engineers during a siege, as soldiers to the General.'[36]

The second person working for change was Charles William Pasley, a promising and intelligent young engineer officer who had seen service in a number of campaigns. He also had very strong views on what was necessary to make the Royal Engineers more effective. As a 29-year-old captain serving during the Walcheren campaign, he felt so strongly that he wrote to Colonel Fyers, Deputy Inspector-General of Fortifications, on 12 May 1809, enclosing his ideas 'on making the Corps more efficient'.[37] Unfortunately for his career, but luckily for the service, he suffered a serious back injury on 14 August 1809, at the siege of Flushing. After a lengthy period of convalescence, Pasley resumed duty in 1811, taking command of the Royal Military Artificer company at Plymouth. Pasley then set his mind to the task of improving the training and effectiveness of his company and over several months made huge improvements. He believed that artificers were required to support engineer officers on operational duty and the RMA in its current state was not capable of doing this. Pasley wrote bluntly and at length on his findings and proposed that a school should be set up to train soldiers who could be deployed with the army to assist in military engineering. In August 1811, John Rowley, Secretary to the Inspector-General of Fortifications, wrote to Pasley:

> On the subject of training the R.M. Artificers to their duties in the field . . . General Morse forwarded the letter you sent him, to the Master-General, with his recommendation . . . I . . . hope that his Lordship will think proper to call upon you to superintend and carry on the system of instruction you have so well pointed out.[38]

Not waiting for any official sanction for his activities, Pasley continued with what he believed was right, but kept his superiors informed of his actions.

> Since I last wrote to your lordship upon this subject, I have employed my spare time entirely in digesting a system of instruction for the use of the young officers of engineers and for the non-commissioned officers and soldiers of the department. When complete, it will be, to the engineer department, what General Dundas' book is to the army. And, though I have no model to follow . . . I have practically proved the efficacy of it by the rapid improvement of the Royal Military Artificers under my command.[39]

Considering that Pasley was only a captain, his correspondence verged on the insubordinate. Writing to Colonel Commandant Mann, the Inspector-General of Fortifications, in January 1812:

> I enclose a memoir upon the state of the engineers department, which will fully explain the grounds upon which I consider it the most inefficient department in His Majesty's Service . . . Not long after the retreat . . . of the British troops employed under Sir John Moore, in a campaign, in which the defects of the department had been fully proved . . . Lord Chatham directed General Morse to give in a plan for forming an establishment of trained sappers and miners, with a view to render the Corps efficient in the Field . . . Major Lefebure had declined the command in Portugal when offered to him, on the avowed plea; that the engineer Establishment in the field was so imperfect, that the officers had nothing before them but a prospect of certain failure and disgrace in every operation of importance . . . At Copenhagen and Flushing, the most mortifying blunders, confusion and delays took place owing to the inefficiency of the department . . . At Badajoz . . . some of our most promising officers of the Corps, either suffered, or actually fell a sacrifice to the defects of the system. Captain Dickenson lost his life [at Badajoz], because he was obliged continually to expose himself on the top of a parapet, showing the men of the working party how to place and picket down fascines . . . As a proof of this I have learned since I wrote you last [sic], that Lord Wellington has lately adopted an expedient for obviating . . . the defective state of the Establishment. For two or three months past, a certain number of soldiers . . . have been trained to sapping and other field duties of the engineer department. If something of the same kind is not Established at home by authority of the Master-General from whom it will naturally be expected that all improvements of the engineer department should originate; I am sorry to say that I feel thoroughly persuaded that the Ordnance Department will soon sink into public contempt and that the consequences of the necessary measures just stated, to which Lord Wellington has been forced to resort for the safety of his army, may prove in the end highly injurious to the honour and interests of the Corps of Royal Engineers, and may tend to set aside the Royal Military Artificers altogether as an [sic] useless and contemptible description of troops which I know that they are generally considered.[40]

Although the tone of the letter was very strong, his views were obviously supported by some of the Ordnance hierarchy as his proposals for setting up a school were well received and being seriously considered. Events in early 1812 were moving fast.

> As General Mann is very desirous that the instruction of the R.M. Artificers in the construction of field works, should be put in train . . . he wishes to see you upon the subject as soon as convenient . . . General Mann wishes you would turn in your mind some outline . . . for him to lay before the Master-General, as to the best means of carrying the system into effect, with some idea if possible of the expense which would attend it upon any given scale.[41]

Pasley's ideas were also being aired by his peers who were serving in the Peninsula. Richard Fletcher wrote to the Inspector-General of Fortifications after the siege of Ciudad Rodrigo in January 1812 that 'the sappers we lately employed were taken from the Third Division, and had received such instruction as time and means afforded, under Captain Burgoyne. They were certainly useful, but far from expert.'[42]

Fletcher also submitted a proposal for the creation of a corps of sappers and miners which was different from Pasley's proposals. They were similar in a number of ways, but clearly developed independently. This leads to the question of whether Fletcher knew of Pasley's proposal, and also if there was any communication between Fletcher and Pasley, as it seems unusual that Fletcher would have submitted a separate proposal at this time if he knew of and agreed with Pasley's. Fletcher's main subordinates, Burgoyne, Squire and Jones, certainly all knew of Pasley's plans and it is inconceivable that Fletcher did not. It appears that Fletcher was proposing a quick-fix solution for immediate implementation by cherry-picking the best soldiers from the Royal Military Artificers and using junior Royal Engineer officers to command them.

Pasley's continued correspondence with the Master-General eventually led to him submitting a proposal to set up the School of Military Engineering. The Inspector-General approved the recommendation and Pasley was asked to take command of the new School of Military Engineering. On 23 April 1812 the Royal Warrant was issued by the Prince Regent authorising the establishment of the school at Chatham under Pasley.[43] The Warrant was signed on the same day that Wellington's dispatch of 7 April was received in London.[44]

The first soldiers from Pasley's school were in the Peninsula before the end of 1812. Though there were still complaints about their skills, they were a major improvement on the performance of the RMA. Apart from training more suited to operational activities, they now came with their own subaltern officers, which removed the problem of the RMA having no constant and consistent leadership. Another consequence of the formation of the school, which appears to have been overlooked by all writers on the subject, was that from 1812, all newly-commissioned Royal Engineer officers were sent to the school to instruct and be instructed on practical field works. The Corps monthly returns state clearly that officers were being sent to Chatham for this purpose.[45] Writing to his sister in May 1812, Pasley's view is clearly explained 'you know I have long had a plan in view of training the young officers and all the N.C. Officers and soldiers to their field duties'.[46] He had used almost identical words in a letter to John Burgoyne in March 1812.[47] Also, in a minute from the meeting of the Board of Ordnance dated 11 May 1812, reference is made to 'the System of Instruction in the Field Duties intended for the junior officers of engineers and the Corps of Military Artificers Sappers and Miners'.[48] Pasley's memoir on the formation of the Royal Sappers and Miners stated that the key role of the engineer officers was the instruction of the soldiers, but went on to say:

> When the officers of engineers are not occupied in military or field duties, they have a course of study laid down for them, calculated to improve them in the science of attack, upon which the art of fortification is founded. They are required to present memoirs relative to the various operations of a siege, stating the number of men, materials and tools, and the distribution of them.[49]

The junior officers typically spent a further four to six months gaining experience of the practical aspects of their profession and also gained valuable insight into the command of the first sappers and miners who were to be sent to the Peninsula. In many cases, these junior officers would travel to the Peninsula in command of the soldiers they had trained with. Pasley also used any other officers who were available to come and teach the new recruits. A testament to the newly-formed establishment was given by Lieutenant Colonel Samuel Dickens, who wrote to Pasley requesting permission to spend a couple of months at the school, 'to take a little instruction' before going out to the Peninsula.[50]

Pasley was keen to eliminate the previous problem of poor discipline by attaching engineer officers permanently to each company of the Royal Sappers and Miners. Whilst he acknowledged that many engineer officers were averse to any form of regimental duties, which they saw as 'drudgery', he saw the introduction of the newly-commissioned junior engineers immediately into the regimental role at Chatham as a way of reducing this view. Pasley also put forward the notion that there should be one title, 'Royal Engineers', for both the officers and the soldiers. He saw the two separate titles as causing a lack of concern in the engineer officers about the actions of the artificers as they took no pride or responsibility for their actions and reputation.[51]

The Engineers' View of their Training

The common view in the army of artillery and engineer officers was that they were studious, stuffy and pedantic. The term 'Scientific Soldier' was a term that was used at this time and the training and education of Ordnance officers differed significantly from the training and education of junior officers in the army. But was this perception based on fact? Were the Ordnance officers better trained? Were they competent to undertake the tasks they would be asked to perform? Did the Ordnance even understand what the requirements were for modern warfare in Europe?

In the eighteenth century, their experience was almost non-existent. Early eighteenth-century campaigns made extensive use of officers from other European nations to provide the specialist engineering services in British armies. More recent operations were focussed on colonial campaigns in India or America, or limited attacks on coastal fortresses often carried out by, or with, the Royal Navy. There was very limited experience of siege warfare in Europe. Wellington was one of the few British generals who had experience of siege warfare, but 'Sepoy' experience counted for little at home.

The engineer officers who were involved in operations in the early years of the nineteenth century were not happy with the training they had received and felt that changes were required. There was resistance from several senior Ordnance officers to the reforms which were being proposed by the younger breed of engineer officer like Pasley, Squire, Lefebure and Burgoyne. Bearing in mind the remarks made above on the Royal Military Academy and the quality of training the cadets received, it is important to note that many of the officers who played prominent roles in the Napoleonic Wars passed through the Royal Military Academy during the period when examination requirements were being lowered to meet the demand for officers.

In most (if not all) cases, the officers themselves complained bitterly about their training and their experiences. One only has to look at the campaigns in which they fought in the period from 1793 to 1810 to realise that they had almost all had nothing but bad experiences at Alexandria, Buenos Ayres, Copenhagen and Walcheren. There was a constant theme of the lack of training engineer officers had received in the practical aspects of their work. Pasley, writing around 1811, set out his views.

> I should have suggested several improvements that appeared to me from my own experience and reflection to be essential . . . I considered the British Army . . . to be incapable of succeeding in a siege, . . . without either having recourse to the barbarous measure in incendiary bombardment, or without an enormous sacrifice of the lives . . . in sanguinary assaults . . . which might be rendered unnecessary by a more efficient organization of the Royal Engineer department, and especially by forming a well-instructed and well-disciplined body of engineer soldiers . . . The better instruction of the junior officers of the Royal Engineers appeared no less essential, for at that time they were not even taught the theory of the attack of fortresses . . . and the examinations for commissions were merely a matter of form, and no genuine test for proficiency. As for practical instruction, they had none, for they were sent on service without ever having seen a fascine or gabion, without the smallest knowledge of the military passage of rivers, of military mining, or any other operation of a siege, excepting what they may pick up from French writers, of which a striking proof occurred in Sir John Moore's retreat, when all attempts to blow up stone bridges . . . made by officers of the Corps, myself amongst others, failed . . . with the exception of only one, which Lieutenant Davy, a very promising young officer, succeeded in completely destroying, but at the expense of his own life, which he lost from not understanding the very simple precautions necessary to insure the safety of the person who fires the train of the mine. For my part, I should not have even known how to make a battery in the attack on Copenhagen, the first siege in which I was employed, but from the information I derived from a French book on the subject.[52]

Jones made a similar point in the preface of his book on the sieges during the Peninsular War, 'In the English language there exists not a single original treatise on sieges; all our knowledge of them is obtained from foreign writers'.[53]

Analysis of the movements of officers on these campaigns shows that there was a small number who repeatedly took part in operations and these officers came to know each other very well and trusted the judgement and discretion of their peers. Their letters over the period on occasions display an almost incandescent rage at the bad planning and organisation of engineering activities. The early years of the nineteenth century saw these officers talking amongst themselves about what needed to be changed. There was recognition that change at home was going to be very slow and they began to discuss how they could make progress themselves. Pasley described how this small group of officers responded to the challenge. The instigator appeared to be Charles Lefebure, who proposed forming a group to foster ideas and knowledge. When Lefebure was killed in April 1810, Burgoyne seems to have taken up the challenge. This was no easy task, as many of the officers were in different locations and planning was over an extended period by letter. In 1810 the 'Society for Procuring Useful Military Information' was formed with an initial membership of six, made up of John Burgoyne, Sebastian Dickenson, George Ross, Edmund Mulcaster, John Jones and John Squire.[54] Its aim was the 'encouragement of military study and engineering'.[55] Membership was by invitation only and restricted to officers 'as are inclined to be of the same way of thinking with ourselves'.[56] One unexpected omission from the initial group was Charles Pasley. He was a logical choice for membership, even if it was for the sole reason of having a UK-based supporter who could collate, disseminate and promote information on the Society's behalf. The probable reason why Pasley was not amongst the founder members was because he was recovering from the injuries he received at Walcheren. Also omitted from the group were the senior engineers in the Peninsula during the period, Richard Fletcher and Howard Elphinstone. Elphinstone was, by this time, back in England, but Fletcher's omission is more surprising. Very little correspondence has survived on the activities of this group. What is clear, however, is the recognition of the need to share experiences and to improve effectiveness in the Corps. That no senior officers were invited to join indicates that the membership did not feel they shared its views.

What is clear is that the skills of the engineers and artificers at the end of the Napoleonic Wars were far greater than they were at the start. The British had a trained and experienced mobile force that was able to meet the demands of the army in 1815 and the years beyond. The demobilisation after the wars slowly eroded this position and the forces that headed for the Crimea thirty-five years later appeared to have forgotten most of what was learnt.

Notes

Abbreviations Used in the Notes
BL = British Library
NA = National Archives
REM = Royal Engineers' Museum
WD = *Wellington's Dispatches*
WSD = *Wellington's Supplementary Dispatches*

Acknowledgements
1. Page, *Intelligence Officer in the Peninsula: Letters & Diaries of Major the Hon. Edward Charles Cocks 1786-1812.*
2. Pen & Sword, 2006.

Introduction
1. NA WO55/977, Letter from Captain Howard Elphinstone, dated 31 July 1808.
2. This is the establishment number, not the actual number of officers serving.
3. Forbes, *History of the Army Ordnance Services*, Vol. 1, p. 173.
4. Ward, *The School of Military Engineering 1812-1909*, Chatham, 1909, p. 4.
5. Pasley, *Course of instruction originally composed for the use of the Royal Engineer Department*, Vol. 2, p. iv.

Chapter 1
1. REM 4201-274, Elphinstone to his wife, 27 July 1808.
2. REM 4201-274, Elphinstone to his wife, 6 August 1808.
3. Landmann, *Recollections of Military Life*, Vol. 2, pp. 93–5.
4. Ibid.
5. Ibid, p. 126.
6. Ibid, p. 127.
7. Ibid, p. 300.
8. REM 4201-274, Elphinstone to his wife, 21 August 1808.
9. NA WO55/977, Landmann to Morse, 17 August 1808 (should be 18 August).
10. NA WO55/977, Landmann to Morse, Vimeiro, 21 August 1808.
11. Landmann, *Recollections of Military Life*, Vol. 2, pp. 310–12.
12. NA WO55/977, Fletcher to Morse, 7 September 1808. A British Pound (£) was made up of 20 Shillings (s).
13. Burnham & McGuigan, *The British Army against Napoleon*, p. 146. Also, Haldane, *Official Letters*, p. 125.
14. NA WO55/977, Fletcher to Morse, *Amity* Transport, 27 July 1808.
15. NA WO55/977, Fletcher to Morse, Oeyras, 7 September 1808.
16. Most references to Fletcher's children mention five, not six. I have used six on the basis that Fletcher himself mentions six in a letter dated 27 July 1808. Two of the children died young and this may account for the discrepancy.
17. NA WO55/977, Fletcher to Morse, 8 October 1808.
18. NA WO55/1561, Fletcher to Morse, 22 October 1808.
19. NA WO55/1561/4.
20. NA WO55/1561, Fletcher to Morse, 22 October 1808.
21. NA WO55/1561/9 Burgoyne's report *en route* from Alhandra to Almeida.
22. NA WO55/958 Fletcher to Mann, Abrantes, 1 November 1808.
23. NA WO55/977, Fletcher to Morse, 26 November 1808.
24. NA WO55/958, Burgoyne to Fletcher, 23 November 1808.
25. BL Add63106, ff. 9-10, Squire to Bunbury, 10 September 1810.

250 Wellington's Engineers

26. Castlereagh, *Correspondence*, Vol. 6, pp. 371–2, 381. The original order from Castlereagh to Dyer, Roche and Patrick dated 19 June 1808. Doyle ordered out 2 July 1808 to accompany released Spanish prisoners.
27. These details taken from Fortescue, *British Army*, Vol. 6, pp. 256–60. These officers included Colonel Sir Thomas Dyer, Major Roche, Captain Patrick, Colonel Charles Doyle, Captain Whittingham and Major Cox.
28. Castlereagh, *Correspondence*, Vol. 6, pp. 416–18.
29. Castlereagh, *Correspondence*, Vol. 6, p. 413.
30. Leith-Hay, *Narrative of the Peninsular War*, 2nd edition, London, 1834.
31. Ibid, Vol. 1, pp. 16–17.
32. BL Add MS41961, f. 92, Pasley to Yorke, 30 August 1808, Castlereagh's letter was dated 26 August 1808. NA WO55/977 Pasley to Morse (probably), 1 September 1808. NA WO55/977 C.W. Pasley to Morse (probably), 1 September 1808.
33. BL Add MS41962, f. 184, Pasley to his brother, 10 February 1809.
34. Leith-Hay, *Narrative of the Peninsular War*, Vol. 1, p. 19.
35. Ibid, p. 22.
36. Ibid, pp. 28–32.
37. NAM 7004-16 f. 4, Pasley to Baird, 1? October 1808.
38. Fortescue, *British Army*, Vol. 6, p. 270.
39. NA WO55/977, Lefebure to Morse, Santander, 7 September 1808.
40. Leith-Hay, *Narrative of the Peninsular War*, Vol. 1, p. 33
41. NA WO55/977, Pasley to Handfield, 21 October 1808.
42. Fortescue, *British Army*, Vol. 6, p. 277.
43. Ibid, pp. 300–3.
44. NA WO30-35-1, Carmichael-Smyth to Baird, 24 November 1808.
45. NA WO55/977, Pasley to Handfield, 21 October 1808.
46. NA WO55/977, Jones to Handfield, 6 November 1808.
47. BL ADD41962, f. 98, Pasley Papers.
48. NAM 7004-16 f. 2, Birch to unknown correspondent, 3 November 1808.
49. NA WO55/977, Jones to Handfield, 6 November 1808.
50. NA WO55/977, Pasley to Lefebure, 4 November 1808.
51. NA WO55/977, Pasley to Handfield, 7 November 1808.
52. NA WO55/977, Pasley to Handfield, 11 November 1808.
53. Moore, *A Narrative of the Campaign of the British Army in Spain*, pp. 59–60.
54. NA WO55/977, Jones to Handfield, 17 November 1808.
55. Jones, *Autobiography*, pp. 22–6; NA WO55/977, Pasley to Handfield, Villa Franca, 6 December 1808.
56. Moore, *Narrative of the Campaign of the British Army in Spain*, p. 63.
57. Ibid, pp. 66–7.
58. Boothby, *Under England's Flag*, pp. 193–5.
59. Ibid, p.195.
60. Wrottesley, *Life of Burgoyne*, p. 30.
61. Boothby, *Under England's Flag*, pp. 200–1; Mulcaster diary, 28 December 1808.
62. Fortescue, *British Army*, Vol. 6, p. 368.
63. NAM 7004-15 f. 16, Birch to Leith, Corunna, 20 December 1808.
64. Boothby, *Under England's Flag*, p. 203.
65. Mulcaster diary, 11 January 1809.
66. Lipscombe, *Wellington's Guns*, p. 68.
67. Boothby, *Under England's Flag*, p. 218.
68. NA WO55/978 Chapman to Morse, Isle of Wight, 16 January 1809.

Chapter 2
1. NA WO55/1561/9, Mulcaster to Fletcher, 19 October 1808, and NA WO55/978, Landmann to Patton, 8 December 1808.
2. BL ADD MS57544, f. 204, Mackenzie to Moore, 13 December 1808.
3. NA WO55/977, Fletcher to Morse, St Julian, 23 September 1808.
4. NA WO55/958, Fletcher to Landmann, Salamanca, 26 November 1808.

Notes 251

5. NA WO55/978, Landmann to Patton, 8 December 1808. Landmann signed his letter, Commanding Royal Engineer.
6. NA WO55/958, Patton to Morse, 21 January 1809.
7. BL ADD MS39201, Mackenzie diary, entry dated 22 February 1809.
8. BL ADD MS39201, Frere to McKenzie, 25 February 1809.
9. NA WO55/958, Liverpool to Landmann, 7 November 1811. WO55/958, Landmann to Morse, 25 November 1811.
10. NA WO55/958, Drummond to Holloway, Gibraltar, 30 January 1809.
11. BL ADD MS39199, Evatt to Mackenzie, Seville, 15 February 1809.
12. NA WO55/958, Neville to Morse, South Street, London, 1 February 1809.
13. NA WO55/958, Fletcher to Morse, Lisbon, 9 April 1809.
14. NA WO55/958, Chapman to Morse, Lisbon, 5 March 1809.
15. NA WO55/958, Chapman to Morse, Lisbon, 22 March 1809.
16. NA WO55/958, Chapman to Morse, Lisbon, 22 March 1809.
17. Rice Jones, *An Engineer Officer under Wellington*, p. 11.
18. Wrottesley, *Life of Burgoyne*, p. 34.
19. NA WO55/978, Fletcher to Morse, London, 22 February 1809.
20. NA WO55/978, Fadden to Slater, 26 February 1809.
21. NA WO55/958, Fletcher to Morse, Lisbon, 3 April 1809.
22. NA WO55/958, Fletcher to Morse, Lisbon, 9 April 1809.
23. WD, Wellesley to Richmond, 14 April 1809. Although Wellesley saw this as a key task, it was not actually done for 18 months.
24. NA WO55/958, Fletcher to Morse, Lisbon, 13 April 1809.
25. NA WO55/958, Fletcher to Morse, Lisbon, 11 April 1809.
26. Rice Jones, *An Engineer Officer under Wellington*, p. 17
27. Mulcaster diary, entry dated 18 April 1809.
28. NA WO55/958, Fletcher to Handfield, Leyria, 24 April 1809.
29. NA WO55/958, Fletcher to Rowley, 4 May 1809.
30. NA WO55/958, Fletcher to Morse, 4 May 1809 and WD, Wellington to Villiers, 7 May 1809.
31. REM 4601-57-1, Emmett's Journal entry dated 4 May 1809.
32. Mulcaster diary, entry for 12 May 1809.
33. NA WO55/958, Fletcher to Morse, 24 May 1809. Connolly, *History of the Corps of Royal Sappers and Miners*, Vol.1, p. 165.
34. REM 4601-74, Fletcher to Burgoyne, 23 May 1809. The report is REM 4601-72.
35. NA WO55/958, Fletcher to Morse, 26 June 1809.
36. NA WO55/978, Fletcher to Morse, 31 May 1809
37. NA WO55/978, Morse to Fyers, 6 July 1809
38. Mulcaster diary, entry for 4 July 1809.
39. Fortescue, *British Army*, Vol.7, p. 213.
40. Mulcaster diary, entry dated 26 July 1809.
41. Rice Jones, *An Engineer Officer under Wellington*, p. 35.
42. Boothby, *A Prisoner of France*, pp. 4–5.
43. NA WO55/1561/6, Report on the defence of Lisbon, 18 August 1809.
44. WD, Wellington to Castlereagh, 25 August 1808; NA WO55/958, Fletcher to Morse, 28 August 1809.
45. WD, Wellington to Castlereagh, Merida, 25 August 1809.
46. WD, Memorandum of the Defence of Portugal, dated 9 March 1809.
47. NA WO55/958, Fletcher to Morse, Merida, 28 August 1809.
48. Mulcaster diary, entry dated 7 October 1809.

Chapter 3
1. Esdaile, *The Peninsular War*, pp. 311–39.
2. WD, Wellington to Castlereagh, 28 August 1809.
3. Thompson (ed), *An Ensign in the Peninsular War, The Letters of John Aitchison*, p. 67.
4. Mulcaster diary, diary entry for 28 April 1809.
5. Rice Jones, *An Engineer Officer under Wellington*, pp. 45–6, entry for 22 October 1809.
6. WSD, Vol. 6, p. 403, Fletcher to Wellington, 15 October 1809.

252 Wellington's Engineers

7. Grehan seems to have missed off the twenty 24-pounders at St Julian.
8. REM 4601-57-1, Emmett's diary, entry for 8 October 1809.
9. There appears to be an error in the printed edition of Jones' book on the Lines. He records the start date of work at Ponte do Rol as 26 March 1810, whereas his diary records the start date as 26 February 1810. Mulcaster's diary notes visiting Thompson as Ponte do Rol on 4 March, so 26 February appears correct.
10. Rice Jones, *An Engineer Officer under Wellington*, p. 47.
11. REM 2001-149-2, Goldfinch to Beresford, Report of the defences of Lisbon.
12. WSD, Vol. 6, pp. 451–8, Fletcher to Wellington, 25 December 1809 and pp. 459–62, 31 December 1809.
13. REM 4601-74, Mulcaster to Burgoyne, 2 January 1810.
14. REM 4201-68, Burgoyne's diary, Vol. 2, 1809, 20 December 1809.
15. REM 4601-74, Mulcaster to Burgoyne, 7 January 1810.
16. Jones, *Journal of Sieges*, Vol. 3, p. 125, 18 February 1810.
17. Ibid, p. 19. Fletcher to Jones, dated 6 July 1810, and also p. 229, where two others (engineers?) were mentioned
18. REM 4601-74, Mulcaster to Burgoyne, 12 November 1810.
19. WSD, Vol. 6, pp. 538–46.
20. NA WO55/958, Fletcher to Morse, 4 July 1810.
21. REM 5501-59-18, Jones to Fletcher, 12 July 1810 and 18 July 1810.
22. Jones, *Journal of Sieges*, Vol. 3, pp. 226–7.
23. Ibid, pp. 230–1.
24. Ibid, p. 92.
25. Ibid, p. 37.
26. Ibid, p. 101.
27. Ibid, p. 122.
28. NA WO55/958, Fletcher to Morse, 2 February 1811.
29. NA WO55/958, Chapman to Morse, 22 March 1809.
30. WD, Wellington to Liverpool, 21 October 1810.
31. Connolly, *History of the Corps of Royal Sappers and Miners*, Vol. 1, p. 170; Oman, *Peninsular War*, Vol. 2, p. 611; Robertson, *Commanding Presence*, p. 172.
32. NA WO55/977, Fletcher to Morse, 29 September 1808.
33. WO55/958, Chapman to Morse, 22 March 1809.
34. WO55/958, Fletcher to Morse, 3 April 1809.
35. WO55/958, Fletcher to Morse, 24 April 1809.
36. WO55/958, Fletcher to Morse, 9 April 1809.
37. WO55/958, Fletcher to Morse, 4 May 1809.
38. WO55/958, Fletcher to Rowley, 4 May 1809.
39. WSD, Vol. 3, p. 219, Coimbra, 7 May 1809.
40. REM 4601-57-1, diary entry for 4 May 1809.
41. NA WO55/1562/2, Fletcher to Morse, 17 October 1808.
42. WSD, Vol. 6, pp. 401–2, Wellington to Castlereagh, 14 October 1809.
43. Rice Jones, *An Engineer Officer under Wellington*, p. 54.
44. REM 5501-59-18, Jones to Fletcher, 18 July 1810.
45. REM 5501-59-18, Jones to Fletcher, 20 July 1810.
46. 7 Sep 1810, Navy decides to withdraw sailors manning signal station; 11 Sep 1810, may need to revert to simple Portuguese telegraph; 2 Oct 1810, Wellington is asking 'are new telegraphs complete'?; 5 Oct 1810 'I am very anxious about our signal posts'; 6 Oct 1810 'Lord W says he will not part with the seamen now, if they are not gone'.
47. Jones, *Journal of Sieges*, p.124, n3.
48. Thompson (ed), *An Ensign in the Peninsular War, The Letters of John Aitchison*, p. 67.
49. Uffindel, *The National Army Museum Book of Wellington's Armies*, p. 85.
50. REM 4601-74, Mulcaster to Burgoyne, 12 November 1809.
51. REM 4501-68, Ross to Dalrymple, 25 April 1810.
52. *Royal Military Chronicle*, Vol. 1, p. 238.
53. Pelet, *The French Campaign in Portugal*, p. 222.
54. BL ADD63106 ff. 3-4, Squire to Bunbury, 27 May 1810.

Notes 253

55. REM 4501-86, Ross to Dalrymple.
56. BL Add63106 ff. 11-12, Squire to Bunbury, 10 October 1810.
57. REM 4201-68, Burgoyne's diary, entry for 1 November 1810.
58. BL Add63106 ff. 13-15.
59. 59. Jones, *Journal of Sieges*, Vol. 3, p. 41.

Chapter 4
1. REM 4201-68, Burgoyne's Journal 1809, Vol. 2, 25 December 1809.
2. REM 4601-72, 2 January 1810, Report by Todd.
3. REM 4601-72, Murray to Burgoyne, 11 January 1810.
4. Wrottesley, *Life and Correspondence of Burgoyne*, p. 94.
5. Perrett, *A Hawk at War* p. 24.
6. Wrottesley, *Life and Correspondence of Burgoyne*, p. 88.
7. Rice Jones, *An Engineer Officer under Wellington*, p. 59.
8. Mulcaster diary, entries for 8 and 9 August 1810.
9. Rice Jones, *An Engineer Officer under Wellington*, p. 65.
10. Mulcaster diary, entries for 19–21 September 1810.
11. WO55/958, Fletcher to Morse, 30 September 1810.
12. REM 4601-72, Burgoyne's papers, Fletcher to Burgoyne, 22 September 1810.
13. Boutflower, *The Journal of an Army Surgeon*, p. 64.
14. BL Add MS63106, ff. 11-12.
15. Wellington to Liverpool, 21 October 1810. This extract taken from *Royal Military Chronicle*, Vol. 1, p. 228.
16. WO55/958, Fletcher to Morse, 4 September 1810.
17. Jones, *Journal of Sieges*, Vol. 3, pp. 28–9.
18. WD, 2nd ed, Vol. 4, p. 317.
19. REM 5501-59-18, diary entry for 19 October 1810. There are a few weeks' diary entries in this folder and this is amongst them.
20. Kincaid, *Adventures in the Rifle Brigade*, p. 17.
21. NA WO55/958, Fletcher to Morse, 26 October 1810.
22. Jones, *Journal of Sieges*, Vol. 3, p. 159, Wellington to Wedekind.
23. Ibid, p. 172, Wellington to Berkeley, 10 November 1810.
24. REM 5501-79, Squire to Fletcher, 20 October 1810.
25. Information from Wikipedia and other sources.
26. John Squire, *A Short Narrative of the late campaign of the British Army under the orders of the Earl of Chatham*, London, 1810.
27. NA WO55/958, Squire to Fletcher, Chamusca, 24 December 1810 and WO55/958, Fletcher to Squire, Cartaxo, 4 January 1811.
28. NA WO55/958, Fletcher to Morse, Cartaxo, 5 January 1811.
29. NA WO55/958, Fletcher to Morse, Cartaxo, 28 February 1811 and 2 March 1811.
30. NA WO55/979, Williams to Fletcher, 8 November 1810.
31. There were several pamphlets produced on their various disagreements, the most notable being, 'Strictures on Napier's History', 'Further Strictures . . .' (both published anonymously in defence on Beresford), Napier's, 'Justification of his third volume', Beresford's refutation of this justification, and Napier's final reply to the refutation.
32. Napier, *History of the War in the Peninsula*, Vol. III, p. 393.
33. Ibid, 1 March 1811, quoted in Appendix X
34. Rousseau, *Journal of D'Urban* , 6 January 1811, p. 173.
35. Ibid, 1 January 1811, p. 171.
36. WD, 2nd Edition, to Beresford, 5 January 1811.
37. Pelet, *Journal*, p. 336.
38. Ibid, p. 351.
39. Rousseau, *Journal of D'Urban* , 20 January 1811, p. 178.
40. REM 5501.59. 1, 2, 3, Jones' Diary, 21 December 1810.
41. All of these are taken from REM 5501.59. 1, 2, 3, Jones' Diary.

Chapter 5

1. WD, Wellington to Liverpool, 7 May 1811. It is interesting to note that Wellington did not have any great desire to take Almeida at this time. It was circumstance, not planning, that led to the blockade.
2. Stanhope, *Notes of Conversations with the Duke of Wellington*, p. 90.
3. F. S. Garwood, 'The Royal Staff Corps', *RE Journal*, June 1943.
4. WD, Wellington to Beresford, 20 March 1811.
5. REM 5501-59, Jones' diary, entry dated, Thomar, 8 March 1811. Also mentioned in REM 4201-68 Burgoyne's diary, 15 March 1811; REM 4601-71, Squire to ?, Arronches, 23 March 1811.
6. McGuffie, *Peninsular Cavalry General*, p. 84.
7. Dickson, *Manuscripts*, Vol. 3, p. 376.
8. Ibid, p. 377.
9. REM 4601-71, Squire to [Fletcher?], Jerumenha, 11 April 1811.
10. Cole's dispatch to Beresford, 16 April 1811, quoted in *Dispatches*.
11. Oman, *Peninsular War*, Vol. 4, p. 274. More recently, Robertson, *A Commanding Presence*, also suggests that Wellington did not have access to a siege train.
12. NA WO55/958, Fletcher to Morse, 16 April 1811.
13. REM 4601-86, Ross to Dalrymple, Olivenza, 25 April 1811.
14. WD, Memorandum 23 April 1811, Vol. 8, pp. 494–6.
15. WD, Wellington to Beresford, 6 May 1811.
16. WD, Wellington acknowledged Castaños' acceptance in a letter to him dated 13 May 1811.
17. J. T. Jones, *Journal of Sieges,* 3rd edition, Vol. 1, p. 12. Unless otherwise stated references to Jones will be from this edition.
18. Ibid, p. 13.
19. REM 5501-59-1, Jones' diary, 8 May 1811. The original diaries are very difficult to read. Copious notes from them were taken by John Hancock, the ex-Curator of the Royal Engineers Museum. Many of my comments are from his notes, not the original diaries.
20. J. T. Jones, *Journal of Sieges*, Vol. 1, pp. 22, 26; REM 5501-59-1, Jones' diary, various entries from 8 to 14 May 1811.
21. Muir, *At Wellington's Right Hand*, p. 193.
22. Ibid, p. 205.
23. Oman, *Peninsular War*, Vol. 4, pp. 282–3.
24. Ibid, facing p. 286.
25. Dickson, *Manuscripts*, Vol. 3, Letter to Maj-Gen Macleod, 21 March 1811, p. 364.
26. Ibid, map of Badajoz and surrounding areas. This map is loose in the 1987 facsimile edition.
27. Rice Jones, *Engineer Officer under Wellington*, p. 100.
28. Fortescue, *British Army*, Vol. 8, p. 143.
29. WD, Wellington to Beresford, Elvas, 20 April 1811.
30. Oman, *Peninsular War*, Vol. 4, pp. 273–4.
31. Dickson, *Manuscripts*, Vol. 3, Letter to Maj-Gen Macleod, p. 364.
32. WD, Wellington to Beresford, Gouvea, 27 March 1811.
33. WD, Wellington to Beresford, Villar Maior, 6 April 1811.
34. Dickson, *Manuscripts*, Vol. 3, pp. 374–5.
35. REM 4601-71 Misc Letters, f. 13. Squire writing on 11 April 1811 dates that 'there are no means at Elvas, and we have not a single platform at our disposal'.
36. WD, Memorandum for Col. Fletcher and Commissary Gen, 9 April 1911. The stores list is detailed in J. T. Jones, *Journal of Sieges*, Vol. 1, p. 345.
37. J. T. Jones, *Journal of Sieges*, Vol. 1, p. 351. The requisition was for fifteen 24-pounder and five 18-pounder guns, with 8,000 roundshot.
38. WD, Wellington to Beresford, Villa Formoso, 10 April 1811.
39. REM 4601-71, Hardinge to Squire, Albuera, 12 April 1811.
40. REM 4601-71, Squire to Hardinge, Olivenza, 13 April 1811.
41. Fortescue, *British Army*, Vol. 8, p. 143.
42. J. T. Jones, *Journal of Sieges*, Vol. 1, p. 18.
43. BL, ADD63106, Squire letters, f. 28, Squire to Bunbury, 30 April 1811.
44. WD, Wellington to Beresford, Celorico, 30 March 1811.

45. WD, Wellington to Beresford, Elvas, 21 April 1811.
46. Dickson, *Manuscripts*, Vol. 3, p. 384, 17 April 1811.
47. REM 4601-71, Squire to Hardinge, Olivenza, 10 April 1811.
48. REM 4601-71, Misc Letters, f.14, Squire to Hardinge, 10 April 1811; f.19, Hardinge to Squire, 20 April 1811.
49. J. T. Jones, *Journal of Sieges*, Vol. 1, p. 348.
50. WSD, Beresford to Wellington, Almendralejo, 3 May 1811.
51. Dickson, *Manuscripts*, Vol. 3, p. 389, letter to Macleod, 1 May 1811; BL, ADD63106, f. 28, Squire Letters, Squire to Bunbury, 30 April 1811.
52. Dickson, *Manuscripts*, Vol. 3, p. 390.
53. Ibid, pp. 389–90.
54. For example, REM 4501-86-4, Ross letters, Ross to Dalrymple, 25 April 1811; BL, ADD63106, Squire letters, f. 28, Squire to Bunbury, 30 April 1811.
55. REM 5501-59-1, Jones' diary, 4–8 May 1811.
56. BL, ADD63106, Squire letters, ff. 31-33, Squire to Bunbury, 17 May 1811.
57. REM 4501-86-4, Ross letters, Ross to Dalrymple, 20 May 1811.
58. REM 4201-68, Burgoyne's diary, 19 May 1811.
59. REM 4601-57-1, Emmet's diary, 7 May 1811.
60. REM 5501-59-1, Jones' diary, 7 May 1811.
61. J. T. Jones, *Journal of Sieges*, Vol. 1, p. 26
62. Rice Jones, *Engineer Officer under Wellington*, pp. 100–3, records the same story as John T. Jones. One was Brigade-Major and the other was the Adjutant for the Royal Engineers at the siege. They would have been working together. The similarity in words is too close for coincidence and clearly one of them has copied their diary from the other.
63. REM 5501-59-1, Jones' diary.
64. REM 4601-71, Squire to Fletcher, 10 May 1811.
65. REM 4501-86-4, Ross letters, Ross to Dalrymple, 20 May 1811.
66. REM 4201-68, Burgoyne's diary, 19 May 1811.
67. Rousseau, *Journal of D'Urban*, p. 213, Oman, *Peninsular War*, Vol. 4, p. 286. Did Oman take this from D'Urban's journal? D'Urban was not actually at Badajoz. He was with Beresford's army.
68. REM 4501-86-4, Ross letters, Ross to Dalrymple, 20 May 1811.
69. REM 5501-59-1, Jones' diary, 11 May 1811.
70. Duncan, *Royal Artillery*, Vol. 2, p. 293.
71. Rice Jones, *An Engineer Officer under Wellington*, p. 103.
72. Oman, *Peninsular War*, Vol. 4, p. 280.
73. Ibid, p. 284.
74. Fortescue says they reported they were ready on 3 May 1811 but there does not appear to be any specific communication to this effect.
75. WSD, Beresford to Wellington, Almendralejo, 3 May 1811.
76. Oman, *Peninsular War*, Vol. 4, pp. 282–3.
77. Three 24-pounders and two 8in howitzers.
78. BL, ADD63106, Squire Letters, f.31, Squire to Bunbury, 17 May 1811.
79. Boutflower, *The Journal of an Army Surgeon*, p. 91.
80. Oman, *Peninsular War*, Vol. 4, p. 286, says that six were injured, but there were only five; Dickinson and Melville killed, and Boteler, Reid and Ross wounded.
81. Rice Jones, *An Engineer Officer under Wellington*, p. 105.
82. J. T. Jones, *Journal of Sieges*, Vol. 1, pp. 30–1.
83. NA WO55/958, Fletcher to Morse, Elvas, 23 May 1811.
84. J. T. Jones, *Journal of Sieges*, Vol. 1, p. 31. Jones provides much of the detail in the following paragraphs.
85. REM 5501-59-1, Jones' diary.
86. Dickson, *Manuscripts*, Vol. 3, p. 394, Dickson to Maj-Gen. Macleod.
87. J. T. Jones, *Journal of Sieges*, Vol. 1, p. 31.
88. Ibid, p. 39 and p. 351, n4.
89. Four field guns were added later to enfilade the bridge and discourage sorties.
90. Three guns were held in reserve.

91. This includes the guns allocated for the attacks on the Pardaleras to Picurina.
92. WSD, Fletcher to Wellington, 3 June 1811.
93. REM 4201-68, Burgoyne's diary, 5 June 1811.
94. BL, ADD63106, Squire Letters, ff. 35-6.
95. WD, letter dated 6 June 1811.
96. Page, *Intelligence Officer in the Peninsula*, p. 115.
97. REM 5501-59-1, Jones' diary, 6 June 1811.
98. Numbers taken from Oman, *Peninsular War*, Vol. 4, p. 429.
99. BL Add MS63166, Squire Letters, 9 March 1811.
100. BL Add MS63106, Squire Letters, 11 March 1811.
101. WD, Wellington to Liverpool, 13 June 1811.
102. Myatt, *British Sieges*, p. 45.
103. J. T. Jones, *Journal of Sieges*, 1st edition, London, 1814, p. 298.
104. Rousseau, *Journal of D'Urban*, p. 222.
105. REM 4501-86-4, Ross Letters, Ross to Dalrymple, 9 June 1811. Lieutenant-General Hew Dalrymple was Ross' great-uncle.
106. Oman, *Peninsular War*, Vol. 4, p. 425; Fortescue, *British Army*, Vol. 8, p. 223.
107. WD, Wellington to Liverpool, 6 June 1811.
108. WD, Wellington to C. Stuart, 8 June 1811.
109. Rousseau, *Journal of D'Urban* , p. 219, notes that a letter from the French Governor of Badajoz was intercepted which said that on 29 May 1811, he had three weeks' bread left.
110. Oman, *Peninsular War*, Vol. 4, p. 419.
111. Fortescue, *British Army*, Vol. 8, p. 221.
112. Ibid, p. 223. Surprisingly, Burgoyne also calls them 'English' in his diary, REM 4201-68, 7 June 1811.
113. REM 4201-68, Burgoyne's diary, entry dated 21 June 1811; Shore, *Engineer Officer under Wellington*, p. 109.
114. Page, *Intelligence Officer in the Peninsula*, p. 124.
115. BL Add MS63106, Squire Letters, 18 June (July?) 1811.
116. F. S. Garwood, 'The Royal Staff Corps', *RE Journal*, June 1943.
117. NA WO55/958, Fletcher to Morse, Elvas, 20 June 1811.
118. REM 4601-74, Burgoyne to Squire, 21 September 1811.
119. Wrottesley, *Life of Burgoyne*, Vol. 1, p. 136.
120. REM 4601-72, Burgoyne to Squire, 20 September 1811.
121. REM 4601-57-1, Emmett's diary, 25 September 1811.
122. Wrottesley, *Life of Burgoyne*, Vol. 1, p. 252.
123. REM 4601-57-1, Emmett's diary, 29 November 1811.
124. BL Add MS63106, note at end of folios, 30 November 1811. Also, Wrottesley, *Life of Burgoyne*, Vol. 1, p. 151.
125. BL Add MS63106, Squire to Bunbury, Portalegre, 4 October 1811.

Chapter 6
1. REM 4501-86, Ross to Dalrymple, 7 January 1812.
2. WD, Wellington to Howarth, 14 May 1811.
3. WD, Wellington to Framingham, Fletcher and Kennedy, 19 July 1811.
4. Dickson, *Manuscripts*, Vol. 3, p. 440. Letter to Wellington dated 9 August 1811. He mentions 115 boats having been dispatched and that another 30–40 are required.
5. Ibid, p. 500.
6. J. T. Jones, *Journal of Sieges*, Vol. 1, p. 89.
7. Ibid, p. 91. Also mentioned in Dickson, *Manuscripts*, Vol. 4, p. 562. This would not affect the attack on the fortress walls, but would stop any sort of counter-battery fire which would increase casualties.
8. Cocks, *An Intelligence Officer in the Peninsula*, p. 162.
9. Although at least two arrived late. Captain Williams and Lieutenant De Salaberry did not arrive until 15 January 1812. J. T. Jones, *Journal of Sieges*, Vol. 1, p. 118.
10. Wrottesley, *Life of Burgoyne*, Vol. 1, p. 91. They eventually arrived on 15 January 1812: J. T. Jones, *Journal of Sieges*, Vol. 1, p. 118.

11. Jones said Fletcher recommended storming the redoubt to Wellington, who agreed. REM 5501-59-2 Jones' diary, 8 January 1812.
12. J. T. Jones, *Journal of Sieges*, Vol. 1, p. 99.
13. Ibid, p. 103.
14. REM 4601-72, Burgoyne to Squire, 16 January 1812.
15. WSD, Vol. 7, p. 153.
16. Dickson, *Manuscripts*, Vol. 4, p. 562, Dickson to MacLeod. The reasons and consequences of the French moves are discussed at length in Oman, *Peninsular War*, Vol. 5, pp. 187–95.
17. Dickson, *Manuscripts*, Vol. 3, p. 534, Dickson to Beresford.
18. Dickson, *Manuscripts*, Vol. 4, p. 562.
19. REM 5501-59-2, Jones' diary, 28 December 1811.
20. REM 4501-86-4, Ross letters, 7 January 1812.
21. WD, Wellington to Richmond, 29 January 1812.
22. Fortescue, *British Army*, Vol. 8, p. 356.
23. Colville, *Portrait of a General*, pp. 83–4.
24. BL, ADD57544, f. 184. Burgoyne to Moore, 10 December 1808.
25. BL, ADD63106, Squire Letters, ff.3-4, Squire to Bunbury, 27 May 1810.
26. BL, ADD41963, ff. 13-16. Squire to Pasley, 3 March 1812. Portalegre.
27. Oman, *Peninsular War*, Vol. 5, p. 165. Fortescue also comments that Dorsenne had no confidence in Barrie. Fortescue, *British Army*, Vol. 8, p. 355.
28. REM 5501-139-1 f. 4. Burgoyne to Pasley, 12 February 1812.
29. Fortescue, *British Army*, Vol. 8, p. 367.
30. Wrottesley, *Life of Burgoyne*, Vol. 1, p. 161. Burgoyne to Squire, 7 February 1812.
31. Ibid, p. 161. Burgoyne to Squire, 7 February 1812.
32. REM 5501-59-2, Jones' diary, 14 January 1812.
33. Wrottesley, *Life of Burgoyne*, Vol. 1, p. 164., and REM 5501-139-1, Burgoyne to Pasley, 12 February 1812.
34. Wrottesley, *Life of Burgoyne*, Vol. 1, p. 164.
35. Ibid, p. 160, 19 January 1812.
36. REM 4601-72 f. 1813/1. Burgoyne to Squire, 16 January 1812.
37. REM 5501-139-1, Burgoyne to Squire, 12 February 1812.
38. Pasley Papers, Add41962, f.197, Burgoyne to Pasley, 26 March 1810.
39. Wrottesley, *Life of Burgoyne*, Vol. 1, p.163. Burgoyne to Squire, 7 February 1812.
40. REM 5501-139, Burgoyne to Squire, 12 February 1812.
41. For example, REM 5501-139-1, Burgoyne to Squire, 12 February 1812; REM 5501-59-2, Jones' diary, 3 January 1812.
42. J. T. Jones, *Autobiography*, p. 48.
43. Fortescue, *British Army*, Vol. 8, p. 365.
44. NA WO3/601, Torrens to Wellington, 21 February 1812. Thanks to Rory Muir for bringing this to my attention.
45. WD, Wellington to Liverpool, 11 February 1812.
46. J. T. Jones, *Autobiography*, p. 51.
47. Ross and Skelton killed. E. R. Mulcaster, Marshall, Macculloch, A. Thompson and Reid wounded. Thompson and Macculloch returned to England.
48. Dickson, *Manuscripts*, Vol. 4, p. 571.
49. Confusingly called 5½in howitzers and 24-pounder howitzers at various times. See WD, Wellington to Hill, 28 Jan 1812 for a description of the pieces. Dickson, *Manuscripts*, Vol. 4, p. 580.
50. J. T. Jones, *Journal of Sieges*, Vol. 1, p. 144.
51. Ibid, pp. 139, 371.
52. Dickson, *Manuscripts*, Vol. 4, p. 585, footnote on letter to Wellington.
53. Myatt, *British Sieges*, p. 82; J. T. Jones, *Journal of Sieges*, Vol. 1, p. 374; Dickson, *Manuscripts*, Vol. 4, p. 599.
54. WSD, Wellington to Wellesley, Elvas, 12 March 1812.
55. J. T. Jones, *Journal of Sieges*, 1st edition, p. 298.
56. REM 5501-59-3, Jones' diary, 25 February 1812.
57. J. T. Jones, *Journal of Sieges*, Vol. 1, p. 376.

258 *Wellington's Engineers*

58. Vetch and two or three other officers were ordered up from Cadiz. Vetch's letters says two other officers, Jones' Journal says three. Vetch did not arrive until 5 April 1812. *RE Journal*, 1 February 1881, p. 26.
59. REM 5501-59-3, Jones' diary, 15 March 1812. Squire in a letter to Bunbury noted that thirteen out of nineteen officers were killed or wounded. This would support the argument that the Cadiz officers arrived late or not at all. BL, ADD63106, Squire letters, ff. 54-55.
60. WSD, Wellington to Piper, 22 and 26 March 1812.
61. J. T. Jones, *Journal of Sieges*, Vol. 1, p. 376.
62. Oman, *Peninsular War*, Vol. 5, p. 239.
63. *RE Journal*, February 1881, p. 30.
64. Oman, *Peninsular War*, Vol. 5, p. 243; J. T. Jones, *Journal of Sieges*, Vol. 1, p. 193.
65. May, *A Few Observations on the mode of attack at Ciudad Rodrigo and Badajoz in 1812 and St Sebastian in 1813*, p. 23. Sunset on 4 April 1812 was 7.06 p.m.
66. *RE Journal*, February 1881, p. 29.
67. MacLeod and Holloway never returned to the Peninsula. Emmett returned in November 1813.
68. Colville, *Portrait of a General*, p. 93.
69. Oman, *Peninsular War*, Vol. 5, p. 270. Oman describes the situation at great length to show that the primary cause of the loss of Badajoz was Napoleon's long-distance meddling.
70. J. T. Jones, *Journal of Sieges*, Vol. 1, p. 403.
71. Colville, *Portrait of a General*, p. 94.
72. WD, Wellington to Liverpool, 7 April 1812 (the dispatch informing Liverpool of the successful assault).
73. *Athenaeum*, 27 April 1889, p. 537, quoting letter from Wellington to Liverpool, 7 April 1812.
74. BL, ADD63106, Squire letters, ff. 54-55, Squire to Bunbury, 8 April 1812
75. WD, Wellington to George Murray, 28 May 1812. Also quoted in Glover, *Peninsular Preparation*, p. 106.
76. J. T. Jones, *Journal of Sieges*, Vol. 1, p. 377; see also pp. 222–6.
77. BL, ADD63106 ff. 54-5, Squire to Bunbury, 8 April 1812.
78. WD, Wellington to Liverpool, 7 April 1812.
79. WO3/601, pp. 276–9, Torrens to Wellington, 21 February 1812.
80. BL, ADD38326 ff. 30-31, Liverpool to Wellington, 28 April 1812.
81. Oman, *Peninsular War*, Vol. 5, p. 256.
82. Myatt, *British Sieges*, p. 116.
83. For example, see Fletcher, Badajoz, 1812, p. 20, and Uffindel, *Wellington's Armies*, p. 107, where the inference is that the infantry would be excused duty in the trenches when there were sufficient artificers trained.
84. WSD, Vol. 7, p. 311, Jones to Chapman, 7 April 1812.
85. Wrottesley, *Life of Burgoyne*, p.182
86. NA WO/55/1561/12, Wedekind to Beresford, 1 March 1812
87. BL, Add MS63106, Squire to Bunbury, 27 April 1812. This was Squire's last letter before he died at Truxillo on 17 May 1812.

Chapter 7
1. REM 4601-74, Burgoyne to Squire, 22 April 1812.
2. Wrottesley, *Life of Burgoyne*, p. 189.
3. Rousseau, *Journal of D'Urban*, p. 254.
4. A detailed description of the construction of the repair is available in Douglas, *Essay on Military Bridges*, 3rd edition, pp. 353–9.
5. WD, Wellington to Liverpool, 28 May 1812.
6. Estimated at four for each howitzer and limber; two for each cart and eight for the ladders carriages. J. T. Jones, *Journal of Sieges*, Vol. 3, pp. 245–6.
7. J. T. Jones, *Journal of Sieges*, Vol. 1, p. 247. Burgoyne used almost identical words in his journal, Wrottesley, *Life of Burgoyne*, p. 313.
8. Porter, *History of the Royal Engineers*, Vol. 1, p. 313.
9. WD, Wellington to Liverpool, 30 June 1812.
10. Wrottesley, *Life of Burgoyne*, Vol. 1, p. 194.

11. NA, WO55/959, Burgoyne's journal of the siege of Fort San Vicente at Salamanca.
12. REM 4601-72, Burgoyne Letters, f. 1812/17, Burgoyne's criticism of the 24-pounder carronades in his report on Burgos is similar to Jones', 'they could not be fired with any accuracy or force'.
13. REM 4601-72, Burgoyne Letters, 1812/17, f.1.
14. Oman, *Peninsular War*, Vol. 6, p. 27.
15. J. T. Jones, *Autobiography*, p. 68.
16. Wrottesley, *Life of Burgoyne*, Vol.1, p. 213.
17. Oman, *Peninsular War*, Vol. 6, p. 27, confusingly says the battery was armed on the night of 23 September 1812. Jones' *Journal of Sieges* and Dickson, *Manuscripts*, say the night of the 22nd/23rd. From reading on in Oman's account from this point the escalade of the same night (22nd) can be believed to also have happened on the 23rd.
18. J. T. Jones, *Journal of Sieges*, Vol. 1, p. 283.
19. Porter, *History of the Royal Engineers*, Vol. 1, p. 322.
20. Dickson, *Manuscripts*, Vol. 4, p. 746.
21. J. T. Jones, *Journal of Sieges*, Vol. 1, p. 297.
22. Ibid, p. 296.
23. J. T. Jones, *Autobiography*, pp. 73–5.
24. BL Add MS41963, Pasley papers, Burgoyne to Pasley, 30 March 1813.
25. J. T. Jones, *Journal of Sieges*, Vol. 1, p. 333.
26. Fortescue, *British Army*, Vol. 8, p. 584.
27. Ibid, p. 226.
28. Ibid, p. 584
29. WD, Wellington to Bathurst, 26 October 1812.
30. J. T. Jones, *Journal of Sieges*, Vol. 1, p. 292.
31. Ibid, p. 335.
32. Wrottesley, *Life of Burgoyne*.
33. REM 4601-72, Burgoyne Letters, 1812/17, f.13.
34. Wrottesley, *Life of Burgoyne*, p. 236.
35. REM 4601-72, Burgoyne Letters, 1812/17, f.13.
36. Porter, *History of the Royal Engineers*, Vol. 1, p. 330.
37. Wrottesley, *Life of Burgoyne*, p. 242.
38. *RE Journal*, January 1890, p. 3.
39. Wrottesley, *Life of Burgoyne*, p. 246.
40. NA WO55/981, Rhodes to Fletcher, 25 November 1812.
41. NA WO55/981, Piper to Fletcher, 25 October 1812.
42. WD, Wellington to Hill, 5 October 1812.
43. NA WO55/981, Hulme to Fletcher, 1 October 1812 and Hulme to Fletcher, 3 December 1812.
44. WD, 2nd Edition, Wellington to Fletcher, Badajoz, 20 December 1812. The names of the officers come from the Wellington Papers, WP1/355.
45. Dickson, *Manuscripts*, Vol. 5, p. 851.
46. WO55/981, Fletcher to Goldfinch, 5 December 1812.

Chapter 8
1. WD, Wellington to Piper, Badajoz, 20 December 1812.
2. Dickson, *Manuscripts*, Vol. 5, p. 830.
3. Ibid, pp. 830–5.
4. WD, Wellington to Dickson, 29 February 1813, Wellington to Beresford 18 April 1813 and 24 April 1813.
5. Made up of six 18-pounders, two spare carriages, six platform wagons, two forges, eighteen ammunition wagons, three store wagons and twenty bullock carts. The brigade was manned by two RA companies, Morrison's and Glubb's. Dickson, *Manuscripts*, Vol. 5, pp. 872–3.
6. WD, Wellington to Conde de la Bispal, 1 May 1813.
7. *RE Journal*, January 1890, p. 7.
8. WD, Wellington to Fisher, Freneda, 4 May 1813.
9. Lipscombe, *Wellington's Guns*, p. 275. Taken from Dickson, *Manuscripts*, Vol. 5, p. 882.
10. Dickson, *Manuscripts*, Vol. 5, p. 882.

260 Wellington's Engineers

11. WD, Wellington to Fletcher, 14 May 1813.
12. WD, Wellington to Graham, 18 May 1813. Thomas Livingstone Mitchell was attached to the QMG's department and employed on surveying and reconnaissance. After the war he was employed for four years sketching the scenes of the many actions for the British government. These maps and drawings were eventually published as *Wyld's Atlas*, the best atlas of the Peninsular War.
13. REM 2001-149-22, Letter from Wright dated 29 May 1813.
14. WD, Wellington to Bathurst, Villadiego, 13 June 1812. Dickson, *Manuscripts*, Vol. 5, p. 908.
15. WSD, Hill to Wellington, Vol. 8, p. 33.
16. J. T. Jones, *Journal of Sieges*, Vol. 2, p. 6.
17. WD, Wellington to Graham, 26 June 1813.
18. WD, Wellington to Dalhousie, 2 July 1813.
19. WSD, Fletcher to Wellington, 11 July 1813.
20. Smith was the senior engineer with Graham's force was before San Sebastian. Fletcher was still coming up from Pamplona. Burgoyne arrived with him on 15 July 1813.
21. Dickson, *Manuscripts*, Vol. 5, p. 960. Dickson clearly records at the end of his diary entry for 12 July 1813, that 'This plan of attack was the proposition of Major Smith.'
22. WSD, Graham to Wellington, 22 July 1813.
23. Dickson, *Manuscripts*, Vol. 5, p. 952.
24. As previously, Jones' Journal is misleading. He lists the full eighteen officers as present throughout the siege, but at least two did not arrive until well into the second siege. Captain Collyer and Lieutenant Wortham did not arrive until 19 August 1813 with a company of RSM. These are all counted in Jones' totals.
25. REM 5501-108-4, Burgoyne's report on the siege, and WSD, Fletcher to Graham, 25 July 1813.
26. WSD, Graham to Wellington, 21 July 1813.
27. Frazer was one who disagreed that the fires would have caused an obstruction. Sabine, *Frazer Letters*, p. 204.
28. Fortescue, *British Army*, Vol. 9, pp. 230–2.
29. Oman, *Peninsular War*, Vol. 6, pp. 583–4.
30. Myatt, *British Sieges*, pp. 162–4.
31. Oman, *Peninsular War*, Vol. 6, pp. 565, 578; Myatt, *British Sieges*, p. 156; Sabine, *Frazer Letters*, p. 185.
32. WSD, Fletcher to Wellington, 29 July 1813.
33. Oman, *Peninsular War*, Vol. 6, p. 585; Fortescue, *British Army*, Vol. 9, p. 232; Sabine, *Frazer Letters*, p. 206; Wrottesley, *Life of Burgoyne*, p. 270.
34. WSD, Fletcher to Wellington, 29 July 1813.
35. Oman, *Peninsular War*, Vol. 6, pp. 575, 578fn.
36. Wrottesley, *Life of Burgoyne*, p. 269.
37. Dickson, *Manuscripts*, Vol. 5, p. 971. *RE Journal*, February 1890, p. 34.
38. Dickson, *Manuscripts*, Vol. 5, p. 973.
39. Sabine, *Frazer Letters*, pp. 198–9. H. D. Jones also thought the breach should have been stormed the first night and waiting for the second breach would add no value. 'Delays are dangerous!!'. *RE Journal*, February 1890, p. 34.
40. Wrottesley, *Life of Burgoyne*, p. 271.
41. J. T. Jones, *Journal of Sieges*, Vol. 2, p. 31; Wrottesley, *Life of Burgoyne*, p. 268.
42. WSD, Graham to Wellington, 29 July 1813.
43. Burgoyne complains about this in his manuscript account of the siege, but it did not make its way into Wrottesley's account. REM 5501-108-4, p. 111.
44. WD, Graham to Wellington, 27 Jul 1813; WSD, Fletcher to Graham, 27 July 1813.
45. Dickson, *Manuscripts*, Vol. 5, p. 973.
46. Sabine, *Frazer Letters*, p. 204.
47. WSD, Graham to Wellington, 24 July 1813.
48. Aspinal-Oglander, Freshly Remembered, pp. 256–7.
49. Quoted in Oman, *Peninsular War*, Vol. 6, p. 583.
50. Ibid, p. 584.
51. Wrottesley, *Life of Burgoyne*, pp. 269–70.

52. J. T. Jones, *Journal of Sieges*, Vol. 2, p. 45.
53. *RE Journal*, January 1890, p. 34. H. D. Jones' journal.
54. Carr-Gomm, *Letters and Journals of Field-Marshal Gomm*, pp. 311–12.
55. Ibid, pp. 314–16.
56. There are similar outspoken comments in the correspondence of most of the key engineers, including Elphinstone, Jones, Pasley, Squire, Burgoyne and Ross.
57. Connolly, *History of the Corps of Sappers and Miners*, pp. 194–7.
58. REM 5501-59-7, p. 65, Wright to Burgoyne, not dated.
59. WD, Wellington to Fletcher, Lesaca, 6 August 1813.
60. WSD, Graham to Wellington, Oyarzun, 14 August 1813.
61. WSD, Graham to Wellington, 28 August 1813 and 28 August 1813.
62. Sabine, *Frazer Letters*, p. 228. Burgoyne makes no mention of this advance battery being ordered.
63. Fletcher, Rhodes and Collyer killed. Burgoyne, Barry and Marshall wounded.
64. There were two officers senior to Burgoyne in the Peninsula, Elphinstone was at Lisbon and Goldfinch was at Pamplona.
65. Wrottesley, *Life of Burgoyne*, p. 273. The footnote on this page suggests that Burgoyne did not like the original plan and offered an alternative to Wellington on 25 July 1813, presumably after the failed assault. I can find no details of this alternate plan, but as mentioned above both Jones and Fletcher were of the view that Wellington wanted to persevere with the original plan of attack. Unfortunately, no-one has explained the reasoning behind the decision to persevere.
66. For example, WD, Wellington to Graham, 16 July 1813, 8:30 p.m.; 20 July 1813, 2 p.m.; 22 July 1813, 9 a.m.
67. *RE Journal*, January 1890, p. 32.
68. Wrottesley, *Life of Burgoyne*, Vol. 1, p. 274.
69. REM 5501-79, Burgoyne to Rowley, 14 October 1813.
70. BL Add MS41963, Pasley Papers, Burgoyne to Pasley, 31 October 1813.
71. Wrottesley, *Life of Burgoyne*, Vol. 1, p. 282.
72. WO55/959 Burgoyne to Mann, 10 September 1813.
73. REM 355.486, Jones *Autobiography*, manuscript, p. 58.
74. REM 4201-274, Elphinstone Letters, 22 March 1813.
75. BL Add41963 f. 131-2, Pasley papers, Burgoyne to Pasley, 24 November 1813.
76. REM 4201-274, Elphinstone to his wife, 13 October 1813.
77. REM 4201-274, Elphinstone to his wife, 16 October 1813.
78. REM 5501-79, Stanway to Burgoyne, 1 November 1813.
79. REM 5501-79, W. Reid to J. T. Jones, 3 November 1813.
80. Porter, *History of the Royal Engineers*, Vol. 1, p. 333.
81. WD, Wellington to Graham, 1 August 1813.
82. WD, Wellington to Bathurst, 8 August 1813.
83. WD, Wellington to Fletcher, Lesaca, 21 August 1813.
84. WSD, Murray to Fletcher Lesaca, 22 August 1813.
85. REM 5501-59-7, Pitts to Burgoyne, Lesaca, 25 August 1813.
86. WD, Wellington to Graham, 9 September 1813.
87. WD, Wellington to Graham, 17 September 1813.
88. WD, Wellington to Bathurst, 19 September 1813.
89. Wrottesley, *Life of Burgoyne*, p. 285.
90. WSD, Wellington to Wellesley, Lesaca, 12 September 1813.
91. Beatson, *The Bidassoa and the Nivelle*, pp. 60–1.

Chapter 9
1. Smith, *Autobiography of Harry Smith*, Vol. 1, p. 142.
2. Beatson, *The Bidassoa and the Nivelle*, p. 67.
3. Wrottesley, *Life of Burgoyne*, Vol. 1, p. 286.
4. WSD, Hope to Wellington, Hendaye, 8 October 1813.
5. REM 5501-79, Reid to Jones, 3 November 1813. REM 5501-139, Reid to Burgoyne, 30 November 1813.

262 Wellington's Engineers

6. REM 4201-274, Elphinstone Letters, 23 October 1813.
7. WSD, Hope to Wellington, 1 November 1813.
8. Wrottesley, *Life of Burgoyne*, p. 287.
9. WSD, Hope to Wellington, Guethary, 12 November 1813.
10. WD, Wellington to Hope, St Pe, 14 November 1813.
11. Connolly, *History of the Royal Corps of Sappers and Miners*, Vol. 1, p. 198.
12. REM 5501-59-7, Pitts to Burgoyne, 1 December 1813.
13. REM 4201-274, 3 November 1813.
14. WSD, Wellington to Hope, 8 December 1813.
15. Wrottesley, *Life of Burgoyne*, Vol. 1, pp. 287–8.
16. ADD MS41963, Pasley Papers, Burgoyne to Pasley, 17 January 1814.
17. Anton, *Retrospective of a Military Life*, p. 88.
18. Sabine, *Frazer Letters*, p. 357.
19. WSD, QMG to Cole, 15 December 1813.
20. REM 5501-59-7, Wright to Burgoyne, 13 December 1813.
21. REM 5501-59-7, H. D. Jones to J. T. Jones, 9 January 1814.
22. REM 4201-274, Elphinstone Letters, 23 January 1814 and 6 February 1814.
23. REM 4201-274, Elphinstone Letters, 16 January 1814. Also see Dickson, *Manuscripts*, Vol. 5, p. 1148.
24. Larpent, *Private Journal*, 3rd Edition, p. 405.
25. WSD Hope to Wellington, 23 February 1814.
26. WSD, Hope to Wellington, 24 February 1813; Penrose to Wellington, 24 February 1814.
27. WSD, Hope to Wellington, 25 February 1813.
28. WD, Wellington to Penrose, 7 February 1813.
29. Porter, *History of the Royal Engineers*, Vol. 1, p. 355.
30. J. T. Jones, *Journal of Sieges*, Vol. 2, pp. 122–3.
31. WD, Wellington to Hope, 2 March 1814.
32. WD Wellington to Hope, 25 February 1814.
33. Larpent, *Private Journal*, pp. 414–15.
34. Havard, *Wellington's Welsh General*, p. 219.
35. WD, Wellington to Bathurst, St Sever, 4 March 1814.
36. WD, Wellington to Hope, St Lys, 26 March 1814
37. Larpent, *Private Journal*, p. 458 (NB not p. 488 as stated in Fortescue). Oman, *Peninsular War*, Vol. 7, p. 48. Fortescue, *History of the British Army*, Vol. 10, p. 67.
38. Sabine, *Frazer Letters*, p. 447.
39. REM 5501-59-7, Wright to Burgoyne, 28 March 1814.
40. REM 5501-59-7, Wright to Burgoyne, 13 April 1814.
41. NA WO55/959, Goldfinch to Elphinstone, 12 April 1814.
42. REM 5501-59-7, Wright to Burgoyne, 13 April 1814.
43. WD, QMG to officer commanding on right bank, 5 April 1814.
44. REM 5501-59-7, Wright to Burgoyne, 13 April 1814.
45. REM 5501-79, Wright to Burgoyne, 10 April 1814.
46. REM 5501-79, Reid to Burgoyne, 8 May 1814.
47. WD, Wellington to Hope, 5 March 1814.
48. WD, Wellington to Hope, 5 March 1814 and 8 March 1814.
49. Wrottesley, *Life of Burgoyne*, p. 297fn.

Appendix 3
1. C. Raeuber, 'Military Topographical Reconnaissance in Portugal, 1810' in Berkeley (ed.), *New Lights on the Peninsular War*, pp. 165–77.
2. Hewitt, *Map of a Nation*.
3. Raeuber, 'Military Topographical Reconnaissance in Portugal, 1810' in Berkeley (ed.), *New Lights on the Peninsular War*, p. 174
4. See Gomez, Velilla and Aguglario, *Tomas Lopez's Geographic Atlas of Spain in the Peninsular War*.
5. Thomas Jefferys, *A New Map Of The Kingdoms Of Spain And Portugal With Their Principal Divisions*, London, 1790.

6. WO55/958, Neville to Rowley, 17 March 1809.
7. BL Add63106, ff.9-10, Squire to Bunbury, 10 September 1810.
8. This is referring to W. G. Elliot RA – *Treatise on the Defence of Portugal*. REM 4601-86, Ross to Dalrymple, 14 December 1810.
9. Taken from Dr John Peaty's presentation to Wellington Congress 2010, 'Wellington's Surveyors and Map-Makers in the Peninsula'.
10. NA 37/10, Scovell Papers. Not dated or signed.
11. Rice Jones, *An Engineer Officer under Wellington*, p. 13.
12. BL Add MS57544, f.204. Mackenzie to Moore, 13 December 1808.
13. Foster, *Sir Thomas Livingstone Mitchell and his World*.
14. NA WO55/1561/9, dated 9 November 1808.
15. Centeno, *O Exercito Aliado Anglo-Português 1808-14*, p. 339.
16. NA WO37/10, Murray to Scovell, 26 September 1808.
17. Centeno, *O Exercito Aliado Anglo-Português 1808-14*, pp. 338–43.

Appendix 4
1. *RE Journal*, January 1890, p. 4.
2. *RE Journal*, June 1943, Article on the Royal Staff Corps 1800–37, pp. 83–4.
3. Leith-Hay, *Narrative of the Peninsular War*, Vol. 1, pp. 300–10.
4. WD, Wellington to Liverpool, Niza, 18 April 1811.
5. NA WO55/959, Fletcher to Morse, 17 October 1811.
6. Based on the details in Dickson, *Manuscripts*, Vol. 5, p. 830.
7. *RE Journal*, January 1890, p. 6.
8. *RE Journal*, 1870, p. 14.

Appendix 5
1. *Royal Military Chronicle*, Vol. 1, part, 1, November 1810, p. 40.
2. Guggisberg, *The Shop*, pp. 1–2.
3. Ibid, pp. 264–5.
4. Ibid, p. 4.
5. Connolly & Edwards, *Roll of Officers of the Corps of Royal Engineers*, p. 10; Guggisberg, *The Shop*, p. 258.
6. W. D. Jones, *Records of the Royal Military Academy*, p. 81.
7. Guggisberg, *The Shop*, pp. 12–13.
8. W. D. Jones, *Records of the Royal Military Academy*, p. 91.
9. Guggisberg, *The Shop*, p. 14.
10. Ibid, p. 15.
11. Ibid, p. 44.
12. W. D. Jones, *Records of the Royal Military Academy*, p. 97.
13. Guggisberg, *The Shop*, p. 15.
14. James, *The Regimental Companion*, p. 38.
15. Duncan, *History of the Royal Regiment of Artillery*, Vol. 1, p. 110.
16. Guggisberg, *The Shop*, pp. 54–5.
17. Ibid, p. 33.
18. W. D. Jones, *Records of the Royal Military Academy*, p. 53.
19. Guggisberg, *The Shop*, p. 35.
20. W. D. Jones, *Records of the Royal Military Academy*, p. 54, 11 March 1795.
21. Ibid, p. 65.
22. Ibid, p. 75.
23. For example, Birch 1793; Lefebure 1793; Elphinstone 1793; Thackeray 1794; Squire 1797; Burgoyne 1798; Goldfinch 1798; J. T. Jones 1798; Pasley 1799; G. C. Ross 1799; Fanshawe 1801; Nicholas 1801; Boothby 1804; E. R. Mulcaster 1804.
24. REM 5501-79, Pasley to J. T. Jones, 3 February 1811.
25. Ward, *The School of Military Engineering*, p. 5.
26. Connolly, *History of the Royal Sappers and Miners*, Vol. 1, pp. 183–4. Warrant for increase signed 28 May 1811.
27. REM 5501-59-1, Jones diary, Vol. 1, entry dated 25 April 1811.

28. Connolly, *History of the Royal Sappers and Miners* Vol. 1, p. 179; J. T. Jones, *Journal of Sieges*, Vol. 1, p. 10.
29. BL, ADD63106, Squire letters, f. 28. Squire also makes mention of artificers (i.e. RMA) and junior officers being trained in a letter of 30 April 1811.
30. REM 5501-59-2, Jones' diary, 9 November 1811.
31. BL, ADD41963, ff.13-16. Squire to Pasley, 3 March 1812. Portalegre.
32. BL, ADD41963, ff. 38-40, Pasley to his sister, 2 May 1812.
33. Wrottesley, *Life of Burgoyne*, Vol. 1, p. 166, Pasley to Burgoyne, 2 March 1812.
34. WD, Wellington to Liverpool, 11 February 1812.
35. *Athenaeum*, 27 April 1889, p. 537, Wellington to Liverpool, 7 April 1812.
36. BL, ADD63106, Squire Letters, ff. 54-5, 8 April 1812.
37. BL, ADD41962, f. 149. Pasley Papers, Pasley to Fyers, 12 May 1809.
38. REM 4601-79, f. 49, John Rowley to Pasley, 6 August 1811.
39. BL, ADD41962, Pasley Papers, ff. 359-60, Pasley to Lord Mulgrave, 11 December 1811.
40. BL, ADD41963, Pasley Papers, ff. 1-2, Pasley to Gother Mann, 18 January 1812.
41. BL, ADD41963, Pasley Papers, ff. 9-10, John Rowley to Pasley, 17 February 1812.
42. Wrottesley, *Life of Burgoyne*, Vol. 1, p. 164, Fletcher to IGF, 29 January 1812.
43. Ward, *The School of Military Engineering*, p. 5.
44. *Royal Military Chronicle*, May 1812, Gazette dated 24 April 1812, announcing dispatch received previous day.
45. See WO54/252 for officers commissioned in 1812.
46. BL, ADD41962, Pasley papers, ff. 38-40, Pasley to his sister, 2 May 1812.
47. Wrottesley, *Life of Burgoyne*, Vol. 1, p. 166, Pasley to Burgoyne, 2 March 1812.
48. WO47/291, 11 May 1812.
49. REM 4501-65, 'Memoir relative to the Royal Sappers and Miners No 1, 1813'.
50. BL, ADD41963, Pasley papers, ff.60-61, Dickens to Pasley, 4 September 1812. Dickens had been CRE at Malta from 1800 to 1812, then returning to England. According to the returns, he was on leave at this time, before returning to Malta in February 1813.
51. REM 4501-65. These comments are taken from Pasley's 'Memoir relative to the Sappers and Miners'.
52. Kealey, *General Sir Charles William Pasley*, p. 13, quoting Pasley, talking about planned content of second part of his Essay.
53. J. T. Jones, *Journal of Sieges*, 1st edition, p. ix.
54. Kealey, *General Sir Charles William Pasley*, p. 9.
55. REM 5501-79, Burgoyne to Squire, 4 January 1811.
56. REM 2201-79, Dickenson to Burgoyne, 9 January 1811.

Bibliography

Primary Unpublished Sources

National Archives
PRO30/35/1	Correspondence of James Carmichael Smyth 1805–37.
WO17/2770	Engineers' monthly returns Aug 1813–Dec 1815.
WO25/3913	Engineer Officer Records 1796–1860.
WO30/35/1	Diary of James Carmichael-Smyth 1808–15.
WO44/612	Misc. Engineer correspondence.
WO54/240	Engineers' Commission Books 1755–80.
WO54/241	Engineers' Commission Books 1797–1805.
WO54/242	Engineers' Commission Books 1805–11.
WO54/243	Engineers' Commission Books 1811–21.
WO54/251	Returns of Officers 1805–9.
WO54/252	Returns of Officers 1810–14.
WO54/253	Returns of Officers 1815–19.
WO55/958	Engineer papers 1798–11.
WO55/959	Engineer papers 1812–46.
WO55/977-984	Royal Engineer papers 1808–15

National Army Museum
1970-04-16-9	Letters of various Officers including John Birch; C. W. Pasley; J. F. Burgoyne.
1999-06-149	Diaries of Lieut. William Staveley R.S.C.
2004-05-26	Military Engineering in the Peninsular War 1808-1814. A Digest of References by Maj. J. T. Hancock.
6807/102	Tylden's MS record on Pontoon Train 1814.

British Library
ADD36306	LETTERS (186) from Arthur Wellesley, Viscount, afterwards Duke of, Wellington, Commander-in-chief of the Forces in Portugal, to Lieut.-General Sir William Carr Beresford, Marshal in the Portuguese service.
ADD41766	GENERAL Sir Charles William Pasley, K.C.B. his family and his career' by his grandson, Col. John Charles Tyler, Royal Engineers; 1929.
ADD41961-5	Pasley Papers 1807-1828: Vols. I–IV. Correspondence, family and professional, of Sir C. W. Pasley. Four volumes: 41961. Vol. I 9 Oct. 1784–25 Dec. 1806. 41962. Vol. II 31 Jan. 1807–29 Dec. 1811. 41963. Vol. III 18 Jan. 1812–27 Dec. 1828, n.d. 41964. Vol. IV.
ADD57544	Supplementary Moore Papers.
ADD63106	Letters of John Squire RE to Sir Henry Bunbury, 1810–12.
ADD63108	Bunbury Corresp (Misc Letters on Nap. Wars).

Royal Engineers' Museum
2001.149	Misc RE letters.
2001.150	Ordnance General Orders.
2001.151	Misc RE Letters.
3801.15.3	Letter from Rice Jones Ciudad Rodrigo 20 Jan 1812.
4201.68	Sir John Fox Burgoyne's Diaries (several).
4201.274	Letters from Howard Elphinstone to his wife.
4201.305	Peninsular Letters of Landmann and Fanshawe 1808–10.
4501.65	Memoirs relating to the Royal Sappers and Miners, 1813.
4501.86.4	Letters from Captain George Ross to Sir Hew Dalrymple.

266 Wellington's Engineers

4601.29	Account of throwing bridge across Adour in 1814.
4601.57.1	Emmett's Peninsular Diary 1809–14.
4601.71	Misc letters of Sir Richard Fletcher.
4601.72	Misc letters from Burgoyne.
5501.52	Notebook of Capt West on river crossings in the Peninsula.
5501.59.1,2,3	J. T. Jones' Diaries from 1810–12.
5501.59.4	Fletcher's Letter book, Nov 1810 – Feb 1811.
5501.59.5	Fletcher's Letter book, Oct 1811 – Oct 1812.
5501.59.6	Reid's notes on the siege of Burgos.
5501.59.7	Letters written to Burgoyne by Squire, Pitts and Wright.
5501.59.8	Letters of Fletcher and Jones related to Torres Vedras.
5501.59.10	Letters to J. T. Jones RE, by his brother Harry D. Jones RE.
5501.59.18	Book of letters on Torres Vedras.
5501.59.21 to 31	Various letters.
5501.79	Letters of RE officers, Peninsula, Egypt and Crimea.
5501.106	Notebook of Harry D. Jones Oct 1812 – Feb 1814.
5501.108.4,5	Burgoyne's diary and sketch of Siege of San Sebastian.
5501.108.6,7	Letters from Moore and Wellington to Burgoyne.
5501.108.8	Instructions on lines of Torres Vedras.
5501.123.1, 2, 3	Reports written by H. D .Jones
5501.134	Notebook of Charles Rochfort Scott R.S.C.
5501.139	Various letters on the Peninsular War.
5501.139.1	Letter from Burgoyne to Pasley on siege of Ciudad Rodrigo.
5501.139.3,4	Letters to/from Fitzroy Somerset regarding ranks.
7708.15	Oldfield papers (info on brigade equipment and pontoon train).
7804.16	Diary of Gustavus Nicholls 1799–1810.
8902.01	Nicholas' Diary from the siege of Cadiz.
9312.13.2	Letter from A. J. Wortham on Siege of San Sebastian.
9312.13.3	Letter from Goldfinch to Morse on battles around Nive and Bayonne (+map).

In the possession of Vernon Merritt, Tunbridge Wells
The Diary of Edmund Mulcaster RE, covering the period from December 1808 to September 1810.
Various letters written by Lancelot Machell RE, December 1809 to May 1813.

Primary Published Sources

Anton, J.,	*Retrospective of a Military Life*, Edinburgh, 1841.
Boothby, C.,	*A Prisoner of France*, London, 1898.
Boothby, C.,	*Under England's Flag from 1804-1809*, London, 1900.
Boutflower, C.,	*The Journal of an Army Surgeon during the Peninsular War*, privately printed, n.d.
Bunbury, H.,	*Narratives of Some Passages in the Great War with France from 1799 to 1810. By Lt General Sir Henry Bunbury formerly Quartermaster-General to the Army in the Mediterranean*, London, 1854.
Carr-Gomm, F. C.,	*The Letters and Journals of Field-Marshal Sir William Maynard Gomm from 1799 to Waterloo 1815*, London, 1881.
Castlereagh, Marquess of,	*Correspondence, Dispatches and other papers of Viscount Castlereagh*, 12 vols, London, 1851.
Dickson, A.,	*The Dickson Manuscripts*, 5 vols, Cambridge, 1987, reprint of 1905 Woolwich edition.
Gurwood, J.,	*Dispatches of the Duke of Wellington*, 1st edition, 12 vols, London, 1834–8.
Gurwood, J.,	*Dispatches of the Duke of Wellington*, 2nd edition, 8 vols, London, 1852.
Haldane, H.,	*Official Letters written by Lieut-Col. Henry Haldane to the Masters-General of his Majesty's Ordnance since the year 1802*, London, 1807.
Henegan, R. D.,	*Seven Years Campaigning in the Peninsula and the Netherlands*, 2 vols, Stroud, 2005.

James, Charles,	*The Regimental Companion; containing the Relative Duties of Every Officer in the British Army*, London, 1800.
Jones, J. T.,	*Journal of the Sieges undertaken by the Allies in Spain in the years 1811 and 1812 with Notes*, 1st edition, London, 1814.
Jones, J. T.,	*Journal of the Sieges carried on by the army under the Duke of Wellington in Spain Between the Years 1811 to 1814*, 2nd edition, 2 vols, London, 1827.
Jones, J. T.,	*Journal of the Sieges carried on by the army under the Duke of Wellington in Spain Between the Years 1811 to 1814; with Notes and Additions also Memoranda Relative to the Lines Thrown Up to Cover Lisbon in 1810*, 3rd edition, 3 vols, London, 1846.
Jones, J. T.,	*The Military Autobiography of Major-General John T. Jones*, London, 1853. Twelve copies only, privately published for family use.
Jones, Rice,	*An Engineer Officer under Wellington in the Peninsula*, Huntingdon, 1986.
Kincaid, J.,	*Adventures in the Rifle Brigade and Random Shots of a Rifleman (abridged)*, Glasgow, 1981.
Landmann, G.,	*Recollections of Military Life 1806-1808*, 2 vols, London, 1854.
Lamare, J. B.,	*Relation des Sieges et Defences D'Olivenza, de Badajoz et de Campo Mayor en 1811 et 1812*, Paris, 1825.
Lamare, J. B.,	*An account of the second defence of the fortress of Badajoz by the French in 1812. Translated by an Officer of the Royal Engineers*, Chatham, 1824.
Leith-Hay, A.,	*A Narrative of the Peninsular War*, 2 vols, London, 1834.
May, J.,	*A Few Observations on the Mode of Attack and Employment of Heavy Artillery at Ciudad Rodrigo and Badajoz, in 1812, and St Sebastian in 1813*, London, 1819.
McGuffie, T. H. (ed.),	*Peninsular Cavalry General: The Correspondence of Lieutenant General Robert Ballard Long*, London, 1951.
Muir, R.,	*At Wellington's Right Hand. The Letters of Lieutenant-Colonel Sir Alexander Gordon 1808-1815*, Stroud, 2003.
Page, J. V.,	*Intelligence Officer in the Peninsula. The Letters and Diaries of Major the Hon. Edward Charles Cocks 1786-1812*, Tunbridge Wells, 1986.
Pasley, C. W.,	*Essay on the Military Policy and institutions of the British Empire, Part 1*, London, 1810.
Pasley, C. W.,	*Course of instruction originally composed for the use of the Royal Engineer Department*, 3 vols, Chatham, 1814–17.
Pelet, J. J.,	*A Hawk at War: The Peninsular War Reminiscences of General Sir Thomas Brotherton*, Chippenham, 1986.
Perrett, B. (ed.),	*The French Campaign in Portugal 1810-1811*, Minneapolis, 1973.
Rousseau, I. J. (ed.),	*The Peninsular War Journal of Sir Benjamin D'Urban*, London, 1988.
Sabine, E.,	*Letters of Colonel Sir Augustus Frazer, K.C.B., commanding the Royal Horse Artillery in the army under the Duke of Wellington written during the Peninsular and Waterloo campaigns*, Uckfield, 2001.
Smith, G. C.,	*Autobiography of Lieutenant General Sir Harry Smith*, 2 vols, London, 1901.
Squire, John,	*A Short Narrative of the late campaign of the British Army under the orders of the Earl of Chatham*, London, 1810.
Thompson, W. (ed),	*An Ensign in the Peninsular War, The Letters of John Aitchison*, London, 1981.
Wellington, Duke of,	*Supplementary Dispatches of the Duke of Wellington*, 15 vols, London, 1858–72.
Whinyates, F. A.,	*Letters written by Lieut.-General Thomas Dyneley C.B., R.A., While on Active Service Between the years 1806 and 1815*, reprinted London, 1984.

Secondary Published Sources

Aspinal-Oglander, C.	*Freshly Remembered; The Story of Thomas Graham*, London, 1956.
Belmas, J.,	*Journaux des siéges faits ou soutenous par les français dans la Péninsule, de 1807 à 1814*, 4 vols, Paris, 1836.
Berkeley, A. (ed.),	*New Lights on the Peninsular War. International Congress on the Iberian Peninsula, Selected Papers 1780-1840*, Lisbon, 1991.
Batty, Robert,	*The Campaign in the Western Pyrenees*, reprinted Cambridge, 1983.
Beatson, F. C.,	*The Bidassoa and the Nivelle*, London, 1931.
Brewer, J.,	*The Sinews of Power. War, Money and the English State 1689–1783*, London, 1989.
Burnham, R. & McGuigan, R.	*The British Army against Napoleon, Facts, Lists and Trivia 1805-15*, Barnsley, 2010.
Centeno, J.,	*O Exercito Aliado Anglo-Português 1808-14*, Lisbon, 2011.
Colville, J.,	*Portrait of a General*, Salisbury, 1980.
Connolly, T. W. J.,	*History of the Corps of Royal Sappers and Miners*, 2 vols, London, 1855.
Connolly, T.W.J, & Edwards, R.F.,	*Roll of Officers of the Corps of Royal Engineers From 1660 to 1898*, Royal Engineers Institute, Chatham, 1898.
Douglas, H.,	*An Essay on the Principles and Construction of Military Bridges*, 1st edition, London, 1816.
Douglas, H.,	*An Essay on the Principles and Construction of Military Bridges*, 3rd edition, London, 1853.
Duncan, F.,	*History of the Royal Regiment of Artillery*, 2 vols, London, 1873.
Esdaile, C.,	*The Peninsular War*, London, 2002.
Fletcher, I.,	*In Hell Before Daylight. The Siege and Storming of the Fortress of Badajoz, 16 March to 6 April 1812*, London, 1984.
Fletcher, I (ed.),	*The Peninsular War. Aspects of the Struggle for the Iberian Peninsula*, Staplehurst, 1998.
Fletcher, I.,	*Badajoz 1812*, Oxford, 1999.
Forbes, A.,	*A History of the Army Ordnance Services*, 2 vols, London, 1929.
Fortescue, J.,	*History of the British Army*, 13 vols & 7 map vols, London, 1899–1930.
Foster, W. C.,	*Sir Thomas Livingstone Mitchell and his World 1792-1855*, Sydney, Australia, 1985.
Gates, D.,	*Warfare in the 19th Century*, Basingstoke, 2001.
Glover, M.,	*Wellington's Army in the Peninsula 1808-1814*, Newton Abbot, 1977.
Glover, R.,	*Peninsular Preparation. The Reform of the British Army 1795-1809*, Cambridge, 1963.
Glover, R.,	*Britain at Bay. Defence against Bonaparte 1803-14*, London, 1973.
Gomex, C., Velilla, C. & Manzano-Agugliaro, F.	*Tomas Lopez's Geographic Atlas of Spain in the Peninsular War*, Universidad Politechnica de Madrid, 2011.
Gregory, D.,	*No Ordinary General. Lieutenant-General Sir Henry Bunbury (1778-1860) The Best Soldier Historian*, New Jersey, 1999.
Grehan, J.,	*The Lines of Torres Vedras*, Staplehurst, 2000.
Griffiths, P. (ed.),	*A History of the Peninsular War, Volume IX, Modern Studies of the War in Spain and Portugal 1808-1814*, London, 1999.
Guggisberg, F. G.,	*The Shop, The Story of the Royal Military Academy*, London, 1900.
Hall, C. D.,	*British Strategy in the Napoleonic Wars 1803-1815*, Manchester, 1992.
Hall, C. D.,	*Wellington's Navy. Sea Power and the Peninsular War 1807-1814*, London, 2004.
Hall, J.,	*The Biographical Dictionary of British Officers Killed and Wounded, 1808-1814*, London, 1998.
Haythornthwaite, P. J.	*The Armies of Wellington*, London, 1994.
Hewitt, Rachel,	*Map of a Nation. A Biography of the Ordnance Survey*, Kindle edition, 2011.

Bibliography

Horward, D., *Napoleon and Iberia, The Twin sieges of Ciudad Rodrigo and Almeida, 1810*, London, 1994.
Jenkins, J. *Martial Achievements of Great Britain and her Allies from 1799 to 1815,* Ken Trotman reprint, Cambridge, 2008.
Jones, J. T., *Account of the War in Spain and Portugal and the South of France From 1808 to 1814 Inclusive*, 2nd edition, 2 vols, London, 1821.
Jones, W. D., *Records of the Royal Military Academy*, Woolwich, 1851.
Kealey, P. H., *General Sir Charles William Pasley KCB, FRS, Colonel-Commandant RE 1780-1861,* London, 1930.
Larpent, F. S., *Private Journal of Judge Advocate Larpent, attached to the Head Quarters of Lord Wellington during the Peninsular War from 1812 to its close*, 3rd edition, London, 1854.
Le Marchant, D., *Memoirs of the late Major-General Le Marchant 1766-1812*, Staplehurst, 1997.
Lipscombe, N., *Wellington's Guns: The Untold Story of Wellington and his Artillery in the Peninsula and at Waterloo*, Oxford, 2013.
Monteiro, M. (ed.), *The Lines of Torres Vedras. A Defence System to the North of Lisbon*, Torres Vedras, 2011.
Moore, J. C., *A Narrative of the Campaign of the British Army in Spain Commanded by His Excellency Lieut-General Sir John Moore*, London, 1809.
Muir, R., *Britain and the Defeat of Napoleon. 1807-1815*, Yale, 1996.
Myatt, F., *British Sieges of the Peninsular War*, Tunbridge Wells, 1987.
Myatt, F., *Peninsular General: Sir Thomas Picton 1758-1815*, Newton Abbott, 1980.
Napier, W. F. P., *History of the War in the Peninsula and in the South of France from the Year 1807 to the Year 1814*, 1st edition, 6 vols, London, 1828–40.
Norris, A. H. & Bremner, R. W., *The Lines of Torres Vedras. The First Three Lines and Fortifications South of the Tagus*, 2nd edition, Lisbon, 1980.
Oman, C. W. C., *A History of the Peninsular War*, 7 vols, Oxford, 1902–30.
Oman, C. W. C., *Wellington's Army 1809-1814*, London, 1986.
Porter, R., *History of the Royal Corps of Engineers. Volume 1,* Woolwich, 1889.
Robertson, I., *A Commanding Presence: Wellington in the Peninsula 1808-1814: Logistics-Strategy-Survival*, Stroud, 2008.
Stanhope, Earl of, *Notes of Conversations with the Duke of Wellington*, London, 1938.
Teissèdre (ed.), *Relations de Sièges en Espagne*, Paris, 2000.
Thompson, M. S., *The Fatal Hill. The Allied Campaign under Beresford in Southern Spain in 1811*, Sunderland, 2002.
Thoumine, R. H., *Scientific Soldier. A Life of General Le Marchant 1766-1812*, London, 1968.
Tyler, J., *A Study of the Royal Engineer Organisation*, Chatham, 1897.
Uffindel, A., *The National Army Museum Book of Wellington's Armies. Britain's Campaigns in the Peninsula and at Waterloo 1808-1815*, London, 2003.
Ward, B. R., *The School of Military Engineering 1812-1909*, Chatham, 1909.
Ward, S. G. P., *Wellington's Headquarters*, Oxford, 1957.
Woolgar, C. M. (ed.), *Wellington Studies I*, Southampton, 1996.
Wrottesley, G., *Life and Correspondence of Field Marshal Sir John Burgoyne*, 2 vols, London, 1873.

Theses

Chilcott, C., *Maintaining the British Army; 1793-1820*, PhD Thesis, University of the West of England, 2005.
Redgrave, T. M. O., *Wellington's Logistical Arrangements in the Peninsular War 1809-1814*, PhD Thesis, King's College London, n.d.

Romans, M.,	*Professionalism and the Development of Military Intelligence in Wellington's Army 1809-14*, PhD Thesis, Southampton, 2005.
Thompson, M. S.,	*The Rise of the Scientific Soldier as seen through the performance of the Royal Engineers in the early 19th Century*, 2009.
Vichness, S.,	*Marshal of Portugal: The Military Career of William Carr Beresford*, PhD Thesis, Florida State University, 1976.

Journals

British Army Review	Fursden, H., 'River crossing in the Peninsular War', *British Army Review*, No. 26, 1967.
JSAHR	*Journal of the Society of Army Historical Research*. Various dates incl, Vol. 27, 1949, pp. 50–60 which gives details of the British officers in the Portuguese army from Challis' index.
Royal Engineer Journal	• Shore, H. V., 'Letters from the Peninsula during 1812-14. Letters of Rice Jones RE', *RE Journal*, July 1912. • Vetch, J., 'Letters from an Officer of the Royal Engineers in the Peninsula 26/10/1810 – 18/3/1813', *RE Journal*, Oct–Dec 1880 & Jan–Mar 1881. • Beresford, C. F. C., 'Diary of Sir Harry Jones 1812–1814', *RE Journal*, Jan/Feb 1890. • Hancock, J. T., 'Study of the failure of the Pontoon bridge at Toulouse in 1814', *RE Journal* Vol. 90, 1976, pp 167–71. • 'Lord Wellington's Instructions on the construction of the Lines of Torres Vedras, 20th Oct 1809', *RE Journal*, November 1911, pp. 285–8. • Pasley, C. W., 'Memoir relative to the School of Military Engineering and the Royal Sappers and Miners', *RE Journal*, July 1911, pp. 3–8. • Jones, J. T., 'A Report on Torres Vedras', *RE Journal*, Apr 1911, pp. 265–8. • Garwood, F. S., 'The Royal Staff Corps', *RE Journal*, June 1943, pp. 81–96, 247–60.
Royal Engineer Professional Papers	• Jones, H. D., 'The Defence of Cadiz', Vol. 3, pp. 75–101. • Reid, W., 'On Intrenchments as support in battle', Vol. 2, pp 2–10. • Reid, W., 'On Assaults', Vol 1, pp. 3–18. • Reid, W., 'On Destruction of Stone Bridges', Vol. 1, pp. 148–50. • Sandham, H., 'Memoir of Lieut.-General Sir Harry D Jones', Vol. 16, pp. ix–xiv.
Royal Military Chronicle	First series, 7 vols, London, 1811–13.
USJ	*United Service Journal*, various dates, London, 1829–41.

Index

Abrantes 15–16, 29, 32–3, 39–40, 51, 53, 56, 59, 77, 97, 142, 156, 160, 208, 222, 249
Acland, General Wroth Palmer, 12–13
Adour, river, 182, 190, 203, 225–8, 231
  bridging of, 194–8
Agueda, river, 39, 117, 121, 143, 225
Aitchson, John, 47, 64
Alagon, river, 39–40, 160
Alba de Tormes, 25, 162
Albuera, 87, 102, 104, 106
Alcantara, 38–40, 78, 145–6, 157, 196, 220, 222–3, 225, 227–8
Alcobaça, 11, 37
Alhandra, 50–2, 54, 61, 73–6, 82
Almada, 35, 50, 57, 156
Almaraz, 16–17, 40–1, 43, 144–5, 156–7, 160, 195, 222–3, 225, 227–8
Almeida, 14–16, 57, 69, 70–2, 85, 89, 94, 116, 121–2, 129, 133, 138, 143, 146–7, 160, 208, 224–5
Alten, General, 89–90, 144, 187
Alverca, 72
Anderson, Henry RE, 2
Anstruther, General Robert, 12
Arroyo dos Molinos, 118
Astorga, 17, 21, 24–5
Avila, 17, 155
Arruda, 50
Arzobispo, 41, 43, 223

Badajoz, 4, 17, 43, 45, 48–50, 69, 84–98, 100–5, 107–8, 110–14, 120, 124–6, 128–31, 133–42, 144, 149, 152, 154–9, 172–3, 177, 179, 192, 208, 224–5, 228, 231, 239–241, 243
  first siege, 88–105
  second siege, 105–13
  third siege, 129–41
Baird, General Sir David, 17, 19–21, 24–5, 27, 181
Ballesteros, Spanish General, 91

Bayonne, 189–91, 194–7, 203–4
Bayonne islands, 69
Benavente, 25–6, 223
Benavente, on river Tagus, 82
Beresford, General William Carr, 33, 37, 49, 51, 58–60, 64, 80–1, 85–7, 90–1, 93–4, 96–106, 111, 174, 189–92, 198, 201–2
Berkeley, Admiral George, 57, 63, 65, 76, 129–30
Berlingas islands, 69
Bidassoa, river, 163, 182–8, 192, 225, 232, crossing of, 186–7
Birch, John Francis RE, 18–9, 21–23, 26
Blake, Spanish General, 19–23, 91, 114
Board of Ordnance 1–2, 4–5, 7, 11, 13, 20–1, 24, 30, 32, 34, 39–40, 56, 79, 128, 141, 156, 181, 184, 204–7, 209, 233, 245
Boothby, Charles RE, 15, 25–8, 34, 36, 38, 42
Boteler, Richard RE, 9, 17, 143, 179, 193
bridges,
  cask bridge, 87, 225, 227
  floating bridge, *see* flying bridge
  flying bridge, 29, 41, 86, 90, 105, 132, 137, 224, 227
  rope bridge, 160, 228
  suspension bridge, 145, 157
  trestle bridge, 85, 121, 187–9, 225, 227
Broderick, British General, 18
Bryce, Alexander RE, 14
Bucellas, 50, 75
Burgos, 21, 127, 156–7, 159, 163, 177, 225
  siege of 148–54
Bussaco, 65, 72
Bunbury, Henry, 56, 64, 66–8, 73, 118

272 Wellington's Engineers

Burgoyne, John RE, 3, 9, 14, 16–17, 25–6, 34, 36–9, 42, 50–2, 64, 66–7, 69–73, 75, 113, 116–18, 122–8, 131, 140–9, 152–5, 158, 161, 164–5, 167, 169, 170, 172, 176, 178–81, 183–5, 187–9, 191–2, 194, 197, 199, 202, 204, 206–7, 210–11, 220, 227, 239–40, 244–6, 248
  Wellington complains about, 183–5
Burrard, General Harry, 9, 12–14, 16

Cadiz 1, 30–2, 34, 45, 131, 134, 136, 158–60, 208, 217, 258
Cairns, Robert RA, 161
Calahandrix, 54, 75
Calder, Sub-Lieut RSM, 191
Cambo, 190–2
Campo Mayor, 69, 85, 104, 113–14
Canning, George, 18, 43, 47
Carmichal-Smyth, James RE, 21
Caroll, Military Agent, 23–4
Carta Militar, 17, 217–18
Castanheira, 48, 51, 54
Castaños, Spanish General, 19–22, 25, 91, 93, 131
Castello Branco, 17, 69, 142
Castlereagh, Robert, 18–20, 43, 47, 65
Caya, river, 89–90, 102, 105, 113–14
Celorico, 72
Chapman, Stephen RE, 28, 32–4, 36–7, 39, 43, 45, 48, 56, 58–60, 70, 72, 206, 209
Ciudad Rodrigo, 4, 14, 16–17, 69–70, 85, 88, 96, 106, 117, 130, 133–4, 136–7, 140, 142–3, 149, 155–6, 159, 166, 172–3, 177, 179, 208, 220, 225, 240, 244
  siege of, 120–9
Coa, river, 72, 85, 115, 224–5
Cocks, Charles, 72, 108, 114, 121
Coimbra, 16–17, 37, 40, 59, 61, 70–3
Colborne, John, 15, 122, 125
Colville, General Charles, 124, 136, 190
Convention of Cintra, 14, 15, 46, 217
Corps of Guides, 7, 221

Corunna, 9, 15, 17–18, 20–1, 31, 39, 48–9, 162, 209, 223
  retreat and battle, 23–8
Craddock, Sir John, British General, 30, 32–3, 36–7, 209
Craufurd, General Robert, 24, 43, 69, 71–2, 78–81, 206–7
Cris, river, 70, 73
Cuesta, Spanish General, 39–43

Dalrymple, Hew, British General, 14, 30, 64, 66
Dão, river, 70, 73
D'Arcy, Robert RE, 14
D'España, General Carlos, 118, 143
D'Urban, Benjamin, 48, 81–2, 101, 111
Davy, Henry RE, 27, 223, 247
De Butts, Augustus RE, 14
Dickens, Samuel RE, 245
Dickson, Alexander RA, 64, 87, 89, 93–8, 101–2, 105–8, 111, 124, 129, 130, 144, 146, 150, 154, 158, 160, 163, 165–6, 169–71, 177, 180, 184 193, 201, 207, 210
Dickinson, Sebastian RE, 75, 109, 243, 248
Douro, river, 17, 37, 39, 86, 118, 143, 145, 155, 157, 160–2
Doyle, Military Agent, 18–19, 22–3
Dundas, Robert RSC, 52

El Bolden, 117–18
Elgin Marbles, 78
Ellicombe, Charles RE, 122–3, 126, 188, 193
Eliot, William RA, 218
Elphinstone, Howard RE, 2–3, 9–13, 37, 158–9, 179–81, 187, 189, 192–4, 197, 199, 200, 202–4, 206–7, 209–10, 246, 248
Elvas, 14–17, 69, 87, 89–91, 93–7, 105–6, 110, 112–14, 129–30, 145, 157, 160, 208, 239
Emmett, Anthony, RE, 32, 37, 50, 60, 69, 117, 118

English, Frederick RE, 9, 11, 199–202
Ericeira, 50–1, 64
Esla, River, 25–6, 162
Evatt, Henry RE, 31
Evelegh, Captain RA, 27

Faden, mapmaker, 17, 34, 217–18
Fane, General, 10–11
Fletcher, Richard, RE 2–3, 9, 13–17, 21, 26–7, 29–30, 34–46, 48–52, 54–61, 68, 70, 72–4, 76, 78–82, 85, 89, 91–4, 97–9, 101–4, 106–7, 116, 118, 121, 123–4, 126–32, 134, 136, 140–2, 149, 153, 155–9, 161–9, 171, 174, 176–7, 179–80, 182–3, 188, 192–3, 206–7, 209–10, 217, 229, 231, 237, 244, 246, 248
 seniority, 14
 injured at Badajoz, 132
 returns to England, 158–9
 death, 176
 opinions, 179–80
Forster, William RE, 9, 15, 26, 42, 50, 55, 75, 85, 95, 99, 108–9
Frazer, Augustus RA, 164, 169–72, 175, 187, 192, 198–9
Freixadas, 7
Fuentes de Oñoro, 83, 105, 114–15, 224–5
Fyers, Edward RE, 32, 42
Fyers, William RE, 42, 242

Garonne, river, 198, 200–1, 204, 226
Gibraltar 2–3, 6, 9, 14–15, 30–1, 45, 208–9
Girard, French General, 118
Goldfinch, Henry RE, 32–3, 38, 42, 45, 51–2, 57, 69, 75, 77, 158, 163–4, 179, 191, 194, 200–2, 209
Gordon, Alexander, 92, 104
Graham, Sir Thomas, 162–5, 167, 169–72, 174–7, 182–5, 197
Guadiana, river, 45, 69, 84–91, 95–9, 103, 106, 111, 113–14, 129, 131–2, 144, 160, 224–5, 229
Guarda, 72

Hamilton, George RE, 34, 36, 38, 51
Henderson, George RE, 157–8, 190, 192
Hill, General Rowland, 16, 37, 73–4, 78, 80, 118–19, 140, 142, 144–5, 156–7, 162–4, 174, 189–92, 197, 200, 202
Hookham-Frere, 23–5, 31
Hope, General John, 14, 16–17, 27–8, 187–91, 194–5, 197–8, 203–4
Hulme, John RE, 75, 77, 157, 161, 163
Hunt, Richard RE, 109–10
Hustler, Robert RE, 31

Irun, 182–3, 186–7

Jerumenha, 69, 86–9, 91, 97, 102, 104, 113–14
Jones, Harry RE, 155, 160–2, 168–70, 172, 177, 192, 222, 230
Jones, John RE, 18, 52, 55, 58–9, 61, 68, 70, 74–5, 85, 91, 121, 124, 128, 141, 149, 151, 155, 164, 165, 170, 178, 179, 206, 238, 247–8
Jones, Rice RE, 3, 32–3, 36–7, 41–2, 45, 48, 51, 55, 57, 60–1, 70, 72, 77, 93, 104, 113
Junot, General Andoche, 10, 12–13, 58, 75, 216–17

La Conception, Almeida, 69–70
Landmann, George RE, 3, 9–15, 29–31, 36, 59, 209
Larpent, Francis, 172, 194, 199
Lascelles, Thomas RE, 114
Latour-Maubourg, General, 87, 114
Lefebure, Charles RE, 18–22, 24, 243, 246, 248
Leith, General, 18–21, 23–4
Leith, Royal Navy, 61, 63
Leith-Hay, Andrew, 19, 77, 145, 227
Lewis, Thomas RE, 168
Linhares, 72
Liverpool, Lord, 31, 64–5, 74, 85, 91, 96, 102, 108, 128, 136, 139, 141, 145, 241

Lopez, mapmaker, 34, 217

Machell, Lancelot RE, 168
Mackenzie, General Alexander, 29–31, 39, 42, 219
Macleod, George RE, 113, 116, 128–9
Madrid, 17, 20–1, 25, 148, 159, 217, 223
Mafra, 50–1, 75, 218
Mann, Gother RE, 243–4
Marmont, French Marshal, 113–14, 117–18, 123, 133, 136–8, 142, 146–8, 239
Marshall, Anthony RE, 143, 157
Massena, French Marshal, 54, 59, 65, 67–8, 75–7, 80, 82–5, 105–7, 113, 116, 217, 224
Maya, 173, 182–4, 186
Meineke, George KGL Engineer, 17, 77, 82
Melhuish, Samuel RE, 196
Mendizabal, Spanish General, 84, 87
Mercer, Alexander RE, 240
Mercer, Cavalier RE, 9
Merida, 17, 84–5, 113, 132, 143–4, 156–8, 225
Mitchell, Thomas, 162, 220
Mondego Bay, 1, 2, 9, 13
Mondego, river, 39, 72–3
Monte Agraça, *see* Sobral
Moore, Sir John, 3, 9, 14–18, 21, 23–9, 43, 46, 66, 78, 209, 219, 224, 243, 247
Montachique, 49–50
Morse, Robert RE, 68, 135, 240, 242–3
Mudge, Richard RE, 41
Mulcaster, Edmund RE, 9, 11–12, 15, 26–9, 36–8, 40–2, 45, 50–2, 55, 64, 70–3, 75, 82, 108, 123, 135, 246, 248
Mulcaster, Frederick RE, 34
Murray George QMG, 27, 48, 66, 160, 183, 194, 219–20

Napier, William, 19, 53, 80, 81, 199
Ney, French Marshal, 19, 75

Nive, river, 190–3, 225, 231
Nivelle, river, 186, 188–90, 225, 231

Olivenza, 82, 84, 87–8, 96–7, 105, 114
Oporto, 9, 33, 35, 37–40, 42, 46, 51, 61, 120, 122, 129, 223

Paget, General, 25–6
Palafox, Spanish General, 20–2
Palmela, 37, 60
Pamplona, 163–5, 174, 176, 183–4, 187–8
Pancorbo, 163
Pardaleras, Fort Badajoz, 90, 92–3, 98–101, 105–6, 138
Parker, Edward RE, 198
Pasley, Charles William RE, 6, 18–21, 23–4, 27, 34–5, 39, 66, 117, 124, 126, 141, 164–5, 178, 187
  military education, 238, 240, 242, 244–250
Patton, Peter RE, 1, 9, 15, 30, 32, 51, 59, 108–9, 156, 209
Pelet, Jean, French Officer, 65, 77, 82,
Peniche, 14, 30, 36, 50, 53, 59, 69, 208
Pero Negro, 61, 74, 76
Phillipon, French Governor of Badajoz, 87, 105, 113, 137, 139
Pickering, Commissary, 52
Picton, General Sir Thomas, 3, 106, 134–5, 198, 269
Picurina, Fort Badajoz,
  first siege, 89, 90, 92, 98–102
  second siege, 105–6
  third siege, 130–1, 133, 140
Piper, Robert RE, 75, 132, 157, 160, 187, 230
Pisuerga, river, 155
Pitts, Thomas RE, 146, 149–50, 152, 154–5, 164, 178, 181–3, 187, 189, 197
Plasencia, 17, 40, 41, 43
Ponte de Murcella, 72, 85, 224, 227
Ponte do Rol, 50, 61, 73
pontoons, 7, 29, 41, 86–7, 98, 129–32, 137, 142, 144, 157, 160–3, 182, 184–92,

194–5, 197–202, 206, 222–3, 225–7, 228–31
Popham, Admiral Home, 61–2
Portugal, defence of, 43–5
Portuguese artificers, 160, 167, 189
Portuguese engineers, 7, 8, 29, 40, 51, 55, 58, 116, 219
  Bellegarde, Luiz Maximo, 55
  Caula, Carlos Frederico Bernado de, 116
  Costa, Neves, 7, 49, 58
  D'Eca, Lourenco Homem da Cunha, 55, 217
  Sousa, Manuel Joaquim Brandao, 55
Portuguese seamen, 7, 75, 160, 197
Power, Robert RE, 190
Preval, French émigré engineer, 13
Pringle, John RE, 143, 156–7
Punhete, 29, 69, 77, 80–2, 222–3

Reid, William RE, 100, 118, 143, 146–7, 149–50, 152, 154–5, 167–8, 187, 196, 203
Rhodes, Charles RE, 156
Rivellas, stream Badajoz, 99, 108, 137
rivers, improving navigation, 118, 157
Rivers, Charles RE, 196
RMA, *see* Royal Military Artificers
Robe, Alexander RE, 196
Roliça, 11, 13, 46, 218
Romana, Spanish General, 20, 24
Roncesvalles, 173–4, 182–3, 187
Ross, George RE, 50, 63–4, 66, 75, 89, 101, 111, 116, 118, 120, 122, 125–7, 143, 218, 239
Rowley, John RE, 14, 242
Royal Artillery 2–3, 13, 31, 39, 161, 169, 193, 230–2, 237
Royal Military Academy, 205, 233–8
Royal Military Artificers 1, 6, 34, 38, 54, 97, 121–2, 131, 134, 149, 226, 238–44
Royal Sappers and Miners 1, 6, 140–1, 166, 173, 176–7, 187, 189, 190, 196, 226, 241–2, 245
Royal Staff Corps 1, 7, 8, 32, 41, 52, 69, 85, 113–15, 121, 123, 145, 155, 157, 182, 186–8, 190, 194–6, 205, 220, 223–7, 229, 238
RSC, *see* Royal Staff Corps
RSM, *see* Royal Sappers and Miners

Salamanca, 16–18, 23–5, 125, 140, 144–8, 154–7, 159, 162, 222
Santander, 18–19, 21–4, 164
Santarem, 33, 75–7, 82
San Christobal, Fort Badajoz, 89–93, 97–101, 103–8, 110–12, 125
San Marcial, 182–3, 185–6
San Sebastian, 121, 163–6, 168, 171, 173–4, 176, 178–9, 181–5, 189, 192
Sappers and Miners, volunteers, 95, 97, 106, 116–17, 127, 131, 133, 149
Savage, Henry RE, 196
School of Military Engineering, 238–46
Scott, Charles RSC, 227
Scovell, George, 7, 221
Setuval, 15, 30, 32, 37, 48, 53, 54, 59, 60, 94
Sherbrooke, General John, 32, 42, 45
signal post, *see* telegraph
Skelton, Thomas RE, 123, 126
Slade, William RE, 157–8, 196
Smith, Charles Felix RE, 163, 165, 169, 182–3
Smith, William Davies RE, 9
Sobral, 36, 49–51, 54–6, 61, 64, 74, 75, 76, 82
Sorauren, 173, 182
Soult, French Marshal, 25, 33, 37, 42–3, 80, 82, 84, 91, 96–7, 102, 104–6, 111, 113–4, 133, 136–8, 140, 146, 167–8, 173–4, 176, 182–3, 186, 188, 191, 194, 198, 202–3, 223
Squire, John RE, 3, 9, 14, 17, 34–5, 56, 64, 66–8, 73, 75, 77–82, 85, 87, 89, 94–7, 99–101, 104, 109, 115, 117–19, 124, 126, 131, 139–40, 142–4, 206–7, 216, 218, 240–1, 244, 246, 248
  experience, 78

argument with Craufurd, 78–80
defences on Tagus, 80–2
death, 143
St Jean De Luz, 189–90, 203
St Julian, 14, 37, 48, 49–51, 54, 57, 60–1, 64, 142
Stanway, Frank RE, 9, 15, 33, 39, 42, 45, 50, 56, 59, 75, 78, 133, 163, 174, 176, 181, 185
Sturgeon, Henry RSC, 7, 123, 145–6, 151, 155, 157, 196–7, 207, 220, 225, 227–8

Talavera, 40–3, 46, 223
Tallia, Jose, Portuguese Engineer, 85
Tamega, river, 39
Tapp, Hammond RE, 143, 168, 197
telegraph, 49, 61–3, 70, 72, 84, 165
Thomson, Alexander RE, 32, 33, 38, 50, 55, 72, 75, 154
Tietar, river, 39–41, 223
Todd, Alexander RSC, 41, 69, 115, 145, 157, 182–3, 186–9, 195–7, 220, 227–8
Toro, 25, 155
Torres Vedras, 7, 33, 46–7, 49–67, 70, 72, 74–6, 84–5, 154, 159, 206, 208, 218, 224
building of Lines, 45–68
occupation of Lines, 73–6
Trench, Samuel RE, 75, 116
Truxillo, 17, 43, 114, 143–4
Tudela, 20, 25, 155

Ustaritz, 190–2

Valladolid, 25, 148, 154–5
Vetch, James RE, 133–4
Via Longa, 50, 52, 56–7
Vigo, 17, 25–6, 32, 69
Villa Velha, 15, 29, 76, 142, 222
Vimeiro, 12–14, 46
Vincent, French Engineer, 49, 58, 216
Vitoria, 24, 163–5, 184, 225, 230

Walcheren, 14, 35, 47, 78, 242, 246
Wedekind, Charles, KGL Engineer, 32, 33, 36, 50, 60, 76–7, 87–8, 142, 156
Wellesley, Arthur, *see* Wellington
Wellesley, Henry, 43, 65
Wellington, Duke of, viii, 1–5, 7, 9–14, 34–5, 37, 39–61, 63–7, 69–74, 76–94, 96–9, 102–8, 110–15, 117–69, 171–95, 197–210, 216, 218–21, 223–6, 229, 232, 241, 243–4, 246
Wells, John Neave, RE 1, 9, 11–13, 16–17, 187, 192
West, George RE, 196, 227
Whitelocke, British General, 78
Williams, John RE, 9, 15, 32, 36, 39, 50, 55, 59, 80, 149–50, 152
Wilson, General Sir Robert, 39–40
Worthy, Major RSC, 32
Wright, Peter RE, 123, 144, 160, 162, 174, 183, 187, 192, 199–202

Zamora, 17, 25, 155, 161, 163
Zezere, river, 29, 33, 40, 80–2